Human Rights, Religion and International Law

In this book, Kerry O'Halloran analyses a subject of international interest – religion – and examines related contemporary issues from a human rights perspective. The book takes the view that while the impact of Islamic State violence has dramatically demonstrated the destructive power of religious extremism for contemporary Western societies, there are also good grounds for the latter to examine the extent to which their laws and policies – nationally and internationally – are contributing to religion's currently destabilising social role. It makes the case for a fuller understanding of the role of religion or belief and argues for a rebalancing of the functional relationship between Church and State both nationally and internationally.

Beginning with an overview of religion, including an examination of key concepts and constructs, the chapters go on to outline the international framework of related human rights provisions and note the extent of their ratification. It proceeds by identifying a set of themes – such as the constitutional positioning of religion; law and policy in relation to secularism; faith schools; equality legislation and the religious exemption; and the tension between free speech and religion – and undertakes a comparative evaluation of how these and other themes indicate significant differences in six leading common-law jurisdictions as illustrated by their associated legislation and case law. It then considers why this should be and assesses any implications arising.

This book will be of great interest to students and scholars in the fields of law, religious studies, political science, human rights and social policy.

Kerry O'Halloran was Adjunct Professor at the Australian Centre for Philanthropy and Nonprofit Studies, QUT, Australia, from 2004 through 2017.

Human Rights and International Law

Series Editor: Professor Surya P. Subedi, OBE, QC (Hon)

Professor Surya P. Subedi, OBE, QC (Hon) is Professor of International Law, University of Leeds, member of the Institut de Droit International and former UN Special Rapporteur for human rights in Cambodia.

This series will explore human rights law's place within the international legal order, offering much-needed interdisciplinary and global perspectives on human rights' increasingly central role in the development and implementation of international law and policy.

Human Rights and International Law is committed to providing critical and contextual accounts of human rights' relationship with international law theory and practice. To achieve this, volumes in the series will take a thematic approach that focuses on major debates in the field, looking at how human rights impacts on areas as diverse and divisive as security, terrorism, climate change, refugee law, migration, bioethics, natural resources and international trade.

Exploring the interaction, interrelationship and potential conflicts between human rights and other branches of international law, books in the series will address both historical development and contemporary contexts before outlining the most urgent questions facing scholars and policy makers today.

Available titles:

Human Rights and Charity Law
Kerry O'Halloran

Human Rights, Religion and International Law
Kerry O'Halloran

Adoption Law and Human Rights: International Perspectives
Kerry O'Halloran

Forthcoming titles:

The Right to Truth in International Law
Victims' Rights in Human Rights and International Criminal Law
Melanie Klinkner and Howard Davis

www.routledge.com/Human-Rights-and-International-Law/book-series/HRIL

Human Rights, Religion and International Law

Kerry O'Halloran

Routledge
Taylor & Francis Group
LONDON AND NEW YORK

First published 2019 by Routledge

2 Park Square, Milton Park, Abingdon, Oxfordshire OX14 4RN
52 Vanderbilt Avenue, New York, NY 10017

Routledge is an imprint of the Taylor & Francis Group, an informa business

First issued in paperback 2020

British Library Cataloguing-in-Publication Data
A catalogue record for this book is available from the British Library

Library of Congress Cataloging-in-Publication Data
Names: O'Halloran, Kerry, author.
Title: Human rights, religion and international law/Kerry O'Halloran.
Description: Abingdon, Oxon; New York, NY: Routledge, 2019. | Series: Human rights and international law
Identifiers: LCCN 2018039359 | ISBN 9780815393573 (hbk) | ISBN 9781351188357 (ebk)
Subjects: LCSH: Freedom of religion (International law) | Freedom of religion – English-speaking countries.
Classification: LCC K3258. O36 2019 | DDC 341.4/832—dc23
LC record available at https://lccn.loc.gov/2018039359

ISBN: 978-0-8153-9357-3 (hbk)
ISBN: 978-0-367-51995-7 (pbk)

Typeset in Galliard
by Apex CoVantage, LLC

Contents

Acknowledgements

I remain very grateful for the support and companionship provided by the Australian Centre for Philanthropy and Nonprofit Studies, my academic base as Adjunct Professor for 13 years ending in December 2017. This book owes much to the groundwork laid in earlier publications completed while in that post. These include *The Church of England: Charity Law & Human Rights*,[1] *Religion, Charity and Human Rights*[2] and *Religious Discrimination and Cultural Context*.[3] Given the not dissimilar subject matter and related case law, focused on the same jurisdictions, there is inevitably some degree of overlap, and I thank the publishers concerned for their understanding.

There were many who contributed along the way to making this a better book. Particular thanks are due to those who offered comment on draft chapters or related text, particularly Neil Foster,[4] (Australia); Frank Cranmer[5] (England and Wales); Gerard Whyte[6] (Ireland); Fred Gedicks[7] (USA); and Matthew Harrington[8] (Canada). Their thoughtful contributions and encouragement have meant a lot, and this book and its author would have suffered without them.

It is a privilege to make this third contribution to the series *Human Rights and International Law*, edited by Professor Surya P. Subedi. I am very thankful to Routledge for commissioning the book and for the editorial diligence of Alex Buckley, who has seen it through to completion. Responsibility for any mistakes, inconsistencies or other faults, and for all views expressed, must unfortunately rest wholly with me.

Any list of dues owed that failed to include the huge debt of gratitude I feel for the support, advice, humour and wine supplied unstintingly by Elizabeth would be most remiss. Thanks for all that and much more.

Notes

1 Springer, 2014.
2 Cambridge University Press, 2014.
3 Cambridge University Press, 2018.
4 Associate Professor, Newcastle Law School, the University of Newcastle, Australia.
5 Research Fellow at the Centre for Law & Religion, Cardiff and Director, Central Lobby Consultants.
6 Professor of Law, Trinity College Dublin, Ireland.
7 Professor of Law, J. Reuben Clark Law School, Brigham Young University, USA.
8 Professeur, Faculté de droit, Université de Montréal, Canada.

Introduction

> It is axiomatic that human rights are universal, inalienable, indivisible, interdependent and interrelated. It should be no surprise, then, that human rights commonly interact with one another. Sometimes they are mutually reinforcing. Sometimes they intersect in ways that create tensions or conflicts. This is all the more likely in a pluralistic society with a diversity of beliefs and values. This diversity adds further weight to the international law requirement to accommodate human rights that are in tension.[1]

The body of human rights can indeed be seen as a complex but coherent unity: a mutuality of rights, each interwoven with others, none having precedence. Religion, once a stand-alone area of privilege, is now – along with equality, justice and other staples of democracy – more commonly viewed, at least in legal terms, as simply one of the core fundamental rights the exercise and balancing of which are essential to the stability and growth of civil society. However, the tensions are real, not just within human rights but also between the body of international law and other frames of reference.

In the contemporary pluralist societies of the developed common law nations, tensions between human rights can often lead to conflict – perhaps particularly between the freedoms of religion and expression. In addition, the levelling effect of equality legislation, reinforced by the discrimination prohibition, is generating its own genre of tensions, most obviously when religion is conflated with cultural mores, typically giving rise to confrontational disputes on abortion, gay marriage and transgender issues. These 'culture wars' – developed and fermented in the United States over recent decades – are now very much to the fore in that country and are becoming so elsewhere as the pushback against permissive laws governing matters of sexuality and gender gathers momentum. Moreover, as graphically demonstrated by a resurgent Islamic fundamentalism and the associated rippling effect of regime instability, religion in recent years has acquired a new and aggressive global political profile – and risks reigniting an old one.[2] The response of Western nations – including execution by drone strikes abroad and repressive surveillance at home – presents an ever- increasing threat to the coherence and authority of international human rights law. At a time when respect for human rights is sorely needed, the devaluing of that currency internationally, coupled with the confused morality resulting from the application of national equality legislation, is questioning their relevance. At the heart of what is rapidly becoming a crisis for at least the weighting given to human rights, if not also for their legitimacy, lies religion.

This book explores jurisdictional differences in the intersect between religion and other human rights as illustrated in the case law of five developed common-law nations. The latter have been selected for study mainly because they subscribe to much the same set of international human rights treaties, conventions and protocols – and of course have a shared legal tradition and Christian cultural heritage – which facilitates direct comparative analysis. In addition, the governments of these nations adhere, ostensibly, to the doctrine of 'State neutrality' toward religion – meaning that they undertake to treat all religions and secularism equally – which suggests that their legal systems are most likely to provide comparable evidence of interaction between religion and human rights. Also, however, their varying engagement in 'the global war against terror' and in the resultant migrant crisis – both with distinctly Muslim characteristics – clearly positions them at the sharp end of the human rights/religion juncture.

It should perhaps be acknowledged at the outset that some might argue that to speak of religion in contradistinction to human rights – as the title of this book suggests – is a false dichotomy. Religion and human rights are surely one and the same. Further, it could be maintained that this interweaving has in fact been very positive: our civilisation owes much to religion. It has served as a singularly important part of civilizations. A book which dwells on case law will miss the positive and largely unseen contribution of religion as, by definition, such a book necessarily deals with contentious litigation concerning difficult issues which are unrepresentative of religion's primary functions. The distinction between the public and private aspects of religion will be lost: in particular, the public benefit of transcendental beliefs that instil private solace, preserve values and foster community cohesion will be overlooked. Such a book can only be expected to present a rather negative picture. Admittedly, there is some truth in this. However, the growth and increased political salience of secularism, combined with the dilution and fragmentation of religious belief and its recent reprise by Islamic fundamentalists into medieval barbarism, is arguably altering the standing of religion relative to other human rights at least in the developed common-law jurisdictions. Rather suddenly it has become both justifiable and necessary to focus squarely on the dark side of religion and the negative aspects of its interaction with human rights.

A further caveat needs to be addressed: the particular human rights this book has elected to focus upon; given their number and range, choices needed to be made. It would seem logical, in a necessarily short book, to restrict consideration to those rights which bear most directly upon religion and on religiously loaded matters (e.g. abortion and gay marriage). Adopting such an approach means that the human rights of central importance are rights to the freedoms of thought and belief, to speech and to association. Equality rights are also hugely important in this context as they cross-cut so many other rights (e.g. women's reproductive rights, marriage rights) and have crucial significance in relation to religion and religious organisations in certain specific settings such as employment and education.

Human Rights, Religion and International Law consists of eight chapters. Part I is a background section of two chapters. The first deals with concepts, constructs and parameters that identify and explain the core principles and legal definitions. The second introduces the main international human rights instruments, notes the points at which human rights and religion intersect and outlines a thematic structure for conducting the jurisdictional comparative analysis. Part II, which constitutes the bulk of the book, deals with contemporary international perspectives and in five chapters focuses in turn on England and Wales, Ireland, the United States of America, Canada and Australia. These jurisdiction-specific chapters closely follow the same format: an overview of the relevant legal framework; a consideration of the intersect between religion/human rights and the interests of the State; a broad study of the law governing the freedom of religion and its capacity to traverse other fundamental human rights such as the freedoms of expression and association; and a more particular case law analysis of contemporary tensions in the relationship between equality legislation, human rights and religion. Part III, the final section, of one chapter, concludes the book by drawing from Part II material to examine the nature of the tensions in the present relationship between human rights law and religion law, to consider the significance of cultural context and to reflect upon the relevance of contemporary politics.

The tight constraints on length have forced the book to focus on contemporary law, ignoring historical background, policy development and the current role of bodies established to promote and mediate government programmes in relation to religion and to humanitarian aid at home and abroad. This has necessarily imposed restrictions preventing anything more than a sketched outline of a subject deserving a much more thorough examination.

Kerry O'Halloran
White Park Bay, UK
Autumn 2018
kerry.ohalloranwpb@gmail.com

Notes

1 Australian Human Rights Commission, *Religious Freedom Review*, 2018, at para. 3. see further at: https://www.humanrights.gov.au/submissions/religious-freedom-review-2018

2 See Polk, W.R., *Crusade and Jihad*, Yale University Press, New Haven, CT, USA, 2018.

Part I

Background

1 Concepts, constructs and parameters

Introduction

In 1958, on the 10th anniversary of the Universal Declaration of Human Rights (UDHR), Mrs Eleanor Roosevelt gave a speech to the United Nations (UN) in which she was at pains to stress that human rights were not abstract principles but were to be found:[1]

> in small places, close to home . . . they are the world of the individual person; the neighbourhood he lives in; the school or college he attends; the factory, farm, or office where he works. Such are the places where every man, woman, and child seeks equal justice, equal opportunity, equal dignity without discrimination.

In the 60 years that have since elapsed, the foundations laid by the UDHR have come to support an ever-growing body of national and international human rights law, together with equality and non-discrimination legislation and voluminous associated jurisprudence. Despite the varying national recognition given to human rights, and the enormous social changes that have occurred in the intervening years, the above observation of Mrs. Roosevelt remains accurate. As will become evident in the jurisdiction-specific chapters of Part II, it remains the case that human rights issues continue to arise with most frequency in everyday settings such as the workplace, high street or classroom. What she could not have foreseen, is the sheer volume and variety of such issues now impacting upon courts and regulators in all those jurisdictions.

In order to give a sense of perspective, this book begins with a brief overview of the historical background: the cultural heritage uniting the common-law nations and a snapshot of human rights, religion and the relationship between them as this might have been perceived around the time when the above speech was given. Having established a common baseline for the five Part II jurisdictions, the chapter then considers the role now played by such shared characteristics in these modern pluralistic societies. This involves a consideration of related policy developments.

The common-law cultural heritage

The legacy of cultural assets, bequeathed by England to the common-law nations that once constituted the British Empire, includes language, customs and associated social mores; Christianity; the common law and accompanying judicial system; parliamentary democracy; and methods of administration and governance. Of particular significance for present purposes is the bequest of Christianity as the institutional religion and its evolving role with the State.

Christianity, theocratic rule and moral imperatives

Theocratic rule provided the environment in which the relationship between Church and State was first formulated in England. When this was transferred by colonialism, it established the presumptive dominance of Christianity, its institutions and moral imperatives; a proposed structure for Church/State relationships; and a model for the social role of religion. As the Part II chapters illustrate, the way these relationships have worked out has distanced those jurisdictions from that initial model and, to some extent, from each other.

Marriage and family

Moral imperatives were always prominent in the law relating to the family: generally as regards marriage and procreation but particularly so in relation to sexuality; their importance to both Church and State was underpinned by transgressions – such as blasphemy or heresy – being labelled as a 'sin' by one and punished as a criminal offence by the other. As Lord Finlay LC commented in *Bowman v. Secular Society Ltd.*, when reflecting on previous centuries of case law:[2]

> It has been repeatedly laid down by the Courts that Christianity is part of the law of the land, and it is the fact that our civil polity is to a large extent based upon the Christian religion. This is notably so with regard to the law of marriage and the law affecting the family.[3]

He was quite clear that up until then the courts would have considered themselves bound by such principles when called upon to interpret the meaning of 'religion'.[4] The distinctively Christian dimension to those principles included: monogamous, heterosexual marriage for life; the sanctity of marriage to the exclusion of non-marital sex, any children thereof, and unmarried partnerships; the criminalisation of abortion, homosexuality and suicide; and the rejection of a Darwinian approach to the meaning of 'life'. These principles now provide the grounds for those traditional religious beliefs that challenge the changes being driven by equality and human rights legislation.

What remained largely unseen but constituted the bulk of that Christian heritage was: the body of values, ethics and principles, distilled from the gospels and scriptures, ingrained and passed on from one generation to the next, that shaped a communal sense of right and wrong; a felt duty to demonstrate Christianity not just in ritual acts of worship but also through public good works as embodied in the law of charity[5], which governed charitable action on behalf of neighbours and community; perhaps also attitudes of acceptance toward the status quo; and the freedom to privately pray, to make personal commitments of faith and atonement. This common morality imprinted on the nations concerned, over the centuries, a shared understanding of marriage and family, of actions that are sinful or virtuous.

Christianity and culture

The English language and associated social customs have always been the primary recognisable features of the bonds that unify this most developed group of common-law jurisdictions. Among the other more conspicuous aspects of their shared culture is the mosaic of Catholic and Protestant churches that have spread much the same web of parishes, ministers/priests and parishioners across the common-law jurisdictions. These continue to be highly visible reminders of the Christian religion that forms the underpinning foundations of the common-law cultural legacy. The shared culture not only came to permeate archives of legislation, particularly family law, but was infused throughout the institutional infrastructure of schools, workplaces and health and social care systems and deeply affected all citizens – whether or not they were religious.[6] The shared culture is clearly evident in centuries of cultural output – in literature, music, art and sculpture – and it developed to provide a shared cultural umbrella for the common-law jurisdictions presently being considered.

Governments in the common-law jurisdictions have traditionally sought to support and sustain their cultural legacy. Layers of statutes, accreted over the centuries, are saturated with assumptions specific to culture and religious heritage, invariably of a Christian nature. This was reinforced by legislating to: assert and protect emblems, icons, language and traditions; endorse related values and principles, and develop an aligned social policy; police boundaries; and safeguard that cultural identity from being swamped or eroded by unplanned immigration.

The 'culture wars'

As the social cohesion provided by a shared Christian heritage has faded, there has been a tendency, at least in the developed nations, for this to be offset by groups forming to pursue their separate sets of morality-based interests. At best, relationships between these groups are tense, and at worst they can become confrontational – as in the current competition between the religious and the secularists, between fundamentalists and mainstream adherents, between the traditional organised religions, and between traditional religions and a proliferating and mutating range of new forms of belief. This reductionist tendency, responsible for proliferating 'islands of exclusivity',[7] is now commonly referred to as 'the culture wars'.

In its current phase, the phenomenon originated in the US, where it evolved from a number of morality-laden issues, including the death penalty, gun laws, abortion and homosexuality. These were often linked to 'life' and/or sexuality.[8] The related moralising extended most recently to reach gay marriage, transgender matters, assisted death, genetic engineering, DNA patenting, cloning and stem cell research – issues which now constitute the heartland of the culture wars. There is little prospect of any retreat from these front-line issues and every likelihood of new fronts opening up; indeed, the indications in the US are that equality and anti-discrimination legislation is serving to drive a socially divisive pushback on areas such as gay marriage.

The culture wars matter, as the present writer has explained elsewhere,[9] not only because of their social disruption but also because they seem to function as a proxy for clashes of religious beliefs. Religion in the jurisdictions being considered is becoming steadily more culturally sublimated: its characteristics are being nuanced and diffused throughout various public activities and forums – employment, education, health care and so on – rather than represented in institutional places of worship. The sublimation may then surface as in the form of an expedient artifice: religious discrimination, generated in fact by religion or belief, may be passed off as an objection to sexual orientation (e.g. the refusal of bakers with strong religious views to bake celebratory cakes for gay couples) or concern for animal welfare (e.g. an objection to the non-stunning of animals slaughtered for food). To a large extent, such 'domestication' of a traditionally polarising source of social unrest has served to defuse its potency: culture war sophistication gradually displacing overt religious discrimination and removing any excuse for sectarianism; a fluctuating agenda of moral imperatives substituting for blunt religious confrontation. However, because of this proxy role, the culture wars can intersect with human rights – mostly on issues where there is a fusion of sexuality and religion – when rights such as the freedom of expression may then be engaged.

The common law and the role of the judiciary

Prevailing in England since the 12th century, before being exported to its colonies, the common law was grounded on the rights and duties of the individual.[10] Often referred to as 'judge made law' it was derived not from the prescribed directives of statute but from tradition, custom and judicial precedent as embodied in rules and interpreted and applied by the judiciary adopting an inquisitorial approach on a case-by-case basis. Consequently, it was heavily reliant on established case precedents.

The common law: a shared tradition

The common law made no provision for class or community actions. There was no sense of collective legal interests. It consisted merely of categories of causes actionable by or against individuals, leaving the latter to fit his or her complaint to an established cause. This approach – listing subjects available for legal redress and permitting subsequent empirical extension by analogy – proved to be problematic. Its grindingly logical approach led to the law being constrained by the rigidity of the specified and corralled by established case precedents, where any development to meet emerging needs could only be achieved by painstakingly distinguishing the facts of new cases from those of the old. The result was a reliance on endless lists and categorisation, producing a consequent patchwork effect rather than a coherent body of law.

However, reliance on the doctrine of precedent did facilitate the growth, to some degree, of a shared jurisprudence between common-law jurisdictions, reinforced historically by the role of the Privy Council. The judiciary in one common-law jurisdiction would consider it reasonable to apply a principle drawn from a case precedent established in another when there was a matching category of circumstances.[11] This, for example, occurred not infrequently in charity law cases where the judiciary for centuries were most often drawing from a pooled jurisprudence established in line with principles formulated under the auspices of the English Statute of Charitable Uses 1601. A shared cultural context, infused with Christian morality and common-law principles, most probably prepared the ground for a not dissimilar jurisdictional response to international human rights and their interaction with religion.

Rights

Legal rights provide for assertive action in the courts by individuals or legal entities for alleged breach of specific rights as established in national legislation and/or in international conventions. Legal rights and corresponding legal duties, usually underpinned by moral authority and enforced by legal powers, form the basis for national legal systems and are characterised by: acknowledgment of specific rights held by individuals or entities; a process for obtaining formal recognition of entitlement; objective adjudication on alleged breach and appropriate recompense; and a process for enforcement. Certain rights have gained international recognition as being of greater importance than others. These are embodied in various international treaties, conventions, protocols and so on, some of which are directly binding upon signatory States. Others have been legislatively incorporated into national law (see Chapter 2). While providing specific remedies for specific unlawful acts, legal rights also contribute to generally reinforcing the currency of human rights norms and to the building of human rights-compliant practices. On the other hand, it may also be argued that an adversarial pursuit of legal rights as a means of dealing with complex social problems can lead to a strategic failure to 'see the wood for the trees' and generate fractious social divisiveness.

Background

From the outset – in the American and French revolutions of the late 18th century – human rights were locked into citizenship and into a strained relationship with religion. Both social upheavals had sought, among other things, to break the institutionalised Church/State theocratic model of government and assert the rights of citizens to a greater measure of independence and equality. This was forcefully asserted in the US Declaration of Independence on 4 July 1776:

> We hold these truths to be self-evident, that all men are created equal, that they are endowed by their Creator with certain unalienable Rights, that among these are Life, Liberty and the pursuit of Happiness.

Although the French Revolution, launched in 1789, drew significantly from the American experience, it went a step further. The French rejection of religion, in effect a rejection of the Catholic Church, lasted into modern times and, together with an ideological insistence on equality as an incident of citizenship, was instrumental in paving the way for human rights.

Not until after the brutalisation of two world wars, the exposure of the Catholic Church's dalliance with fascism and the harrowing futility of experiments with ideology did sovereign States come together in Paris on 10 December 1948, under the auspices of the UN General Assembly, to adopt the Universal Declaration of Human Rights (UDHR) and thereby lay the foundations for contemporary international human rights.

Citizenship and human rights

The signature hallmark of human rights lies in the fact that they are vested uniformly in each human being and bring an entitlement: to exercise any such right in the context of relationships either with other human beings or with the State and to appeal to supranational authorities to have that entitlement enforced should the State fail in its legal obligation to respect such rights. While the first can be interpreted as an incident of citizenship, derived from nationality, the second introduces a tension with citizenship, as it authorises a transcending of the citizen/State relationship when necessary to ensure the protection or enforcement of human rights.

Initially, and for nearly two centuries, the 'rights of man' as articulated in both the American and French revolutions were interpreted as the rights of citizens vested in them by virtue of their nationality and assured of protection by the authorities of their sovereign nation State as part of an agreed 'social contract'. Not until the mid-20th century, in the face of irrefutable evidence of the extent of disempowerment inflicted upon citizens – by religion, ideology and nation States – did human rights come to be viewed as being vested in human beings as such rather than by virtue of their being citizens. More recently, the impact of globalisation and mass migration, accelerated by the phenomenon of 'Stateless persons' and the volume of cases determined on a supranational basis, have caused many to see yet further erosion in the relationship between citizenship and human rights. Paradoxically, others take quite the opposite view and argue that the concept of 'citizen' is no longer tied to the nation State but has been re-branded to become 'citizen of the World' precisely because of the uniform, increasingly comprehensive and supranational effect of human rights.[12] A variation of this outlook suggests that citizenship itself is no longer relevant: by establishing transcendent norms, this growing body of rights has become so fundamentally important that it is rapidly attaining the status of a new religion. Having eaten into the space formerly reserved for religious beliefs, a new global superstructure of moral verities is being built and progressively refined while Western society stoically views the displacement of institutional religion as inevitable, a consequence of its tarnished public role being slowly replaced by private piety.

Initial formulation of international human rights and freedoms

Thirty years of essentially religious wars in Europe came to an end with the signing of the Treaty of Westphalia in 1648. This, in effect, ended centuries of both feudal theocratic rule and supranational religious allegiances. The Treaty has been hailed as inaugurating the modern era because it rested upon a multinational agreement, committing sovereign States to respect each other's independent territory and to respect the responsibility of each ruler for ensuring the protection of those religions within it. This marked a significant step in establishing the concept of 'a comity of nations', and also, by breaking the overriding power of religion, it marked the beginnings of secularism. Exactly three centuries later, following more wars that devastated Europe and elsewhere, the Universal Declaration of Human Rights (UDHR) sought to revive the 1648 initiative. The 30 fundamental rights entrenched in the UDHR provided the foundations for the development of all subsequent human rights and include the following which have a particular relevance for religion and are therefore the focus of attention throughout this book.

Right to justice

Access to justice, as guaranteed under Articles 6–11 of the UDHR, is central to the rule of law and a prerequisite for the recognition and enforcement of all other rights. This composite right is of fundamental importance, encompassing an entitlement to equality before the law and to equality of protection by it. Included within its scope is the right to: access a legal system; receive a presumption of innocence and a fair trial; and to receive due process. It requires: relevant information to be available that can be readily understood; appropriate processes and proceedings to exist; an opportunity to obtain such resources as may necessary for effective representation; the proceedings to be conducted independently, fairly, with a right of appeal; and that the outcome is fully and fairly enforced. It is a right that must not be diluted or subverted by diverting a claimant to a parallel religious tribunal or process. In particular, a Shari'a court is unable to provide the requisite impartiality and human rights-compliant remedies required to satisfy this right.

Right to life

This most basic of all human rights was established by Article 3 of the UDHR. It declares that everyone has the right to life, liberty and security of person, and it is unqualified.

In a religious context, this right has a particular relevance for issues relating to abortion, IVF and medically assisted death.

Right to freedom of religion

Article 18 of the UDHR declared the right to freedom of thought, conscience and religion. Enjoyment of this right is necessarily entangled with such other rights and freedoms as those of expression, association and assembly. It includes the right: to have, to adopt or to change a religion or belief; to exercise religion or belief publicly or privately, alone or with others; and to exercise religion or belief in worship, teaching, practice and observance. It also provides for the right to have no religion and to have non-religious beliefs protected. Needless to say, the right to change religion is in direct conflict with the Muslim ruling on apostasy.

Right to freedom of expression

Article 19 of the UDHR establishes the right to articulate opinions and ideas without fear of retaliation, censorship or sanction, and directs that it may be exercised through any media and regardless of frontiers. As one of the principal hallmarks of a democratic society, this right is particularly important for those who need to advocate on behalf of a cause, to comment on events or to challenge an abuse of power. It often functions with other rights such as the freedoms of religion or association. Because it rests on a presumption of permissiveness, it facilitates the growth of a tolerant and pluralist society. In particular, it licences the public manifestation of religious belief, religious identity and the exchange of religious and secular views.

Right to freedom of association

Initially established by Article 20 of the UDHR, this right is crucial for those who wish to join with others to form a legal entity in order to act collectively in pursuit of a common lawful interest. The freedom of association protects the collective pursuit of common goals. It also provides for the right not to be compelled to belong to an association. Essentially it protects the discretion of an individual to form, join or leave an association without interference from the State. This right is crucial for religious organisations, but its exercise by individuals who wish to leave such an organisation can prove difficult in the context of some religions, communities and ethnic groups.

Right to marry and found a family

Article 16 of the UDHR provides for the right of men and women of a marriageable age to marry and to found a family in accordance with their national law without hindrance due to race, nationality or religion. It is specifically made conditional upon the free and full consent of the spouses who are thereafter – for the duration of their marriage and at time of dissolution – entitled to equal rights. Any child born to the parties during their marriage is held to be part of that family. The right to found a family is absolute. The State is required to protect the family unit and cannot interfere with it. There is no legal obligation for the State to provide the services that may be necessary for the right to be exercised, but any State intervention in family affairs is required to be in accordance with the obligation to respect the private and family life of the family's members. The second part of the right, namely, 'to found a family', was clearly intended to be construed as dependant upon first exercising 'the right to marry'. Marriage would confer legal status on 'family' and vest the spouses with reciprocal duties, parental obligations, inheritance rights and so on.

The definition of 'family' has always been of importance to religions, some of which permit arranged marriages, underage marriages or seek to impose constraints on 'marrying out'.

Right to education

As stated in Article 26 of the UDHR, this right establishes that everyone has a right to education, accessible without cost at least until the secondary stage, including a parental right to determine their child's religious education. It is a vitally important right, as it provides a gateway for personal social success and economic security and also the means for facilitating an intergenerational transfer of culture, values and beliefs. Education is understood to mean the provision of factual information, objectively and impartially taught, including health and safety information relating to sex and the facts of life.

This right is specifically required to be exercised in a manner that promotes understanding, tolerance and friendship among all religious groups, which carries particular implications for faith schools.

Right to employment

Article 23 of the UDHR establishes that everyone has a right to employment on reasonable terms. This is a right, not a duty. Individuals are free to choose not to work. No one should be prevented by others from seeking employment, and the right is exercisable in relation to employment in general, not in relation to any particular type of employment.

Neither a religious organisation nor a religious individual are entitled to impose restrictions upon others as to whether or not they may work, nor when they may do so, the type of work they should seek, or the type of clothing they should wear if employed.

Right to equality and non-discrimination

Article 7 of the UDHR is unequivocal in its pronouncement that all are equal before the law, all are entitled without any discrimination to equal protection of the law and all are entitled to equal protection against any discrimination or any incitement to discrimination. This may be read in conjunction with the blanket provision in Article 2 that everyone is entitled to enjoy all UDHR rights and freedoms without distinction of any kind – such as religion – or due to any form of status. This fundamental principle of entitlement to equality and non-discrimination is drawn from similar expressions in both the French Declaration of the Rights of Man and the US Fourteenth Amendment.

For religious organisations and for those of religious belief, the equality and non-discrimination provisions often present difficulties – particularly in the context of employment – which require them to seek exemption from universal constraints that adversely affect their religious freedom.

Religion and beliefs

For millennia, 'religion' has been understood as a concentration of immutable doctrines, rituals and modes of worship, commanding the commitment of its adherents. However, this is no longer necessarily the case. Within a generation or two, if largely within the developed nations, it has been redefined. Now, 'religion' and 'belief' must accommodate not just the traditional institutional religions and an infinite variety of belief systems but also atheists, agnostics and pagans.

Institutional religions

The basic indices, traditionally employed by the judiciary to differentiate a religious entity from all others, have been a belief in a 'supreme being' together with a shared commitment to faith and worship.

Christianity, Judaism and Islam are among the oldest of extant religions. Each is monotheistic with accompanying doctrines and rituals of worship. Other prominent religions with well-established histories include Buddhists, Hindus and Sikhs; these tend to be non- or multi-theistic, with rituals being of central importance. In addition, there are a large and fluctuating number of organisations with a varying quotient of religious characteristics of which Mormons, Scientologists, Druze and Zoroastrians are perhaps the most notable. Then there are religious type groupings that derive from and represent a particular ethnic culture, such as may be found among the Indigenous people of Australia, Canada and elsewhere. Many of these are of ancient origin, preceding Christianity, in which theism is merged with nature.

Doctrines, tenets and so on

A body of core doctrines, creeds or tenets have traditionally been held to comprise the essence of a religion: serving to affirm the beliefs that commit and bind the members as adherents of a particular religion and to differentiate it from all others. However, while Lord Halsbury's observation that "speaking generally, one would say that the identity of a religious community described as a Church must consist in the unity of its doctrines"[13] remains accurate in relation to the more institutional religions, it is less so as regards the many new bodies adhering to philosophical or other belief systems.

New religions

The modern spin-offs from core religions are innumerable: all accommodate an ever-growing number of splinter groups and sects. Christianity, initially fractured into its Roman Catholic, Orthodox and Protestant branches, has since embraced many distinct bodies, including Methodists, Baptists, Plymouth Brethren, Lutherans, Quakers, the Latter-Day Saints (Mormons), Jehovah's Witnesses and the Christian Reformed Church. Protestantism alone comprises some 33,000 different denominations.[14] Hinduism includes Vaishnavism, Shaivism and Shaktism, while Islam has divided into Sunni, Shia, Ahmadiyya and other branches. Some, for example, evangelical Christian churches and strains of Islam, have so refined their beliefs or reduced them to fundamentalist precepts that they face rejection by their parent religion; in others, adherents have developed individual interpretations of their religion's basic beliefs.

In addition, there is a swathe of those such as the Bahá'í, Krishna Consciousness and Falun Gong that share a more spiritualist dimension.

Cults

Cults have little in common with religion other than commitment to a central belief, nor with each other except for a common tendency toward having a charismatic leader, abnormal rituals and the practice of 'brainwashing' its members. There are many dozens of such groups in existence, ranging from New Age mystics to fundamentalist evangelical groups, all of which are easier to join than to leave. The Branch Davidians, for example, many of whom died in an armed confrontation with State authorities in Waco, Texas, in 1993, was such a cult.

Modern definitions

The right of an individual, organisation or community, in public or private, to manifest religion or belief or the lack thereof, and to change that religion or belief, is well established in all Part II jurisdictions. However, the parameters of that right – to freedom of religion or belief – are dependant upon judicial interpretations of 'religion', 'belief' and 'manifest'.

'Religion'

There is currently no agreed-upon definition of 'religion' in international law. However, as the UN Special Rapporteur on Religion or Belief has pointed out:[15]

> [T]he scope of what is protected by the right to freedom of religion or belief must be construed broadly, covering theistic, non-theistic and atheistic beliefs, as well as the right not to profess any religion or belief. It is, therefore, not limited to traditional, mainstream or "recognized" religions and practices.

The traditional religions continue to be readily recognisable although, as noted above, over the past century or so they have generated many subsidiaries and sects and are constantly being joined by new groups each with their own singular interpretation of 'religion'.

'Beliefs'

The word 'belief' applies not just to convictions of a religious nature but also more generally to those which are personal, political, philosophical or moral. The proliferation and infinite variety of new forms of belief that seemed to spring up in the aftermath of the 1960s hippy culture challenged judicial efforts to find a test that could be uniformly applicable to identify those that approximated a 'religious belief'. These included many, like the Freemasons, who espoused philosophical principles but differed from religion by not having a theistic component and by being less reliant upon the supernatural. They shared with religion the fact that the belief of adherents rested on a commitment to a set of principles which informed their world view. At first the regulatory approach adopted was to judge the new in accordance with the accepted specification of the old: the traditional need for doctrines, tenets, worship, celebrants and so on that typified collective religious belief was used as a template for assessing whether new forms conformed to that model. This was defeated by the diversity and mutation of belief systems and also by the perceived unfair advantage in terms of public credence that might be gained by those modelled on traditional religions.[16] However, while there was widespread consensus that an individual's religious beliefs must be ascertained by examining personal convictions[17] and related conduct, there was less certainty as to how much credence should be attached to subjective interpretations as determinative of religious adherence (the 'tooth fairy' problem).

Indigenous beliefs

A challenging factor for this book, not to be overlooked, is the presence of Indigenous people in four of the six Part II jurisdictions. Despite the analytical difficulties involved, there can be no doubt that the concepts and beliefs of an Indigenous culture offer a sufficiently valid and coherent parallel to those of

Christianity, for example, to warrant equal consideration and require the same assessment as to how they intersect with human rights. The core spiritual beliefs, customs and rituals are as varied as the aboriginal cultures that produced them. Although they have been in existence for longer than Christianity, it is now probably impossible to know the extent to which they have been altered by exposure to centuries of Christian missionaries and proselytism. All have been the subject of 19th century legally enforced intervention by Christian religious organisations, the nature and effects of which would now be condemned as constituting a violation of their human rights. All are also now recognised in international law as having rights which they are entitled to have protected.[18]

"Manifestation" of religion or belief

The right to freedom of religion includes the right to manifest it alone and in private, or in public and in the company of fellow believers, subject only to the condition that the manifestation is lawful and does not intrude upon the rights of others. It is closely associated with the right to freedom of expression and is often contentious when it takes the form of a private expression of religious belief – such as praying or wearing religion-specific clothing – and is exercised publicly, for example, in the workplace or classroom.

Religion and beliefs: balancing public and private interests

Religious beliefs, as experienced by an individual, are clearly entirely personal, a matter of private piety: the interests served are confined to him or her, save to the extent that, by example, they may influence others. Should such an individual or a religious organisation choose to manifest their religious beliefs by engaging in public activities intended to give effect to them, then that activity becomes a matter of wider interest. However, this may not be optional. Jurgen Habermas argues that for the religious individual as for the religious organisation, doctrinal beliefs require private piety to be given effect through public conduct – "ye shall know them by their fruits".[19] Because religious dogma leaves both unable to compromise, this imposes an additional burden upon them and therefore society should make special allowances. He suggests that "the liberal State must not transform the requisite institutional separation of religion and politics into an undue mental and psychological burden for those of its citizens who follow a faith".[20]

The social role of religion and beliefs

In addition to manifesting beliefs in acts of collective worship, prayer or other ceremonial activities with and for their adherents, religious organisations also have a well-earned reputation for engaging in good works for the general public benefit. Their contribution to establishing social coherence and a network of institutions in all Part II jurisdictions is inestimable. The foundations of the present educational, health and social care services were laid more by Church than

State, while the churches, schools, universities and hospital complexes provided the basic framework for building communities, assisted by a unifying Christian ethos and architecture. Indeed, the distinctive pastoral landscape of a Church of England parish became the familiar, self-referencing, socially consolidating context for communities throughout the British Empire; on a different scale, much the same can presumably be said for other more locality-based distinctive religious communities such as the Amish. As physical manifestations of virtuous principles, as deliverers of public benefit services and as institutions representing their interests on issues to government and the public, religious organisations are undoubtedly players in the public domain. However, they have a proven capacity not just for community building but also for promoting social division. As has been noted "religion can bind communities together; but it can also emphasise their differences".[21]

Bridging and bonding

The capacity to emphasise difference is only too apparent in the vast range of religious buildings, artefacts, activities and services and so on, the cumulative effect of which is to advertise the separateness, exclusiveness and competitiveness of each religion, its associated organisations and their respective sets of adherents. For non-Christians in the Part II jurisdictions, the prominence of so much venerable Christian architecture and customs, coupled with the symbols, emblems and national anthems that link Church and State must be perceived as intimidating. Indeed, the spread of Islamic mosques, minarets and burquas – though on a comparatively very minor scale – may instil the same reaction in non-Muslims.

Being essentially a member-benefit activity, religion is constrained by the exclusiveness of adherents' commitments and their consequent rejection of those adhering to all other religious beliefs or to none. Experiences in many parts of the world from Sarajevo to Belfast to Baghdad provide evidence of religion's capacity to further the 'bonding' form of social capital at the price of the 'bridging'.[22] Clearly, religion accompanied by proselytism, can serve to emphasise differences, accentuate the marginalisation of minority groups and exacerbate any tendencies toward polarisation.

Religion and equality legislation

Equality legislation, anti-discrimination provisions and human rights more broadly have brought new challenges to religious organisations and their adherents. In particular, the levelling effect of statutory equality requirements, even with carve-outs reserved for the religious, is quite confrontational for those who firmly believe in the transcendental and protest that to be equated with secularists is to entirely miss the point. Indeed, religious beliefs and human rights are mutually exclusive in certain areas. Religious organisations are fundamentally unable, for example, to reconcile traditional theological precepts of marriage as a lifelong monogamous and heterosexual union with the contemporary human rights recognition of it as a union that may encompass homosexual relationships: the orthodox view of marriage, central to Christian religious belief, stands in blunt opposition to the modern statutory requirement that it and gay marriage be respected as equal before the law.

Church and State

As society in a common-law context became less theocratic, with boundaries emerging between the spheres of interest of Church and State, so the shared ground for their continued mutual support became less based on matters of religious doctrine. While this had been the case in the US from the time of the Declaration of Independence, the loosening of the Church/State relationship also became a feature of governance arrangements in all common-law jurisdictions except in England, where the 'established' Church retained its constitutional links with Crown and government. Although scaled back, what did not change was the social role of Christianity, its institutions, customs and vernacular throughout those jurisdictions.

The doctrine of State neutrality

The formal separation of Church and State provides the best possible guarantee that government and the courts will ensure that public life is neutral, free from the undue influence of religion or secularism, and that the legal integrity and autonomy of the citizen is not *a priori* compromised. However, not all nations make such provision, and in the Part II common-law jurisdictions the traditional role of Christianity, its institutions and customary social role continues to have an authoritative presence.

The principle that the State must adopt a neutral approach to religion and religious matters suggests that in law the State should be both 'religion blind' by treating religion as it would anything else, and make no distinction between religions, treating all of them and secularism with equal impartiality. However, as pointed out by Ahdar and Leigh,[23] the 'religion blind' approach is problematic in that 'equality of form can be accompanied by inequality of effect'.[24] Legislation intended to apply universally to all citizens may impose an undue burden upon a particular religious minority. Moreover, an approach that requires religious values and principles to be treated in law the same as those of a secular organisation results in the protest from religious organisations that to do so is perverse: their values are transcendent. Not only are they intended to be different from those that inform secular matters but also, by definition, adherents have no option but to adhere to them; to be a religious person is to accept and give effect, throughout the course of their daily life, to values that transcend secular concerns. It is argued that by insisting on parity the State is diluting or dismissing the values that our civilisation has been founded upon.

State cultural identity

The doctrine requiring the State to treat all religions and non-religions equally may adversely affect national cultural identity. Many States have dense and deep ties with a particular religion and, arguably, their governments have a duty of care to protect it from being disproportionately damaged by laws and policies driven by the neutrality doctrine. A conflation of culture and religion, often enduring over centuries, has done much to shape national identity; particularly in Europe and the Middle East. Some States, such as England, continue to have formal constitutional arrangements with a designated 'established' church in which one specific religion is clearly preferenced above all others. There is an argument that the doctrine imposes such an additional burden upon the primary traditional religion – because of the collateral damage to cultural integrity – relative to all other religions and faiths, that its application may constitute a form of religious discrimination.

Secularism

Secularism[25] can be interpreted as licencing the State to assume responsibility for all decision-making, facilities, administrative systems and processes associated with matters in the public interest without concessions to a religion or religions, nor with any input from religious organisations. While this clearly would not accommodate State religion, or any State preferencing of religion (e.g. favouring Christianity over Islam), there is doubt as to whether it extends to suggesting that religion per se, or religions, or religious values should not be recognised and respected by the State; though not for Jurgen Habermas, who urges that the State "must not discourage religious persons and communities from also expressing themselves politically as such".[26]

Secularism may also be interpreted as affording religion protection from the State. This might be understood, in the Part II jurisdictions, as starting with constitutional arrangements that clearly separate Church and State. The State would then function impartially toward all religions: it would not question the veracity of their beliefs, doctrines or modes of worship; nor would it interfere in their governance or staffing arrangements. It would permit scope for missionary work, proselytism and conscientious objection to be available to those with or without religious beliefs on equal terms. This would seem to accord with the Habermas argument that:[27]

> The principle of separation of Church and State demands that the institution of the State operate with strict impartiality vis-a-vis religious communities; parliaments, courts, and the administration must not violate the prescription not to privilege one side at the cost of another. But this principle is to be distinguished from the laicist demand that the State should defer from adopting any political stance which would support or constrain religion per se, even if this affects all religious communities equally. That would amount to an overly narrow interpretation of the separation of State and Church. At

the same time, the rejection of secularism must not succumb to leaving the door wide open for revisions that would undermine the principle itself.

Islands of exclusivity

A variation of the above approach, championed by Essau,[28] is to establish safe zones for religious organisations and adherents which would permit such entities to be exempted from the constraints of equality and anti-discrimination legislation where such constraints could be shown to have a direct adverse impact upon their beliefs. Rivers, in his masterly *The Law of Organised Religions*, has given this his support, stating that:[29]

> While the State may legitimately adopt a particular, more or less controversial, conception of equality, it should not impose such a conception uniformly on the whole of civil society. Protection from uniform State ideologies is one of the main points of collective religious liberty.

There will be few who will disagree with their joint views about the dangers of giving permission for the State to impose an ideology – any ideology. However, balance is everything, and if there is to be a veto by religious entities on matters of equality that are binding on the rest of society, its exercise must somehow be conditional upon this being demonstrably compliant with the best interests of that society, particularly if tax exemption and/or government funding is involved.

Government support for religious organisations

Secularism suggests that government funding and or tax exemption or any form of support or privilege would either not be available to any religious organisation or would be available equally to all and to their secular counterparts. In practice, this is often not the case.

Government funding

A very significant proportion of the funding needed by religious organisations comes from government, most often in the form of tax exemptions but also as grants for service provision. Whether on a domestic basis or as overseas aid, it is often the case that the only possible service providers on hand to address concentrations of social need are those operated by churches or other faith-based organisations.

Regulatory control

Traditionally, religious organisations have very largely been excepted or exempted from government regulatory control.

Testamentary privilege

The law in the Part II jurisdictions has traditionally permitted testators to attach religiously discriminating conditions to gifts made in wills, a privilege which mostly continues in effect.

Modern policy formulation: religion and human rights

All developed countries now have complex religious environments in which previously dominant institutional religions are losing ground to secularism and, more mundanely, to the immediacy of social-media distractions. The traditional social role of religion is being eroded and fragmented by an ever-growing proliferation of new quasi-religions and belief systems, while fundamentalism, particularly from within Islam, is a growing threat. For the pluralist Part II jurisdictions, the challenge of finding and protecting a sound basis for civil society is one that requires the State to accommodate an unstable mix of religious and cultural affiliations.

Revival of the nation State

Although often foretold, the demise the nation State – as an inevitable consequence of globalisation, or of the forming of supranational conglomerates such as the European Union, or due to the fading of national cultures in the face of multimedia output and escalating foreign travel – may prove to have been premature. Indications are that it is currently undergoing something of a revival. Despite the incremental harmonisation introduced by an increasingly extensive matrix of human rights and decades of associated jurisprudence, arguably any trends toward a more coherent social order are superficial. Also worrying is the realisation that the ongoing 2015/16 migrant crisis triggered a reflexive national protectionism (with some notable exceptions) rather than a coordinated international humanitarian response. From eastern Europe to the US, politics have witnessed a distinct lurch to the right as the Western democracies introduce citizenship tests, advocate tighter border controls and the forced repatriation of migrants.

State sovereignty

The concept of State sovereignty has morphed from a reference to ruler control over people and territory within borders respected by other countries to a reference to the sovereignty of the people within a State: from the absolute right of a sovereign ruler – *'l'etat, c'est moi'* – to the elective rights of citizens. This represents a shift in focus away from the closed, exclusive powers of a ruler to the more open, sharing will of the people. Parliamentary democracy in the Part II jurisdictions has gradually facilitated the sort of cross-border arrangements that would previously have compromised State sovereignty.

Among the many incentives that have promoted increased transnational power sharing – trade and security being to the fore – has been a recognition of the need to protect vulnerable minorities, including religious organisations, their adherents and non-believers wherever they may be, from persecution. The mediation of a human rights paradigm, conferring protection upon a person from unwarranted State constraint and stratified in accordance with the 30 areas of protection recognised initially in the UDHR (as subsequently expanded), into the law governing the 'comity of nations' has imposed limits on State sovereignty. When a State can be seen to be abusing its responsibilities as guardian of citizens rights – as most recently in the gassing of civilians in Douma by the Syrian State armed forces – then the Western democracies will consider that an international obligation to enforce human rights trumps the obligation to respect State sovereignty. This idea is a principle clearly demonstrated by international armed intervention in Kosovo, and it is one now represented by an impressive body of treaties, conventions and protocols and an accompanying network of international institutions.

Foreign policy

Unquestionably the impact of globalisation, aided by the internet, together with a matrix of international agreements on human rights and other matters, as supported by a multilateral web of institutions, have woven the doctrine of 'comity of nations' into a much denser and more complicated reality than could possibly have been foreseen when initially formulated in the early post-Westphalian era. Security concerns have done much to incentivise this transformation.

'Global war on terror'

Since the 9/11 attacks in 2001, it has been estimated that the US counterterrorism response has led to a situation where, as of 2018, its security forces have a presence in 76 countries or 39 percent of those on the planet.[30] Among other things, this provides a measure of how little importance is now attached to the principle of State sovereignty and indicates the scope of transnational penetration in pursuance of a perceived moral imperative, even if not mandated by the UN. It raises serious questions regarding human rights violations associated with practices such as unilateral targeted executions by drone strikes. For present purposes, the main significance of the US led, and largely US conducted, 'global war on terror' is that it has been waged almost exclusively in Muslim countries where very many innocent civilians have been killed and much social infrastructure destroyed, causing large-scale population displacement.

The migrant crisis

This phenomenon – depicted as the greatest transborder movement of people since World War II – has seen waves of uprooted and homeless families, mostly

Muslims, arrive in various European countries and in those of North America. The sudden influx of such a volume of dependant foreigners has sharply accentuated the usual culture clashes and triggered an acute awareness in the host countries of domestic cultural norms and values usually taken for granted. Consequently, government uncertainty regarding the balance to be struck between support of its national culture, including traditional religious affiliation, or in support of multiculturalism would seem to be tipping toward the former and a resurgent 'nation State' ethos. A revival of interest in asserting and protecting national cultural identity is now emerging as a legitimate government goal. While this is an understandable response to the scale of current migratory activity, the totalitarian challenge of ISIS and the threat of Islamic domestic terrorism, it carries with it profound implications for how Western nations – especially the Part II jurisdictions – respond to the human rights of migrants.

Domestic policy

The international engagement of Part II jurisdictions (excepting Ireland) with Islamic extremism is adding to the destabilising pressures that seem to be converging on both the domestic practice of human rights and the traditional social role of religion.

Domestic terrorism

The concentrated use of aerial bombing on targets in Muslim countries has played a considerable role in triggering population displacement and in driving waves of migrants into the Part II jurisdictions and elsewhere.[31] In addition, 'home-grown' Islamic terrorism is generating a cycle of security issues that constrain human rights and risk exacerbating domestic insecurity. In response to the United Nations Security Council Resolution 1373,[32] most common-law nations and others have in recent years introduced domestic antiterrorism legislation, policies and practices, and these have increased the tension between different religious/cultural communities and added to the sense of alienation felt by many Western Muslim citizens already aggrieved by media coverage of devastated Muslim cities. As the Special Rapporteur has warned: "[P]olicies that are adopted to enhance the capacity of security forces to combat terrorism by limiting fundamental rights, such as the rights to freedom of expression, association and peaceful assembly, often have dire consequences for the enjoyment of the right to freedom of religion or belief".[33]

Government initiatives in relation to religion

All developed Western countries, and probably many others, have introduced laws, policies and practices, and have established specific agencies, to promote religious pluralism and a better mutual understanding between religious communities and between them and secularists. In a climate dominated by fear of

Islamic terrorism, where there are indications that cultural/religious pluralism is struggling to absorb large numbers of Muslim migrants and is under threat from religious fundamentalist tendencies, governments are now giving more attention to religious matters and related human rights than ever before. Part of the challenge concerns the balance to be struck between intervention designed to bolster pluralism and positively address the insecurity of Muslim citizens and accommodate new Muslim migrants and intervention designed to protect the established national culture. Political consensus is necessary to develop a 'cultural synthesis' approach which, while recognising and protecting a nation's cultural identity, also proactively seeks to give recognition and space to other cultures within national borders and promotes the building of bridges with minority cultural groups. A varying degree of political willingness to pursue such an approach is becoming very evident among the Part II jurisdictions.

Conclusion

Internationally, there is little evidence that the acceptance and spread of human rights, accompanied by the institutional network provided by the UN and ancillary bodies, has gained sufficient traction to prevent, reduce or bring an end to social upheaval, crimes against humanity or international warfare: measuring international acceptance of human rights by the steadily increasing range of related treaties, conventions and so on, and by the number of State signatories may be illusory. Arguably, the marked disconnect between signing and implementing human rights instruments is now approaching the existential, but then neither does religion currently offer much in the way of grounds for optimism. The revival of Islamic fundamentalism may not have produced the promised caliphate, but it did bring an unforeseen scale of destruction, not just in Iraq but in many other Muslim countries, with a reach that extended into the heart of cities in the Western developed world. As the religious tensions in the Middle East and North Africa – between Shia and Sunni Muslims, between Muslims and Jews and Muslims and ethnic groups – draw in the leading developed nations, there is every reason to doubt whether religion in the immediate future can be a force for good in the international arena.

Domestically, the proliferation of both human rights and various forms of religion and beliefs may be contributing to the fragmentation of our contemporary 'selfie' society. Their interaction, particularly as regards equality and non-discrimination, while undoubtedly increasing awareness of and respect for difference, may also be drawing attention to and generating a touchiness toward public manifestations of religious or cultural differences. All Part II jurisdictions have for some years been multifaith, multicultural and committed to human rights, so it should now be possible to establish whether or to what extent the response of their legal systems to a spectrum of contemporary religion-related issues is human rights-compliant. The rest of this book is largely concerned with identifying and weighing such case law evidence as there may be to aid that line of enquiry.

Notes

1 As quoted by Ignatieff, M., *The Ordinary Virtues: Moral Order in a Divided World*, Harvard University Press, Cambridge, MA, 2017, at p. 196, citing the Church Peace Union (now the Carnegie Council), *In Your Hands: A Guide for Community Action on the 10th Anniversary of the UDHR*, New York, 1958.
2 [1917] AC 406 (H.L.).
3 Ibid., citing: *Briggs v. Hartley* (1850) 19 L. J. (Ch.) 416; *Cowan v. Milbourn* (1867) L. R. 2 Ex. 230; *De Costa v. De Paz* (1754) 2 Swanst, 487; and *In re Bedford Charity* (1819) 2 Swanst. 470, 527.
4 A long catalogue of cases beginning with *De Costa v. De Paz* (1754) 2 Swans 487, Chancery, including *Lawrence v. Smith, Murray v. Benbow* (1822) *The Times* (2 Feb. 1822), *Briggs v. Hartley* (1850) 19 L. J. (Ch.) 416, and ending with *Pare v. Clegg* (1861) 29 Beav 589, 54 ER 756, established that "the Courts will not help in the promotion of objects contrary to the Christian religion".
5 The Statute of Charitable Uses 1601 (43 Eliz. 1, c.4) governed four centuries of shared provision by charitable entities, most usually religious organisations, throughout the common law jurisdictions.
6 Laws, L.J. acknowledged as much in *McFarlane v. Relate Avon Ltd.* [2010] IRLR 872; 29 BHRC 249 when he observed that "the Judaeo-Christian tradition, stretching over many centuries, has no doubt exerted a profound influence upon the judgment of lawmakers as to the objective merits of this or that social policy", at para. 23.
7 See Esau, A.J., '"Islands of Exclusivity": Religious Organisations and Employment Discrimination', *UBC Law Review*, Vol. 33, 2000, at p. 719.
8 See for example, Sands, K.M. (ed.), *God Forbid: Religion and Sex in American Public Life*, Oxford University Press, New York, 2000.
9 O'Halloran, K., *Religious Discrimination and Cultural Context*, Cambridge University Press, Cambridge, 2018, at pp. 510–515.
10 See Blackstone, Sir William, *Commentaries on the Laws of England*, Clarendon Press, Oxford, 1765–1769.
11 Most notably permitting the cross-jurisdiction adoption of principles such as *audi alteram partem, nemo judex debet esse in proprio sua causa*, and *res judicata*.
12 See for example, Benhabib, S., *The Rights of Others: Aliens, Residents and Citizens*, Cambridge University Press, Cambridge, 2004.
13 *Free Church of Scotland v. Overtoun* [1904] AC 515, HL (Sc), per Lord Halsbury LC at pp. 612–613.
14 Barrett, D.B., Kurian, G.T. and Johnson, T.M., *World Christian Encyclopedia: A Comparative Survey of Churches and Religions in the Modern World* (2nd ed.), Oxford University Press, New York, 2001.
15 See Report of the UN Special Rapporteur on Freedom of Religion or Belief, 2017, at para. 26.
16 *Gillette v. United States* [1971] USSC 45; (1971) 401 US 437, 28 Law Ed (2d) 168.
17 See in the US, *United States v. Seeger* [1965] USSC 49, 13 Law Ed (2d) 733.
18 See the UN Declaration on the Rights of Indigenous Peoples, 2006.
19 Matthew 7:16, part of the Sermon on the Mount ('fruits' meaning deeds or works).
20 Habermas, J., 'Religion in the Public Sphere', *European Journal of Philosophy*, Vol. 14:1, 2006, at pp. 1–25, p. 9.
21 *Gallagher v. Church of Jesus Christ of Latter-Day Saints* [2008] 1 WLR 1852, 1867, per Lord Scott of Foscote, at para. 51.
22 See Puttnam, R., *Bowling Alone*, Simon and Schuster, New York, 2000. See also Çelik, G., 'Breakpoint or Binder: Religious Engagement in Dutch Civil Society', *Journal of Civil Society*, Vol. 9:3, 2013, at pp. 248–267.

23 Ahdar, R. and Leigh, I., *Religious Freedom in the Liberal State* (2nd ed.), Oxford University Press, Oxford, 2013, at pp. 113–114.
24 Ibid., citing Barry, B., *Culture and Equality: An Egalitarian Critique of Multiculturalism*, Polity Press, Cambridge, 2001, at pp. 18, 258.
25 The term 'secularism' was first coined by George Jacob Holyoake (1817–1906).
26 Habermas, J., 'Religion in the Public Sphere', *European Journal of Philosophy*, Vol. 14:1, 2006, at pp. 1–25, pp. 9–10.
27 Ibid., at p. 9.
28 Esau, A.J., '"Islands of Exclusivity": Religious Organisations and Employment Discrimination', *UBC Law Review*, 33, 2000, 719. See also Esau, A.J., 'Islands of Exclusivity Revisited: Religious Organizations, Employment Discrimination and *Heintz v. Christian Horizons*', *Canadian Labour & Employment Law Journal*, Vol. 15, 2009–2010, at p. 389.
29 See Rivers, J., *The Law of Organised Religions*, Oxford University Press, Oxford, 2010, at p. 136.
30 See further Brown University's Watson Institute for International and Public Affairs, at: http://watson.brown.edu/costsofwar/.
31 While other factors have also been in play – including failure of the 'Arab Spring', climate change, the Shia/Sunni/Ahmdiyya split within Islam and basic economics – the trauma and destruction inflicted for many years by Western airpower has undoubtedly been a lead cause of population displacement in many Muslim countries.
32 On 28 September 2001, the UN Security Council unanimously adopted a wide-ranging, comprehensive resolution with steps and strategies to combat international terrorism.
33 See Report of the UN Special Rapporteur on Freedom of Religion or Belief, A/HRC/34/50, 2017, at para. 37.

2 International conventions, protocols and ECtHR/HRC case law

Introduction

The Council of Europe in its Recommendation concerning religion[1] declared that "States must require religious leaders to take an unambiguous stand in favour of the precedence of human rights, as set forth in the European Convention of Human Rights (ECHR), over any religious principle".[2] It is therefore unsurprising that a tension between human rights and religion is very evident in the case law generated by the HRC and the ECtHR.

This chapter outlines the contemporary framework of international treaties, conventions, protocols and so on that address the human rights/religion relationship, notes the key rights and freedoms with relevance for religion and identifies the related courts and regulatory bodies. It examines and discusses the evolving principles established by rulings of the European Court of Human Rights (ECtHR) and the Human Rights Committee (HRC) in relation to issues arising on the State/religion interface. It considers the impact of equality legislation and the nature and extent of the religious exemption. This leads into the identification of themes from case law that can focus a comparative evaluation of the religion and human rights in the jurisdiction-specific chapters of Part II.

Framework of relevant international conventions and protocols

There is no such thing as a fixed international framework of law governing religion and human rights more generally. There is, however, a growing corpus of international treaties, conventions and protocols variously impacting on religion, some of which are commonly binding on all nations and all binding on a few, together with a body of related jurisprudence which binds some but provides a common point of reference for all. Their internationalism is evidenced not only by signed treaties and so on between countries but also by the internalising of those same provisions into the domestic law of many nations and their consequent application through local, regional and national courts.

The core religion related conventions

The contemporary body of human rights, growing from the 1948 Universal Declaration and achieving near global consolidation with the 1966 Covenant, now forms a complex, interrelated, indivisible and constantly evolving system of law.

The Universal Declaration of Human Rights (UDHR) 1948

This provided the foundation for all subsequent international human rights instruments. In the ensuing decades, it has prompted the incorporation of such rights into the legal systems of 165 countries, including each of the five nations studied in Part II. Although without a designated enforcement mechanism, it is now accepted that the UDHR imposes an obligation upon the governments of all signatory States to ensure respect for the full body of rights.

The European Convention on Human Rights (ECHR) 1950

The UDHR was subsequently enlarged by the ECHR[3] which, as the court noted in *Tyrer v. the United Kingdom*,[4] "is a living instrument which . . . must be interpreted in the light of present-day conditions". Since then, human rights have been constantly evoked, with the related rulings by the ECtHR growing to form a considerable body of ever-evolving governing principles. Article 6 of the Treaty of the European Union imposes a requirement that all EU law respect the fundamental rights guaranteed by the ECHR.

Article 9 provides for freedom of thought, conscience and religion, including the right: to change religion or belief; to exercise religion or belief publicly or privately, alone or with others; to exercise religion or belief in worship, teaching, practice and observance, and it also provides for the right to have no religion and to have non-religious beliefs protected. It is a qualified right, and as such, the freedom to manifest a religion or belief can be limited, or subject to 'interference', so long as that limitation: is prescribed by law, is necessary and proportionate and pursues a legitimate aim (namely, the interests of public safety, the protection of public order, health or morals, or the protection of the rights and freedoms of others). It is a right restricted to public authorities or those acting on behalf of a public body. Article 14 broadly prohibits discrimination "on any ground", including religion.

The International Covenant on Civil and Political Rights (ICCPR) 1966

This has become particularly relevant because of its wide international application and the accompanying monitoring provided by the United Nations Human Rights Committee (HRCommittee). Together with the Optional Protocol, it has now been ratified by some 169 countries, all of which are required under Article 21 to "respect" ICCPR rights, many being prescriptive, and to "ensure" that citizens have access to them and to an effective remedy for any violation. Most countries have fully incorporated the Covenant into domestic law. Article 18(1) declares the right to freedom of religion, a right in which "[t]he terms 'belief' and 'religion' are to be broadly construed," as "Article 18 is not limited in its application to traditional religions or to religions and beliefs with institutional characteristics or practices analogous to those of traditional religions".[5] Further, in advice with direct relevance for traditional religions and their reliance upon doctrines and tenets, the UN HRCommittee, echoing the above dictum of the ECtHR, has stated that "the Covenant should be interpreted as a living instrument and the rights protected under it should be applied in context and in the light of present-day conditions".[6] In particular, the Covenant mandates that domestic law must prohibit any discrimination[7] and that the advocacy of national, racial or religious hatred shall similarly be prohibited.[8] ICCPR rights and freedoms are so closely intertwined that a breach of any one typically also engages others. The ICCPR, together with the UDHR and the ICESCR, are sometimes collectively referred to as the International Bill of Human Rights.

The European Charter of Fundamental Rights 2000

Proclaimed in Nice in December 2000, the Charter is important because of the explicit non-discrimination provisions in Article 21 (1): "Any discrimination based on any ground such as sex, race, colour, ethnic or social origin, genetic features, language, religion or belief, political or other opinion, membership of a national minority, property, birth, disability, age or sexual orientation shall be prohibited".

The United Nations Declaration on the Rights of Indigenous Peoples (UNDRIP) 2006

For three of the five Part II jurisdictions – Canada, Australia (also New Zealand) and the US (CANZUS) – UNDRIP[9] is singularly important, Article 12 of which declares:

> Indigenous peoples have the right to manifest, practice, develop and teach their spiritual and religious traditions, customs and ceremonies; the right to maintain, protect, and have access in privacy to their religious and cultural sites; the right to the use and control of their ceremonial objects; and the right to the repatriation of their human remains. States shall seek to enable the access and/or repatriation of ceremonial objects and human remains in their possession through fair, transparent and effective mechanisms developed in conjunction with indigenous peoples concerned.

Article 34 adds that "indigenous peoples have the right to promote, develop and maintain their institutional structures and their distinctive customs, spirituality, traditions, procedures, practices and, in the cases where they exist, juridical systems or customs, in accordance with international human rights standards". Although the CANZUS nations did ultimately endorse the Declaration, they did so subject to the same objections raised when they voted against it.[10] UNDRIP has been said to codify "Indigenous historical grievances, contemporary challenges and socio-economic, political and cultural aspirations".[11]

Other relevant international instruments

In addition to the above, for present purposes the following can be regarded as the essential constituents of the international framework of conventions, protocols and so on which now bring human rights to bear upon matters of religion and belief: the International Covenant on Economic, Social and Cultural Rights (ICESCR) 1976; the United Nations Convention on the Rights of the Child (UNCROC) 1989; the Convention on the Elimination of All Forms of Discrimination against Women (CEDAW) 1979; the Declaration on the Elimination of All Forms of Intolerance and of Discrimination Based on Religion or Belief 1981; and the UN Resolutions on the Elimination of All Forms of Religious Intolerance 1981 and 1993, which assign related responsibilities to a Special Rapporteur.

An ever-growing list of international treaties, conventions, protocols and so on are constantly enlarging the number of bodies and themes which interface with national law governing religion and human rights. These include: the International Labour Organisation Discrimination (Employment and Occupation) Convention, the Universal Declaration on the Human Genome and Human Rights 1997 and the International Convention on the Rights of Persons with Disabilities 2006. The International Convention on the Elimination of Race Discrimination (ICERD) 1969 can have a particular relevance in countries which do not have specific religious discrimination legislation. In Article 5(d) it provides for:

vii the right to freedom of thought, conscience and religion; and
viii the right to freedom of opinion and expression.

As regards Europe, a series of Directives binding upon the UK and Ireland also have an influence on religion. Of particular importance is Council Directive 2000/78/EC of 27 November 2000 (establishing a general framework for equal treatment in employment and occupation), which gives direct protection against discrimination in employment based on religion or belief (see further below). Also important are: the European Social Charter 1965 and 1996, which guarantees fundamental social and economic rights; the Charter of Fundamental Rights of the European Union 2000; the Race Equality Directive 2000/43/EC; the European Council Directive 2000/78 EC; the Recast Gender Directive 2006/54/EC on equal treatment in employment; the Gender Directive 2004/113/EC dealing with sex equality in goods and services; and the General Comments issued by the HRC. In July 2008 the European Commission published a proposal for an anti-discrimination directive covering goods and services in the four remaining grounds – age, sexual orientation, religion or belief and disability – as yet not finalised.

Other regional human rights instruments with a direct bearing on religion are the American Convention on Human Rights, Article 12, and the African Charter on Human and Peoples' Rights, Article 8. Also of relevance is the Principles on the Application of International Human Rights Law in Relation to Sexual Orientation and Gender Identity (the Yogyakarta Principles), which state that sexual orientation and gender identity are integral to every person's dignity and humanity and must not be the basis for discrimination or abuse.

International bodies with a brief for religion

One effect of subscribing to a supranational body of jurisprudence accompanied by some enforcing authority, however slight, is to promote an evolving degree of uniformity in the national application of human rights law and a corresponding reduction in its unilateral interpretation.

The Council of Europe

The Council of Europe, among other things, works to promote consistency in the domestic laws of its 47 member States. It is known primarily for producing the 1950 Convention for the Protection of Human Rights and Fundamental Freedoms, which provides safeguards for private and family life (Article 8) and guarantees the right to marry and found a family (Article 12).

Commissioner for human rights

Established in 1999, this is an independent and non-judicial officer who functions in an ambassadorial capacity on behalf of the Council of Europe by engaging with member States to raise awareness about human rights issues and to promote the development of national human rights structures.

The European committee of social rights

This body monitors national compliance with the European Social Charter through its Collective Complaints Procedure and through national reports submitted by the contracting party States. Its decisions and conclusions, though unenforceable, must be respected by the States concerned.

The United Nations

Founded in 1945 to promote international cooperation and prevent further wars, the United Nations (UN) is now the world's largest and most powerful human rights organisation. It works on behalf of its almost 200 member States to maintain international peace and security, conciliate disputes, promote human rights, foster social and economic development, protect the environment and provide humanitarian aid in cases of famine, natural disaster and armed conflict. In Article 55(c) of its founding Charter, the UN declares that its objective is to "promote universal respect for, and observance of, human rights and fundamental freedoms for all without distinction as to race, sex, language or religion".

The UN took an early stand against discrimination that conflates religious and racial prejudices with its 1978 Declaration on Race and Racial Prejudice, which recognised that "religious intolerance motivated by racist considerations" was a form of racism.[12] In addition to the UDHR, it has been responsible for formulating such foundational human rights instruments as the 1966 International Covenant on Civil and Political Rights, together with the International Covenant on Economic, Social and Cultural Rights, the Convention on the Rights of the Child 1989 and the Declaration on the Rights of Indigenous People 2006.

The UN Human Rights Council (HRC)

This body was established in 2006 when it replaced the UN Commission on Human Rights, which was formed in 1946. This subsidiary of the General Assembly works with the High Commissioner on behalf of its 47 HRC member States to oversee human rights issues for the UN. Among the many human rights themes addressed by the Council are those relating to women's rights, LGBT rights and the rights of racial and ethnic minorities. For present purposes, the operative provision is Article 18(2), which declares that 'no one shall be subject to coercion which would impair his freedom to have or to adopt a religion or belief of his choice'. It assigns responsibility for identifying existing and emerging obstacles to the enjoyment of the right to freedom of religion or belief to a Special Rapporteur on the Freedom of Religion and Belief. The Rapporteur reports to the Council and presents recommendations on ways and means to overcome such obstacles. Resolution 16/18, initially introduced in March 2011 at the UN Human Rights Council by the Organisation of Islamic Cooperation, called upon UN member states to combat "intolerance, negative stereotyping and stigmatisation of, and discrimination, incitement to violence and violence against, persons based on religion or belief".

A working group, drawn from the 47 member States, meets three times a year to conduct the Universal Review Process, which monitors implementation of the Covenant by the 193 UN State parties, considers national progress and sets new goals. This process requires submission of national progress reports every four years which are then subject to HRC examination; the results of the examination are summarised in the HRC's 'Concluding Observations'.

UN general comments

The committee for each of the treaty bodies[13] publishes from time to time a 'General Comments' briefing paper which interprets its respective treaty provisions, addresses trends and emerging issues and provides related guidance.

Since 1981 the ICCPR committee has issued General Comments which offer guidance as to the interpretation of particular Covenant provisions and the implications of emerging trends.[14] Of particular note is `General Comment No 22 (see further below).

Courts, commissions and other regulatory bodies

There are a proliferating number of bodies, some with adjudicatory authority, that form a network which does not purport to administer international justice but does weave normative threads of legal principles and processes that make a contribution in that direction.

The European Court of Justice (CJEU)

Officially the Court of Justice of the European Union (CJEU), and normally referred to as the ECJ, it has two constituents: the European Court of Justice (ECJ) and the General Court, which hear complaints against the institutions of the EU from individuals and member States. This, the highest court in the European Union on matters of European Union law, was established in 1952 with the role of ensuring that EU law is interpreted and applied fully and consistently throughout the EU. It adjudicates on legal disputes arising between national governments and EU institutions, enforces decisions taken and settles compensation for any entity that has had their interests harmed as a result of the action or inaction of the EU.

The European Court of Human Rights (ECtHR)

Described as "the most successful international human rights adjudication and enforcement regime in the world today",[15] the ECtHR rules on issues arising from the domestic litigation generated by 47 member States of the Council of Europe, including the UK and Ireland, concerning alleged violations of rights enshrined in the European Convention on Human Rights and its protocols. In making its determinations, the ECtHR is guided by principles such as 'proportionality', 'compatibility with democracy' and 'a margin of appreciation'. The first requires a fair balance to be struck between the demands of the general interests of the community and the requirements of the protection of the individual's fundamental rights.[16] The ECtHR looks at the interference complained of in the light of the case as a whole to determine whether the alleged interference is "prescribed by law" and was: (i) for a legitimate aim which is important enough to justify interfering with a fundamental right, (ii) rationally connected to achieving that aim, (iii) no more than reasonably necessary to achieve it, and (iv) in the light of this, striking a fair balance between the rights of the individual and the interests of the community.[17] It imports a liberal measure of balance and tolerance.[18] Frequently the ECtHR can be seen applying the second principle – is this form of State intervention necessary in a democratic society?[19] The third permits States a degree of latitude in their interpretation of human rights obligations.[20] Each State enjoys a margin of appreciation when assessing what constitutes 'discrimination' and the extent to which differences in otherwise similar situations may justify a corresponding difference in treatment. This principle is not above reproach and has attracted criticism.[21]

The Venice commission

This organ of the Council of Europe was established in 1990 and has a membership of 60 member States (the 47 members of the Council of Europe plus 13 others). Its primary task is to assist and advise individual countries in constitutional matters in order to improve functioning of democratic institutions and the protection of human rights. It does so by appointing a working group of rapporteurs to advise national authorities on relevant issues.

The United Nations Human Rights Committee (HRCommittee)

Composed of a body of 18 independent experts that meet three times a year, the HRCommittee was established under Article 28 of the ICCPR. It provides an independent and impartial monitoring function by reporting on implementation of the Covenant by the 193 UN member States and on issues arising for any of the State parties to Optional Protocols 1 and 2.

The Committee requires State parties to ensure that domestic law provides "all the necessary safeguards required to prevent the restriction of Covenant rights beyond the limits permissible under the Covenant".[22] In addition, under Optional Protocol 1, which has 35 signatories and 116 States parties (as of January 2018), the HRCommittee exercises a quasi-judicial function whereby it considers and determines alleged breaches of Covenant provisions in proceedings brought by individuals.[23]

The Convention on the Elimination of Discrimination against Women (CEDAW)

The Committee on the Elimination of All Forms of Discrimination against Women monitors implementation of the Convention which was adopted in 1979 by the United Nations General Assembly. The Committee reviews and makes recommendations on national reports submitted by the States parties within one year of their ratification or accession of the Convention, and thereafter every four years.

Human rights commissions

It has been customary for human rights issues, including religious discrimination, to be regulated by a designated national or regional Human Rights Commission, with a right of appeal to the appropriate court. As equality and non-discrimination legislation has grown, it is now not uncommon for all litigation relating to alleged inequity, inequality or discrimination to be assigned, in the first instance, to the same unified administrative body.

Other

The Committee for the Elimination of Racial Discrimination monitors compliance with the UN's International Convention on the Elimination of All Forms of Racial Discrimination (ICERD). In its General Recommendation XXIX, the Committee strongly reaffirmed that discrimination based on descent in Article 1 of ICERD includes discrimination "against members of communities based on forms of social stratification such as caste and analogous systems which nullify or impair their equal enjoyment of human rights". The Committee on Economic, Social and Cultural Rights provides a corresponding monitoring role in relation to ICESCR provisions. Also relevant is the Advisory Committee on the Framework Convention for the Protection of National Minorities (FCNM), a monitoring body of the Council of Europe, and the Equal Rights Coalition of 30 nations founded in 2016 to promote and protect the rights of the LGBT community around the world.

International reports

In 2006 the UN General Assembly introduced the above-mentioned Universal Periodic Review process[24] which applies uniformly to each of the 193 UN Member States, including those presently being considered. It provides an opportunity for each State to make a periodic declaration to the Human Rights Council regarding the actions taken to improve human rights in its country – including protection against religious discrimination – to receive comment from its peer signatory States and to agree on goals for the next review. This process operates in conjunction with the Principles relating to the Status of National Institutions (the Paris Principles), adopted by UN General Assembly in 1993[25] which set out the minimum standards required from national human rights institutions if they are to be considered credible and to operate effectively. In order to be effective and awarded 'A status', national human rights institutions must be independent, adequately funded and have a broad human rights mandate.

While UNCROC has no designated enforcement mechanism, the Committee on the Rights of the Child (CRC) does make recommendations to States, on the basis of reports filed with it under Article 44, for improvements in national law and practice. This audit mechanism provides a useful tool for promoting transparency and accountability and for benchmarking developments in national law while also facilitating international comparative assessments.

The UN Committee on the Rights of Persons with Disabilities (CRPD) has criticised the UN Human Rights Committee, which wants to create a right to abortion on the grounds of foetal abnormality. CRPD stated that "laws which explicitly allow for abortion on grounds of impairment violate the Convention on the Rights of Persons with Disabilities".

There are many other organisations, such as Human Rights Watch and Amnesty International, which also issue reports.

The State and the human rights/religion intersect

The role and functions of the State intersect with human rights at many points, and this is mostly mutually reinforcing. However, some human rights specifically recognise circumstances in which religion, religious individuals or religious organisations may need and be entitled to legal protection by or from the State.

Balancing the interests of Church and State

Protecting the freedom of religion and belief from State interference is the primary objective of Article 9 of the European Convention on Human Rights (ECHR). This is reinforced by Article 14 which protects against State discrimination in the enjoyment of any ECHR on grounds that include religion and belief.

Any consideration of a balancing of the interests of religion and State has to begin with an acknowledgment that all Part II jurisdictions have inherited a legacy of Christian culture which remains very visibly imprinted on their societies. While the ECtHR has ruled that State protection of its religious/cultural identity is legitimate,[26] this particular identity cannot be perceived as being anything other than intimidating for secularists and for those of non-Christian beliefs. The need for such a balancing exercise also applies in relation to the interests of secularism and religion *per se*. This was acknowledged by the ECtHR in *Folgerø & Others v. Norway*[27] when again, and importantly for this book, it found that a State had a legitimate interest in protecting its established cultural identity from being neutralised by the secularism of its institutions. The court then held that the compulsory teaching of religious knowledge in State schools, which concentrated on Christianity to the detriment of other religions, was justified given that Christianity had long been a significant component of that culture. The extent to which the ECtHR had retreated from the secular high ground of earlier rulings became evident in *Lautsi v. Italy*[28] (see further below).

At the very least, the State is required, under Articles 9 and 14 of the ECHR as supported by Article 1 of the First Protocol, to ensure protection against religious discrimination. This is repeated in a number of international conventions, protocols and so on,[29] including Articles 2(1) and 26 of the ICCPR, which bind every signatory nation to prohibit discrimination on the basis of religion, while Article 20(2) provides that "any advocacy of national, racial or religious hatred that constitutes incitement to discrimination, hostility or violence shall be prohibited by law". The ECtHR has held that Article 14 is not limited to cases where a State treats differently persons in analogous situations without providing an objective and reasonable justification but is "also violated when States without an objective and reasonable justification fail to treat differently persons whose situations are significantly different".[30]

State- and religion-related terrorism

Article 18(3) of the ICCPR, in conjunction with other international instruments, requires security measures to be human rights-compliant. However, ISIS terrorism and the scale of the ongoing migrant crisis, which began in 2015 and saw waves of refugees escaping from Islamic countries such as Libya, Afghanistan, Iraq and Syria – devastated by ISIS, by western armed intervention, by local religious/ethnic conflicts (particularly between Shia and Sunni communities) and by climate change – have prompted intrusive domestic measures from Western governments. While some of these can seriously violate basic human rights – such as rights to fair trial, liberty and freedom from torture – other more general constraints, warns the Special Rapporteur, are also likely as are the resulting negative impacts on a democratic society:[31]

> Policies that are adopted to enhance the capacity of security forces to combat terrorism by limiting fundamental rights, such as the rights to freedom of expression, association and peaceful assembly, often have dire consequences for the enjoyment of the right to freedom of religion or belief.

State neutrality

The rulings of the ECtHR[32] have established that the State must adopt a neutral stance in relation to religious matters[33] in order to ensure the preservation of pluralism and the proper functioning of democracy.[34] In so doing the State is assured of enjoying a wide margin of appreciation – at least when issues arise for adjudication by the EctHR,[35] though not if determined by the HRC.

The State is required to treat all religious groups equally. As the ECtHR declared in *Religionsgemeinschaft der Zeugen Jehovas and Others v. Austria*:[36] "[T]he obligation under Article 9 of the Convention . . . on the State's authorities (is) to remain neutral in the exercise of their powers in this domain (and) requires therefore that if a State sets up a framework for conferring legal personality on religious groups to which a specific status is linked, all religious groups which so wish must have a fair opportunity to apply for this status and the criteria established must be applied in a non-discriminatory manner". This approach was further emphasised in *Savez Crkava "Riječ života" and Others v. Croatia*[37] when the court noted that "the State had a duty to remain neutral and impartial in exercising its regulatory power in the sphere of religious freedom and in its relations with different religions, denominations and beliefs".[38]

Christian symbols/prayers in State facilities

The presence of such overt expressions of a particular religion/culture gave rise to issues in *Folgerø & Others v. Norway*[39] (see further below) and earlier in *Valsamis v. Greece*.[40] In both cases the ECtHR found that the mandatory exposure of pupils to symbols and rituals in State schools did not constitute a violation of their parents' rights under either Article 9 or Article 2 of Protocol No. 1.

The issue is also one which occasionally surfaces in the context of an official requirement to swear an oath before undertaking certain responsibilities. So, in *Buscarini and Others v. San Marino*,[41] some members of Parliament, as a prerequisite to taking up their duties, had to swear an oath on the Bible, while in *Alexandridis v. Greece*,[42] a court 'swearing-in' procedure was an official requirement. In both, the Court held that there had been a violation of Article 9 because such a procedure was tantamount to obliging them to swear allegiance to a particular religion. Article 9 was found to be similarly violated in *Dimitras and Others v. Greece*[43] by an obligation imposed on the applicants, as witnesses in a number of sets of judicial proceedings, to disclose their religious convictions in order to avoid having to take an oath on the Bible.

Protecting religion from the State

Concern regarding the Church/State relationship has often and for many decades, in some countries for centuries, been focused mainly on a perceived need to protect the former from the latter. Arguably, the momentum given to this concern by the growth of a more assertive secularism has eased in recent years as reflected in ECtHR rulings which indicate a readiness to recognise a State right to take positive measures to defend its cultural heritage – including the status of its traditional primary religion.

Intervention in Church affairs

ECtHR rulings have established that the State is prevented from intervening in: the decisions of religious communities to admit or exclude members;[44] doctrinal differences within the membership[45] and the freedom to choose employees according to criteria specific to the religious community.[46]

The ECtHR has been particularly firm in cautioning the State against intervening in doctrinal matters: "[T]he State's duty of neutrality and impartiality [among beliefs] is incompatible with any power on the State's part to assess the legitimacy of religious beliefs and requires the State to ensure mutual tolerance between opposing groups".[47] In *Manoussakis v. Greece*,[48] it ruled that "the right to freedom of religion . . . excludes any discretion on the part of the State to determine whether religious beliefs or the means used to express such beliefs are legitimate".[49] It must restrict intrusion solely to establishing that the commitment to a religion or belief is held with cogency, seriousness, cohesion and importance.[50] The subsequent ECtHR rulings in the German cases of *Obst*[51] and *Schüth*[52] seemed to be inconsistent with this approach, as although both were factually similar, they had different outcomes, thus suggesting that the court had engaged in a weighting of the relative importance of religious beliefs and thereby breached the autonomy of the Church (see further below). The more recent ruling in *İzzettin Doğan and Others v. Turkey*[53] reaffirmed the *Manoussakis* approach.

State protection of Indigenous beliefs/culture

The right to a cultural identity is given explicit recognition under Articles 8, 9 and 11 of the ECHR, while Article 27 of the ICCPR specifically recognises the right of minorities to maintain their own culture, language and religion. A right to protection is to be found in the Framework Convention for the Protection of National Minorities but is asserted mainly by Article 12 of the UN Declaration on the Rights of Indigenous Peoples. Related issues often come before the court as a consequence of State intervention in the way of life of the Roma or of the Traveller community, and the advice of the ECtHR in *Chapman v. the United Kingdom*[54] holds true as a general principle governing the relationship between the State and Indigenous people:[55]

> [A]lthough the fact of belonging to a minority with a traditional lifestyle different from that of the majority does not confer an immunity from general laws intended to safeguard the assets of the community as a whole, such as the environment, it may have an incidence on the manner in which such laws are to be implemented.

Other principles of similar general application formulated by that court include: in *Muñoz Díaz v. Spain*,[56] that "the force of the collective beliefs of a community that is well-defined culturally cannot be ignored"; in *R.B. v. Hungary*,[57] that "any negative stereotyping of a group, when it reaches a certain level, is capable of impacting on the group's sense of identity"; in *Ciubotaru v. Moldova*,[58] that "an individual's ethnic identity constitutes an essential aspect of his or her private life"; and in *Izzetin Doğan and Others v. Turkey*,[59] it stressed the importance of "the right of a religious community to an autonomous existence".

State protection of its traditional religious/cultural identity

Article 9 is subject to the significant caveat that it cannot be allowed to diminish the role of a faith or a Church with which the population of a specific country has been historically and culturally associated:[60] while "new" religious communities cannot be disadvantaged relative to traditional religious organisations, the State has a right to take steps to protect its cultural heritage, including any religion which may have traditionally formed part of that heritage.

A judicial concern to ensure that the established cultural identity of a member State does not become neutralised by the secularism of its institutions is evident in the case law.[61] In *Folgerø & Others v. Norway*,[62] for example, which concerned an objection to the compulsory teaching in State schools of religious knowledge that concentrated on Christianity to the detriment of other religions, the ECtHR ruled in favour of the right of the State to protect its cultural and religious identity. That same year, in *Hasan and Eylem Zengin v. Turkey*,[63] the court applied the same approach when it ruled that "greater priority [given] to knowledge of Islam" was justified by "the fact that, notwithstanding the State's secular nature, Islam is the majority religion practised in Turkey". Again, in *Lautsi v. Italy*,[64] which focused on the religious discrimination – as perceived by secularist parents – represented by a crucifix in every classroom of the school in which their child was a pupil, the ECtHR found that this was permissible, as "a European court should not be called upon to bankrupt centuries of European tradition . . . this court ought to be ever cautious in taking liberties with other people's liberties, including the liberty of cherishing their own cultural imprinting".[65] An approach which seem to harden further in *Martinez v. Spain*,[66] when a 'married priest' who taught Roman Catholicism in a State school, unsuccessfully alleged that the non-renewal of his contract was due to the publicity given to his situation as a married priest, and thus conflicted with his rights under Article 9. The decision of the ECtHR, albeit by a very narrow majority, supported the religious autonomy of the Spanish Catholic Church. The Special Rapporteur has warned that this approach is not without its risks for a democratic society, as "many Governments promote certain religions in order to define and demark their national or cultural identity".[67]

There is also evidence of the ECtHR adopting a more balanced approach as in *Akdaş v. Turkey*,[68] when it stressed that it is frequently necessary "to take into consideration the existence, within a single State, of various cultural, religious, civil or philosophical communities", a rationale it reiterated in *Mansur Yalçın & Ors v. Turkey*.[69]

State preferencing of religion and religious organisations

In the eyes of many secularists, and others, the statutory privileges granted to those who are religious constitute a form of reverse religious discrimination and, as such, compromise the basic human rights of all citizens.

The 'religious' exemption

That religion and associated organisations are entitled to a degree of autonomy is recognised in the UN Declaration on Religious Intolerance, which provides for the right to "train, appoint, elect, or designate by succession appropriate leaders" and the right to "establish and maintain appropriate charitable and humanitarian institutions".[70] This right was relied upon until 2012 by the Catholic Church to claim that its priests were appointed on the basis of a 'vocational calling' rather than as secular employees, thereby enabling the Church to disclaim employer responsibility for the sexual abuse of children perpetrated by many priests.

The right to appoint clergy and fill other key leadership posts, free from the restrictions of anti-discrimination and equality law, has been extended to permit similar staff appointments in religious service provision entities such as hospitals, schools and so on and to restrict access to services, schools and social care facilities owned by religious organisations. The extent to which such an extension is permissible – exempting the selection of ancillary staff such as cleaners, janitors, gardeners and so on from such legislative provisions – varies somewhat across the common-law jurisdictions but is challenged in all by secularists and others. The challenge is perhaps strongest in Germany where, as illustrated in the above-mentioned *Schüth*[71] case, a body of jurisprudence has established that the State is entitled, and obliged, to intervene in such internal Church employment disputes; if it did not intervene, an aspect of German labour law would become "clericalized", a rationale seemingly endorsed by the ECtHR, in that instance, in a decision which may prove to have value as a precedent on which to base further challenges.

Regulatory privileges

Traditionally, institutions of the Church have been spared regulatory intervention from those of the State. There is no mandatory registration requirement for religious organisations, without which there is no basis for regulatory monitoring; they have generally been left to regulate their own affairs. Only if religious entities choose to opt into universally applicable processes – by seeking incorporation or tax exemption status – will they then become subject to the associated but perfunctory regulatory requirements.

Tax privileges

Religious organisations, churches and their associated service provision emanations tend to automatically qualify for exemption from most taxes on the basis of State recognition of their legally presumed public benefit status. Of the few cases heard by the ECtHR, three concerned France and the tax exemption entitlement of religious organisations, in respect of which judgments were handed down at the beginning of 2013.[72] In all three, the organisations had initially been found to be in breach of relevant tax requirements due to their receiving direct donations, which had resulted in loss of exemption status and the imposition of harsh financial penalties. Their appeal rested on the argument that requiring them to pay tax on direct donations infringed their right to manifest and exercise their freedom of religion, contrary to Article 9. The ECtHR upheld their appeal, ruling that direct donations were a major source of funding of a religious body and that taxing them might have an impact on its ability to conduct its religious activities. This decision was in keeping with an earlier ruling[73] in which the court had held that the amount of money demanded from the Jehovah's Witnesses by the French tax authorities had constituted an interference with their right to manifest under Article 9 because it had the effect of reducing the vital resources of the Association.

Testamentary privileges

The law has for centuries permitted testators to make religiously discriminating dispositions. Throughout the 20th century, and continuing if to a variable extent at present, bequests to next-of-kin on condition, for example, that they do or do not marry someone of a specified religion, have been exempted from equality and non-discrimination laws. In many common law countries there continues to be no legislative provision explicitly prohibiting such violations of universally accepted non-discrimination principles.

State funding of faith-based facilities and services

The issue of whether religious organisations should receive direct government funding, and if so, which organisations and on what basis, has long been contentious. The common-law jurisdictions presently being considered tend to have either an 'established' Church or a network of institutional religions, and the extent to which the State uses this as a vehicle for delivering public services is a matter that will be explored in Part II.

Religion and the freedoms of association and expression: ECtHR/HRC rulings

The fundamental right to religious freedom has for many generations been securely established in all developed nations, but the legal definition of what constitutes 'religion' and 'belief' in contemporary society has greatly changed, and this has had consequences for other human rights. Arguably, these have been of greatest significance for the freedoms of association and expression, as can be seen in the rulings of the ECtHR and the HRCommittee.

Freedom of religion

The right to freedom of religion is proclaimed in Articles 18 of the UDHR and the ICCPR, replicated in Article 9(1) of the ECHR and reinforced by the ICESCR and by Article 10 of the Charter of Fundamental Rights of the European Union. Most usually, reliance is placed on the clear declaration of the right in Article 9(1) of the ECHR:

> Everyone has the right to freedom of thought, conscience and religion; this right includes freedom to change his religion or belief and freedom, either alone or in community with others and in public or private, to manifest his religion or belief, in worship, teaching, practice and observance.

This is supplemented by Article 14:

> The enjoyment of the rights and freedoms set forth in [the] Convention shall be secured without discrimination on any ground such as sex, race, colour, language, religion, political or other opinion, national or social origin, association with a national minority, property, birth or other status.

The right is applied internationally by Article 18 of the ICCPR, of which Article 18(3) provides that the freedom to manifest one's religion or beliefs may be subject only to such limitations as are prescribed by law and are necessary to protect public safety, order, health, morals or the fundamental rights and freedoms of others. Article 18 rights are non-derogable, even at times of national emergency, and are reinforced by Articles 2 and 26; the Article 27 right of religious minorities to protection for their culture and religious practices may also be relevant. The UN HRCommittee, in General Comment 22, emphasises that:

> 2. Article 18 protects theistic, non-theistic and atheistic beliefs, as well as the right not to profess any religion or belief. The terms "belief" and "religion" are to be broadly construed. Article 18 is not limited in its application to traditional religions or to religions and beliefs with institutional characteristics or practices analogous to those of traditional religions.
>
> 5. The Committee observes that the freedom to "have or to adopt" a religion or belief necessarily entails the freedom to choose a religion or belief, including the right to replace one's current religion or belief with another or to adopt atheistic views, as well as the right to retain one's religion or belief.

It also notes that "the concept of worship extends to ritual and ceremonial acts giving direct expression to belief, as well as various practices integral to such acts, including the building of places of worship, the use of ritual formulae and objects, the display of symbols, and the observance of holidays and days of rest".[74] It clearly also extends to provide protection for non-coercive proselytism. It is restated in many national constitutions and statutes, ultimately providing the governing source of authority for national courts and regulatory bodies. The interpretation and developmental significance of this right has evolved with ECtHR case law and HRCommittee rulings.

'Religion'

Until 1995, the European Commission on Human Rights denied almost all applications for a hearing from religions that could be called "new", "minority", or "nontraditional".[75] Even now, all Conventions and the ECtHR refrain from providing a definition of 'religion'. However, the ECtHR requires that any interpretation be applied objectively, have reasonable justification[76] and be non-discriminatory; any difference in treatment must comply with strict standards. Further, in *Campbell and Cosans v. United Kingdom*,[77] it ruled that theistic beliefs are not essential to satisfy a legal definition of 'religion' and has since accepted that Jehovah's Witnesses, the Church of Scientology and the Moon sect are protected by Article 9(1) of the Convention, as are pacifists, druids, vegans and atheists. The HRC in General Comment 22 has stated, as noted above in reference to Article 18 of the ICCPR, that the protection afforded to 'religion' or 'belief' encompasses "theistic, non-theistic and atheistic beliefs, as well as the right not to profess any religion or belief".[78]

'Beliefs'

The ECtHR has found that the veracity of a 'belief' is to be determined by having regard to its cogency, seriousness and cohesion and its importance to the holder.[79] It extends to ideas and philosophical convictions of all kinds[80] and could, for example, include pacifism and conscientious objection. This interpretation is also proclaimed in the European Directive on Race, issued in 2000.[81]

Indigenous beliefs

Although Article 12 of UNDRIP recognises the right of Indigenous people to spiritual and religious beliefs as a collective right, this remains a controversial topic for four of the Part II jurisdictions, as it is in many other countries, because such beliefs are invariably entangled with land ownership. Spiritual beliefs tend to be associated with nature and to involve the topographical features of the land where their ancestors have lived for many generations and which may well find protection under Protocol No. 1, Article 1, of the ECHR.[82] The conflation of religious belief with land ownership – or land usage over millennia – can make this an area where human rights, religion and the State come into sharp conflict.

Manifestation of religion or belief

The Declaration on the Elimination of All Forms of Intolerance and of Discrimination Based on Religion or Belief 1981 protects the manifestation of religion or belief, including: worshipping and assembling, and maintaining places for this purpose; establishing and maintaining charitable or humanitarian institutions; practicing religious rites and customs; writing and disseminating religious publications; teaching religion and belief; soliciting voluntary financial support; the training and appointment of religions leaders in accordance with the requirements and standards of the religion or belief; observing religious holidays and ceremonies; and communicating with individuals and communities on matters of religion and belief. This interpretation has been reinforced by the HRC advice that the right to manifest religion or belief, in Article 9(1) of the ECHR, should be interpreted to "include not only ceremonial acts but also such customs as the observance of dietary regulations, the wearing of distinctive clothing or headcoverings, participation in rituals associated with certain stages of life, and the use of a particular language customarily spoken by a group".[83] Article 9 also specifically includes the right to conscientious objection.

Under Article 9(2), the right to manifest is made subject to the rights of others, a conditional right of exercise that is replicated in the ICCPR:[84] Article 18(1) establishes the right to manifest, and Article 18(3) makes it subject to restrictions in specified circumstances. The ECtHR has ruled that the right includes the freedom to manifest one's religion alone and in private, in community with others[85] or in public and within the circle of those whose faith one shared.[86] However, in exercising that freedom, an applicant "may need to take his specific situation into account".[87] As the court ruled in *Kosteski v. 'The Former Yugoslav Republic of Macedonia'*,[88] protection is not afforded to every act motivated or inspired by a religion or belief. In that instance, it was not persuaded that attendance at a Muslim festival was a manifestation of the applicant's beliefs that warranted such protection. Manifestation issues now often arise where there has been a clash between the right to freedom of religion and the right not to be discriminated against on the grounds of sexual orientation.

In General Comment 22, at para 8, the HRCommittee noted the wide application of rights protected by Article 18:[89]

> The Committee observes that the concept of morals derives from many social, philosophical and religious traditions; consequently, limitations on the freedom to manifest a religion or belief for the purpose of protecting morals must be based on principles not deriving from a single tradition.

It has stressed that the State may interfere in the right to manifest a religion or belief but only if it can show that this was 'prescribed by law' and 'necessary to protect public safety, order, health, or morals or the fundamental rights and freedoms of others'. This threshold results in a heavy onus being placed upon the State to justify any such action. In *Jakobski v. Poland*,[90] for example, the ECtHR ruled that it was unlawful for prison authorities to deny a Buddhist prisoner a vegetarian diet even though such a diet was not strictly required by Buddhism; it was sufficient and not unreasonable that the prisoner believed it necessary to manifest his beliefs in that way.

Religious discrimination

Article 14 of the ECHR broadly prohibits discrimination "on any ground", including religion; it takes effect solely in relation to the enjoyment of the rights and freedoms safeguarded by other Convention provisions.[91] It is supported by: Article 9 of the ECHR, by Article 1 of the First Protocol and also by CEDAW and the ICCPR.[92] Article 1 of Protocol 12 to the ECHR, which came into force for those States that ratified it on 1 April 2005, provides for a free-standing right to non-discrimination, irrespective of whether the difference in treatment engages another Convention right. It therefore provides for protection equivalent to non-discrimination guarantees in ICERD and the ICCPR.

Articles 2(1) and 26 of the latter bind every signatory nation in relation to discrimination on the basis of religion. Article 27 gives an assurance that minority groups are entitled to profess and practice their own religion, while Article 20(2) provides that "any advocacy of national, racial or religious hatred that constitutes incitement to discrimination, hostility or violence shall be prohibited by law". Article 14 is further reinforced by the Employment Framework Council Directive 2000/78/EC, the purpose of which, as stated in Article 1, is to "lay down a general framework for combating discrimination on the further grounds of religion or belief, disability, age or sexual orientation, as regards employment and occupation". Also relevant is the International Labour Organisation Discrimination (Employment and Occupation) Convention 1958 (ILOC),[93] which provides in Article 1.2 an exemption relating to the employment of people by "religious institutions", where discrimination is "required by the tenets and doctrines of the religion, is not arbitrary, is consistently applied" or "is an inherent requirement of a particular job".

One of the most important UN documents protecting religious freedom is the UN Declaration on the Elimination of All Forms of Intolerance and of Discrimination Based on Religion or Belief 1981, particularly in Articles 2 and 6. Article 2 defines religious discrimination as:

> Any distinction, exclusion, restriction or preference based on religion or belief and having as its purpose or as its effect nullification or impairment of the recognition, enjoyment or exercise of human rights and fundamental freedoms on an equal basis.

Article 6 states that a religious community's joint or shared expression of beliefs is protected equally with the individual's right. In addition to elaborating upon the right to 'manifest' one's religion in Article 18,[94] the Declaration sets out in considerable detail what the international community regards as basic standards for protection of religious freedom, and in Article 3 cautions that "discrimination between human beings on grounds of religion or belief constitutes an affront to human dignity".

Freedom of association

The right of individuals to meet, or form associations, for the purposes of worship, religious teaching or for any other religion-related reason, is long established and was acknowledged in Article 20 of the UDHR and also in Article 18(1) of the ICCPR by the phrase 'in community with others', as restated in Article 22. It was enhanced in Article 11 of the ECHR and ultimately significantly enlarged by the ICESCR. UNCROC, in Article 15, also recognises among the rights of the child a right to freedom of association. As illustrated by *Handyside v. The United Kingdom*,[95] it includes the right to associate for purposes of advocacy or dissent. The exercise of this right is subject only to such constraints as may be necessary in a democratic society.

Both the HRCommittee and the ECtHR have been alert to the dangers inherent in State policies which seek to control religious associations or target certain associations for restrictive measures. The HRCommittee in *Malakhovsky v. Belarus*[96] ruled that State bureaucracy, which unduly delayed and then refused to register a religious community, thereby preventing it from acquiring the legal status of a 'religious association', had unlawfully obstructed the latter's religious activities and violated their rights under Article 18 of the ICCPR. While the ECtHR has issued rulings condemning government bans on public demonstrations by LGBT groups,[97] it has also ruled that if an association's activities constitute widespread intimidation, the association can be lawfully banned.[98] The State closure of the Jumah Mosque Congregation gave the court an opportunity to consider the juxtaposition of the rights to freedom of religion and the freedom of association.[99] The closure was based on the fact that while the organisation purported to be a non-government organisation delivering community support services, it was in fact engaging in religious activities and functioning as a religious organisation (registration requirements differentiated between the two) when it was prohibited from doing so. The ECtHR warned that:[100]

> citizens should be able to form a legal entity in order to act collectively in a field of mutual interest is one of the most important aspects of the right to freedom of association, without which that right would be deprived of any meaning. The way in which national legislation enshrines this freedom and its practical application by the authorities reveals the state of democracy in the country concerned.

This message was reiterated with some emphasis in *Genov v. Bulgaria*[101] when the ECtHR ruled that the autonomy of religious communities was essential to pluralism in a democratic society and was therefore at the very heart of the protection afforded by Article 9.

The 'positive action' provisions

Positive action is permitted if it is a proportionate means of addressing the disadvantages of a group with shared protected characteristics and if it serves to encourage a more proportionate take-up in activities or services by members of such a protected group. It may come into play where a group is perceived to be socially or economically disadvantaged or subject to systemic discrimination.

Freedom of expression

This right, as initially declared in Article 19 of the UDHR, was subsequently reinforced and further developed by Article 10 of the ECHR and Article 19 of the ICCPR. While Article 19(2) of the ICCPR states the general freedom of expression, under Article 19(3) this is made subject to "the interests of other persons or to those of the community as a whole", which permits restrictions when they are: (i) "provided by law," and (ii) "necessary" for (iii) "respect of the rights or reputations of others" or for "the protection of national security or of public order or of public health or morals". So, for example, the exercise of this right is subject to the duty to protect the welfare of minors from sexual exploitation.[102] There is no uniform definition of hate speech in international law. Article 20(2) states that any "advocacy of national, racial or religious hatred that constitutes incitement to discrimination, hostility or violence shall be prohibited by law". The right to freedom of expression necessarily engages other rights such as the right to access information and the right to freedom of assembly.[103]

Religiously motivated conduct

A manifestation of religion or belief is not permissible if it's likely to cause alarm or distress. For example, in *Vejdeland and Others v. Sweden*[104] the ECtHR applied hate speech principles in relation to sexual orientation issues. While in *Fränklin-Beentjes and CEFLU-Luz da Floresta v. the Netherlands*,[105] which concerned the seizure and confiscation of a quantity of *ayahuasca*, a hallucinogenic substance consumed during ceremonies in the religion known as the "Santo Daime Church", the ECtHR decided that the confiscation, taken under drugs legislation, had been "necessary in a democratic society" for the protection of health.

Religious apparel

Many and varied permutations of this interpretation of the right to manifest religion have appeared before both the HRCommittee and the ECtHR, though with some difference in approach. In *Hudoyberganova v. Uzbekistan*,[106] the former ruled that the decision of a university to exclude a student for her refusal to remove her hijab in class constituted a breach of Article 18 of the ICCPR and similarly in *Singh v. France*,[107] which concerned the expulsion of a Sikh boy from school for wearing a *keski* in accordance with his religious beliefs. The ECtHR, in *Ahmet Arslan and others v. Turkey*,[108] found that the State had not established a satisfactory reason for imposing a prohibition on the wearing of religious clothing in public spaces and failed to demonstrate that the restriction was necessary in a democratic society. The clothing in question did not conceal the face, and the prohibition was "expressly based on the religious connotation of the clothing in question".[109] However, in *Leyla Sahin v. Turkey*,[110] a university rule barring students who refused to remove their head coverings from attending classes or exams was held not to violate such rights on the grounds that the domestic policy of secularism was the paramount consideration. Similarly, in *Dogru v. France*[111] and *Kervanci v. France*,[112] the ECtHR upheld the expulsion of two girls from schools where they had refused to remove their Islamic headscarves, ruling that such State action was not a violation of the private right to manifest one's religion under Article 9.

In recent years, the French 'burqua ban' would seem to have furthered judicial inconsistency as regards the perceived human rights implications. In *S.A.S.*

v. France,[113] the ECtHR examined the proposition that wearing clothing which concealed the face in public is incompatible with the "ground rules of social communication". In upholding the right of the State to introduce such a law, the court noted that "the respondent State is seeking to protect a principle of interaction between individuals, which in its view is essential for the expression not only of pluralism, but also of tolerance and broadmindedness without which there is no democratic society". Contrary to the HRCommittee approach in the above *Hudoyberganova* case, the ECtHR accepted the State's submission that the law pursued two legitimate aims: public safety[114] and respect for the minimum set of values of an open and democratic society.[115] In *Samira Achbita & Anor v. G4S Secure Solutions NV*[116] and in *Bougnaoui v. Micropole SA*[117]the ECJ reached different conclusions on much the same issue concerning Muslim employees wearing headscarves: rejecting and affirming the appeals respectively.

Proselytism

Article 18 of the ICCPR provides protection for proselytism. When, as in *Leven v. Kazakhstan*,[118] State regulations constrain preaching, then the HRCommittee will consider this to constitute a breach of Article 18. Similarly, the ECtHR ruled, in *Kokkinakis v. Greece*[119] and *Manoussakis v. Greece*,[120] respectively, that the Greek anti-proselytism law impermissibly interfered with freedom of religion and "the right to freedom of religion . . . excludes any discretion on the part of the State to determine whether religious beliefs or the means used to express such beliefs are legitimate". As Justice Pettiti commented in *Kokkinakis*, "[R]eligion is one of the foundations of a democratic society within the meaning of the Convention and the pluralism that cannot be disassociated from a democratic society depends on religious freedom". The HRCommittee has consistently adopted the same approach.[121]

In *D.H. v. Czech Republic*,[122] the ECtHR considered that the Islamic veil was a "powerful external symbol" capable of having a proselytising effect, at least on very young children. However, where the symbols manifesting religious beliefs are of a passive nature – as in *Lautsi v. Italy*[123] – it would seem that they are not held to constitute indoctrination or misplaced proselytism, and should be accommodated.

Blasphemy

Articles 18 and 19 of the ICCPR, which protect the freedom of expression, do so in terms which do not prohibit blasphemy laws. The offence of blasphemy remains on the statute books in 59 countries, including some common-law jurisdictions[124] but is now mostly significant in an Islamic context where expressions of irreverence toward Muhammad can have serious consequences. Those consequences can include death. Many in Pakistan have been killed for that offense. Blasphemy laws are also significant to 21st century protests, violence and death in Europe where those judged to have insulted or acted with disrespect toward the prophet Muhammad have been attacked by his followers. The Charlie Hebdo massacre in Paris is the most memorable and invidious response to perceived blasphemy.[125] The Rabat Plan of Action calls for the repeal of all anti-blasphemy laws on the grounds that "such laws stifle and unduly inhibit both the right to freedom of expression and the right to freedom of religion or belief".[126]

Conscientious objection

State respect for those who express their commitment to religion, belief or moral values by refusing to undertake certain duties is explicitly mandated by Article 18(1) of the ICCPR. Although initially denied by the HRCommittee,[127] it was subsequently acknowledged by that body in General Comment No. 22:[128]

> The Covenant does not explicitly refer to a right to conscientious objection, but the Committee believes that such a right can be derived from Article 18.

This was recognised in *J.P. v. Canada*[129] and in cases such as *Min-Kyu Jeong et al. v. Republic of Korea*[130] when conscientious objection was treated as providing grounds for exemption from service in the armed forces.[131] Indeed, the claims of individual citizens to such exemption have been brought before the courts over many decades.[132] Not until *Bayatyan v. Armenia*,[133] however, was it determined that such claims could also find protection under Article 9. This case concerned a Jehovah's Witness who alleged that his conviction for refusal to serve in the army had violated his right to freedom of thought, conscience and religion. The ECtHR then took the view that opposition to military service, where it is motivated by a serious and insurmountable conflict between the obligation to serve in the army and a person's conscience or his deeply and genuinely held religious or other beliefs, constitutes a conviction or belief of sufficient cogency, seriousness, cohesion and importance to attract the guarantees of Article 9(1).[134] An interesting corollary to this legal elevation of the right to assert individual conscientiousness is that there is a corresponding duty on the individual to exercise it: 'obeying orders' is no longer a passport for exemption. Bringing conscientious objection within the ambit of Article 9(1) is important as, within that provision, freedom of conscience is recognised as an absolute right in contrast to the conditional rights of 9(2).

The protection of Article 9 extends to conscientious objection in other contexts and inevitably raises questions as to its potential scope. This in fact occurred some 40 years ago in *Kjeldsen*,[135] a case which rested on a conscientious objection to mandatory sex education for teenagers in public schools. The ECtHR then interpreted Article 2 of the First Protocol as not granting parents any right to object, on moral grounds, to educational content or practices, if these were developed in an "objective, neutral and pluralistic manner". A claim to be excused from service provision on the grounds of conscientious objection frequently occurs in relation to abortion (see further below).

Human rights, equality and religion: the ECtHR/HRC rulings

Equality and non-discrimination are wholly part of the body of international human rights. Such, however, has been the impact of related domestic legislation, regulatory rulings and the sheer volume of case law in recent years that this sector shows signs of developing into a distinct species of human rights law. In all modern democratic nations, the intersection of the human right to equality and to freedom of religion results in allegations of discriminatory treatment in everyday settings. These are located, as Mrs Eleanor Roosevelt noted 60 years ago,[136] primarily in the family, in education and in the workplace. They are now being brought before the courts or regulatory bodies under the provisions of equality legislation. The pattern and trend of issues arising on the fraught interface of human rights, religion and equality – as illustrated in the rulings of the ECtHR and the HRCommittee – provide a baseline for the Part II comparative jurisdictional analysis.

Right of access to justice

The human rights requirement that the State put in place an impartial legal process providing equality of access to justice (UDHR, Articles 6–11; ECHR, Article 6) applies to religion, its adherents and organisations as much as it does to any other entity. Article 10 of the former requires proper processes to be available for accessing justice and addresses such matters as: that relevant information is available and can be readily understood; that appropriate processes and proceedings exist and are accessible; that proceedings are held before an independent and impartial tribunal; that free legal aid and advice are available where necessary, with adequate representation and without undue delay; that the proceedings are conducted independently, fairly and with a right of appeal; and that the outcome is fully and fairly enforced.

Religious law and courts

Secular law has had a parallel religious counterpart for centuries: all Part II jurisdictions accommodate religious law, such as the Islamic *Shari'a*, Jewish *halakha* and Christian canon law; though the secular has a contemporary social application and a national jurisdiction, the religious tends to be unrestricted by such boundaries. While the status of such religious law requires protection in the light of the ECtHR ruling in *Manoussakis v. Greece*,[137] when it warned that there was no "discretion on the part of the State to determine whether religious beliefs *or the means used to express such beliefs* are legitimate",[138] the Special Rapporteur's warning is arguably more apposite: "[D]enominational family laws frequently reflect and reinforce inequalities between men and women concerning marriage, child rearing, custody, maintenance, inheritance and other areas of family life".[139]

The tension between denominational laws and domestic statute law, particularly on family matters, gives rise to issues in all democratic societies. In terms of the requirement that statutory laws have precedence – for example, as regards divorce or same-sex marriage – it questions the competence of the State to challenge related theological beliefs and inevitably by doing so also questions the doctrine of State neutrality.

Shari'a law

The right to due process can at times conflict with the freedom of religion and belief; often this occurs in the context of employment law or equality and non-discrimination law. It is particularly prone to doing so when statutory processes are bypassed as citizens turn, or are turned, to religious law or to ethnic religious/cultural customs and practices; the Islamic *mahr* agreement ('bride price' or dowry, payable to the wife on divorce), for example, is no substitute for judicial distribution of assets following statutory matrimonial proceedings. In *Soha Sahyouni v. Raja Mamisch*,[140] the ECJ considered a husband's dissolution of his marriage by having his representative pronounce the divorce formula before the religious Shari'a court in Syria, which then declared the couple divorced, leaving his wife entitled to a once-off financial payment in accordance with Shari'a law. The court found that a divorce resulting from the unilateral declaration of one spouse before a religious court had the legal status of a 'private' divorce and is not recognised under EU law. This ECJ ruling represents an interesting benchmark for the right of the State to intervene in religious matters, necessarily weighing theological beliefs relating to marriage and interfering in Church autonomy, which must have implications for the established ECtHR defence of the State neutrality doctrine.

Moreover, the *Hudud* (or *Hadd*) offences – which include sex outside marriage, theft and drinking alcohol – are punishable by penalties such as stoning, flogging or the amputation of a limb; abjured by most Muslims, these are clearly not human rights-compliant and no matter how important in theological terms, they cannot hope to shelter behind any such doctrine.

Right to life

Initially established by Article 3 of the UDHR, there are circumstances in which the basic human right to life can conflict with religious beliefs.

Abortion, contraception

UNCROC is unequivocal in asserting the rights of the child: the Preamble states that the rights contained in the Convention apply to children both before and after birth; Article 3 requires that in all actions relating to children the interests of the child must be a "primary consideration", while Article 6 recognises that every child has the right to life. The latter is also asserted in Article 1 of the ICCPR, while the status of the unborn child as acknowledged in Article 2(1) of the ECHR has been considered, if to non-committal effect, by the ECtHR.[141] The reason why the ECtHR has been unable to rule definitively on matters affecting the status of a foetus lies in the different religious traditions of constituent member States which have correspondingly different definitions of when life begins.

Ultimately, however, it is difficult to square the human rights of a child, born or unborn, with those of a woman to contraception and abortion as has been demonstrated in the ECtHR struggle to balance "on the one hand, the need to ensure protection of the foetus and, on the other hand, the woman's interests".[142] To date the ECtHR has declined to recognise any 'right to abortion'[143] (though the Article 8 right to private life does extend to respect for decisions to become a parent or not).[144]

Refusing medical treatment

In *Jehovah's Witnesses v. the Russian Federation*[145] the ECtHR found that the essence of Article 8 of the ECHR lay in the protection provided for private life and human dignity, and therefore it accommodated the right of individuals to refuse, for religious reasons, the offer of life-saving blood transfusions: the law must respect personal autonomy. The risks incurred were a matter for private, not public, concern. This approach is now firmly established in international law.

Medically assisted death

Article 2 of the ECHR, like Article 3 of the UDHR, enshrines a duty to protect life. Human rights, however, is a work in progress which evolves in keeping with developments in knowledge and circumstances and in relation to cultural context. This process recently brought the ECtHR to the view that a 'right to die' must be viewed in conjunction with that of personal dignity protected by Article 8 of the ECHR, a combination that allows for a right to die, if not to medical assistance in doing so, in closely defined circumstances.[146] The governing principle, as the court then proclaimed, is that "an individual's right to decide by what means and at what point his or her life will end, provided he or she is capable of freely reaching a decision on this question and acting in consequence, is one of the aspects of the right to private life within the meaning of Article 8 of the Convention".[147] The ECtHR most recently gave further consideration to end-of-life issues in *Lambert and Others v. France*.[148] It then noted that the Article 2 duty to protect human life consisted of both positive and negative obligations: to take appropriate steps to safeguard lives and to refrain from the 'intentional' taking of life. It concluded that as long as therapeutic abstention was not about taking life intentionally, there would be no violation of the negative obligation to "refrain from the 'intentional' taking of life".

Right to marry and found a family

Recognised under Articles 12 of the UDHR and the ECHR, this right is reinforced by Articles 17 of both and greatly enlarged by Article 8 of the latter, which has a particularly wide reach. The protection it extends to 'private and family life' includes personal dignity and could conceivably encompass private religious activity. It embraces, under Article 16 of the ICCPR, a right to an authentic and autonomous identity. The limitations exercisable by the State as set out in Article 8(2)[149] – necessary in a democratic society in the interests of national security, public safety or the economic well-being of the country, for the prevention of disorder or crime, for the protection of health or morals, or for the protection of the rights and freedoms of others – may similarly impose boundaries upon personal religious activity.

Marriage and family relationships

In *Schalk and Kopf v. Austria*,[150] while the ECtHR found that it could not force States to make marriage available for same-sex couples,[151] it noted that the right to marry is granted to "men and women", and includes the right to found a family, which could be interpreted as granting the right to two men or two women, because, as the court observed, all other Convention rights are granted to "everyone". Curiously, the recognition of a right to marry does not extend to what might be viewed as its corollary – a right to divorce.[152]

Same-sex marriage

Until the latter part of the 20th century, homosexuality was a criminal offence in many developed nations, as it continues to be elsewhere. Not until the ECtHR ruling in *Dudgeon v. The United Kingdom*[153] did equality and non-discrimination principles signal a sea change.[154] In *Oliari*[155] the ECtHR ruled that State failure to provide same-sex couples with any kind of legally recognised civil union violated their human rights. In its judgment, the court noted that "same-sex couples are just as capable as different-sex couples of entering into stable, committed relationships". More recently, *Oliari* has been followed by not dissimilar rulings in *Pajić v. Croatia*,[156] *Aldeguer Tomás v. Spain*[157] and *Taddeucci and McCall v. Italy*.[158] However, the right to legal recognition of a same-sex relationship stopped short of an entitlement to marry, as the court made clear in 2018 when it approved a ruling – based on Article 12 of the ECHR – that "there is no right to homosexual marriage".[159]

Sexuality and gender

Article 26 of the ICCPR affords general recognition and protection to all suffering from discrimination, while Articles 8 (right to respect for private and family life) and 12 (right to found a family) of the ECHR are also clearly engaged when it comes to recognition of the legal rights of transsexuals. Sexual orientation and gender identity are included among prohibited grounds of discrimination under international human rights law, and therefore it is unlawful to make any distinction of people's rights based on the fact that they are lesbian, gay, bisexual or transgender.

The record of ECtHR rulings giving recognition to the rights of transsexuals probably began with *B. v. France*[160] and *Christine Goodwin v. United Kingdom*,[161] when in both cases the court found there had been a violation of Article 8 of the ECHR. Additionally, in *Goodwin*, it found that Article 12 – the right to marry and found a family – had also been breached and ruled that "it finds no justification for barring the transsexual [person] from enjoying the right to marry under any circumstances". Since then the ECtHR has gradually extended its recognition of transsexual rights.[162]

The 'Yogyakarta principles',[163] compiled in 2007 by the International Commission of Jurists together with the International Service for Human Rights, provide a specific yardstick for examining and comparing the progress made by Part II jurisdictions in relation to such issues.

Assisted reproduction, adoption, surrogacy and genetic engineering

Maternity, in most developed Western nations, has largely become a chosen option. Pregnancy may not only be avoided or terminated as above but may be achieved by artificial insemination, bypassed through the use of adoption or pursued via surrogacy. All of this has rendered the choice to parent a gender-free option available as much to single persons and same-sex couples as to others. However, as the ECtHR pointed out in *Sijakova v. The Former Yugoslav Republic of Macedonia*,[164] neither the right to marry and to found a family, nor the right to private and family life, nor any other right guaranteed by the Convention implies a right to procreation. This approach was evident in *S. H. and others v. Austria*,[165] which concerned the Austrian ban on using sperm and ova donations for IVF treatment. In confirming the ban, the court restored the concepts of 'natural procreation' and 'natural family' as the basic foundations for the parenting model known to the law. It re-established the traditional rule – *mater semper certa est* (the mother is always certain) – in a decision that imposes constraints on the future use of IVF, not to mention surrogacy.

Recent advances in science and medicine have opened up debate on human cloning, eugenics and the long-term impact of genetic technology on cultural mores and racial diversity. In *Oliver Brüstle v. Greenpeace e.V*,[166] the plaintiff sought a patent for cells produced from human embryonic stem cells for use in the treatment of neurological diseases. This prompted the ECJ to examine the definition of a human embryo and the legal protection available in respect of biotechnological inventions. Ultimately the court, in a watershed judgment which gives precedence to religious precepts over scientific research, ruled that an invention is non-patentable if any of the necessary steps regarding its implementation result in the destruction of human embryos, or if the invention is used in the destruction of future embryos. The ECJ followed up in 2018 with a not dissimilar approach when it ruled that genetically edited plants (usually to improve crop yield and eliminate weaknesses) and animals must be made subject to the same regulatory regime as all other GM organisms.[167]

Right to employment

Established initially under Article 23 of the UDHR, this right was considerably expanded by Articles 6 and 7 of the ICESCR and includes references to an entitlement to a favourable working environment. It has also been developed by equality and non-discrimination legislation and case law. The ICESCR specifically requires State parties to ensure that enumerated rights – for example, to work, to training, to equal pay, to join trade unions – can be enjoyed without discrimination of any kind, specifically including religious discrimination. The intersection of the human right to be employed and the right to religious freedom are matters governed chiefly by Article 9 of the ECHR and the Framework Equality Directive 2000/78/EC; the latter stipulates that only in very limited circumstances will a characteristic related, in particular, to religion constitute a genuine and determining occupational requirement. These provisions have the effect of exempting religious organisations and persons of religious belief from the constraints of much equality legislation.

Hiring/firing staff and religious beliefs

As regards religious organisations, the law permits employers whose ethos is based on religion or belief a right to impose related occupational requirements upon employees.[168] The intersection of human rights, religion and employment law was illustrated in the different outcomes of two factually similar ECtHR cases: *Obst v.Germany*[169] and *Schüth v. Germany*.[170] Both cases concerned the dismissal of officials from their posts in religious organisations on grounds of breaches of contract caused by adultery; the former dismissal was upheld, while the latter was overturned. The difference in outcome reflected a difference in the relative importance of the posts to respective core religious beliefs of the employing organisation. In *Obst*, because the official occupied a leadership post in the Mormon Church, a public representative of its core mission, his conduct could be construed as a serious violation of religious belief which set an example to followers that undermined the employer's basic beliefs. In *Schüth*, the official was employed as an organ player, a role that was merely ancillary to the employing organisation's core mission, and consequently the same conduct would have had proportionately less impact. Much turns on the strength of the link between the nature of the defendant's conduct, the centrality of the particular belief to the religion and the importance of the defendant's role as a representative of the employing religious organisation.[171]

As regards secular organisations, the law recognises the right of employees to bring personal religious beliefs into the workplace, provided this does not infringe the rights of others nor negatively impact upon the working environment. This is balanced by the responsibility of individuals to choose occupations which do not fundamentally conflict with their beliefs and to accept that, once employed, their religious beliefs are not grounds for refusal to undertake the duties of a post to which they were appointed. In *Kottinenen v. Finland*,[172] for example, the ECtHR upheld an employer's right to dismiss a Seventh-Day Adventist who had refused to continue working after sunset on Fridays as required by his contract. In *Kosteski v. 'The Former Yugoslav Republic of Macedonia'*,[173] the ECtHR did not find it unreasonable that an employer might regard absence without permission or apparent justification – to attend a Muslim festival – as a disciplinary matter. However, in the leading case of *Eweida and others v. the United Kingdom*,[174] the ECtHR found a violation of the applicant's right to manifest her religion by wearing a cross on a necklace because such use was discreet and there was no evidence that it had breached the rights of others.

Accommodating religious beliefs/practices in the workplace

As the ECtHR reasoned in *Achbita*:[175]

> While an employee cannot "leave" his sex, skin colour, ethnicity, sexual orientation, age or disability "at the door" upon entering his employer's premises, he may be expected to moderate the exercise of his religion in the workplace, be this in relation to religious practices, religiously motivated behaviour or (as in the present case) his clothing.

However, a line is crossed when an employee overtly proselytises in the workplace – both because this may infringe the rights of colleagues to privacy or harassment and because it may cause disruption in the workplace. It may also damage the employer's public image and thereby negatively affect the business.[176] Following the ECJ ruling in *Bougnaoui*,[177] it will also be crossed when the wearing of religion-specific clothing (an Islamic scarf) cannot be considered to be a 'genuine and determining occupational requirement' dictated by the nature of the occupational activities concerned or by the context in which they are carried out.

Right to education

Initially stated in Article 26 of the UDHR and subsequently in Articles 18(1) and (4) of the ICCPR, the right to education is reinforced by Articles 18 of the ICCPR and 13 of the ICESCR.

Together with Article 2 of Protocol 1, as monitored by the HRC, these provisions provides a wide ambit of protection for the right of parents to determine the religious education of their children,[178] including adherents of a minority religion.[179] Article 13 of the ICESCR provides for a right of parental choice of school and a right to ensure that their child's religious and moral education conforms to their own beliefs. Some UNCROC provisions are also relevant: Article 14 requires respect for the child's right to freedom of thought, conscience and religion; Article 20 states that where alternative care arrangements are provided, due regard shall be paid to the desirability of continuity in a child's upbringing and to the child's ethnic, religious, cultural and linguistic background, while Article 30 establishes the right of children from such background or of indigenous origin to profess and practise their religion and maintain their culture. In the collective and pedagogical teaching environment of a classroom, this right is one which often gives rise to tensions as secularists and others protest that their rights – for example, to freedom of expression – are being infringed.

Government funding and religious education: general overview

The fact that a considerable proportion of current educational service provision is borne by religious organisations is unsurprising given their record of establishing most basic social services and their continuing unique institutional presence across most communities in all developed nations. Many such organisations are necessarily in receipt of State funding, which can generate contention from their secular counterparts as well as expose them to sanctions for ECHR violations.[180] As the ECtHR warned in *Sychev v. Ukraine*,[181] "the exercise of State powers which affects Convention rights and freedoms raises an issue of State responsibility regardless of the form in which these powers happen to be exercised, be it for instance by a body whose activities are regulated by private law".

Educational facilities: religion, staffing and pupil access

The recent case of *Osmanoglu and Kocabas v. Switzerland*,[182] a landmark ECtHR ruling, recognised the State right to give primacy to its traditional cultural heritage in a school curriculum context. It concerned Muslim parents of Turkish heritage living in Switzerland who, in accordance with their religious beliefs, would not permit their daughters to attend compulsory mixed-sex swimming lessons which were part of the Swiss national curriculum. The court acknowledged that the human rights of the parents were being interfered with but denied that this amounted to a violation of their human rights under Article 9. It observed that "the children's interest in a full education, facilitating their successful social integration according to local customs and norms, took precedence over the parents' wish to have their daughters exempted from mixed swimming lessons and that the children's interest in attending swimming lessons was not just to learn to swim, but above all to take part in that activity with all the other pupils, with no exception on account of the children's origin or their parents' religious or philosophical convictions". The court unanimously found that the Swiss authorities had the right to facilitate "successful social integration according to local customs and mores" and had behaved legitimately by "seeking to protect foreign pupils from any form of social exclusion," and that this took precedence over parents' preferences.

State schools, religion and educational content

The HRC has stated, in General Comment No. 22 on Article 18, that:[183]

> 6. [. . .]The Committee notes that public education that includes instruction in a particular religion or belief is inconsistent with article 18.4 unless provision is made for non-discriminatory exemptions or alternatives that would accommodate the wishes of parents and guardians.

This was reinforced by a ECtHR ruling that while a State is under no obligation to provide religious teaching in public schools, should it choose to do so, in order to conform to the neutrality doctrine and to avoid breaching the Article 14 prohibition on discrimination, it is obliged to ensure that pupils of all faiths receive equal religious teaching.[184]

In *Folgerø v. Norway*,[185] the Grand Chamber held that the requirement in Article 2 of Protocol 1 that parental "religious and philosophical convictions" must be respected is crucial because it aims at:

> safeguarding the possibility of pluralism in education which possibility is essential for the preservation of the "democratic society" as conceived by the Convention. In view of the power of the modern State, it is above all through State teaching that this aim must be realised. . . . The verb "respect" means more than "acknowledge" or "take into account". In addition to a primarily negative undertaking, it implies some positive obligation on the part of the State.

The Grand Chamber noted, in what for this book is a most important judgment, that Norway gave Christianity much more attention than any other religion or belief but held that this was legitimate given the State's margin of appreciation and "the place occupied by Christianity in the national history and tradition" of Norway: if this was "a departure from the principles of pluralism and objectivity", then it was a justified one. Subsequently, in *Mansur Yalçın & Ors v. Turkey*,[186] the ECtHR commented that pupils must not be forced to participate in a particular form of worship or exposed to religious indoctrination.[187]

Faith schools

While Article 2 of Protocol No. 1 provides explicit authority for establishing faith schools as a means of giving effect to the parental right to determine the religious education of their children, this is also protected by Articles 18 of the ICCPR and 14(3) of the Charter of Fundamental Rights of the European Union. For secularists and others, the exclusiveness of faith schools can give rise to issues, including investing State funding to establish premises and staffing; discrimination in pupil admissions and staff appointments; skewing curriculums in favour of religious belief; and the corresponding alignment of school ethos and values in regard to issues such as gay marriage, abortion and so on.

Right to non-discrimination in service provision

Article 2 of the UDHR, as enlarged in Article 14 of the ECHR and supported by Article 2 of the ICCPR, provides for the right not to be discriminated against. It requires any difference in treatment to be objectively and reasonably justified. This is amplified further in Article 26 of the ICCPR, which declares that everyone is entitled to equality before the law and to equal protection by the law, without discrimination due to religion, among other grounds. These international provisions, underpinned by decades of rulings by the ECtHR and echoed by national equality legislation and decisions of regulatory bodies, require that services be accessed and provided without barriers created by any form of legally prohibited discrimination. Contemporary issues often present in the form of a conflation of sexual orientation and religious belief.

Provision by religious organisations

Public benefit services provided by religious organisations, including hospitals, schools and residential care facilities, are increasingly being drawn into the ambit of equality legislation. This raises issues regarding their entitlement to claim exemption from constraints that burden their competitors. Some such organisations have chosen to withdraw services rather than accept equality principles that compromise their beliefs.

Provision of public services

Public benefit services – for example, in schools and in health and social care facilities – are required to be delivered in a manner wholly compliant with all human rights, equality and non-discrimination legislation, whether delivered by a government agency or by a body funded and contracted to do so on behalf of government. This leaves little room for public officials in such facilities to claim exemption, on grounds of conscientious objection, from any service delivery requirements of their post.[188] In *Francesco Sessa v. Italy*,[189] for example, the ECtHR dismissed the complaint of a Jewish lawyer that the refusal to adjourn a case in which he was to provide representation services to a date which did not coincide with the Jewish holidays of Yom Kippur and Sukkot was an interference with his right to manifest his religion. The court considered that such interference was justified on grounds of the protection of the rights and freedoms of others – and in particular the public's right to the proper administration of justice. More recently, the ECtHR has ruled that there is a right to non-discrimination in the provision of public religious services.[190]

Private goods and service provision

The intersection of religion and equality/non-discrimination statutory requirements is very evident in the contemporary case law concerning commercial service provision of all developed nations.

Service denial on grounds of conscientious objection

Protection for matters of personal conscience can be found under Article 9(1) of the ECHR, as has been demonstrated in: opposition to abortion services;[191] opinions on the benefits of alternative medicine;[192] and refusal to work on registering homosexual civil unions.[193] However, there are limits. For example, the ECtHR has repeatedly found no violation of Article 9 in cases where a conscientious objector has protested that laws of universal application unduly burden their particular religious beliefs, as, for example, when a citizen refused to pay taxes because some of the revenue would fund abortions[194] or when a Sikh motorcyclist refused to wear a crash helmet as this would entail removing his turban.[195]

The ECtHR outlined the governing principles in *Pichon and Sajous v. France*,[196] when it gave the following explanation for its ruling that two pharmacists who refused to sell contraceptives had gone beyond legally permissible limits by seeking to impose their beliefs on the public: "[A]s long as the sale of contraceptives is legal and occurs on medical prescription nowhere other than in a pharmacy, the applicants cannot give precedence to their religious beliefs and impose them on others as justification for their refusal to sell such products". It reiterated its view expressed earlier in *R.R. v. Poland*[197] that Article 9 does not protect all acts motivated by religion or belief. This approach has since been adopted by the European Committee of Social Rights when, in *FAFCE v. Sweden*,[198] it rejected a claim that women could be denied access to legal abortion services by health professionals on the grounds of the latter's conscientious objection to the provision of such services, stressing that the Charter "does not impose on States a positive obligation to provide a right to conscientious objection for health care workers". This decision is in keeping with its earlier ruling in *IPPF v. Italy*[199] that the primary purpose of Article 11 of the Charter is to guarantee individuals' access to adequate health care and not to protect the interests of health care providers; when it comes to reproductive health care the primary rights holders under the Charter are women, not their doctors.

Broadcasting services

Although protected under Article 10(2) of the ECHR, the right to freedom of speech is subject to a duty to avoid gratuitous offensiveness or profanity to those of religious belief.[200] While the latter, as demonstrated in *Otto-Preminger-Institut v. Austria*,[201] may have to tolerate a level of offensiveness, there is no requirement to accept views that amount to a malicious violation of the spirit of tolerance. The

ECtHR then held that there was an obligation to avoid, as far as possible, expressions that were gratuitously offensive.[202] Similarly, in *Wingrove v. The United Kingdom*,[203] which concerned a soft-porn video purportedly depicting the erotic fantasies of St Teresa, entitled 'Visions of Ecstasy', the ECtHR considered the ban imposed by the regulatory authority as justified in a democratic society and therefore compliant with Article 10(2) of the Convention.

Conclusion

As the Special Rapporteur has noted: "[F]reedom of religion or belief rightly has been termed a 'gateway' to other freedoms, including freedom of expression and freedom of peaceful assembly and association . . . there can be no free religious community life without respect for those other freedoms".[204]

This chapter sketched an outline for structuring a thematic analysis of the legal relationship between religion and human rights in the Part II jurisdictions. Having taken the Special Rapporteur's observation together with Mrs Roosevelt's reference to human rights being found in "the world of the individual person; the neighbourhood he lives in; the school or college he attends; the factory, farm, or office where he works",[205] as a reasonable rationale for focusing the jurisdictional enquiry, the resulting format was then duly applied to explore the relationship between human rights, religion and international law. Doing so from a European perspective was necessary because most relevant international law originated there, resulting in several decades of case law and guiding principles which have a direct bearing on two of the five jurisdictions being considered.

As a preliminary, the chapter examined the international legal framework and the nature of the State relationship with religion and human rights, as ultimately this sets the parameters for the working out of all related public and private domestic law. It then concentrated on the case law illustrating the relationship between the freedoms of religion and those of expression and association before turning to focus on the case law illustrating the type of issues arising on the religion/human rights in everyday community life in settings such as education, the workplace and health care. This exercise revealed a number of interesting themes that will serve as touchstones or reference points for the Part II comparative analysis of jurisdictions. These include: the State right to give primacy to its traditional religion/cultural heritage;[206] protection of religion from the State;[207] the religious exemption;[208] the right to right to manifest religious belief in public;[209] parental rights in relation to children's religious upbringing;[210] right to medically assisted death;[211] conscientious objection as grounds for a refusal of service provision;[212] and the importance of the proportionality principle.[213]

Notes

1 Council of Europe, Parliamentary Assembly, *State, Religion, Secularity and Human Rights*, Recommendation 1804 (2007).

2 Ibid., at para. 17.

3 The diverse constituency of the ECHR's 47 member States includes Russia, Turkey, Iceland and Azerbaijan.
4 Application No. 5856/72, (1978). Wording derived from Article 31 of the Vienna Convention on the Law of Treaties, 23 May 1969, United Nations Treaty Series, Vol. 1155, at p. 331.
5 See General Comment No. 22, UN Doc. CCPC/C/21/Rev.1/Add/4L.
6 Citing Article 31 of the Vienna Convention on the Law of Treaties, 1969.
7 Article 26.
8 Article 20.
9 The United Nations Declaration on the Rights of Indigenous Peoples was adopted by the General Assembly on Thursday, 13 September 2007, by a majority of 144 States. There were four votes against: Australia, Canada, New Zealand and the United States.
10 See Gover, G., 'Settler – State Political Theory, "CANZUS" and the UN Declaration on the Rights of Indigenous Peoples', *European Journal of International Law*, Vol. 26:2, 2015, at pp. 345–373.
11 See Coates, K. and Mitchell, T. (eds.), 'From Aspiration to Inspiration: UNDRIP Finding Deep Traction in Indigenous Communities', 2013, at: www.cigionline.org/articles/aspiration-inspiration-undrip-finding-deep-traction-indigenous-communities.
12 Followed in 2001 by the Council of Europe's First Additional Protocol to the Cybercrime Convention, which defines 'racist and xenophobic material' as including "religion if used as a pretext" for racial/ethnic discrimination.
13 ICCPR, CESCR, CERD, CEDAW, CAT, CRC, CMW, CRPD and the CED.
14 The authority for which lies in the Provisional Rules of Procedure, Rule 70(3).
15 Moravcsik, A.,'The Origins of Human Rights Regimes: Democratic Delegation in Postwar Europe', *International Organization*, Vol. 54:2, 2000 at pp. 217–252.
16 See *Olson v. Sweden (No. 1)* (1988) 11 EHRR 299; *Sporrong v. Sweden* [1982] 5 EHRR 35, at para. 69; *Tsirlis and Kouloumpas v. Greece* (1997) 25 EHRR 198, at para. 116; *Razgar v. Secretary of State for Home Department* [2004] UKHL 27, at para. 20; and see, *Kozac v. Poland* [2010] ECHR 280 (2010) 51 EHRR 16.
17 See *Huang v. Secretary of State for the Home Department* [2007] 2 AC 167, at para. 19; *R (Quila) v. Secretary of State for the Home Department* [2012] 1 AC 621, at para. 45; and *Bank Mellat v. HM Treasury (No. 2)* [2013] UKSC 39 [2013] 3 WLR 179, 222, at para. 20.
18 See *Refah Partisi v. Turkey* (2003) 37 EHRR 1 [2003] ECHR 87.
19 See *Olson v. Sweden (No. 1)*, op. cit., where it is explained that to be justifiable such interference must be "relevant and sufficient; it must meet a pressing social need; and it must be proportionate to the need".
20 See, for example, *Lithgow v. United Kingdom* (1986) 8 EHRR 329, *Fredin v. Sweden* (1991) 13 EHRR 784, *Abdulaziz, Cabales and Balkandali v. United Kingdom* (1985) 7 EHRR 471.
21 Letsas, G., 'Two Concepts of the Margin of Appreciation', *Oxford Journal of Legal Studies*, Vol. 26:4, 2006 at pp. 705–732.
22 Sri Lanka CCPR A/50/40 (1995) 445; Sri Lanka CCPR CCPR/CO/79/LKA (2003) 7. See also Tunisia CCPR A/42/40 (1987) 137; Slovakia CCPR A/52/40 (1997) 383.
23 See further Tyagi, Y., *The UN Human Rights Committee, Practice and Procedure*, Cambridge University Press, Cambridge, 2010.
24 Established by UN General Assembly resolution 60/251 of 3 April 2006, it aims to review national human rights performance at four yearly intervals.
25 See *National Institutions for the Promotion and Protection of Human Rights*, UN Doc A/RES/48/134 (20th December 1993).

26 *Members of the Gldani Congregation of the Jehovah's Witnesses and Others v. Georgia*, Application No. 71156/01 (2007).
27 Application No. 15472/02 (2007).
28 Application No. 30814/06 (2011).
29 See also the International Labour Organisation Discrimination (Employment and Occupation) Convention 1958 (ILOC), the UN Declaration on the Elimination of All Forms of Intolerance and of Discrimination Based on Religion or Belief, and the Employment Framework Council Directive 2000/78/EC.
30 *Thlimmenos v. Greece* (2001) 31 EHRR 411, at para. 44.
31 See Report of the UN Special Rapporteur on Freedom of Religion or Belief, A/HRC/34/50, 2017, at para. 37.
32 See, for example, *Dahlab v. Switzerland*, Application No. 42393/98 (2001) and *Leyla Sahin v. Turkey*, Application No. 44774/98 (2005).
33 For an analysis of the relationship between religion, the right to religious freedom and democracy, see Boyle, K., 'Human Rights, Religion and Democracy: The Refah Party Case', *Essex Human Rights Review*, Vol. 1:1, 2004.
34 *Metropolitan Church of Bessarabia and Others v. Moldova*, Application No. 45701/99, §§ 115–16, ECHR 2001-XII.
35 *Cha'are Shalom Ve Tsedek v. France* [GC], Application No. 27417/95, § 84, ECHR 2000-VII.
36 Application No. 40825/98 [2008] ECHR 762, at para 92. Also see *Bayatyan v. Armenia,* Application No. 23459/03 (2011); *S.A.S. v. France,* Application No. 43835/11 (2014); and *Lautsi and Others v. Italy*, Application No. 30814/06 (2011).
37 Application No. 7798/08 (2010).
38 Ibid., at para. 88.
39 Application No. 15472/02 (2007).
40 (1996) *Reports of Judgments and Decisions* 1996-VI.
41 Application No. 24645/94 § 34, ECHR 1999-I.
42 Application No. 19516/06 (2008).
43 Application Nos. 42837/06, 3237/07, 3269/07, 35793/07 and 6099/08 (2010).
44 *Svyato-Mykhaylivska Parafiya v. Ukraine*, Application No. 77703/01 (2007).
45 *Holy Synod of the Bulgarian Orthodox Church (Metropolitan Inokentiy) and Others*, Application Nos. 412/03 and 35677/04 (2009); *Karlsson v. Sweden*, Application No. 12356/86 (1988); *Spetz and Others v. Sweden*, Application No. 20402/92 (1994); and *Williamson v. the United Kingdom*, Application No. 27008/95 (1995).
46 *Obst v.Germany*, Application No. 425/03 (2010).
47 *Refah Partisi (The Welfare Party) and Others v. Turkey*, Application Nos. 41340/98, 41342/98, 41343/98 and 41344/98 (2003), at para. 91. Also, see *Bayatyan v. Armenia* [2011] 234/9/ 03.
48 (18748/91) (1996) 21 EHRR CD3.
49 See also *Hasan and Chaush v. Bulgaria*, op. cit.
50 *Eweida and Others v. the United Kingdom*, Application Nos., 48420/10, 59842/10, 51671/10 and 36516/10 (2013).
51 *Obst v.Germany*, op. cit.
52 *Schüth v. Germany*, Application No. 1620/03 (2010).
53 Application No. 62649/10 (2016).
54 Application No. 27238/95 (2001).
55 Ibid., at para. 96.
56 Application No. 49151/07 (2009).
57 Application No. 64602/12 (2016).

58 Application No. 27138/04 (2010).
59 Application No. 62649/10 (2016).
60 *Members of the Gldani Congregation of Jehovah's Witnesses and Others v. Georgia*, Application No. 71156/01 (2007).
61 Ibid.
62 Application No. 15472/02 (2007).
63 [2007] ECHR 787.
64 Application No. 30814/06 (2011).
65 Ibid., per Bonello, J., at para. 1.2.
66 Application No. 36286/14 (2016).
67 See Report of the UN Special Rapporteur on Freedom of Religion or Belief, A/HRC/34/50, 2017, at para. 28.
68 Application No. 41056/04 (2010).
69 *Mansur Yalçın & Ors v. Turkey* [2014] ECHR 938, at para. 68.
70 The UN Declaration on the Elimination of All Forms of Intolerance and of Discrimination Based on Religion or Belief, Article 6(g) and (b), respectively.
71 *Schüth v. Germany*, Application No. 1620/03 (2010).
72 *Association Cultuelle du Temple Pyramide v. France* 50471/07 – HEJUD [2013] ECHR 105, (31 January 2013), *Association des Chevaliers du Lotus D'Or v. France 50615/07* – HEJUD [2013] ECHR 104, (31 January 2013), and *Eglise Evangelique Missionnaire and Salaûn v. France* 25502/07 – HEJUD [2013] ECHR 107, (31 January 2013). See further at: www.lawandreligionuk.com/2013/02/06/taxation-and-religious-organisations-three-french-cases-at-the-ecthr/.
73 *Fédération Chrétienne des Témoins de Jéhovah de France v. France* [2001] No. 53430/99, (6 November 2001).
74 See the UN Human Rights Committee, *General Comment No. 22: Article 18 (Freedom of Thought, Conscience and Religion)*, 30 July 1993, at para. 4.
75 See Gunn, T.J., 'Adjudicating Rights of Conscience Under the European Convention on Human Rights', in Van der Vyver, J.D., and Witte, J.D. (eds.), *Religious Human Rights in Global Perspective: Legal Perspectives*, Martinus Nijhoff, The Hague, 1996, at p. 311.
76 See, for example, *Tsirlis and Kouloumpas v. Greece* (1997) 25 EHRR 198. See also the *Belgian Linguistic Case* (1968)(No. 2) 1 EHRR 252.
77 [1982] 4 EHRR 293. See also *Arrowsmith v. United Kingdom* [1978] 3 EHRR 218.
78 General Comment No. 22, UN Doc CCPR/C/21/Rev.1/Add.4, [8].
79 See *Campbell and Cosans v. United Kingdom* (1982) Application No. 7511/76, 4 EHRR 293, at para. 36.
80 See *Knudsen v. Norway*, Application No. 11045/84 (1985).
81 Both the European Directive on Race and the Employment Framework Council Directive ('the Article 13 Directives') were issued in 2000.
82 *Debelianovi v. Bulgaria*, Application No. 61951/00 (2007).
83 Ibid., note 78.
84 Ibid.
85 *Süveges v. Hungary*, Application No. 50255/12 (2016).
86 See, for example, *Perry v. Latvia*, Application No. 30273/03 (2007).
87 *Kalac v. Turkey* [1997] EHRR 552, at para. 27.
88 3 April 2006 ECHR.
89 As cited in *Viktor Leven v. Kazakhstan*, Communication No. 2131/2012, CCPR/C/112/D/2131/2012 (2014).
90 [2010] 30 BHRC 417. Also see *Bayatyan v. Armenia* [2011] 23459/03.
91 See *Schmidt v. Germany* [1994] EHRR 513, 526, at para. 22.

92 Opened for signature by General Assembly resolution 2200A (XXI) of December 16, 1966 and entered into force 23 March 1976. As of March 2012 the Covenant had 74 signatories and 167 parties.
93 Adopted by the General Conference of the International Labour Organisation on 25 June 1958 and came into effect on 15 June 1960. As of May 2011 the Convention had been ratified by 169 out of ILO 183 members.
94 GA Res 36/55, UN GAOR, 36th sess, UN Doc A/36/684 (1981).
95 (5493/72) [1976] ECHR 5.
96 Communication No. 1207/2003, CCPR/C/84/D/1207/2003 (2005).
97 *Bączkowski and Others v. Poland*, Application No.1543/06 (2007); *Alekseyev v. Russia*, Application Nos. 4916/07, 25924/08 and 14599/09 (2010); and *Genderdoc-M v. Moldova*, Application No. 9106/06 (2012).
98 *Vona v. Hungary,* Application No. 35943/10 (2013).
99 See *Juma Mosque Congregation & Ors v. Azerbaijan,* Application No. 15405/04 (2013) and *Islam-Ittihad Association & Ors v. Azerbaijan,* Application No. 5548/05 (2014).
100 Ibid., at para. 39.
101 Application No. 40524/09 (2017), at para. 35.
102 See *Mouvement raëlien suisse v. Switzerland,* Application No. 16354/06 (2012); *Vejdeland and Others v. Sweden*, Application No. 1813/07 (2012); and *Bayev and Others v. Russia*, Application No. 67667/09 (2017).
103 See *Kivenmaa v. Finland*, Communication No. 412/1990, CCPR/C/50/D/412/1990 (1994).
104 Application No. 1813/07 (2012).
105 Application No. 28167/07 (2014).
106 Communication No. 931/2000, CCPR/C/82/D/931/2000, (November 2004).
107 Communication No. 1852/2008, CCPR/C/106/D/1852/2008 (2012).
108 Application No. 41135/98 (2010).
109 Ibid., at paras. 136, 151.
110 Application No. 44774/98 (2005).
111 Application No. 27058/05 (2008).
112 Application No. 31645/04 (2010).
113 Application No. 43835/11 (2014).
114 See also *Phull v. France,* Application No. 35753/03 (2008), which upheld the right of airport security officials to require removal of turban, in sharp contrast to *Ranjit Singh v. France*, Communication No. 1876/2009, when the Human Rights Committee found a requirement to remove a turban for an identification photo violated the right to freedom of religion under the ICCPR; and *El Morsli v. France,* Application No. 15585/06 (2008), right to deny entry to French consulate on refusal to remove veil in front of a man for an identity check.
115 See also *Ebrahimian v. France*, Application No. 64846/11 (2015), when the ECtHR upheld the nonrenewal of a contract in respect of a hospital social worker who refused to remove her Islamic headscarf, ruling that this was legitimate because every public servant has the duty to assure the neutrality of public services and State secularism.
116 [2016] EUECJ C-157/15, (31 May 2016).
117 [2016] EUECJ C-188/15 EU:C:2016:553, (13 July 2016).
118 Communication No. 2131/2012. CCPR/C1112/D/2131/2012, (21 October 2014).
119 (A/260-A) (1994) 17 EHRR 397.
120 (18748/91) (1996) 21 EHRR CD3.
121 See, for example, *Immaculate Joseph et al v. Sri Lanka*, Communication No. 1249/2004/, CCPR/C/85/D/1249/2004 (2005).

122 Application No. 42393/98, 2001-V ECtHR 449.
123 Application No. 30814/06, ECtHR, (18 March 2011).
124 See 2011 Pew Research Centre report at: www.pewforum.org/2011/08/09/rising-restrictions-on-religion6/.
125 On 7 January 2015, two Islamic gunmen attacked the Paris office of the satirical magazine Charlie Hebdo, killing eight staff and others.
126 See Report of the UN Special Rapporteur on Freedom of Religion or Belief, 2017, at para. 18.
127 *L.T.K. v. Finland*, Communication No. 185/1984, CCPR/C/OP/2 (1990).
128 At para. 11.
129 Communication No. 446/1991, CCPR/C/43/D/446/1991 (1991).
130 Communication Nos. 1642-1741/2007, CCPR/C/101/D/1642-1741/2007 (2011).
131 See General Comment 22, para. 3. See also *Atasoy and Sarkut v. Turkey*, Communication Nos. 1853/2008 and 1854/2008, CCPR/C/104/D/1853-1854/2008 (2012) and *Jong-nam Kim et al v. The Republic of Korea*, Communication Nos. 1786/2008, CCPR/C/106/D/1786/2008 (2012).
132 The HRC's decision in *J.P. v. Canada*, Communication No. 446/1991, was the first time, albeit *obiter dictum*, it accepted that Article 18 of the ICCPR afforded protection to conscientious objectors.
133 [2011] 234/9/ 03.
134 *Bayatyan v. Armenia*, op. cit., at para. 110.
135 *Kjeldsen, Busk Madsen and Pedersen v. Denmark*, Application Nos. 5095/71; 5920/72; 5926/72 (1976).
136 See Ignatieff, M., *The Ordinary Virtues: Moral order in a Divided World*, Harvard University Press, Cambridge, MA, 2017, at p. 196, citing the Church Peace Union (now the Carnegie Council), *In Your Hands: A Guide for Community Action on the 10*th *Anniversary of the UDHR*, New York, 1958.
137 Application No. 18748/91 (1996) 21 EHRR CD3.
138 See also *Hasan and Chaush v. Bulgaria*, op. cit.
139 See Report of the UN Special Rapporteur on Freedom of Religion or Belief, A/HRC/34/50, 2017, at para. 40.
140 Case C-372/16 (2017). See further Cranmer, F., 'EU recognition of *Shari'a* divorce decrees: *Sahyouni*' in *Law & Religion UK*, 18 September 2017, at: www.lawandreligionuk.com/2017/09/18/eu-recognition-of-sharia-divorce-decrees-sahyouni/.
141 *Paton v. United Kingdom* (1980) 3 EHRR 308.
142 See *Boso v. Italy*, Application No. 50490/99, Eur. Ct. H.R. 846 (2002). Note that in *Parrillo v. Italy*, Application No. 46470/11 (2015), the ECtHR, applying the margin of appreciation rule, recognised that a State could take steps to protect the right to life of an embryo.
143 *P. & S. v. Poland*, Application No. 57375/08 (2012), at para. 99.
144 *Evans v. the United Kingdom*, Application No. 6339/05, § 71, ECHR 2007-IV.
145 Application No. 302/02 (2010).
146 *Haas v. Switzerland* (2014) 58 EHRR 7, para. 51.
147 Ibid., at para. 51. See also *Koch v. Germany* (2013) 56 EHRR 6, paras. 46 and 51, and *Gross v. Switzerland* (2014) 58 EHRR 7, para. 60.
148 Application No. 46043/14 (2015).
149 See also Article 29 of the UDHR.
150 Application No. 30141/04, Council of Europe: European Court of Human Rights, (24 June 2010).
151 A matter left to individual States: *Parry v. the United Kingdom*, Application No. 42971/05 (2006).

152 *Johnston and Others v. Ireland*, 1986, Series A no. 112 and *Babiarz v. Poland*, Application Nos. 1955/10 and 8923/12.
153 Application No. 7525/76 (1981).
154 Note that, as of 2018, 6 EU States make no provision for same-sex marriage: Romania, Poland, Slovakia, Bulgaria, Lithuania and Latvia.
155 *Oliari & Ors v. Italy* [2015] ECHR 716.
156 Application No. 68453/13 (2016).
157 Application No. 35214/09 (2016).
158 Application No. 51362/09 (2016).
159 *Relu Adrian Coman and Others v. Romania*, C-673/16, per Advocate General Melchior Wathelet (11 January 2018).
160 Application No. 13343/87 (1992).
161 *Christine Goodwin v. United Kingdom*, Application No. 28957/95 (2002).
162 See, for example: *Schlumpf v. Switzerland*, Application No. 29002/06 (2009); *P.V. v. Spain*, Application No. 35159/09 (2010); and *P. v. Portugal*, Application No. 56027/09 (2011).
163 See 'Principles on the Application of International Human Rights Law in Relation to Sexual Orientation and Gender Identity' as updated in 2017. See further at: www.refworld.org/pdfid/4a783aed2.pdf.
164 Application No. 67914/01 (2003).
165 Application No. 57813/00 (2011).
166 ECJ, Case C-34/10 (2011).
167 ECJ Case C-528/16, *Confédération paysanne and Others v. Premier ministre and Ministre de l'Agriculture, de l'Agroalimentaire et de la Forêt.*
168 *Lombardi Vallauri v. Italy*, Application No. 39128/05 (2009).
169 Application No. 425/03 (2010).
170 Application No. 1620/03 (2010).
171 See *Rommelfanger v. Germany*, Application No. 12242/86 (1989).
172 (1996) 87 DR 68. See also *Stedman v. United Kingdom* (1997) 23 EHRR CD 168.
173 Application No. 55170/00 (2006).
174 Op. cit.
175 *Samira Achbita & Anor v. G4S Secure Solutions NV*, op. cit., at para. 116.
176 *Larissis and Others v. Greece*, Application Nos. 23372/94, 26377/94 and 26378/94. Also, *Dahlab v. Switzerland (dec.)*, Application No. 42393/98, ECHR 2001-V.
177 C – 188 /15 *Bougnaoui and Association de défense des droits de l'homme (ADDH) v. Micropole Univers* (2017).
178 This Protocol was established on 20.3.1952. The leading case on Protocol 1 Article 2 is *Belgian Linguistic* (1968) 1 EHRR 252. See also *Folgerø and Others v. Norway*, Application No. 15472/02 (2007), *Hasan and Eylem Zengin v. Turkey*, Application No.1448/04 (2007) and *Appel-Irrgang and Others v. Germany*, Application No. 45216/07 (2009).
179 *Mansur Yalcin and Others v. Turkey*, Application No. 21163/11 (2016) and *Sofuoglu and Others v. Turkey*, Application No. 21163/11 (2014).
180 *Storck v. Germany*, 2005-V Eur. Ct. H.R.
181 Application No. 4773/02 (2005) (unreported), at: www.echr.coe.int/echr/.
182 Application No. 29086/12 (2017).
183 See HRC, General Comment No. 22, on Freedom of Thought, Conscience or Religion, at para. 6 (adopted at the Forty-eighth Session of the Human Rights Committee, on 30 July 1993). Note also the Committee of Ministers' Recommendation Rec. 5 (2010) which encourages "safeguarding the right of children and youth to education in a safe environment, free from violence, bullying, social exclusion or other forms of discriminatory and degrading

treatment related to sexual orientation or gender identity" (para. 31 of the Recommendation).

184 *Savez crkava « Riječ života » and Others v. Croatia*, Application No. 7798/08 (2010).

185 [2007] ECHR 546.

186 [2014] ECHR 938.

187 Ibid., at para. 64.

188 *Eweida and others v. United Kingdom* [2013] IRLR 231.

189 Application No. 28790/08 (2012).

190 *Doogan and Others v. Turkey*, Application No. 62649/10 (2016).

191 *Knudsen v. Norway*, Application No. 11045/84 (1985).

192 *Nyyssönen v. Finland*, Application No. 30406/96 (1998).

193 *Eweida and Others v. the United Kingdom* Application Nos. 48420/10, 59842/10, 51671/10 and 36516/10 (2013).

194 *Bouessel du Bourg v. France,* Application No. 20747/92 (1993).

195 *X. v. the United Kingdom*, Application No. 8160/78 (1981).

196 Application No. 49853/99 (2001).

197 Application No. 27617/04 (2011).

198 Complaint No. 99/2013 (2015).

199 Complaint No. 87/2012 (2014).

200 *Otto-Preminger-Institut v. Austria,* Series A no. 295-A (1994), at paras. 46, 47, 49.

201 Series A no. 295-A, (20 September 1994).

202 Ibid., at paras. 46–50.

203 (19/1995/525/611), 25 November 1996.

204 See A/HRC/34/50, at para. 33.

205 As quoted by Ignatieff, M., *The Ordinary Virtues: Moral Order in a Divided World*, 2017, at p. 196, op. cit.

206 *Osmanoglu and Kocabas v. Switzerland*, Application No. 29086/12 (2017).

207 *İzzettin Doğan and Others v. Turkey*, Application No. 62649/10 (2016).

208 *Obst v. Germany*, Application No. 425/03 (2010).

209 *Eweida and others v. the United Kingdom*, Application Nos. 48420/10, 36516/10, 51671/10, 59842/10 – HEJUD [2013] ECHR 37.

210 *Folgerø v. Norway* [2007] ECHR 546.

211 *Haas v. Switzerland* (2014) 58 EHRR 7.

212 *FAFCE v. Sweden*, Complaint No. 99/2013 (2015).

213 See *Olson v. Sweden (No. 1)* (1988) 11 EHRR 299 and further at f/n 16.

Part II

Law, policy & practice

3 England & Wales

Introduction

As secularism outgrows religion and the latter becomes more diverse and fragmented, the citizens in England and Wales are becoming steadily more human rights-oriented. Mostly, this is apparent in the general upsurge in litigation concerning equality and discrimination, but it is also evident in the volume of issues coming before the courts and other regulatory bodies which police the interface between religion and human rights.

This chapter models the approach to be adopted in each of the following four chapters. It begins by setting out the domestic legal framework relating to religion, outlines the extent of commitment to related international provisions and considers any relevant international human rights reports. It then systematically examines in turn a sequence of distinct themes relating to the religion/human rights interface (identified in the preceding chapter) and related domestic case law. Firstly, it deals with the Church/State relationship. Secondly, it addresses the main issues arising in relation to the freedoms of religion, expression and association, giving particular attention to the tension between freedom of speech and religious manifestation. Thirdly and finally, the chapter concludes with a review of the equality-driven case law emanating from such contexts as health care, employment and education.

While this chapter is entitled "England and Wales", to a very large extent the law outlined in the following pages may be taken as broadly representative of the three jurisdictions that comprise the UK. Where this is clearly not the case, as for example, in relation to the *locus standi* of the Church of England or abortion in Northern Ireland, every effort is made to draw attention to that fact as appropriate in the text.

Current legal framework

The UK administers and is subject to a body of human rights, international and domestic, which has its genesis in that foundation document, the Universal Declaration of Human Rights (UDHR) 1950.

International legislation

Since becoming one of the first countries to ratify the UDHR, the UK has become a party to a range of treaties, conventions and protocols of which the most relevant for present purposes are: the European Convention on Human Rights (ECHR), ratified in 1951; the International Covenant on Civil and Political Rights (ICCPR), ratified in 1976 with certain reservations and declarations but not adoption of Optional Protocol 1;[1] the International Covenant on Economic, Social and Cultural Rights (ICESCR), ratified in 1976; the International Convention on the Elimination of Race Discrimination (ICERD), to which the UK is a signatory nation; the International Convention on the Rights of the Child (ICRC), ratified in 1991; the UN Convention on the Elimination of All Forms of Discrimination against Women (CEDAW), ratified in 1986 with its Optional Protocol; and the Convention on the Rights of Persons with Disabilities (CRPD), which it ratified in 2009.

More specifically, the main components of this framework with relevance for religion are Articles 9 and 14 of the ECHR, as applied in conjunction with Article 18 of the ICCPR, and the EU Council Directive 2000/78/E.

Domestic legislation

Essentially, while the right to freedom of religion may be traced back to the Magna Carta in 1215,[2] UK human rights law derives from the governing principles outlined in the United Nations Declaration of Human Rights, as enlarged in the European Convention and the International Covenant, and subsequently established by the Human Rights Act 1998, the Employment Equality (Religion or Belief) Regulations 2003 and the Equality Act 2010.

The Human Rights Act 1998

The European Convention on Human Rights (ECHR) was applied in this jurisdiction by the Human Rights Act (HRA) 1998.[3] Section 1 specifically incorporates: the rights and fundamental freedoms set out in Articles 2–12 and 14 of the Convention; Articles 1–3 of the First Protocol; and Article 1 of the Thirteenth Protocol, as read with Articles 16–18 of the Convention (see further Chapter 2).

The employment equality (religion or belief) regulations 2003

This statute made it unlawful for employers to discriminate on the grounds of religion or belief and enacted in UK law the religion or belief provisions of the Framework Equal Treatment Directive (2000/78/EC); these legislative provisions were subsequently consolidated in the Equality Act 2010, Sched 2.

The Equality Act 2010

This prohibits unfair treatment in the UK on any of nine 'protected grounds', which include religion or belief, whether occurring: in the workplace, when providing goods, facilities and services, when exercising public functions, in the disposal and management of premises, or in education and by associations (such as private clubs), and whether the discrimination is direct, indirect or takes the form of harassment or victimisation. Schedule 9, paragraph 2 (giving effect to Article 4 of the above-mentioned Framework Equality Directive 2000/78/EC), deals with employment 'for the purposes of an organised religion'[4] and provides certain exemptions from the non-discrimination provisions of employment law.

Religion is treated the same as any other 'protected characteristic'. The Act offers protection for individuals; indeed, it was the view of the Court of Appeal in *Mba v. London Borough of Merton*[5] that group disadvantage was not covered under the Equality Act.[6] It also gives effect to the Employment Equality Directive 2000/78/EC, which protects against direct and indirect discrimination, harassment and victimisation perpetrated on the grounds of religion or belief.

Other legislation

The Crime and Disorder Act 1998, as amended,[7] created specific offences of racially and religiously aggravated crime based on the offences of wounding, assault, damage, harassment, threatening or abusive behaviour and stalking. The Racial and Religious Hatred Act 2006 prohibits "incitement to religious hatred"[8] but does not define religion or what constitutes a religious belief. The Protection from Harassment Act 1997 is important, as is the Public Order Act 1986 amended by the 2006 Act, which created new offences: s.29B(i) provided that 'a person who uses threatening words or behaviour, or displays any written material which is threatening, is guilty of an offence if he intends thereby to stir up religious hatred'; subject to the caveat in s.29J that this does not prohibit or restrict discussion, criticism or expressions of antipathy, dislike, ridicule, insult or abuse of particular religions, beliefs or practices of adherents, or proselytising.

International courts and regulatory bodies

EU membership brought with it a requirement that the UK accept the superior jurisdiction of the ECtHR and the CJEU. Importantly, the UK will continue to be subject to the jurisdiction of the ECtHR after Brexit. The established accountability to other international committees will also continue.

The European Court of Human Rights (ECtHR)

The ECtHR hears complaints alleging violations of rights enshrined in the Convention and its protocols. In making its determinations, the court is guided by principles such as: 'proportionality' and 'compatibility with democracy'.[9] Its decisions are reached in the light of 'a margin of appreciation' which permits States a degree of latitude in their interpretation of human rights obligations[10] (see further Chapter 2).

The Human Rights Committee (HRC)

The HRC monitors progress made on promoting human rights and provides an update every four years on achievements and clarifies further goals (see further Chapter 2).

Other fora

The European Court of Justice (CJEU) and various other bodies established by their respective international conventions to monitor implementation might also be relevant (see further Chapter 2).

Domestic courts and regulatory bodies

The Equality and Human Rights Commission (EHRC), established by the Equality Act 2006, acts as the regulator in respect of issues – including those relating to religion – which arise under the Equality Act 2010. The Employment Tribunal determines allegations of rights abuse in the workplace from which a right of appeal lies to the Employment Appeal Tribunal (EAT). Human rights issues, including those involving religion, are mainly resolved by these regulatory bodies, but many are adjudicated in the county court and High court and some go on appeal to the Appeal Court and possibly on to the Supreme Court (UKSC).

International reports on human rights in the UK

The US government, in its 2016 report on human rights in the UK, noted its concern with certain matters, including the following with relevance for religion/ human rights: "an increase in hate crimes based on ethnicity, disability, anti-Semitism, and religion".[11] In September 2017, the HRC issued its third Universal Periodic Review report on UK progress in respect of its human rights record.[12] This contained 227 recommendations for improvements which mainly addressed perceived shortcomings in the statutory protection available to children, migrants, ethnic and religious minority groups and as regards people-trafficking, hate crimes and discrimination.

The State and the human rights/religion intersect

England and Wales, the only common-law jurisdiction presently being considered that has an 'established' church, illustrates the truth of the Special Rapporteur's observation that "privileged religions also exist under the auspices of 'secular'

States".[13] Anglican canon law has been assimilated into national law, which gives it, and Protestantism more broadly, a favoured legal status relative to all other religions. Specific constitutional arrangements have for centuries granted a role to the 'established' Church of England, differentiating its status from all other religions, beliefs and non-beliefs with resulting consequences for human rights.

Balancing the interests of Church and State

Munby J, in *X v. X*,[14] succinctly explained this balancing act as follows: "[A]lthough historically this country is part of the Christian west, and although it has an established church which is Christian, I sit as a secular judge serving a multi-cultural community". The balance to be struck was made clear in *McFarlane v. Relate Avon Ltd*,[15] when Lord Carey, the former Archbishop of Canterbury, sought to intervene by making suggestions as to the desired composition of the court (suggestions deemed by Laws LJ to be "deeply inimical to the public interest")[16] and the need to address what he perceived to be an alleged "lack of sensitivity to religious belief"[17] by the judiciary when dealing with such cases. In response, Laws LJ drew attention to two principles generally considered to be central to liberal democracy: that the State should remain neutral in relation to religion and that public policy should be rigorously secular. He pointed out that:[18]

> In a free constitution such as ours there is an important distinction to be drawn between the law's protection of the right to hold and express a belief and the law's protection of that belief's substance or content. The common law and ECHR Article 9 offer vigorous protection of the Christian's right (and every other person's right) to hold and express his or her beliefs. And so they should. By contrast they do not, and should not, offer any protection whatever of the substance or content of those beliefs on the ground only that they are based on religious precepts. These are twin conditions of a free society.

He added "the conferment of any legal protection or preference upon a particular substantive moral position on the ground only that it is espoused by the adherents of a particular faith, however long its tradition, however rich its culture, is deeply unprincipled".[19]

State- and religion-related terrorism

Being engaged for many years in warfare in largely Muslim countries, and having suffered related domestic terrorist attacks dating back to the Lockerbie bombing, including the London atrocities in 2005 and 2017, the UK now has in place a sophisticated range of antiterrorism measures. Government has introduced security and antiterrorism legislation, surveillance and accelerated deportation measures, a review of multicultural policies and a new policy emphasis on preventing radicalisation and building a closer rapprochement between local government and Muslim communities. This approach balanced a strategy to prevent radicalisation[20] with specific counterterrorism legislation.[21]

State neutrality

The principle that the law must treat all religions equally has been established since at least *Re Pinion (deceased)*[22] when it was held that "the court cannot discriminate between religions". It was reiterated more vigorously by Laws J, in *McFarlane* below, when continuing his peroration against religious preferencing he advised that:[23]

> We do not live in a society where all the people share uniform religious beliefs. The precepts of any one religion – any belief system – cannot, by force of their religious origins, sound any louder in the general law than the precepts of any other. If they did, those out in the cold would be less than citizens; and our constitution would be on the way to a theocracy.

Nevertheless, given the fact of an enduring 'established' church, "it seems difficult, if not impossible, to conceive of an official 'State religion' that in practice does not have adverse effects on religious minorities, thus discriminating against their members".[24]

Christian symbols/prayers in State facilities

In February 2012, the High Court in *NSS v. Bideford Town Council*[25] ruled that it was not lawful, under s.111 of the Local Government Act 1972, for the Council to continue with its long-standing practice of holding prayers at the beginning of meetings. Prayer, Ouseley J ruled, is a private matter that has no place in the formal proceedings of a legal assembly. In response to the ruling, the government promptly introduced amending legislation with the effect that councils wanting to continue holding formal prayers could do so. Three years later the Commission on Religion and Belief in British Public Life advised that "the legal requirement for schools to hold acts of collective worship should be repealed".[26] These skirmishes indicate that the continuation of settled and familiar Christian rituals in State facilities cannot be taken for granted.

Protecting religion from the State

In *Wachmann*,[27] when explaining why the court would not examine Jewish doctrines, reference was made to the dangers of "straying across the well recognised divide between Church and State".

Intervention in Church disputes

The above warning, reiterated in *R(E) v. Governing Body of JFS*,[28] that "it has been long understood that it is not the business of the courts to intervene in matters of religion" and again in *Johns & Anor, R (on the application of) v. Derby City Council & Anor*[29] that "a secular judge must be wary of straying across the well-recognised divide between Church and State", was explored further by Neuberger PSC in *Shergill v. Khaira.*[30] He then explained that while the court does not adjudicate on the truth of religious beliefs nor on the validity of particular rites, nonetheless "the court addresses questions of religious belief and practice where its jurisdiction is invoked either to enforce the contractual rights of members of a community against other members or its governing body or to ensure that property held on trust is used for the purposes of the trust". Consequently, as regards the present dispute, he warned that unless the parties were able to resolve their differences, "the court may have to adjudicate upon matters of religious doctrine and practice in order to determine who are the trustees entitled to administer the trusts".[31]

State protection of its traditional religious/cultural identity

As the 'established Church', the Church of England has been singled out by the State as having a distinct and superior status and one which formally binds it to the State. The fact that – under the Marriage (Same-Sex Couples) Act 2013, accompanied by amendments to the Equalities Act 2010 – it is relieved of any duty to conduct gay marriages (as is the Church in Wales) is further evidence of its singular *locus standi* as representing the nation's religious/cultural identity.[32].

State preferencing of religious organisations

The UK has accrued an impressive body of law privileging religious organisations and adherents, some of which is now undergoing revision.

The religious exemption

A body representing an 'organised religion' is permitted, under the Equality Act 2010,[33] to impose explicitly discriminatory restrictions on employment opportunities in relation to gender, marital status and sexual orientation.[34] An employer with an ethos based on religion or belief is permitted to discriminate on the grounds of religion or belief[35] if it is an occupational requirement for the particular post, is genuine and determining and, having regard to that ethos and the nature or context of the work, the application of the requirement is a proportionate means of achieving a legitimate aim. Because of the narrowing effect of the 'determining' requirement, this exemption was virtually restricted to employing religious organisations,[36] causing the European Commission, in November 2009, to issue a 'Reasoned Opinion to the United Kingdom' expressing its view that the exceptions to the principle of non-discrimination on the basis of sexual orientation for religious employers were broader than that permitted by the directive.[37]

Schedule 23, para 2 of the same Act, allows 'organisations relating to a religion or belief' – but without a commercial sole or main purpose (unlike in the US following the *Hobby Lobby* ruling) – to discriminate on the grounds of religion or belief or sexual orientation in the way they operate. Their purpose must be to: practise, advance or teach, or enable adherents to receive a benefit, or engage in an activity 'within the framework of that religion or belief'; or to foster or maintain good relations between persons of different religions or belief. Such organisations may exercise religious discrimination when: determining membership of the organisation, participation in its activities, use of its premises or 'the provision of goods, facilities or services in the course of activities undertaken by the organisation'. Such a restriction may be imposed either because of the purposes of the organisation or to avoid causing offence on grounds of its religion or belief to adherents. However, it must be exercised reasonably.

Additionally, the sexual orientation provisions of the Equality Act 2010 allow a religious organisation to restrict provision of a service to persons of one sex or to separate services for persons of each sex – but only if this is necessary to comply with the doctrines of the religion or to be for the purpose of avoiding conflict with the strongly held religious convictions of a significant number of the religion's followers.[38] An organisation cannot lawfully discriminate in the provision of goods and services on the grounds of sexual orientation, where such provision is undertaken on behalf of a public body.

Regulatory privileges

Religious entities have traditionally been very largely left to be self-regulating. Until the early 21st century, this was the only common-law jurisdiction with a charity-specific regulator and, as virtually all churches and religious organisations had charitable status, it fell to that regulator – the Charity Commission for England and Wales – to assume responsibility for such entities. However, there was an established practice of treating them as 'excepted' from the standard requirements applied to all other charities.[39] This designation of 'excepted' is now set to continue until at least 2021, as will, therefore, the current lax regulatory regime.

Tax privileges

Religious organisations and their outworkings – schools, hospitals and social care facilities and so on – have traditionally enjoyed charitable status, accompanied by automatic tax exemption (though not from VAT). Being exempt from the tax burden, solely on grounds of religious status, is viewed by many of those on whom the obligation rests to make up the resulting deficit in tax revenues as an outdated concession to the right to religious freedom. There is an argument that, given the evidence of sexual abuse perpetrated by such organisations, this should negate an automatic entitlement to privileges denied to their secular counterparts. Coincidentally, perhaps, alone among the common-law jurisdictions, the UK has recently made their continued right to tax exemption dependent upon proof of satisfying a public benefit test.

Testamentary privileges

The long tradition of State preferencing of religion continues to be evident in the practice of permitting gifts and trusts, most usually created by testators but occasionally by donors, to be made subject to a religiously discriminating condition: usually requiring a prospective beneficiary to commit to or renounce a specified religion, and often set in the context of marriage and/or the upbringing of children.[40] This approach permitted many instances where donor-imposed religious constraints were respected[41] and conditions that restrained religion (either requiring or prohibiting the practice of a particular religion) or marriage (either requiring or prohibiting marriage to a person of a particular religious persuasion, ethnicity or class) were, and continue to be, almost always judicially endorsed.

State funding of faith-based facilities and services

The UK in recent decades has experienced a dramatic shrinking of the State owing to the shedding of many governmental functions as the provision and delivery of many public services has transferred to other sectors, such as religious organisations, as they have a unique nationwide institutional network. This transfer has been accompanied by considerable uncertainty as to whether 'public functions' paid for by public funds but contracted out by government retain their public character for the purposes of the United Kingdom's Human Rights Act 1998,[42] but there is no doubt about the scale of public benefit service provision now delivered by religious organisations.

Education services provide a good example of such government-funded provision.

According to the Dept of Education, there are 6,814 faith-based schools (faith schools), constituting 34 percent of the maintained sector, of which about 67 percent are Church of England and 29 percent are Catholic.[43] Most often they receive government grants of up to 90 percent of capital costs of the buildings and 100 percent of running costs (including teachers' salaries). Inevitably, the majority of State funding for faith schools goes to the Church of England, as does that for chaplaincy services. In *National Union of Teachers v. Governing Body of St Mary's Church of England (Aided) Junior School*,[44] the Court of Appeal found that the Church of England school was in the State system and that the governors were a body charged by the State with the running of the school and were exercising their functions with a view to securing provision by the school of the national curriculum. In these circumstances, the governors were to be regarded as an emanation of the State for the purposes of the doctrine of direct effect.[45]

Until 2002, the only chaplains employed by the Prison Service were Christian chaplains. Since then, it has also provided prisoners with Christian, Jewish and Muslim chaplains.

Religion and the freedoms of association and expression

The Human Rights Act 1998 and the Equality Act 2010 provide the main statutory parameters for the human rights/religion intersect.

Freedom of religion

Guaranteed by the Human Rights Act 1998, s.9, this "right and fundamental freedom" is incorporated along with other provisions of international instruments into UK domestic law (see further Chapter 2). As in all democracies, the right to freedom of religion or belief is in practice dependent upon judicial elucidation of key legal terms, the nature of the balance struck between Church and State and the privileges and exemptions granted to religious organisations and to their adherents.

Definitions

While there are no legislative definitions of key legal terms, the UK case law reveals the extent of judicial efforts to bridge this gap.

- 'Religion'

Over time, judicial rulings have extended the traditional interpretation of 'religion' to accommodate non-theistic, multitheistic and philosophical beliefs. More recently, the Equality Act has broadly declared that it includes any religion; any religious or philosophical belief; a lack of religion; and a lack of belief. As regards the latter, Dyson PSC has emphasised that "the right *not* to hold the protected beliefs is a fundamental right which is recognised in international and human rights law and . . . the Convention too. There is nothing marginal about it".[46]

In *R (on the application of Hodkin and another) v. Registrar General of Births, Deaths and Marriages*,[47] Toulson JSC explained that:[48]

> religion should not be confined to religions which recognise a supreme deity. First and foremost, to do so would be a form of religious discrimination unacceptable in today's society. It would exclude Buddhism, along with other faiths such as Jainism, Taoism, Theosophy and part of Hinduism. . . . I would describe religion in summary as a spiritual or non-secular belief system, held by a group of adherents, which claims to explain mankind's place in the universe and relationship with the infinite, and to teach its adherents how they are to live their lives in conformity with the spiritual understanding associated with the belief system.

Accordingly, belief in a 'supreme being', the practice of worship and adherence to a specific body of doctrines, tenets and so on are no longer essential to the definition of 'religion'.

- 'Beliefs'

In *Willamson*,[49] Walker JSC asserted that "pacifism, vegetarianism and total abstinence from alcohol are uncontroversial examples of beliefs which would fall within Article 9".[50] As Nicholls JSC explained:[51]

> Article 9 embraces freedom of thought, conscience and religion. The atheist, the agnostic, and the sceptic are as much entitled to freedom to hold and manifest their beliefs as the theist. These beliefs are placed on an equal footing for the purpose of this guaranteed freedom.

In *McClintock v. Department of Constitutional Affairs*,[52] Elias P reiterated the established view of the ECtHR that "the test for determining whether views can properly be considered to fall into the category of a philosophical belief is whether they have sufficient cogency, seriousness, cohesion and importance and are worthy of respect in a democratic society".[53] Subsequently, the 2003 Employment Equality (Religion or Belief) Regulations, para. 2(1), declared that " 'belief' means any religious or philosophical belief", but not until *Grainger v. Nicholson*[54] did the judiciary provide guidance as to how this term was to be interpreted. Burton J in the course of that appeal hearing[55] then suggested the following criteria should be applied to determine whether a "belief" met the requirements in Article 9 of the ECHR:

i The belief must be genuinely held.
ii It must be a belief and not, as in *McClintock*, an opinion or viewpoint based on the present state of information available.
iii It must be a belief as to a weighty and substantial aspect of human life and behaviour.
iv It must attain a certain level of cogency, seriousness, cohesion and importance.
v It must be worthy of respect in a democratic society, be not incompatible with human dignity and not conflict with the fundamental rights of others (paragraph 36 of *Campbell*[56] and paragraph 23 of *Williamson*).[57]

Whereas in the past a person could be construed as having a religious belief by the mere fact of their belonging to a church, which carried an implied commitment to its doctrines, now it is the demonstrable sincerity of an individual's beliefs that is the crucial legal determinant.[58] However, due attention must be given to the judicial warning regarding the inherent contradictions and dangers for legal objectivity in attaching undue weight to subjectively perceived 'truths'.[59] The views expressed above by Nicholls LJ in *Williamson*[60] were echoed by EAT in *Eweida*[61] that "it is not necessary for a belief to be shared by others in order for it to be a religious belief",[62] by Bingham LJ in *Begum*[63] and by the comment of Baroness Hale for the Court of Appeal in *Ghai*[64] that "it matters not for present purposes whether it is a universal, orthodox or unusual belief".

Manifestation of religion or belief

As the Equality and Human Rights Commission has explained:[65]

> Manifestations of a religion or belief could include treating certain days as days for worship or rest; following a certain dress code; following a particular diet; or carrying out or avoiding certain practices. There is not always a clear line between holding a religion or belief and the manifestation of that religion or belief. Placing limitations on a person's right to manifest their religion or belief may amount to unlawful discrimination; this would usually amount to indirect discrimination.

This right to hold and to manifest a religion or belief is also subject to the caveats that any manifestation does not violate the human rights of others; and that the person concerned takes responsibility for having knowingly placing themselves in a position where their principles might be compromised. Regarding the latter, as Weatherup J put it in *Christian Institute*,[66] "in exercising his freedom to manifest his religion, an applicant may need to take his specific situation into account".[67] This rationale would seem to have been in play in *Cherfi*,[68] *Chaplin*[69] and *Playfoot*[70] – where in each case the claimants had knowingly placed themselves in positions which could potentially compromise their beliefs – but has been blunted somewhat by the ECtHR ruling in *Eweida* that "the better approach would be to weigh that possibility in the overall balance when considering whether or not the restriction was proportionate".[71]

Religious discrimination

UK law recognises four types of religious discrimination: direct, indirect, harassment or victimisation.[72] The first takes the form of unequal treatment whereby some are directly treated less favourably than others because of their religious beliefs.[73] The second incidentally disadvantages a certain religious group, as when a service provider's provision, criterion or practice imposes restrictions that affect their ability to access services available to others.[74] The third results from 'whistleblower' circumstances involving a complaint about religious discrimination, while the fourth is behaviour that may include physical attack, verbal abuse or causing discomfort because of a religious or racial difference.

The Equality Act 2010, Schedule 9, provides exemptions and exceptions from the general prohibition against discrimination. These are variable in nature and differ in application depending on the 'protected characteristic' to which the discrimination relates. This inconsistency could be circumvented by an alternative model based on the theory of religious autonomy, a concept recognised by human rights law.[75]

Freedom of association

The right of individuals to meet, or form associations, for the purposes of worship, religious teaching or any other religion-related reasons, is long established. However, difficulties arise when the activities of any such association conflict with the human rights given effect in equality and non-discrimination legislation.[76]

The 'positive action' provisions

Introduced by the Equality Act 2010, s.158, the positive action provisions provide specific opportunities for intervention in circumstances that would otherwise constitute unlawful discrimination.[77] Those identified as belonging to a group sharing one or more of the protected characteristics[78] (e.g. Muslim women, Afro-Caribbean schoolboys) may for that reason justifiably attract additional State resources.[79] Positive action is only lawful if the statutory criteria are met: it must be 'reasonably thought' that one of the conditions applies, such as disadvantage or disproportionately low participation. It permits, for example, targeted bursaries and scholarships where the potential recipients share a particular religious faith or belief.

Freedom of expression

In recent years, as recourse to YouTube, blogging and tweeting has become endemic, the intersect between this right and freedom of religion has become highly sensitive, particularly so after the Charlie Hebdo[80] massacre.

Religiously motivated conduct

Posters declaring "Islam out of Britain",[81] or a Christian preacher displaying signs reading "Stop Immorality", "Stop Homosexuality" and "Stop Lesbianism",[82] being clearly religiously motivated and alarmist, have been prohibited. However, an exercise of free speech such as publication of *The Satanic Verses*[83] is permissible even if it incites lethal religious hatred outside the jurisdiction. Recently, charges against a preacher who had berated Islam in a sermon on the internet were dismissed on the grounds that such conduct was not so grossly offensive that it forfeited the protection given to the freedoms of speech and religion under the ECHR.[84] While there is an argument that prohibiting incitement to religious hatred, through the Racial and Religious Hatred Act 2009, is open to abuse because it offers a means to censor genuine debate, this is countered by some with the view that not outlawing such behaviour may permit the reckless insulting of the religious and incite lethal responses.

Religious apparel

The UK has never sought to legally prohibit the public wearing of turbans, other headwear or items of apparel that denote religious affiliation. Problems do arise, however, and then there is an onus on the wearer to show a sincere conviction that the particular item is a necessary and appropriate manifestation – not of any particular doctrine of that religion/belief – but is required by their interpretation of it. That there are limits to the latitude permitted to such subjective interpretation was demonstrated in *Playfoot (a minor), R (on the application of) v. Millais School*,[85] when the court found that an item of jewellery (a 'purity ring') was "representative of a moral stance and not a necessary symbol of Christian faith"; though, arguably, a 'moral stance' should be sufficient to attract judicial protection under Article 9 of the ECHR.

In *Begum*,[86] the House of Lords considered the wish of a schoolgirl to wear the jilbab in keeping with the professed religious beliefs of herself and her family, despite the prohibition on doing so in the school dress code. While the court upheld her right to believe that her religion required her to wear the jilbab, it nevertheless considered that the school had been entitled to reject her right to manifest her belief in that way. In choosing to attend Denbigh High School, Ms Begum had chosen to accept the limitations imposed by the school's dress code. In *Noah v. Sarah Desrosiers (trading as Wedge)*,[87] a Muslim applying for a hairdressing position was held to have suffered indirect discrimination when her employer warned that she would be required to remove her hijab while at work, if appointed. The employment tribunal found that there was an onus on the employer to produce evidence that the wearing of the headscarf would have an adverse effect on the business. In the absence of any such evidence, the requirement was found not to be justified. Some years later, in the not dissimilar case of *Begum v. Barley Lane Montessori Day Nursery*,[88] a Muslim claimed that she had suffered religious discrimination at a job interview when told that she would not be permitted to wear a jilbab of appropriate length and therefore had been unable to accept the post. The EAT concluded that the prospective employer was justified in considering that the particular length of the jilbab might constitute a tripping hazard to staff or to the children in their care. Again, in *Chaplin v. Royal Devon & Exeter Hospital NHS Foundation Trust*[89] – which concerned a nurse who refused on religious grounds to stop wearing a crucifix with her uniform, contrary to the Trust's health and safety policy – the court found that the nurse had not been subjected to direct or indirect discrimination, as the Trust had tried to make a reasonable accommodation by suggesting that she wear the crucifix as a brooch or attached to her name-badge lanyard.[90]

If a restriction is ostensibly neutral but has a disproportionate effect on an ethnic minority, then it must be justified. This was evident in *R (Watkins-Singh) v. Aberdale Girls' High School*,[91] where the school ban on wearing jewellery was held to impose a particular constraint on Sikh pupils. In *Azmi*,[92] the court upheld the earlier Employment Tribunal finding that the beliefs of the claimant – a classroom-based bilingual support worker – concerning the veil were "genuine and held by a sizeable minority of Muslim women".[93] It found that the restriction on wearing the niqab was a neutral rule which put the claimant at a disadvantage, but was justified as it was a proportionate measure given the interests of the children in having the best possible education. The school had examined the effects of teaching with the niqab in place and had evidence to show that, in those circumstances, the indirect discrimination was justified. That there are limits to judicial tolerance of dress as a manifestation of belief was apparent at London's Blackfriars Crown Court when Murphy J, commenting that "the niqab has become the elephant in the courtroom", ruled that a Muslim woman defendant should remove her niqab when giving evidence.

However, it was *Eweida v. British Airways PLC*[94] that most clearly marked a turning point. Ms Eweida, a committed Christian working for British Airways in a customer service area, had wanted to display a small cross around her neck, contrary to BA policy that no jewellery was to be visible. She claimed that BA's refusal to allow this was indirect discrimination. On appeal to the EctHR,[95] it was held that British Airways had breached Ms Eweida's human rights, in particular her right to freedom of thought, conscience and religion, adding that "there was no evidence that the wearing of other, previously authorised items of religious clothing, such as turbans and hijabs, by other employees, had any negative impact on British Airways' brand or image".[96]

Blasphemy and proselytism

Proselytising or 'spreading the word' has always been an activity recognised in law as being for the public benefit.[97] In *Redmond-Bate v. DPP*,[98] the provocative views of three fundamentalist Christian preachers, which had generated a heated response from a crowd and threatened to 'disturb the peace', were found to be permissible. As Sedley LJ commented:

> Free speech includes not only the inoffensive but the irritating, the contentious, the eccentric, the heretical, the unwelcome and the provocative provided it does not tend to provoke violence. Freedom only to speak inoffensively is not worth having.

Traditional principles, or prejudices, were finally swept away by the Criminal Justice and Immigration Act 2008, which abolished the common-law offences of blasphemy and blasphemous libel.

Conscientious objection

In this jurisdiction, the principle of freedom of conscience dates back to 1757. Although conscientious objection was not specifically mentioned in the Military Service Act of 1916, which introduced compulsory conscription, acknowledgement was given to those whose "objection genuinely rests on religious or moral convictions". The Human Rights Act 1998 gave the principle explicit recognition in the declaration that "everyone has the right to freedom of thought, conscience and religion".

In the above-mentioned *Eweida* case,[99] the court noted that religious freedom "is primarily a matter of individual thought and conscience" and took the view that the appellant's desire to wear a cross openly was a sincere manifestation of her religious beliefs (see further below).

Human rights, equality and religion: the case law

As noted by Toulson JSC:[100]

> Religion and English law meet today at various points. . . . Individuals have a right to freedom of thought, conscience and religion under Article 9 of the European Convention. They enjoy the right not to be discriminated against on grounds of religion or belief under EU Council Directive 2000/78/EC and under domestic equality legislation.

In practice, it is the latter which generates most contemporary case law. In the UK, for the most part, the relevant legal framework is provided by the Equality Act 2010, the associated Regulations supplemented, to a lesser extent, by the racial hatred and antiterrorism legislation.

Right of access to justice

Parallel systems of justice can give rise to problems, particularly – as in family law matters – when traditional patriarchal values governing religious systems inhibit female access to statutorily defined legal rights.

Religious law and courts

The Church of England has always had its own internal consistory courts for settling disputes affecting members. For centuries, the Beth Din network of private tribunals have sought to resolve civil disputes arising among Jews, while Shari'a law is attracting a growing constituency as a resource for resolving issues arising in an Islamic cultural context. These religious courts offer mediation on marital disputes, family matters and finance:[101] their legal authority lies in the Arbitration Act 1996, and the secular courts will enforce an arbitration award by a religious tribunal in such circumstances.[102] The role of religious minority tribunals can be controversial: there can be pressure on potential litigants to seek religious mediation services instead of initiating statutory proceedings. When any such pressure results in a denial of access to statutory proceedings, possibly as a consequence of religious beliefs, then there will have been a breach of statutory and ECHR provisions[103]

Shari'a law

The Islamic Shari'a Council, established in the 1980s, has between 35 and 80 Islamic tribunals operating in the country dealing with several hundred cases of marriage and divorce per month.[104] The disparity between Shari'a law and national law has been a matter of government concern:[105] not least because an estimated 100,000 Muslim women have undergone unregistered Shari'a marriage ceremonies which leave them unable to avail of statutory divorce proceedings, as they have not been married in accordance with statute law, and are thus left dependent upon petitioning the Shari'a Council for mediation.[106]

Right to life

The Human Rights Act 1998, Article 2, guarantees that everyone's life will be protected by law.

Abortion, contraception

The current law in the UK (excepting Northern Ireland)[107] permits abortions to be carried out up to the 24th week of pregnancy, subject to certain requirements, but if medically necessitated they may be carried out at any stage if the birth presents a serious risk to the mother's health; the mother's physical health and mental health may be taken into account when estimating that risk. The attendant legal issues rarely come before the courts – because the governing Abortion Act 1967 (revised 1990) is quite permissive in scope.[108] However, they recently surfaced in Scotland in *Greater Glasgow Health Board v. Doogan and Wood*,[109] which concerned two Catholic midwives who had refused, on religious grounds, to work as required by their employing hospital in its abortion clinic: a refusal not accepted by their managers. As it turned out, the court did not need to consider the possible issue of religious discrimination as it was sufficient to resolve the case, upholding the Health Board's right to direct the involvement of midwives in abortion procedures, by relying on a narrow interpretation of what constituted 'participate' for the purpose of the conscientious objection provisions of s.4 of the Abortion Act 1967 with the caveat that "it may be reasonable to expect an employer to accommodate an employee's objections". More recently, religion and abortion were entangled in the *Matter of an Application for Judicial Review by the NI Human Rights Commission*,[110] which dealt with the right to abortion as governed by the Abortion Act 1967 and the Offences against the Person Act 1861. The effect of this legislation meant that medical staff carrying out abortions could be jailed unless the life of the woman concerned was directly under threat or if there would be lasting, long-term negative effects on her mental or physical health from continuing with her pregnancy. It also had the effect of discriminating against women in Northern Ireland by denying them access to the abortion services available to other female UK citizens. On appeal to the Supreme Court, the case was dismissed for lack of standing, but a majority did consider that the current law was disproportionate and incompatible with Article 8 of the ECHR.[111]

Refusing medical treatment

R v. Senior[112] concerned a member of the Peculiar People sect who was convicted of the manslaughter of his baby by neglect, as he had refused to provide the child with medical aid or medicine, believing that to do so would show insufficient faith in God and the power of prayer. Since then, British courts have consistently upheld the right of a child to life despite parental refusal to authorise life-saving treatment, an issue which most usually involves Jehovah's Witnesses and blood products.[113]

Medically assisted death

Parliament and the judiciary have repeatedly resisted appeals for UK law to recognise a right to assisted suicide, even in cases of extreme and terminal suffering. As Hoffmann LJ commented in *Bland*,[114] "those who adhere to religious faiths which believe in the sanctity of all God's creation and in particular that human life was created in the image of God himself will have no difficulty with the concept of the intrinsic value of human life". This view was later echoed by Steyn LJ in *Pretty v. DPP*:[115]

> There is a conviction that human life is sacred and that the corollary is that euthanasia and assisted suicide are always wrong. This view is supported by the Roman Catholic Church, Islam and other religions.

Again, in *Nicklinson & Anor R (on the application of) (Rev 1)*,[116] the court concluded by finding that s.2(1) of the Suicide Act 1961 could not be aligned with s.3(1) of the Human Rights Act 1998 in such a way as to remove the culpability of those who assist others to commit suicide. In short, the law in the UK is now wholly compliant with the above Article 3, though not with ECtHR developments (see further Chapter 2).

Right to marriage and to found a family

The Human Rights Act 1998, Article 12, guarantees the right to marry to men and women of marriageable age and the right to found a family, a right extended to same-gender couples who contract civil partnerships in accordance with the Gender Recognition Act 2004 and the Marriage (Same-Sex Couples) Act 2013.

Marriage and family relationships

UK law has, in the main, long since adjusted to accommodate a definition of 'family' which includes unmarried couples, non-marital children and more recently, lesbian or homosexual relationships,[117] but for some UK citizens, their religious beliefs prevent an acceptance of this definition.

The resulting tensions within the UK Islamic communities have been demonstrated by 'honour' crimes in which the victims are almost always Muslim women. There were 11,000 such cases recorded in this jurisdiction between 2010 and 2014, including forced marriages, desertion of abusive husbands, female genital mutilations (FGM), abductions, beatings and murders. The persistence of FGM, though not exclusive to Muslims, is a particularly worrying phenomenon. A total of 5,702 cases were recorded for 2015, the first year of mandatory reporting by health officials, but as of 2018, there still has to be a successful prosecution for a practice so well known and legally prohibited for decades.

The non-compliance of Islamic religious beliefs with human rights has also been evident in the many cases involving Muslim male sexual abuse of non-Muslim women. As the independent inquiry 'Child Sexual Exploitation in Rotherham'[118] revealed, this was clearly illustrated by the gangs of Asian men who abused some 1,400 young Caucasian girls over a 16-year period: the perpetrators were Muslim males, and Muslim girls were not among their victims.

Same-sex marriage

In giving effect to equality principles, the Marriage (Same-Sex Couples) Act 2013 ended the statutory monopoly of that institution by heterosexual couples and broadened yet further the legal interpretation of 'family'. The 2013 Act also positions the Church of England at the centre of a human rights controversy. As the established Church, it is relieved, by amendments to the Equality Act 2010, of any duty to conduct gay marriages. It is thereby required to operate in a discriminatory fashion to the detriment of all Anglican same-sex couples wishing to marry.[119]

Sexuality and gender

Legal recognition of the right of transsexuals not to be discriminated against has a long history in which the ECtHR initially endorsed domestic statutory law and declined such recognition.[120] This changed with the *Christine Goodwin* case,[121] when the ECtHR ruled in favour of a transsexual who sought legal recognition of her new gender identity because of "the changing conditions within the respondent State and within Contracting States generally" and "evolving convergence as to the standards to be achieved" in the context of official recognition of post-operative transsexual gender identity.[122]

Since the Gender Recognition Act 2004 came into effect, transgender persons have been able to acquire official documentary evidence – for example, an amended birth certificate – of their changed genetic identity, and since 2010 gender reassignment has been included as a protected characteristic in the Equality Act. A notable feature of the 2004 Act – unlike comparable legislative provisions elsewhere – is that a record of a gender identity change is not conditional upon proof of completed surgical procedures.

Assisted reproduction, adoption, surrogacy and genetic engineering

The introduction of IVF treatment, now governed by the Human Fertilisation and Embryology Act 1990 (as amended in 2008), inaugurated an era of fertility research and treatment featuring "cloned embryos" and stem cell research that has greatly facilitated human and animal reproduction. This brought with it controversy as to the morality of such intervention, which to some amounted to artificially "manufacturing" life.

Right to employment

This right, which generates considerable litigation in the UK, is governed by the Equality Act 2010.[123]

Hiring/firing staff and religious beliefs

While religious organisations are exempt from the full rigour of the Equality Act when hiring and firing staff, they are not wholly at liberty to ignore the basic aspects of the right to employment. They are not, for example, entitled to establish a 'closed shop' exclusively favouring persons of a designated religion or belief. This was clearly illustrated in *Hinder & Sheridan v. Prospects for People with Learning Disabilities*,[124] which concerned a Christian organisation that introduced a policy limiting staff recruitment to practicing Christians for the vast majority of roles on the basis that those in particular posts might have to lead prayers or give spiritual guidance and told existing non-Christian employees that they were no longer eligible for promotion. The Tribunal found that not every job in a Christian organisation needed to be done by Christians, that the 2003 Regulations required a job evaluation to be undertaken for every post and held that the policy constituted unlawful discrimination. In *Reaney v. Hereford Diocesan Board of Finance*,[125] the Tribunal found that it was not unreasonable that a religious organisation should stipulate a requirement of celibacy when interviewing a homosexual candidate for position of youth worker; this could be said to be in compliance with its religious doctrines. However, having decided that he was the best candidate and that he met the celibacy requirement, the organisation had then been unreasonable in refusing to employ him.

A religious organisation is legislatively permitted to discriminate by expressly restricting staff recruitment when religious belief is a genuine occupational requirement for a particular post.[126] *McNab v. Glasgow City Council*,[127] for example, concerned an atheist maths teacher in a Roman Catholic High School who had never been promoted, failed in his head of department application and then decided to apply for a post of Acting Principal Teacher of Pastoral Care but was not interviewed. Both the Tribunal and the EAT concluded that being a Catholic could not be a 'genuine and determining' occupational requirement for the post and that the plaintiff had therefore suffered direct discrimination under the Employment Equality (Religion or Belief) Regulations 2003. On the other hand, when a Muslim plaintiff alleged religious discrimination following his failure to secure the post of finance administrator, in an organisation that required an applicant incumbent to be "a practicing Christian committed to the objectives and the values" of the organisation, the Tribunal had little difficulty in dismissing the allegation on finding that being a practicing Christian was a genuine occupational requirement and that employing a non-Christian would have had a very significant adverse affect on the organisation's ethos.[128]

In a secular context, the hiring and firing of employees was initially considered to be a matter governed solely by the contractual terms of employment which were routinely invoked to nullify any subsequent claim that duties could not be undertaken for reasons of religious belief. For example, in *Esson v. London Transport Executive*,[129] the appeal of a Seventh-Day Adventist, dismissed after trying to take Saturdays off for religious reasons, was rejected, with the court ruling that it was his duty to reconcile the 'insurmountable conflict' between his religious beliefs and his contractual obligations. In *Ahmad v. Inner London Education Authority*,[130] the Court of Appeal held that the right to freedom of thought, conscience and religion, as established by Article 9 of the ECHR, did not entitle an employee to be absent from work for the purpose of religious worship in breach of contract; subsequently upheld by the ECtHR.[131] Again, in *Stedman v. UK*,[132] a dismissal for refusal to work on a Sunday was held not to constitute a breach of the right to freedom of religion: the employee's freedom to resign in effect guaranteed her Convention rights.

Much the same approach was adopted toward public service employees. In *Ladele v. London Borough of Islington*,[133] the Court of Appeal considered the firing of Ms Ladele, a Christian marriage registrar, who refused to be involved in registering same-sex "civil partnerships" in accordance with newly introduced statutory procedures. The court took the view that the registration process was a public service with significant human rights implications for the community and that the administration of that process formed part of Ms Ladele's contractual duties. Dismissing her appeal, the court noted: "[T]he effect on Ms Ladele of implementing the policy did not impinge on her religious beliefs; she remained free to hold those beliefs, and free to worship as she wished".[134] Similarly, in *McFarlane v. Relate Avon Ltd*,[135] which concerned a relationship counsellor who had been dismissed when he indicated to his employer that he did not approve of same-sex relationships on biblical grounds and did not wish to be involved in counselling such couples. The court, following the approach it had earlier adopted in *Ladele*,[136] ruled that Mr M had not suffered religious discrimination. Both decisions were subsequently upheld on appeal to the ECtHR. Again, in *McClintock v. Department of Constitutional Affairs*,[137] which concerned the request of a JP member of a statutory panel – the JP member resigned when his request was refused – that he be excused from officiating in cases where he might have to decide whether same-sex partners should adopt children, the EAT found that McClintock had not been disadvantaged because of his religious belief and that, even if he had been, such discrimination would have been justified.

These cases indicate that religious beliefs – or conscientious objection – will not justify a refusal to perform contractual duties if they disproportionately affect the rights of others. The probability of such a disproportionate effect increases where the beliefs are those of a small minority, as was the case in *James v. MSC Cruises Limited*,[138] which concerned a Seventh-Day Adventist who was not prepared to work from sunset on Friday until sunset on Saturday but who failed to mention this during her job interview. She then claimed religious discrimination when the job offer was withdrawn following that disclosure. The Tribunal found that MSC had a 'real business need' for Saturday working and, balancing that against the significance of the disadvantage caused to the complainant, concluded that the business needs outweighed the discriminatory effects on the complainant and so dismissed her claim.

Accommodating religious beliefs/practices in the workplace

The *Eweida* case[139] established that no clear dividing line existed between holding and manifesting a religious belief: in that instance, not untypically, there was a balance to be struck between the conduct of a religious adherent and the impact of that conduct upon others and upon the requirements of their terms of employment. In *Mr H Monaghan v. Leicester Young Men's Christian Association*,[140] the Tribunal considered an instruction from the complainant's manager that he should not seek to convert those using the YMCA's services to Christianity. The Tribunal upheld the manager's action. In *Drew v. Walsall Healthcare NHS Trust*,[141] it upheld the dismissal of a consultant paediatrician whose teamwork was heavily influenced by his faith and included circulating a prayer which he described as a personal inspiration and religious references in his professional communications. In both *Chondol v. Liverpool CC*[142] and *Grace v. Places for Children*,[143] the EAT upheld the firing of staff who were committed Christians, not because of their beliefs but because they had chosen to manifest them in ways that adversely impacted upon others and were inappropriate. Similarly, in *Apelogun-Gabriels v. London Borough of Lambeth*,[144] which concerned an employee who complained of religious discrimination because of his dismissal for distributing 'homophobic material' to co-workers during prayer meetings. The tribunal confirmed that the material was offensive and held that any indirect discrimination involved in his dismissal was justified. In *Haye v. London Borough of Lewisham*,[145] a Christian administrative assistant was held to have been justifiably dismissed after posting similar views about LGBT practices on the Lesbian and Gay Christian Movement's website.

However, in the workplace, as elsewhere, there may be conflict between two human rights: freedom of speech and the freedom to manifest religious belief. In *Smith v. Trafford Housing Trust*,[146] Briggs J considered whether an employer was entitled to discipline an employee, a Christian manager, for posting on Facebook his view that holding civil partnership ceremonies in churches was "an equality too far". While accepting that the complainant could have considered this as homophobic and have been offended, Briggs J found that "her interpretation was not in my view objectively reasonable"[147] and advised that:[148]

> [t]he frank but lawful expression of religious or political views may frequently cause a degree of upset, and even offence, to those with deeply held contrary views, even where none is intended by the speaker. This is a necessary price to be paid for freedom of speech.

As Underhill J explained in *Dhaliwal*,[149] "it is also important not to encourage a culture of hypersensitivity or the imposition of legal liability in respect of every unfortunate phrase".[150]

The importance of the proportionality principle must also be borne in mind. In *Thompson v. Luke Delaney George Stobbart Ltd*,[151] a Jehovah's Witness who had been refused permission for time off work on Sundays had her discrimination claim upheld: the refusal was not proportionate because there were other employees who could have covered the Sunday shift without difficulty. In contrast, a plaintiff of the same religion with the same complaint failed in *Patrick v. IH Sterile Services Ltd*[152] to establish religious discrimination. The Tribunal considered that the employer could justify interference with the plaintiff's right to manifest his religious beliefs, as its contractual obligation to provide sterile laboratory services to its customers on Sundays was a legitimate aim, and sharing out the obligation to work on Sundays equally across the workforce was a proportionate means of achieving it. Similarly, in *Cherfi v. G4S Security Services Ltd*,[153] the refusal of a security guard's request that his working hours be adjusted to facilitate attendance at a mosque for prayer on Fridays was found to be justified and his indirect discrimination claim was unsuccessful. The employer required a certain number of security staff to be on-site during operating hours and had offered a number of alternative options that had been rejected.

Right to education

In this jurisdiction, the right to a religious component in education was established by the Education Act 1944, as amended by the Education Reform Act 1988 and the School Standards and Framework Act 1998. It was accompanied, in the 1994 Act, by a requirement that schools provide opportunities for pupils to engage in acts of collective worship.[154]

Government funding and religious education: general overview

No church or religious organisation receives direct funding for religious purposes from the government. Faith schools, however, which now constitute a third (6,813 as of January 2017) of all schools, receive financial support of up to 90 percent of capital costs and 100 percent of running costs, including salaries. In *R (Fox & Ors) v. Secretary of State for Education*,[155] the plaintiffs successfully contended that the school education syllabus in effect gave priority to religion at the expense of other systems of belief and non-belief. As Warby J then summarised:[156]

> Taken overall, the human rights jurisprudence establishes the following points of relevance to this claim. In carrying out its educational functions the State owes parents a positive duty to respect their religious and philosophical convictions; the State has considerable latitude in deciding exactly how that duty should be performed, having regard among other things to available resources, local conditions and, in particular, the preponderance in its society of particular religious views, and their place in the tradition of the country; thus, the State may legitimately give priority to imparting knowledge of one religion above others, where that religion is practised or adhered to by a majority in society; but the State has a duty to take care that information or knowledge included in the curriculum is conveyed in a pluralistic manner; subject to certain threshold requirements, immaterial here, the State must accord equal respect to different religious convictions, and to non-religious beliefs; it is not entitled to discriminate between religions and beliefs on a qualitative basis; its duties must be performed from a standpoint of neutrality and impartiality as regards the quality and validity of parents' convictions.

As he went on to note, it was permissible for the State to exercise some discernment in how it gave effect to this duty: "[T]he Strasbourg jurisprudence shows that the duty of impartiality and neutrality owed by the State does not require equal air-time to be given to all shades of belief or conviction".[157] However, as that jurisprudence clearly requires religious education in non-faith schools to be "objective, critical and pluralistic"[158] and while "a fair balance allows the State to accord appropriate weight to majority views, but does not permit it to treat the views of minorities in a way that is significantly different at the qualitative level,"[159] therefore such education must also include humanism and other non-religious beliefs.[160]

Educational facilities: religion, staffing and pupil access

The provisions of the 1998 Act distinguish between voluntary-aided and voluntary-controlled schools, community schools, foundation schools and academies: this differentiation has implications for staffing and for financial support. In voluntary controlled or foundation schools with a religious character, religion can be taken into account in appointing the head teacher, and up to a fifth of its teaching staff can be "selected for their fitness and competence" to give religious education in accordance with the tenets of the faith of the school. Voluntary-aided schools can impose religious requirements on all teaching staff and on the criteria for pupil admission. The appointment of ancillary staff can be subject to religious criteria where being of a particular religion or religious denomination is a genuine occupational requirement (GOR).[161]

Staffing and religion was the focus of contention in the above-mentioned *Glasgow City Council v. McNab*,[162] when the EAT upheld a tribunal's decision that an atheist teacher employed by a Catholic school maintained by the Council had suffered direct discrimination. Pupil admission can also prove contentious. In *Mandla (Sewa Singh) and another v. Dowell Lee and others*,[163] a Sikh boy was denied admittance to a private school because he refused to comply with the school uniform requirement to cut his hair and remove his turban: a turban being emblematic of religious/cultural identity, he could not remove it without sacrificing that identity. The House of Lords held that it was unlawful indirect discrimination (albeit racial discrimination under the Race Relations Act 1976) for a headmaster of an independent school to insist on a uniform requirement of short hair and caps for boys, thus excluding Sikhs who wear turbans with long hair; the ruling was echoed in *R (Watkins-Singh)*,[164] above.

The most important case in this field, however, is *R (on the application of E) v. Governing Body of JFS and the Admissions Appeal Panel of JFS*,[165] which concerned the rules of admission to a Jewish school that had, for 52 years, required a child – in accordance with Orthodox Jewish doctrine – to have a mother who was Jewish. In this case, she had converted but that conversion was not recognised by the Chief Rabbi. The issue for the court was whether the school could claim an exemption against a charge of racial discrimination on the grounds of their religious commitments. The High Court ruled that a school that accepts State funding must not discriminate in its admission policy on the basis of ethnicity. Subsequently, the UKSC, in a majority ruling, found that what in the High Court had been characterised as religious grounds were in fact racial grounds, notwithstanding their theological motivation, and no faith school could be excused from the prohibition on race discrimination. More recently, in *The British Humanist Association v. LB of Richmond upon Thames*,[166] the court considered and dismissed a claim that the opening of new Catholic primary and secondary schools would mean operating admissions policies focused predominantly on children who are Catholic rather than being more widely available to children resident in the area.

State schools, religion and educational content

Daily collective prayer or worship of "a wholly or mainly . . . Christian character" is practised in schools in England and Wales. Moreover, the law requires that religious education in State-funded schools be provided for all children between the ages of three and 19, and that it should reflect the predominant place of Christianity while taking into account the teachings and practices of other principal religious groups in the country. This requirement has generated concern. The AHRC Network in its 2015 report took the view that:[167]

> [t]he protection of the right to freedom of religion or belief of those who do not wish to participate is undermined by current practices. There may also be questions of discrimination against those pupils and their families who do wish to have collective worship provided but who are not Christian.

Although all parents have the legal right to request that their children do not participate in religious education, the judiciary have warned that this right offers insufficient protection:[168]

> [A]n opt-out is not an adequate substitute for the provision of an educational programme which accords the parents their right to respect for their convictions. The need to withdraw a child would be a manifestation of the lack of pluralism in question.

The Commission on Religion and Belief in British Public Life has gone even further and commented as follows:

> The arguments in favour of retaining compulsory Christian worship in UK schools are no longer convincing[169] . . . religious practices should not be required in publicly funded schools, but also they should not be prohibited. . . . If the curriculum is objective, fair and balanced, and does not contain elements of confessional instruction or indoctrination, then this teaching should be required in all schools and there is no reason for a legal right to withdraw from learning about religion and belief[170] . . . governments across the UK should repeal requirements for schools to hold acts of collective worship or religious observance . . . recognise the negative practical consequences of selection by religion in schools, and that most religious schools can further their aims without selecting on grounds of religion in their admissions and employment practices; require bodies responsible for school admissions and the employment of staff to take measures to reduce such selection.[171]

Perhaps as a consequence, head teachers would seem to be becoming more lax in fulfilling their legal obligation to provide religious education. A 2017 report issued by the National Association for RE teachers, quoting data obtained under the Freedom of Information Act, disclosed that more than a quarter of England's secondary schools no longer offer religious education.[172] This has led some parents to protest that their statutory rights, and the respect these were entitled to under Protocol 1 Article 2, were being infringed.

Faith schools

Established under the Education Act 1944 as reinforced by s.71 of the School Standards and Framework Act 1998 – giving parents the right to withdraw their children from religious education and collective worship in every maintained school (whether religious or secular) – such schools give full effect to the requirement in Article 2 of Protocol 1 that parents' "religious and philosophical convictions" be respected. They now constitute a third of all UK schools and are overwhelmingly Christian – mostly Church of England or Catholic, though some are Muslim or Sikh. They are attended by nearly one-quarter of all pupils and are exempted by the Equality Act from the general prohibition on religious discrimination.[173] Although faith schools are obliged to follow the National Curriculum, the exemption permits an extensive range of discriminatory practice, including: preferential treatment in terms of funding to become established; permission to discriminate in pupil admissions[174] and staffing;[175] a teaching curriculum skewed in favour of religious belief; and a corresponding alignment of social values in regard to issues such as gay marriage, abortion and so on, though they are not entitled to State subsidised transport.[176]

Islamic schools and madrassas have attracted official concern on human rights grounds.[177] Most recently, in the *Al-Hijrah School case*,[178] this concern focused on a voluntary-aided Islamic, mixed-sex, State school which Ofsted had ruled was breaching the 2010 Equalities Act by strictly segregating pupils from the age of nine, teaching them in different classrooms, making them use separate corridors and play areas and applying this policy also to clubs and school trips. The Court of Appeal found the school's defence of its policy on the grounds of Islamic teaching to be irrelevant, as was the fact that it had parental approval: each child had a statutory right under the 2010 Act to be educated in a non-discriminatory manner. This is an important ruling because it gave clear precedence to rights of equality rather than to religious privilege and may presage further constraints upon the exemptions enjoyed by religious organisations. It prompted Ofsted to declare an intention to scrutinise other schools with similar policies, including several Orthodox Jewish and Christian faith schools. Further initiatives include mandatory registration for all madrasses and for all children who are being home-schooled.

The Commission on Religion and Belief in British Public Life, in its 2015 report, recommended that faith schools "should take measures to reduce selection of pupils and staff on grounds of religion".[179] It has warned:[180]

> In England successive governments have claimed in recent years that faith schools and free schools create and promote social inclusion which leads to cohesion and integration. However, in our view it is not clear that segregation of young people into faith schools has promoted greater cohesion or that it has not in fact been socially divisive and led rather to greater misunderstanding and tension. Selection by religion segregates children not only according to religious heritage but also, frequently and in effect, by ethnicity and socio-economic background. This undermines equality of opportunity and incentivises parents to be insincere about their religious affiliation and practice. . . . Bodies responsible for school admissions should take measures to reduce selection on grounds of religion in State-funded schools.

Right to non-discrimination in service provision

The right to non-discrimination in service provision, enlarged and now given effect by ECHR case law and the Equality Act 2010, protects against discrimination in the supply of goods and services, including accommodation, as well as in employment, occupation and vocational training. It is one which not infrequently generates litigation when service provision is refused on religious grounds.

Provision by religious organisations

The *Catholic Care* case provides a stark example of what can happen when human rights collide: in this instance, equality and the freedom of religion. It concerned the refusal of that adoption agency to provide its services to same-sex cohabiting couples or civil partners (or to unmarried couples), on the basis that to do so would be contrary to the tenets of the Catholic Church. In the High Court, Briggs J advised that the services could be restricted on the basis of sexual orientation only if the restriction amounted to a proportionate means of achieving a legitimate aim. The regulatory authority concluded that this test was not satisfied, reasoning that religious conviction was insufficient to justify the discrimination by the charity because of the public nature of its activities. This decision was then appealed to the First-tier Tribunal (Charity)[181] where it was dismissed following the Tribunal's finding that the charity had failed to meet the statutory test imposed by s.193 of the Equality Act 2010 requiring it to demonstrate that the less favourable treatment it proposed to offer same-sex couples would constitute a proportionate means of achieving its legitimate aim of providing suitable adoptive parents for a significant number of 'hard to place' children.[182]

Provision of public services

R (on the application of Johns) v. Derby City Council[183] concerned members of the Pentecostal Church, with strong religious views against homosexuality, who had been rejected as foster carers by Derbyshire County Council. Their claim that their beliefs were not a legitimate fostering concern, that these beliefs would not impede them from offering a foster-care service and that their rejection constituted religious discrimination by the Council, were dismissed by the court. Munby LJ, following the decisions in *Ladele* and *McFarlane*, reasoned that the rejection was due to their stance on sexual orientation, not because of their religious belief, and that the Council was entitled, indeed required, to ensure that its public service provision was compliant with equality and non-discrimination legislation. That rationale was subsequently endorsed by the ECtHR which ruled, in relation to both applicants, that their employer pursued a legitimate aim – to provide public services without discrimination.[184] The ECtHR considered that the right not to be discriminated against on the ground of sexual orientation was protected by the ECHR.

Private goods and service provision

The same conflation of sexual mores and religious belief permeates equality case law in the private sector. For example, in *Bull v. Hall and Preddy*,[185] the UKSC confirmed that it was unlawful discrimination for Christian hotel owners to refuse a double-bedded room to a same-sex couple and dismissed their argument that they should not be compelled to run their business in a way which conflicts with their deeply held religious beliefs. Again, among a number of similar cases, the court in *Black and Morgan v. Wilkinson*[186] held that a same-sex couple requesting a double bedroom, who were neither married nor in a civil partnership, had been unlawfully discriminated against on the grounds of their sexual orientation in breach of regulation 4 of the Equality Act (Sexual Orientation) Regulations 2007. The court pointedly emphasised that "the application of the regulations to the defendant's bed and breakfast establishment does not prevent her from holding her religious beliefs".

Where the service provider is expected not only to provide a service but, in doing so, to express support for a position with which they disagree, then it might be argued that the right to freedom of expression comes into play. Such a scenario arose in the Northern Ireland 'gay cake' case.[187] The court at first-instance ruled that it was unlawful direct discrimination on grounds of sexual orientation for a bakery owned by two Christians to refuse to bake a cake which had printed on it a picture of "Bert and Ernie" and the caption "Support Gay Marriage". Morgan LCJ for the Court of Appeal, in upholding that ruling, weighed considerations of equality and religious freedom:[188]

> To prohibit the provision of a message on a cake supportive of gay marriage on the basis of religious belief is to permit direct discrimination. If businesses were free to choose what services to provide to the gay community on the basis of religious belief the potential for arbitrary abuse would be substantial.

However, when finally determined by the UKSC,[189] that court took a different view. It considered that the central issue was the right to freedom of expression. Overturning the earlier decisions, the UKSC found that there had been no discrimination: neither political nor based on sexual orientation. As Lady Hale put it, on behalf of a unanimous bench:[190]

> The objection was not to Mr Lee because he, or anyone with whom he associated, held a political opinion supporting gay marriage. The objection was to being required to promote the message on the cake. The less favourable treatment was afforded to the message not to the man . . . what matters is that by being required to produce the cake they were being required to express a message with which they deeply disagreed . . . the bakery would have refused to supply this particular cake to anyone, whatever their personal characteristics. So there was no discrimination on grounds of sexual orientation.

Service denial on grounds of conscientious objection

Health and social care professionals, in the UK as elsewhere, are with increasing frequency being penalised for refusing to engage with public services that offend their consciences. In response, the Conscientious Objection (Medical Activities) Bill 2017 was introduced in Parliament as a private Peer's bill to clarify the rights of conscientious objection for medical professionals, protecting them from participating in medical procedures – such as IVF or abortion – to which their beliefs are opposed.

Broadcasting services

Publishing by way of broadcasting is not legally required to be inoffensive to the sensitivities of an individual or group.[191] In *Sunday Times v. the United Kingdom (no. 1)*,[192] and *Handyside v. the United Kingdom*,[193] the EctHR considered that the protection of Article 10 extended to the broadcasting of religious advertisements that "offend, shock or disturb". Most recently, a 60-second advertisement based on the Lord's Prayer, due to be shown immediately before *Star Wars: The Force Awakens*, was banned by the cinemas concerned on the grounds that it was likely to cause offence. This elicited the following admonition from the Equality and Human Rights Commission:[194]

> Freedom to hold a religion and freedom to express ideas are essential British values. . . . There is no right not to be offended in the UK; what is offensive is very subjective and lies in the eye of the beholder.

Conclusion

For present purposes, the most obvious distinguishing feature of this jurisdiction is the fact that for many centuries it has had an 'established' church. The Church of England continues to be formally bound to the State with all the ancillary complications that this relationship has traditionally entailed. Consequently, those belonging to other religions and to none may well be justified in taking the view that the privileges granted to that Church compromise both their right to freedom of religion and the principle of State neutrality. The *locus standi* of the Church of England, however, is only one aspect of the deeply Christian cultural heritage embodied in the language, laws, literature, architecture, music and artwork of this country: a heritage which it has very largely succeeded, over the centuries, in transplanting to all other Part II jurisdictions, though all others have chosen to reject an 'established' church. Paradoxically, this leadership is currently being reversed: the UK, the progenitor common-law jurisdiction, is now showing every sign of espousing secularism rather than religion.

The transition from a mainly Christian nation to one that has become steadily more secularist has not been without challenges along the religion/human rights transect. The promotion of pluralism naively overlooked the need to recognise and make appropriate arrangements to accommodate the very different values and beliefs of non-Christian religious groups. The problems represented only too graphically in the Rotherham scandal and in the non-prosecution of FGM cases revealed the extent to which policy was blind to the realities of religious/cultural difference. Arguably, the current policy drive to facilitate the opening of more 'faith' schools stands a good chance of compounding a problem of polarised religious/cultural communities.

There is some evidence of an awareness to build in corrective measures. So, for example, that the UK, alone among the common-law jurisdictions, has recently made the continued right of religious organisations to tax exemption conditional, upon evidence of their now satisfying a public benefit test, seems appropriate in the light of past evidence to the contrary. Also, the current private Peer initiative to introduce Conscientious Objection (Medical Activities) legislation would seem to indicate an awareness that it would be prudent to avoid a policy drift that might exacerbate social polarisation.

Notes

1 See Moon, G., 'Complying with Its International Human Rights Obligations: The United Kingdom and Article 26 of the International Covenant on Civil and Political Rights', *European Human Rights Law Review*, Vol. 8:3, at pp. 283–307.
2 Magna Carta, signed by the King as head of State, contained the clause "that the English Church is to be free and to have all its rights fully and its liberties entirely".
3 Note that a Commission has for some years been engaged in reviewing the case for a national Bill of Rights, see further at: http://aka.justice.gov.uk/downloads/about/cbr/second-consultation/cbr-second-consultation.pdf.
4 See also Equality Act 2010, Sch. 12, para. 5; (Designation of Institutions with a Religious Ethos) (England and Wales) Order 2010, SI 2010/1915.
5 [2013] EWCA Civ 1562.
6 See *Chatwal v. Wandsworth Borough Council* [2011] UKEAT 0487/10/0607, where it was noted that there are no settled criteria for what constitutes a 'group'.
7 As amended by the Anti-Terrorism, Crime and Security Act 2001 and the Protection of Freedoms Act 2012.
8 See also *Abrahams v. Cavey* [1968] 1 QB 479, at pp. 481–482.
9 See *Refah Partisi v. Turkey* (2003) 37 EHRR 1 [2003] ECHR 87, when the ECtHR ruled that Shari'a law is not consistent with democracy and therefore the Turkish government was justified in banning a political party seeking to introduce such law.
10 See, for example, *Lithgow v. United Kingdom* (1986) 8 EHRR 329; *Fredin v. Sweden* (1991) 13 EHRR 784; *Abdulaziz, Cabales and Balkandali v. United Kingdom* (1985) 7 EHRR 471.
11 See further 'Executive Summary', at p. 1, at: www.state.gov/documents/organization/265700.pdf.
12 See further at: https://documents-dds-ny.un.org/doc/UNDOC/GEN/G17/192/15/PDF/G1719215.pdf?OpenElement.
13 See Report of the UN Special Rapporteur on Freedom of Religion or Belief, A/HRC/34/50, 2017, at para. 28.
14 [2002] 1 FLR 508, at para. 12.
15 [2010] IRLR 872; 29 BHRC 249.
16 Ibid., at para. 26.

17 Ibid., at para. 20.
18 Ibid., at para. 22.
19 Ibid., at para. 23.
20 The 'Prevent Strategy', see further at: www.gov.uk/government/publications/counter-terrorism-strategy-contest.
21 For example, the Protection of Freedoms Act 2012 and the Terrorism Prevention and Investigations Measures Act 2011.
22 [1965] Ch. 85. See also *Nelan v. Downes* (1917) 23 CLR 546.
23 *McFarlane v. Relate Avon Ltd*, op. cit., at para. 24.
24 See Bielefeldt, H., 'Report of the Special Rapporteur on Freedom of Religion or Belief', presented to the UN General Assembly, Human Rights Council Nineteenth session, 22 December 2011.
25 [2012] EWHC 175 (Admin).
26 Commission on Religion and Belief in British Public Life, *Living with Difference: Community, Diversity and the Common Good*, the Woolf Institute, Cambridge, 2015, at p. 8.
27 *R (Wachmann) v. Chief Rabbi of the United Hebrew Congregations of Great Britain and the Commonwealth* [1992] 2 All ER 249 at pp. 255–256. See also *Shergill & Ors v. Khaira & Ors* [2014] UKSC 33.
28 [2010] IRLR 136, per Hope DPSC, at para.157.
29 [2011] EWHC 375 (Admin) at p. 41.
30 [2014] UKSC 33, at paras. 45–59.
31 Ibid., at para. 59.
32 The Church of England will be able of its own accord, under the Church of England Assembly (Powers) Act 1919, to bring legislation before Parliament to rescind its exemptions and 'opt in'.
33 The Equality Act 2010, Schedule 9, at para. 2.
34 Ibid., at Sched. 9. Also, see the School Standards Framework Act 1998, s.60, which provides that foundation or voluntary schools with a religious character can give preference in employment, remuneration and promotion to teachers whose beliefs are in accordance with the tenets of that religion.
35 See further Sandberg, R. and Doe, N., 'Religious Exemptions in Discrimination Law', *Cambridge Law Journal*, Vol. 66:2, 2007.
36 See *R (on the application of Amicus) v. Secretary of State for Trade and Industry* [2004] IRLR 430 QBD [2004] EWHC 860 (Admin).
37 See Reasoned opinion to the UK, 2009, at: http://europa.eu/rapid/press-release_IP-09-1778_en.htm?locale=en.
38 Equality Act 2010, Sched. 23, S. 2 (7) and s.2(9).
39 Under the Charities (Exception from Registration) Regulations 1996 (author acknowledges advice from Frank Cranmer on this matter; note to author, 18 July 2018).
40 See further Grattan, S. and Conway, H., 'Testamentary Conditions in Restraint of Religion in the Twenty-First Century: An Anglo-Canadian Perspective', *McGill Law Journal*, Vol. 50, 2005, at p. 50, McGill L.J. 511.
41 Re Lysaght [1966] Ch. 191 and Re Dominion Students Trust [1947] 1 Ch. 183.
42 See, for example, *YL v. Birmingham City Council* [2007] UKHL 27 [2008] 1 A.C. 95.
43 See further at: www.education.gov.uk/aboutdfe/foi/disclosuresaboutschools/a0065446/maintained-faith-schools.
44 [1997] 3 CMLR 630.
45 See *Cali & Figli SrL v. SEPG* [1997] ECR I-1547 [1997] 5 CMLR 484, at para. 23.
46 *RT (Zimbabwe) & Ors v. Secretary of State for the Home Department* [2012] UKSC 38, at para. 42.

47 [2013] UKSC 77.
48 Ibid., at paras. 51, 57.
49 *R (Williamson) v. Secretary of State for Education and Employment* [2005] 2 AC 246.
50 Ibid., at para. 55.
51 Ibid., at para. 24.
52 [2008] IRLR 29.
53 Ibid., at para. 41.
54 [2010] IRLR 4 (EAT).
55 Ibid., at para. 24.
56 *Campbell and Cosans v. United Kingdom* [1983] ECHR 3.
57 *R (Williamson) v. Secretary of State for Education and Employment*, op. cit.
58 See *Christian Institute and Others v. Office of First Minister and Deputy First Minister*, Neutral Citation no. [2007] NIQB 66, per Wetherup, J., at para. 48.
59 *McFarlane v. Relate Avon Ltd* [2010] EWCA Civ 880; [2010] IRLR 872, per Laws, L.J., at paras. 23–24.
60 [2005] UKHL 15 [2005] 2 AC 246 (HL), at para. 75. An approach very much in keeping with the views expressed by Lord Greene MR in *Re Samuel* [1942] 1 Ch. 1, CA, at p. 17.
61 [2010] EWCA Civ80 (12 February 2010). Oxford University Press, 2012, at p. 14.
62 *Eweida v. British Airways* [2008] UKEAT 0123, 08, 2011 (EAT), at para. 29.
63 *R (On the application of Begum (by her litigation friend, Rahman)) v. Headteacher and Governors of Denbigh High School* [2006] UKHL 15 (HL), at para. 18.
64 *Ghai, R (on the application of) v. Newcastle City Council & Ors* [2010] EWCA Civ 59.
65 See EHRC, 'Code of Practice on Employment', 2011, at para. 2.61.
66 *Christian Institute and Others v. Office of First Minister and Deputy First Minister*, op. cit.
67 Citing *Kalac v. Turkey* [1997] EHRR 552, at para. 27.
68 *Cherfi v. G4S Security Services Ltd* [2011] UKEAT 0379 10 2405, (24 May 2011).
69 *Chaplin v. Royal Devon & Exeter Hospital NHS Foundation Trust* [2010] ET 1702886/2009. Similarly in *X v. UK*, No. 7992/77, 14 DR 234 (1978).
70 Playfoot (a minor), R (on the application of v. Millais School) [2007] EWHC 1698.
71 *Eweida and Others v. UK* [2013] ECHR 37, at para. 83. Author acknowledges advice from Frank Cranmer on this matter (email comments 27 January 2017).
72 See the Equality Act 2010, which gives effect to the Employment Equality Directive 2000/78/EC.
73 See, for example, *Showboat Entertainment Centre Ltd v. Owens* [1984] IRLR 7 (EAT) and *Weathersfield Ltd v. Sargent* [1999] IRLR 94 (CA).
74 See, for example, *Eweida v. British Airways* (2010), EWCA Civ. 80, at para. 6. See also *Azmi v. Kirkless M.C.* [2007] ICR 1154.
75 See, for example: *Hasan and Chaush v. Bulgaria*, app. 30985/96; *Svyato-Mykhaylivska Parafiya v. Ukraine*, Application No. 77703/01; and *Sindicatul "Pastorul cel Bun" v. Romania*, Application No. 3220/09.
76 See, for example, *Catholic Care (Diocese of Leeds) v. The Charity Commission for England and Wales* [2011] EqLR 597.
77 See also the Employment Equality Directive 2000/78/EC, Art 2(2)(b).
78 The "protected characteristics" being age, disability, gender reassignment, marriage and civil partnership, pregnancy and maternity, race, religion or belief, sex and sexual orientation.
79 See *R (Kaur and Shah) v. Ealing LBC* [2008] EWHC 2062 (Admin).

80 In Paris on 7 January 2015, ten journalist staff of the Charlie Hebdo magazine were killed by Islamic gunmen.
81 *Norwood v. DPP* [2003] EWHC 1564.
82 *Hammond v. DPP* [2004] EWHC 69 (Admin).
83 Rushdie, S., *The Satanic Verses*, St Martin's Press, Picador, 2002 (1988, 1st ed.). Also, see the more recent controversy relating to Corso, S., *The Jewel of Medina*, Beaufort Books, US, 2008.
84 *DPP v. McConnell* [2016] NIMag 1.
85 [2007] EWHC 1698.
86 *R (On the application of Begum (by her litigation friend, Rahman) v. Headteacher and Governors of Denbigh High School* [2006] UKHL 15 (HL).
87 ET 2201867/2007.
88 UKEAT/0309/13/RN, 2015.
89 [2010] ET 1702886/2009.
90 Author acknowledges advice from Frank Cranmer on this matter (note to author, 18 July 2018).
91 [2008] EWHC 1865 [2008] 3 FCR 203.
92 *Azmi v. Kirkless Metropolitan Borough Council* [2007] UKEAT/009/07.
93 Ibid., at para. 101.
94 [2010] EWCA Civ 80.
95 *Eweida v. United Kingdom* [2013] ECHR 37.
96 Ibid., at para. 94.
97 *Commissioners for Special Purposes of the Income Tax Act v. Pemsel* [1891] AC 531 (H.L.).
98 [2000] HRLR 249.
99 *Eweida v. British Airways PLC*, op. cit.
100 See *R (on the application of Hodkin and another) v. Registrar General of Births, Deaths and Marriages* [2013] UKSC 77, per Toulson, J.S.C., at paras. 32–33.
101 Douglas, G., et al, 'Social Cohesion and Civil Law: Marriage, Divorce and Religious Courts', Cardiff Law School, 2011 at: www.law.cf.ac.uk/clr/Social%20Cohesion%20and%20Civil%20Law%20Full%20Report.pdf.
102 *Kohn v. Wagschal & Ors* [2007] EWCA Civ 1022. Author acknowledges advice from Frank Cranmer on this matter (note to author, 18 July 2018).
103 See, for example, *Smith and Grady v. United Kingdom*, 29 E.H.R.R. 493 (1999); *Costello-Roberts v. United Kingdom*, 247-C Eur. Ct. H.R. (ser. A) (1993).
104 See the Siddiqui report, *Applying Shari'a Law in England and Wales: Independent Review*, Home Office, 2018, at: www.gov.uk/government/publications/applying-sharia-law-in-england-and-wales-independent-review.
105 See the Casey report: *A Review into Opportunity and Integration*, Ministry of Housing, Communities and Local Government, 2016, at: www.gov.uk/government/uploads/system/uploads/attachment_data/file/575973/The_Casey_Review_Report.pdf.
106 See the Siddiqui Report and the Government's response, at: www.gov.uk/government/publications/applying-sharia-law-in-england-and-wales-independent-review.
107 In Northern Ireland abortion is illegal in circumstances where conception results from rape or incest or where there are fatal foetal abnormalities.
108 But not so permissive in Northern Ireland where the Abortion Act 1967 does not apply and abortion is legally permitted only if a woman's life is in danger, or if there is a permanent risk to her mental or physical health.
109 [2014] UKSC 68.
110 [2015] NIQB 96.
111 Human Rights Commission for Judicial Review [2018] UKSC 27.
112 [1899] 1 QB 283.

113 See, for example, *Birmingham Children's NHS Trust v. B & C* [2014] EWHC 531 (Fam); *Re S (A Minor) (Medical Treatment)* [1993] 1 FLR 376 and *Re R (A Minor) (Blood Transfusion)* [1993] 2 FCR 544.
114 Op. cit., at p. 826C-E.
115 *R (Pretty) v. Director of Public Prosecutions* [2002] 1 AC 800, at para. 54.
116 [2014] UKSC 38 on appeal from [2013] EWCA Civ 961.
117 See, for example, *Smith and Grady v. United Kingdom* (2000) 29 EHRR 548 and *Goodwin v. United Kingdom* (2002) 35 EHRR 447.
118 See further at: www.rotherham.gov.uk/downloads/file/1407/independent_inquiry_cse_in_rotherham.
119 Note that in *O'Donoghue and others v. UK* [2010] ECHR Application No. 34848/07, the ECtHR had already identified government exemption of Church of England marriages, from legislative provisions with a general application – the Asylum and Immigration (Treatment of Claimants etc.) Act 2004 – as being in breach of the Article 14 guarantee of freedom from discrimination and as such constituting religious discrimination.
120 See *Rees v. United Kingdom* (1987) 9 EHRR 56; *Cossey v. United Kingdom* (1990) 13 EHRR 622; and *Sheffield and Horsham v. United Kingdom* (1999) 27 EHRR 163.
121 *Christine Goodwin v. United Kingdom*, Application No. 28957/95 (2002).
122 Ibid., at para. 74.
123 See also the Code of Practice on Employment 2011, at paras. 2.50–2.61.
124 [2008] ET 2902090/2006 & 2901366/ 2008.
125 ET/1602844/2006.
126 See, the Framework Directive EC (2000/78), Article 4(2); the Equality Act 2010, Sched 9(2); and the Employment Equality (Religion or Belief) Regulations 2003, Regulation 7(3).
127 UKEATS/0037/06/MT; [2007] IRLR 476. See also *Mayuuf v. The Governing Body of Bishop Challoner Catholic Collegiate School* ET 3202398/04, (December 2005).
128 *Muhammad v. The Leprosy Mission International* ET 2303459/09.
129 [1975] IRLR 48.
130 [1978] QB 36, CA. A decision seemingly followed in *Safouane & Bouterfas v. Joseph Ltd and Hannah* [1996] Case No. 12506/95/LS & 12569/95, when the appeal of two Muslims, dismissed for praying during breaks, was rejected. However, both seem at variance with *JH Walker Ltd v. Hussain* [1996] IRLR 11 EAT, when it was decided that actions taken by an employer causing detriment to Muslims as a class, such as refusal to allow time off for religious holidays, might be held to constitute indirect racial discrimination against those from an ethnic or national origin that is predominantly Muslim.
131 (1982) 4 EHRR 126.
132 *UK* (1997) 23 EHRR CD168, following *Ahmad v. UK* (1981) 4 EHRR 126. Also, see, *Cherfi v. G4S Security Services Ltd* [2011] UKEAT 0379 10 2405 (24 May 2011); and *MBA v. London Borough of Merton* [2013] EWCA Civ 1562.
133 [2009] EWCA (Civ) 1357.
134 Ibid., per Lord Neuberger, at para. 51.
135 [2010] EWCA Civ B1. See also *R(Johns) v. Derby City Council* [2011] EWHC 375 (Admin); [2011] 1 FLR 2094.
136 [2009] EWCA Civ 1357 [2010] IRLR 211.
137 [2008] IRLR 29.
138 No. 2203173/05, (April 2006).
139 *Eweida v. British Airways* PLC[2010] EWCA Civ 80; *Eweida v. United Kingdom* [2013] ECHR 37.
140 (2004), ET Case No. 1901830/04.

141 UKEAT/0378/12/SM, 2013.
142 [2009] UKEAT 0298/08/1102.
143 UKEAT/02/17/13/GE.
144 (2006), ET Case No. 2301976/05.
145 (2010), ET Case No. 2301852/09.
146 [2012] EWHC 3221.
147 Ibid., at para. 85.
148 Ibid., at para. 82.
149 *Richmond Pharmaceuticals v. Dhaliwal* [2009] ICR 724. See also *Land Registry v. Grant* [2011] ICR 1390.
150 *Dhaliwal*, op. cit., at para. 22.
151 [2011] NIFET 00007 11FET, (15 December 2011).
152 ET 3300983/11.
153 [2011] UKEAT 0379_10_2405, (24 May 2011).
154 See further AHRC Network report, *Collective Worship and Religious Observance in Schools: An Evaluation of Law and Policy in the UK*, 2015, at: http://collectiveschoolworship.com/documents/CollectiveWorshipReligiousObservanceAHRCNetworkReport13November2015.pdf.
155 [2015] EWHC 3404 (Admin).
156 Ibid., at para. 39.
157 Ibid., at para. 74.
158 *Kjeldsen, Busk Madsen and Pedersen v. Denmark* (1976) 1 EHRR 711 at 53, citing *Folgerø v. Norway* [2007] ECHR 546.
159 Ibid., at para. 33.
160 See further Pollock, D., 'Objective, Critical and Pluralistic? Religious Education in Non-Faith Schools', in *Law & Religion UK*, 17 June 2016, at: www.lawandreligionuk.com/2016/.
161 Employment Equality (Religion or Belief) Regulations 2003.
162 Op. cit.
163 [1983] 2 AC 548.
164 *R (Watkins-Singh) v. Aberdale Girls' High School* [2008] EWHC 1865 [2008] 3 FCR 203.
165 *R(E) v. Governing Body of JFS* [2010] IRLR 136; [2009] UKSC 15 on appeal from [2009] EWCA Civ 626.
166 [2012] EWHC 3622 (Admin).
167 See AHRC Network report, *Collective Worship and Religious Observance in Schools*, op. cit., at p. 7.
168 See *R (Fox & Ors)*, op. cit., at para. 79.
169 Ibid., at p. 34.
170 Ibid., at p. 36.
171 Ibid., at p. 37.
172 See further at: www.bbc.co.uk/news/education-41282330.
173 Equality Act 2010, Sch. 11, pt 2.
174 See School Admissions Code, 2015, at: www.gov.uk/government/publications/school-admissions-code–2.
175 See School Standards and Framework Act 1998, as amended, at: www.legislation.gov.uk/ukpga/1998/31/contents.
176 *Diocese of Menevia & Others v. City & County of Swansea Council* [2015] EWHC 1436 (Admin).
177 See the Casey report: *A Review into Opportunity and Integration*, HMSO, 2016, at: www.gov.uk/government/uploads/system/uploads/attachment_data/file/575973/The_Casey_Review_Report.pdf.
178 *HM Chief Inspector of Education, Children's Services and Skills v. The Interim Executive Board of Al-Hijrah School* [2017] EWCA Civ 1426.

179 Commission on Religion and Belief in British Public Life, *Living with Difference: Community, Diversity and the Common Good*, the Woolf Institute, Cambridge, 2015, at p. 8.
180 Ibid., at p. 33.
181 *Catholic Care (Diocese of Leeds) v. The Charity Commission for England and Wales* [2011] EqLR 597.
182 See also *St Margaret's Children and Family Care Society v. OSCR* [2014] SCAP App 02/13 which found in favour of the Society on very similar facts.
183 (2011) EWHC 375 (Admin).
184 *Eweida and Others v. United Kingdom* [2013] ECHR 37.
185 [2013] UKSC 73. Also, see the similar case *Black v. Wilkinson* [2013] EWCA Civ 820 [2013] 1 WLR 2490.
186 [2013] EWCA Civ 820.
187 Neutral Citation No. [2015] NICty 2. See also a US decision to the same effect (Chapter 7).
188 *Gareth Lee v. Colin McArthur, Karen McArthur and Ashers Baking Co Ltd*, Neutral Citation [2016] NICA 39 per Morgan, L.C.J., at para. 64.
189 *Lee v. Ashers Baking Company Ltd and others* [2018] UKSC 49.
190 Ibid. at paras, 47, 54 and 62.
191 See further the Ofcom Code, at: www.ofcom.org.uk/tv-radio-and-on-demand/broadcast-codes/broadcast-code/section-four-religion.
192 Series A no. 30, (judgment of 26 April 1979).
193 Series A no. 24, (judgment of 7 December 1976).
194 See further at: www.lawandreligionuk.com/2015/11/24/that-cinema-advert/.

4 Ireland

Introduction

Catholic Ireland, an identity confidently established in previous generations, has faded in recent decades. However, while the institutional authority of Catholicism has undoubtedly been eroded by a mix of internal scandals and the external pressures of globalisation and multiculturalism, a legacy of religious protectionism continues to inhibit the modernisation of family law and public services, particularly in relation to matters of sexuality and education.

This chapter follows the pattern laid down by its predecessor. Beginning with an outline of the relevant international and domestic legal framework, it then examines the law governing the relationship between the State and human rights/religion as evidenced in constitutional provisions, legislation and case law. This leads into a consideration of the key human rights – the freedoms of religion, association and expression – and their interrelationships. The final and largest section reviews the case law generated by issues arising from the overlapping human rights, equality and religious frames of reference.

Current legal framework

In the Republic of Ireland, the law relating to religion and human rights is a fusion of traditional conservative provisions, some recent modernising statutes and a good deal of international legislation. As a wholly committed member of the EU, Ireland has embraced European instruments, enacted its leading human rights declarations and absorbed ECHR and ICCPR jurisprudence.

International legislation

The main constituent parts of this framework are as in England and Wales (see Chapter 3). Essentially, they comprise Articles 9 and 14 of the European Convention on Human Rights as applied in conjunction with international treaties, conventions and protocols,[1] and certain EU Directives,[2] together with decisions of the ECtHR, of the UN HRCommittee and of the European Court of Justice as they interpret directives and rights under the EU Treaty.

The European Convention on Human Rights (ECHR)

The ECHR guarantees religious freedom and prohibits discrimination on religious grounds. It requires that any interpretation of 'religion' be applied objectively, have reasonable justification[3] and be non-discriminatory; any differential treatment must comply with strict standards. Article 14 of the Convention, as supported by Article 9 (the right to freedom of thought, conscience and religion) and by Article 1 of the First Protocol (the right to peaceful enjoyment of property), now have a direct bearing upon Irish domestic law. Moreover, Article 29.4.6 of the Constitution makes express provision for European Union law to prevail over Irish domestic law where the two are in conflict, but only to the extent that such EU law is "necessitated" by Ireland's membership.

Domestic legislation

Constitutional authority and principles are augmented by a not untypical range of equality and non-discrimination legislation.

The Constitution

Bunreacht na hÉireann, the Irish Constitution, was enacted by parliament – the *Oireachtas* – in 1937. Article 44.1 declares that "the State acknowledges that the homage of public worship is due to Almighty God. It shall hold His Name in reverence, and shall respect and honour religion". The fact that a degree of primacy is constitutionally granted to Catholicism was broadly acknowledged by O'Higgins CJ in *Norris v. AG.*[4,5]

Articles 40–44 of the Constitution specifically provide protection for fundamental rights, including freedom of religion and belief. Article 40.1. states:

> All citizens shall, as human persons, be held equal before the law. This shall not be held to mean that the State shall not in its enactments have due regard to differences of capacity, physical and moral, and of social function.

The limitations of this constitutional equality assurance were recognised in the comment offered by Henchy J in *Dillane v. Ireland*:[6]

> When the State . . . makes a discrimination in favour of, or against, a person or category of persons, on the express or implied grounds of a difference of social function the courts will not condemn such discrimination as being in breach of Article 40.1 if it is not arbitrary, capricious, or otherwise not reasonably capable, when objectively viewed in the light of the social function involved, of supporting the selection or classification complained of.

Shortly afterwards, O'Higgins CJ acknowledged that the preferential State treatment of religion could be seen as being among such limitations. In *Norris*,[7] he declared that, as he understood it, the Irish people had proclaimed in the Preamble to the Constitution a "deeply religious conviction and faith and an intention to adopt a Constitution consistent with that conviction and faith and with Christian beliefs". Notwithstanding the declaration in Article 44.2.3 that the State shall not discriminate on religious grounds, a considerable body of case law accruing before and after the O'Higgins pronouncement testifies to such preferential treatment.

The Workplace Relations Act 2015

This legislation governs the rights and responsibilities of employers and employees. It provided a new adjudication process to settle disputes in the workplace by consolidating the various functions of the Labour Relations Commission, the Employment Appeals Tribunal (EAT), the National Employment Rights Authority and the Labour Court into a single body – the Workplace Relations Commission – which commenced in October 2015. There is a right of appeal to the Labour Court with a further appeal, on a point of law only, to the High Court.

The Employment Equality Acts 1998–2015

This legislation came into effect in 1998 and has since been amended by the Equality Act 2004 (exemption for religious bodies is provided in both this and in the Equal Status Act, s.7), the Civil Partnership Act 2010 and other statutes. It provides protection for workers against discrimination, harassment and sexual harassment in the workplace. It promotes equality in the workplace and prohibits discrimination across nine different grounds: gender, civil status, family status, sexual orientation, religion, age, race, disability and membership of the Traveller Community.

The Equal Status Acts 2000–2015

This legislation came into effect on the 25 October 2000 and includes the Equal Status Act 2000, the Equality Act 2004, the Equal Status (Amendment) Act 2012 and the Equality (Miscellaneous Provisions) Act 2015. These statutory provisions prohibit discrimination in employment, housing assistance, vocational training, advertising, collective agreements, the provision of goods and services and other opportunities to which the public generally have access, on any of the above nine grounds.

The Equality Act 2004

This legislation abolished the upper and lower age thresholds, while s.8 broadened the definition of 'harassment' in the 1998 Act.

The European Convention on Human Rights Act 2003[8]

This legislation partially incorporates the ECHR, together with several of its Protocols, into domestic law. Irish courts are consequently instructed: in s.2, that "in interpreting and applying any statutory provision or rule of law, a court shall, in so far as is possible, subject to the rules of law relating to such interpretation and application, do so in a manner compatible with the State's obligations under the Convention provisions";[9] in s.4, that "judicial notice" be taken of the Convention provisions and of judgments of the ECtHR or any decision of the Committee of Ministers established under the Statute of the Council of Europe on any question in respect of which it has jurisdiction; and they must also, when interpreting and applying the Convention provisions, take due account of the principles laid down in such judgments or decisions. Under s.5, a court may make a "declaration of incompatibility" where it finds that legislation or a rule of law is incompatible with the State's obligations under the ECHR, in which case the matter must be referred to the *Oireachtas*.

Other legislation

Other relevant statutes include: the Pensions Act 1990–2008; the Unfair Dismissals Act 1977–2007; the Social Welfare (Miscellaneous Provisions) Act 2004, which prohibits discrimination in the provision of occupational pensions; and the Prohibition of Incitement to Hatred Act 1989, which outlaws hate speech, including incitement to hatred based on *inter alia*, sexual orientation. There have been protests from organisations such as the Irish Council of Civil Liberties regarding the absence of legislation specifically prohibiting religiously motivated hate crimes. Also, and of considerable importance, is the currently pending Equal Status (Admission to School) Bill 2016 (see below).

International courts and regulatory bodies

Ireland, unlike England and Wales, is to continue its EU membership for the foreseeable future and will therefore continue to accept the superior appellate jurisdiction of the ECJ and the ECtHR as well as remain accountable to various international committees for progressing the implementation of convention provisions.

The European Court of Human Rights (ECtHR)

Under s.4 of the European Convention on Human Rights Act 2003, "judicial notice" is required to be taken of ECtHR judgments. In making its determinations, the ECtHR allows States a wide margin of appreciation[10] when it comes to placing limitations on the manifestation of one's religion and belief. In deciding whether there has there been a limitation or interference on the exercise of the applicant's religion, the infringement must be: (a) prescribed by law and (b) necessary in a democratic society[11] for a permissible purpose, that is, directed to a legitimate purpose and proportionate in scope and effect (see further Chapter 2).

The Human Rights Committee (HRC)

This body of independent experts, monitors implementation of the ICCPR. Ireland is required to submit a progress report every four years to which the HRC responds and makes recommendations as to additional goals (see further Chapter 2). In relation to the Optional Protocol 1, Ireland has registered the reservation that it does not accept the competence of the HRCommittee to consider a communication from an individual if the matter has already been considered under another procedure of international investigation or settlement.

Other fora

The bearing of European and other international fora on Irish affairs is much the same as in England and Wales. For present purposes, the European Court of Justice and various other committees established by their respective international conventions to monitor implementation have intermittent relevance (see further Chapter 2).

Domestic courts and regulatory bodies

As elsewhere, in practice, most religion-related disputes are addressed by the national regulator for human rights and equality, though the High Court also plays a well-established role, as will the new Court of Appeal, and occasionally matters with a constitutional dimension will be determined by the Supreme Court.

The Irish Human Rights and Equality Commission (IHREC)

On 1 November 2014, the Equality Authority (established in 1999) and the Irish Human Rights Commission (established in 2000) merged to become the IHREC, which assumed responsibility for regulating matters arising under the Employment Equality and Equal Status legislation and under the Human Rights Commission Act 2000. Its primary function is to protect and promote human rights and equality and to build a culture of respect for human rights, including religious freedom.

The Workplace Relations Commission (WRC)

Established under the Workplace Relations Act 2015, the Commission replaces the Employment Appeals Tribunal and consolidates the functions of many other bodies, including the Labour Relations Commission, Rights

Commissioner Service, Equality Tribunal and the National Employment Rights Authority. It hears cases of reported workplace discrimination, including on the basis of religion, and it operates a blanket anonymity policy when reporting its rulings.

The Labour Court

Equality claims may be heard by the Labour Court on appeal from the WRC.

International reports on human rights in Ireland

The UN has repeatedly criticised Ireland's record on human rights and government inaction on several fronts, many of which are linked to religious values, specifically Catholicism: the treatment of survivors of the Magdalene laundries; the absence of safe and lawful abortion; gender parity; and the rights of transgender people. It has also called upon Ireland to give formal recognition to Travellers as an ethnic group. In July 2014, following its fourth 'universal periodic review' of Ireland's compliance with the ICCPR, the UN HRC advised that Ireland was breaching the fundamental human rights of atheists and members of minority faiths – including freedom of conscience, equality before the law and freedom from discrimination – contrary to the International Covenant on Civil and Political Rights. It reported that both the new abortion legislation and the Constitution must be revised to ensure women who are pregnant as a result of rape, incest or who have a diagnosis of fatal foetal anomaly have access to abortion if they so choose, and called for access to abortion where a woman's health is at risk. It reiterated its "previous concern regarding the highly restrictive circumstances under which women can lawfully have an abortion owing to Article 40.3.3 of the Constitution and its strict interpretation by the State party". The committee also considered Article 41.2, which declares that "by her life within the home a woman gives to the State a support without which the common good cannot be achieved", and guarantees to protect mothers from having to work outside the home "to the neglect of her duties within the home". It recommended that "the State party should take concrete steps . . . to facilitate the amendment of Article 41.2 of the Constitution to render it gender neutral and further encourage greater participation of women in both public and private sectors". It called for two referendums to be held: on abortion and on the place of women in society.

The United Nations Committee on Economic, Social and Cultural Rights has similarly expressed concern regarding: the failure of the Irish State to protect the human rights of atheists and secularists in the Irish Education system; discrimination against women under the right to health; and with regard to the blasphemy laws. Also noteworthy is the 2016 report of the UN Committee on the Rights of the Child which called for an end to compulsory school worship.[12]

The State and the human rights/religion intersect

Article 44.2.3 of the Constitution declares the following:

> The State shall not impose any disabilities or make any discrimination on the grounds of religious profession, belief or status.

As Henchy J remarked, "[T]he primary aim of the constitutional guarantee is to give vitality, independence and freedom to religion",[13] an aim which, arguably, the State has successfully pursued as evidenced by its record of consistently discriminating in favour of religion, specifically Catholicism.

Balancing the interests of Church and State

Until the late 1960s, the State/Church relationship verged on the theocratic; such was the degree of mutual support embodied in the Constitution. Abortion, contraception, homosexuality and divorce were among the 'no-go areas' cordoned off by State laws and Church veto.

State- and religion-related terrorism

Ireland's policy of neutrality has kept it out of active participation with 'the allies' in their wars in Islamic countries: it not only declined to send troops to the Iraq wars but there was strong resistance to the use of its airport at Shannon for the purposes of US troop transport and for 'extraordinary rendition'. Ireland is currently a non-combatant nation for the purposes of the ongoing war against ISIS.

State neutrality

While the Constitution declares that the State may not 'endow' any religion (Article 44.2.2), nor discriminate on religious grounds (Article 44.2.3), it also explicitly asserts the Christian values of the State – derived specifically from Catholic teachings – in the Preamble and elsewhere in various Articles.[14]

Christian symbols/prayers in State facilities

The Constitution requires the President, judges and members of the Council of State to swear a religious oath before taking office (Articles 12, 31, 34). Other religious references include: all authority is held to come from 'the Most Holy Trinity'; obligations are owed to 'our divine Lord Jesus Christ'; and the State is urged to hold the name of God in reverence and to honour and respect religion. While not mentioning Catholicism, such references clearly discriminate in favour of religion, specifically Christianity. This is reinforced by the practice of commencing daily parliamentary business with a prayer calling upon "Christ our

Lord" for guidance, and by the daily transmission of the Angelus by *Raidió Teilifís Éireann*, the State broadcasting company.

Protecting religion from the State

While Article 44 prohibited any State establishment or endowment of religion,[15] or any State discrimination on the basis of religious belief, Article 44.1.3 extended State recognition to:

> the Church of Ireland, the Presbyterian Church in Ireland, the Methodist Church in Ireland, the religious Society of Friends in Ireland, as well as the Jewish Congregations and the other religious denominations existing in Ireland at the date of the coming into operation of this Constitution.

By omitting reference to other religions or beliefs, the Constitution conferred on the State an implied duty to give primacy to the protection of Catholicism and those specified religions.

Intervention in Church disputes

The courts follow case precedents by not inquiring into the inherent validity of a particular religion, nor do they examine the relative merits of different religions. As Henchy J explained in *McGrath and Ó Ruairc v. Trustees of Maynooth College*,[16] the court had no power to intervene in the appointment procedures of religious dominations which were protected by Article 44.2.3 of the Constitution:[17]

> [F]ar from eschewing the internal disabilities and discriminations which flow from the tenets of a particular religion, the State must on occasion recognise and buttress them. For such disabilities and discrimination . . . are part of the texture and essence of the particular religion.

This was an approach confirmed later by Barrington J when considering the relative *locus standi* of the Muslim, Hindu and Jewish religions under Article 44.[18]

State protection of its traditional religious/cultural identity

The Constitution unequivocally commits the State to upholding the nation's declared religious/cultural identity. The Preamble begins with "in the name of the Most Holy Trinity" while Article 6 provides that "all powers of government, legislative, executive and judicial, derive, under God, from the people". Article 44 makes special reference to the Christian nature of the State and pledges the State to uphold its duty to pay "the homage . . . due to Almighty God", and religious values are commended as being of central importance to Irish society. This protective approach to the traditional culture was apparent in *Campaign to Separate Church and State.*,[19] which concerned, among other matters, the presence of

Catholic icons or artwork in classrooms. Barrington J then ruled that publicly funded schools are not obliged "to change the general atmosphere of its school merely to accommodate a child of a different religious persuasion". Again, in *O'Shiel v. Minister for Education*,[20] Laffoy J upheld a requirement that publicly funded schools give preference to employing teachers qualified to teach Irish to a reasonable standard. However, this is counterbalanced to an extent by the observation of Hogan J:[21]

> Article 44.2.1 protects not only the traditional and popular religions and religious denominations – such as, for example, Roman Catholicism, the Church of Ireland and the Presbyterian Church – but perhaps just as importantly, it provides a vital safeguard for minority religions and religious denominations whose tenets are regarded by many as unconventional.

State preferencing of religious organisations

Barrington J, in *Corway v. Independent Newspapers (Ireland) Ltd*,[22] when considering the *locus standi* standing of religions under Art. 44 of the Constitution, commented that it:

> is an express recognition of the separate co-existence of the religious denominations, named and unnamed. It does not prefer one to the other and it does not confer any privilege or impose any disability or diminution of status upon any religious denomination, and it does not permit the State to do so.

The religious exemption

Under the Equal Status Acts 2000–2012, s.7(3)(c), schools may offer preferential admission to pupils of certain religious backgrounds where "the objective of the school is to provide education in an environment which promotes certain religious values", and s.7(2) enables a school to refuse admittance to a pupil who is not of its denomination where it can prove that "the refusal is essential to maintain the ethos of the school". Similarly, under the Employment Equality Acts 1998–2012, s.37(1), a religious, medical or educational institution established for a religious purpose may discriminate where it is reasonable to do so in order to maintain the 'religious ethos' of the institution or is reasonably necessary to avoid undermining that ethos.[23] Unfortunately, there is no definition of 'ethos', though it is reasonably certain that a religious preference may be legitimately exercised in respect of employees, job applicants or pupil admissions, including reserving quotas of places available in certain teaching and nursing institutions, and will include disciplinary action against employees who breach the established standards and traditions of a religious institution.[24]

In *Quinn's Supermarket Ltd v. Attorney General*[25] and in *Re Article 26 and the Employment Equality Bill 1996*,[26] the Supreme Court confirmed that a religious action may be exempt from general laws if a failure to provide an exemption would restrict or prevent the free profession and practice of religion. It is clear, however, that not every "distinction necessary to achieve this overriding objective will be valid".[27] In the latter case, the Supreme Court ruled that it was constitutionally permissible to discriminate on grounds of religious profession, belief or status if this is necessary to "give life and reality" to the constitutional guarantee of freedom of religion.[28]

Regulatory privileges

Religious organisations in Ireland have traditionally been self-regulating. There has never been a requirement for them to register with any government body. Religious status conferred an exemption from the regulations imposed by the Revenue Commissioners, leaving only those that were incorporated amenable to the routine administrative requirements of the Companies Office. The consequences of a lax regulatory regime were recorded in the Ryan Report[29] of the Commission to Inquire into Child Abuse in orphanages and schools and the Murphy Report[30] regarding sexual abuse in the archdiocese of Dublin – both detailing many decades of child abuse perpetrated by Catholic clergy.

The exemption from registration is continued under the Charities Act 2009, s.48(6) of which extends this privilege to an "education body". As many of these are owned and/or managed by religious organisations, this has the effect of enabling them to avoid the levels of fiscal monitoring, regulatory accountability and public transparency now expected of all other charities. Exemption is also evident in the freedom that permits many religious bodies to establish member-only outreach charities: for example, Jah-Jireh homes are charitable facilities established and run wholly and solely to give accommodation and care to members of the Jehovah's Witnesses community.

Tax privileges

Religious organisations in Ireland, unlike in England and Wales, are legally presumed to satisfy the public benefit test and therefore automatically qualify for charitable status and associated tax exemption privileges. Under s.2 of the Charities Act 2009, the definition of "charitable organisation" extends to religious organisations or communities, including, again unlike in England and Wales, 'closed' communities such as convents. The provision goes on to provide an exemption from restrictions solely in favour of "a religious organisation or community, on accommodation and care of members of the organisation or community". As a very large proportion of all charitable entities in this jurisdiction – gifts, donations, bequests, educational and health service facilities, and many other organisations – have religious status, this could be construed as constituting a

State policy of positive discrimination in favour of religion – which, in practice, means mainly Catholicism.

Testamentary privileges

The courts in Ireland, following the precedents established by their English counterparts, similarly endorsed the religious discriminatory preferences of testators. For example, in *Duggan v. Kelly*,[31] a condition against marrying a Papist was upheld and so, in *Re McKenna*,[32] was a condition against marrying a Roman Catholic, while in *Re Knox*[33] the court upheld a condition restricting marriage to a Protestant wife with Protestant parents. Only when the right to make such a conditional testamentary disposition was trumped by what was considered to be a greater duty, such as the educational obligation of parents under Article 42 of the Constitution, did the courts rule religiously discriminatory dispositions invalid.[34]

State funding of faith-based facilities and services

In practice, the policy of providing State funding has been one aimed not directly at assisting religious purposes but toward assisting Roman Catholic organisations most usually in their role as service providers in health care and education. The long-established government practice of funding staff or equipment in mainly Catholic, but partially Protestant, controlled service provision in some hospitals and most schools is set to continue for the foreseeable future (see further below).[35]

In *Campaign to Separate Church and State Ltd*,[36] a challenge to the constitutionality of the State funding of school chaplains was launched by an organisation opposed to State involvement with religion, arguing that this use of funding discriminated against those of non-Christian beliefs and secularists and would be better directed toward improving non-religious education services. The court found that parents had the right to have religious education provided in the schools which their children attend and were not obliged to settle merely for religious 'instruction'. The role of the chaplain helped to provide this extra dimension to the religious education of children and therefore:[37]

> the State by paying the salaries of chaplains in community schools is having regard to the rights of parents vis-a-vis the religious formation of their children and enabling them to exercise their constitutionally recognised rights

and[38]

> the present system is merely a manifestation, under modern conditions, of principles which are recognised and approved by Articles 44 and 42 of the Constitution.

Barrington J concluded his judgment in the Supreme Court by adding two caveats to his decision. First, the system of salaried chaplains had to be available to all community schools of whatever denomination on an equal basis in accordance with their needs, and second, it was constitutionally impermissible for a chaplain to instruct a child in a religion other than the child's own without the knowledge and consent of his or her parents (see further below).

Religion and the freedoms of association and expression

Religion and belief, having remained undefined by Irish legislators and judiciary, are matters that have largely retained their traditional meaning. The interpretation of, and structural relationship between, the freedoms of religion, association and expression have only occasionally attracted judicial attention.

Freedom of religion

The Constitution acknowledges a duty to "respect and honour religion" (Article 44.1), provides for the freedom of conscience and the free profession and practice of religion, subject to public order and morality (Article 44.2.1) and directs that the State must not impose any disabilities or make any discrimination on the ground of religious profession, belief or status (Article 44.2.3). The European Convention on Human Rights Act 2003 incorporates the ECHR provisions, while further protection is available under the EU Charter of Fundamental Rights and Article 18 of the ICCPR.

Definitions

The Constitution makes no express reference to faiths that do not profess belief in a god, nor to polytheistic religions, nor to beliefs of a wider philosophical nature such as humanism. Statute law also provides no definition of what constitutes a 'religion' or 'belief'. Effectively, then, Irish law continues the traditional common-law understanding that such matters rest on a belief in the existence of a Supreme Being and on worship of that Being.

- 'Religion'

As Barrington J explained in *Corway v. Independent Newspapers (Ireland) Ltd*:[39]

> [T]he State acknowledges that the homage of public worship is due to Almighty God. It promises to hold his name in reverence and to respect and honour religion. At the same time it guarantees freedom of conscience, the free profession and practice of religion and equality before the law to all citizens be they Roman Catholics, Protestants, Jews, Muslims, agnostics or atheists.

This interpretation was endorsed by Hogan J in *Temple Street*,[40] when he noted that the State is required to give parity of recognition to Christian and non-Christian religions. However, given the fact that the Constitution leans heavily toward Christianity – particularly Roman Catholicism – there remains some doubt as to the reality of that parity.

A distinctive characteristic of religion in this jurisdiction has been and remains an emphasis on the importance of private piety. Its significance was recognised by Gavan Duffy J in *Maguire v. Attorney General*[41] and in *re Howley*.[42]

- 'Beliefs'

The view that a legal definition of religion could be satisfied by a system of belief not involving faith in a god has never been unequivocally affirmed by the judiciary, and the legislators have clearly chosen not to avail of the opportunity to break with tradition by specifically extending recognition to philosophical beliefs. Attempts to broaden recognition to include recognition for humanism, for example, have failed. However, while Irish statutory law retains the traditional requirement of a belief in god, the case law explicitly extends the constitutional guarantee of freedom of religion beyond monotheistic Christian religions.

Manifestation of religion or belief

The 'free practice' clause in Article 44 of the Constitution is conditional upon its exercise being compliant with other rights – particularly free speech and freedom of association – and from time to time this has arisen for consideration in the Irish courts.[43]

Religious discrimination

The basic principles governing religious discrimination are laid down in the Constitution, particularly Article 44.2.3. However, in *Campaign to Separate Church and State v. Minister for Education*,[44] the Supreme Court upheld the legality of religious discrimination when it found that parents had a constitutional right to have religious education provided in schools. Again, *In the Matter of Article 26 of the Constitution and In the Matter of the Employment Equality Bill, 1996*,[45] the same court concluded that it was permissible, on a constitutional basis, to make distinctions on grounds of religion in certain restricted circumstances when necessary to "give life and reality to the guarantee of free profession and practice of religion".

Currently, the Equal Status Act 2000 provides that 'discrimination' can be taken to occur when a person is treated less favourably than another person is, has been or would be treated in a comparable situation on any of the nine specified grounds. As between any two persons, the discriminatory grounds under s.6(2)(e) include "that one has a different religious belief from the other, or that one has a religious belief and the other has not". The Equality Act 2004, s.85A, in keeping with the Employment Equality Directive 2000/78/EC, states that in addition to "direct" discrimination, there is also indirect victimisation and harassment or sexual harassment.

Freedom of association

The Constitution, Article 40.6.1, protects the right to form an association but makes its exercise subject to legislative requirements protecting public order and morality.[46]

The 'positive action' provisions

The Employment Equality Acts 1998–2011, ss.24(1), 33 and 37(1)(a), together with the Equality Act 2004, ss.15 and 22, all permit positive discrimination on religious grounds by allowing more favourable treatment of employees or prospective employees in religious, educational or medical institutions. This applies not just to accessing jobs but also for more favourable conditions of employment.

The decision in *Quinn's Supermarket* was unequivocally based upon a perceived need to extend 'positive discrimination' to the interests of a religious minority. The plaintiff's argument – that special exemption for Jewish kosher butchers from the Sunday trading laws was discriminatory against non-Jewish shopkeepers – was rejected, though the exemption was struck down on the basis that it went further than was necessary to protect religious freedom. Again, in *Re Article 26 and the Employment Equality Bill 1996*,[47] s.12 of the Bill provided that the prohibition on religious discrimination would not apply to the selection of nurses or primary teachers for employment in any "religious, educational or medical institution which is under the direction or control of a body established for religious purposes". Such institutions were permitted to give "favourable treatment" on grounds of religion to employees, and to prospective employees in terms of recruitment – if necessary "to uphold the religious ethos of the institution".[48] This was termed "positive discrimination" by counsel for the Attorney General, but must now be read subject to s.11 of the 2015 Act.

Freedom of expression

The Constitution, Article 40.6.1, protects the right to free speech, as qualified by the caveat that it may not be used to undermine "public order or morality or the authority of the State".

Religiously motivated conduct

There have been very few rulings on religion-related issues recorded by the Workplace Relations Commission (WRC). However, the 2014–17 proceedings brought by four sibling students attending NUIG were based on alleged violations of their right to freedom of religious expression by college authorities. All four had been active members of two college groups, the Christian Union and Life societies, which promoted "teachings of Christianity" and "sanctity of human life". They claimed that their posters opposing abortion and same-sex marriage were removed by college officials and that they had been subjected to harassment by those officials. Ultimately, the WRC ruled that the complaints were mostly time-barred and all others failed to satisfy the grounds for discrimination, harassment and/or victimisation on grounds of religion under the Equal Status Acts.

Religious apparel

Issues relating to religion-specific clothing worn by employees have generated very few cases in this jurisdiction, although the continuing, if occasional, presence of traditionally attired nuns in schools, hospitals, social care facilities and so on, while reassuring to many is probably experienced as at least incongruous to non-Catholics. The variable spectrum of female Islamic clothing (from hijab to chador and burqua) has not given rise to much controversy. However, in *Tavoraite*,[49] the firm belief of the plaintiff that whereas previously her religious belief did not mandate wearing the hijab, it now did, led to problems in her workplace regarding the effect of the hijab on her capacity to perform her duties. This matter was ultimately settled out of court (see further below).

Blasphemy and proselytism

Article 40.6.1 explicitly criminalised the publication of "blasphemous, seditious, or indecent matter", while the Defamation Act 2009 declared that a person will be guilty of an offence if:

> he or she publishes or utters matter that is grossly abusive or insulting in relation to matters held sacred by any religion, thereby causing outrage among a substantial number of the adherents of that religion, and (b) he or she intends, by the publication or utterance of the matter concerned, to cause such outrage.

This enduring constitutional and statutory ban on blasphemy has been accompanied by a traditionally strong Irish commitment to missionary work in Africa which had proselytism as a central component. Both the constitutional and statutory provisions highlighted the leaning towards a theistic rather than a secular State and both have now been removed by national referendum in 2018.

Conscientious objection

Article 44.2.1 of the Constitution, under the heading "Religion", provides a guarantee that all citizens are entitled to "freedom of conscience . . . subject to public order and morality". Any restriction on this right would have to be rational, intrude as little as possible and be proportionate to the aim it seeks to achieve.[50] As noted in *AM v. Refugee Appeals Tribunal*,[51] the provision has for the most part dealt with freedom of conscience in the religious context.[52] In that case, the court held that s.2 of the Refugee Act 1996 was to be interpreted in accordance with the right to freedom of conscience under the Constitution and required that protection be afforded to a conscientious objector with a well-founded fear of persecution.

Human rights, equality and religion: the case law

Freedom of religion, as protected in both the Constitution and in equality legislation, tends to generate human rights issues when values traditionally associated with it come into conflict with contemporary social mores. In an Irish cultural context, that invariably means mainly in relation to matters such as the public education system, sexuality and aspects of the right to life.

Right of access to justice

There is no constitutional right of access to justice, and statutory law is restrictive in the terms on which provision is made for legal aid and representation in regulatory and judicial proceedings.[53] In July 2015, the UN Committee on Economic, Social and Cultural Rights expressed concern at the lack of legal aid services in Ireland "which prevents especially disadvantaged and marginalised individuals and groups from claiming their rights and obtaining remedies, particularly in the areas of employment, housing and forced evictions, and social welfare benefits".

Religious law and courts

Ecclesiastical authorities, particularly those of the Catholic Church, have traditionally wielded considerable power in family law matters. Although the Law Reform Commission recommended in 1984 that decrees of nullity of marriage granted by an ecclesiastical court of the Catholic Church should no longer be recognised by the national legal system, the Church continues to adjudicate on matrimonial matters and to annul marriages on religious grounds.[54] Such rulings no longer have any civil law effect.

Shari'a law

The Irish Council of Imams, which represents all 14 imams and the 40,000 Muslims in the Republic of Ireland, is campaigning for the introduction of Shari'a law, but unlike in the UK, there is no evidence that Shari'a courts are yet established in this country.

Right to life

This most fundamental of the fundamental human rights has been of central importance to the Irish 'culture wars' in which religion, specifically Catholicism, consistently played an overtly partisan role.

Abortion, contraception

Many hospitals and health care facilities have been built and continue to be managed by Catholic bodies, and consequently the availability of medical treatment has at times been subject to associated religious beliefs: abortion and contraception are two areas where religious sanctions have generated most social controversy.[55] This was particularly so during the 1983 and 2018 national referendums on abortion, the former resulting in the 8th Amendment (which guaranteed the equal right to life of a mother and her unborn child) and the latter in its repeal.

The availability of abortion for Irish women – long prohibited by both the Offences against the Person Act 1861 and Article 40.3.3 of the Constitution – has for some decades been the subject of considerable national[56] and international controversy. In *A, B and C v. Ireland*,[57] for example, the ECtHR considered the rights of a Lithuanian resident in Ireland denied access to abortion and held that a broad margin of appreciation should be accorded to Ireland because of the "acute sensitivity of the moral and ethical issues raised by the question of abortion or as to the importance of the public interest at stake".[58] Interestingly, this was challenged in the dissenting opinion of six judges who considered that such reasoning justified exactly the opposite approach and pointed out that it was "the first time that the court has disregarded the existence of a European consensus on the basis of 'profound moral views'". They argued that the fact that these "moral views" "can override the European consensus, which tends in a completely different direction, is a real and dangerous new departure in the court's caselaw". It is a line of argument that, obviously, calls into question the rationale for the 'margin of appreciation' doctrine. Subsequently, the 2012 insertion of Article 42A into the Constitution with its specific reference to "all children" has been judicially interpreted as intended to extend protection to the unborn, and as a consequence the unborn may be treated as having a right to family life.[59] However, the introduction of the Protection of Life During Pregnancy Act 2013, which provides for the termination of pregnancy in cases where there is a risk of loss of life from physical illness in an emergency or a risk of suicide, was so limited that it effectively denied Irish women access to abortion in circumstances legally permitted in most other developed nations. Mounting public dissatisfaction led to the 2018 national referendum and its decisive vote in favour of abolishing the 8th Amendment, thereby paving the way for legislation that will liberalise the law relating to abortion.[60]

Refusing medical treatment

In *Re A Ward Of Court*,[61] the Supreme Court upheld the right to refuse treatment, even if such a refusal can lead to death, by granting a mother permission to authorise palliative care only for her daughter who was in a persistent vegetative state.

Medically assisted death

While the Criminal Law (Suicide) Act 1993, s.1 decriminalises suicide, s.2 makes it an offence punishable by 14 years imprisonment for anyone to aid, abet, counsel or procure the suicide or attempted suicide of another.

The declaration by Hamilton CJ that "it is important to emphasise that the Court can never sanction steps to terminate life"[62] was reaffirmed more recently by the Supreme Court ruling in *Fleming v. Ireland & ors.*[63] It then determined that right to life in Article 40.3.2 of the Constitution "does not import a right to die".[64] As Denham CJ said of the constitutional protection of the right to life, this cannot logically include a right to terminate that life or have it terminated, as "in the social order contemplated by the Constitution, and the values reflected in it, that would be the antithesis of the right rather than the logical consequence of it".[65] This approach may well leave those who do not subscribe to it feeling that they are being denied access to a human right now recognised by the ECtHR.[66]

Right to marriage and to found a family

The continued shelf life of much of the Offences against the Person Act 1861 speaks volumes in terms of those areas of family law and sexuality-related matters where legislators have feared to tread.[67]

Marriage and family relationships

Article 41.1.1 of the Constitution "recognises the Family as the natural primary and fundamental unit group of Society, and as a moral institution possessing inalienable and imprescriptible rights, antecedent and superior to all positive law", and guarantees its protection by the State; while Article 41.3 declares that "the State pledges itself to guard with special care the institution of marriage, on which the Family is founded, and to protect it against attack". The inescapable corollary is that non-marital families, one-parent families and others are all relatively disadvantaged in the eyes of the Constitution. A whole nexus of issues about the respective rights of parent and child, as compounded by the marital status of those concerned, revolve around this constitutional presumption favouring the marital family. Given that the non-marital family has always attracted less protection in law than the family based on marriage,[68] there is a probability that in that respect the protection afforded human rights in this jurisdiction may be structurally flawed because it is inherently discriminatory in its prejudicial treatment of non-marital parents and children (and, also in its treatment of family units led by single parents or by same gender couples) compared with members of a marital family. This was never clearer than during the middle decades of the 20th century, when the State shamefully colluded with the Church to isolate single mothers as a threat to the institutions of marriage and the family.[69] An 'illegitimate' child was treated by the State as *sui juris* (outside the law) and by the Church as 'lost to God', a formula resulting in immense suffering to untold numbers of unmarried mothers and their children which included a proliferation of private nursing homes in which very many babies died, to be buried in unmarked graves,[70] and from which many others were spirited away to new homes overseas.[71]

Same-sex marriage

In August 2015, the President of Ireland approved legislative provision for same-sex marriage which was duly signed into law as the Thirty-fourth Amendment of the Constitution.[72]

Sexuality and gender

Conservatism in relation to matters of sexuality has a long history in Ireland and has been pivotal to the Irish 'culture wars'. The 'Magdalene Laundries',[73] religious adoption agencies, and mother and baby homes stand as reminders of past human rights abuses resulting from institutionalised attitudes toward religion and sexuality. Not until 1993 was homosexuality decriminalised,[74] and as recently as 2017, new legislation was introduced to criminalise prostitution.[75]

In *Foy v. An t-Ard Chlaraitheoir & Others*,[76] McKechnie J ruled that Irish law was deficient and in breach of international human rights as it failed to provide legal recognition for transgender people. This ruling resulted in the Gender Recognition Act 2015, which now provides legal recognition for the acquired gender of transgender persons and should extend the ambit of legal prohibition from discrimination on sexual grounds.

Assisted reproduction, adoption, surrogacy and genetic engineering

The role of religious organisations in the Irish adoption process has a troubled history in which the human rights of mothers and their children were often routinely violated. For example, recent disclosures regarding the 13,500 adoptions arranged between 1946 and 1969 by the St. Patrick's Guild, a Sisters of Charity adoption society, reveal that in at least 126 cases, the agency fraudulently recorded the adoptive parents' names on the birth certificates of babies born to unmarried mothers. It would seem probable that that as many as 150,000 Irish adoptions might need to be investigated to determine the scale of this human rights abuse.[77]

Surrogacy services are also problematic. The basic rule that the birth mother is the legal mother of the child was reaffirmed by the Supreme Court in *M.R. and D.R. & others -v- An t-Ard- Chlaraitheoir & others.*[78] There is, as yet, no specific legislation governing surrogacy:[79] while not illegal, surrogacy agreements are unenforceable.[80] Consequently, it is estimated that there are now several hundred children living in Ireland born to surrogate mothers whose legal status is uncertain and whose human rights are seriously compromised.[81] This is a state of affairs which, the Supreme Court pointed out, "makes statutory law reform in this area more than urgent",[82] and the issue has not been resolved by the Children and Family Relationships Act 2015.

Whether the law should permit the patenting of inventions which directly use hES cells (human embryonic stem cells), or have used them in their development was initially considered to be constitutionally prohibited. At present, following the High Court ruling in *M.R. v. T.R.*,[83] subsequently confirmed by the Supreme Court,[84] that embryos held in cryopreservation and created outside the womb are not protected under the Constitution, the situation is uncertain. Since then, Bills have been drafted to prevent or otherwise regulate the use of embryos for research, including the Human Tissues Bill 2008, but have never become law.

Right to employment

The law governing this right is to be found in the Constitution, the Workplace Relations Act 2015, the Employment Equality Acts 1998–2015 as amended by the Equality Acts 2004 and 2015 and in various European conventions, protocols and directives.[85]

Hiring/firing staff and religious beliefs

In *Re Article 26 and the Employment Equality Bill 1996*,[86] the Supreme Court was asked to rule on the constitutionality of sections 12 and 37(1) of the Bill which exempted from the statutory ban on religious discrimination in employment any "religious, educational or medical institution which is under the direction or control of a body established for religious purposes or whose objectives include the provision of services in an environment which promotes certain religious values". As mentioned above, it then held that it was constitutionally permissible to discriminate on grounds of religious profession, belief or status – when hiring or firing staff and other such matters – if this is necessary to "give life and reality" to the constitutional guarantee of freedom of religion.[87] Two years later, in *Greally v. Minister for Education (No 2)*,[88] Geoghegan J upheld the constitutionality of a recruitment system for secondary schoolteachers that gave priority to the employment of teachers who had experience teaching in Catholic schools. As the Equality (Miscellaneous Provisions) Act 2015, s.11, further entrenches the central importance of 'religious ethos', the probability is that the above judicially endorsed approach will be maintained with adverse effects on the human rights of staff – for example, belonging to the LGBT community, or divorcees, single parents or persons of another religion or none – hired or fired in the very many schools, hospitals and care facilities controlled by religious organisations. This state of affairs is likely to result in a continuation of criticism that s.37(1) of the Employment Acts 1998–2011 – even as now amended by the 2015 Act – allows for a more generous interpretation of matters exempted from the religious discrimination prohibition than is permitted under Article 26 of the ICCPR and Article 4(2) of the Framework Directive.[89]

Accommodating religious beliefs/practices in the workplace

While this is an employer's duty, the obligation is one that is also shared among employees: there is an acceptance that a degree of give-and-take, compatible with efficient working arrangements, is permissible, subject to a reasonableness test.

In *Tavoraite v. Dunnes Stores*,[90] a Muslim employee had her employment terminated after two years of warnings that, while at work, she was required to conform to the company's dress code and desist from wearing a hijab, despite her protests that this was necessitated by her religious beliefs. The Tribunal hearing ended when the plaintiff reached a settlement with the company. In *Cristian Zamfir v. Lorien Enterprises Limited*,[91] a Romanian Orthodox Christian, employed in a restaurant where he worked largely with Muslim staff, complained about discrimination on the grounds of race. He had initially worked as a kitchen porter, then as a commis chef or pizza chef, but unlike the Muslim staff, he was made to clean the toilets. His complaint, relating to allegations of discrimination on both race and religion, was found to be unjustified as there was no evidence to suggest that he was being singled out for toilet cleaning duties. Although derogatory language was used by staff in the kitchen, this was not such as would constitute harassment. More recently, in 2017, the WRC ruled that a Hindu chef had been unfairly dismissed when he returned to work after disappearing for six weeks on 'prayer leave' for his deceased father. In response to the employer's defence that such cultural practices did not exist in Ireland, the regulator commented that this was "an unusual stance for an employer in a hopefully pluralistic society".

Right to education

Despite contrary constitutional and statutory exhortation, the Irish educational system remains heavily denominational in character.

Article 42.4 of the Constitution requires the State to "provide other educational facilities or institutions with due regard however, for the rights of parents, especially in the matter of religious formation". The Equal Status Acts 2000–2015 provide that an educational establishment shall not discriminate in relation to: (a) the admission or the terms of conditions of admission of a person as a student to the establishment and (c) any other term or condition of participation in the establishment by a student.[92] However, unlike elsewhere, a very large proportion of the buildings and teachers comprising the educational system were and continue to be provided by religious bodies, and all teacher training colleges are denominational. So, although State-funded, education is in practice controlled by religious bodies – almost exclusively Roman Catholic. Singularly, among the Part II jurisdictions currently being studied, the State educational system in Ireland was viewed from its inception as a crucial medium for the intergenerational transfer of denominational values and beliefs – primarily those of Catholicism – and as such the lead role in shaping the ethos of values and beliefs of that system was assumed by Church rather than State; the possibility of moving toward role reversal, to accommodate and reflect the diversity of beliefs in contemporary Irish society, has only slowly emerged in very recent years.

Government funding and religious education: general overview

Article 44.2 of the Constitution declares: "State aid for schools shall not discriminate between schools under the management of different religious denominations". However, the Education Act 1998, s.15(2)(b) confers authority on school 'patrons', to whom Boards of Management are accountable for upholding the ethos of a school. As by far the majority of schools have the Catholic Church, or its representative, as its 'patron', the public school system is, in effect, obliged to maintain a Catholic religious ethos. Moreover, the requirement to provide an 'integrated curriculum' in all Catholic schools ensures that that religious ethos permeates all teaching, which compromises the staff right to freedom of thought, conscience and religion.

Crowley v. Ireland[93] clearly established that the State could support denominationally controlled education in discharging its obligation to provide for free primary education. The issue of the very considerable Catholic influence upon the State education system came before the courts again in *Campaign to Separate Church and State Ltd v. Minister for Education*,[94] when both Barrington and Keane JJ invoked Article 44.2.4 in support of the proposition that the public funding of denominational schools did not constitute an endowment of religion. Barrington J noted that the Constitution distinguished between religious 'education' and religious 'instruction' and that the right of a child not to attend religious instruction at a publicly funded school did not protect that child from being influenced, to some degree, by the religious ethos of the school.

In practice, the national primary school system has remained very largely governed by the Catholic Church since the founding of the State.[95] This necessarily results in the education of most Irish children being delivered through that particular religious ethos, regardless of whether this is compatible with whatever religion is or is not practiced in their family home. Government initiatives to moderate this state of affairs, including the Education (Admissions to Schools) Bill 2016, have recently been launched.[96] In conjunction with the Education Together group, the government aims to open nine new post-primary non-denominational or multi-denominational schools in 2018–2019. Clearly there is some way yet to go before the government could be considered to be adequately protecting the human rights of all non-Catholic pupils and their parents – thereby complying with the advice given by the HRC in General Comment 22 – in its management of religious matters in the public education system.

Educational facilities: religion, staffing and pupil access

Accessing the education services provided by a national educational system controlled by religious bodies can be problematic for any staff or pupils who do not share the beliefs of such bodies.

The Equal Status Act 2000, s.7(3)(c), allows schools, including those in receipt of public funding, to discriminate in admissions on the grounds of religion where the objective is to provide education in an environment which promotes certain religious values. However, s.3(1) of the 2003 Act places a statutory duty on "organs of the State" to "perform its functions in a manner compatible with the State's obligations under the Convention provisions" unless there is a law stating that this is not required. There is thus a presumption that public bodies will respect the requirements of the ECHR. Arguably, given that the ownership of most schools rests with the Catholic Church, as does the management and delivery of educational services, the role of that Church in the national education system for children in Ireland could be construed as that of a public body, and while functioning as such, it cannot avail of the statutory exemption provided for religious bodies, and full Convention compliance would be required.[97] As noted above, this does not happen in practice, which leaves the Irish public education of children open to the challenge that it allows religion to compromise human rights.

The fact that pupil access is a systemic and ongoing problem became obvious when, in February 2016, the United Nations Committee on the Rights of the Child issued a report which urged Ireland to "expeditiously undertake concrete measures to significantly increase the availability of non-denominational or multidenominational schools and to amend the existing legislative framework to eliminate discrimination in school admissions, including the Equal Status Act". The report concluded that "schools are continuing to practice discriminatory admissions policies on the basis of the child's religion" and the Committee said it remained "concerned at the very small number of non-denominational schools". One aspect of that problem is evident in the long-standing grievance felt by the small and scattered Protestant community. To be assured that their children receive an education within an appropriate religious ethos, many Protestant parents – unlike their Catholic neighbours – must send their children to expensive boarding schools and are forced to rely on the discretionary benevolence of their local churches and charities to pay the fees.

That staff access can also problematic was demonstrated the 2010 case of Michelle McKeever, a member of the Church of Ireland. A Catholic school, which had offered Ms McKeever a permanent teaching post, withdrew the offer following a post-interview phone call in which she was questioned about holding a certificate in religious studies – a compulsory requirement of the Irish Catholic Bishops' Conference for teachers working in Catholic-managed primary schools. The Equality Tribunal found that she had suffered direct religious discrimination, because of her membership of the Church of Ireland, and awarded her maximum compensation. The case is important as it sounds a warning to all employers that they will be liable to a similar legal sanction in circumstances where their action results in the human rights of an employee – for example, as a member of the LGBT community – being violated. Where staff conduct publicly breaches the religious ethos of their employer, as in *Flynn v. Power*,[98] then they are unprotected, as they bear responsibility for having knowingly placed themselves in a position where accepting that ethos was part of their terms and conditions of employment.

State schools, religion and educational content

In *Campaign to Separate Church and State Ltd*,[99] the court considered the right of a child not to receive religious instruction: that such a child was suffering discrimination by being burdened with instruction that was detrimental to their needs as a non-believer or believer in another religion. Both Barrington and Keane JJ were of the view that Article 44.2.4 imposed a duty upon any school receiving government funding to provide alternative arrangements for such a child. This was reinforced in the above-mentioned 2016 report issued by the United Nations Committee on the Rights of the Child, which recommended that Ireland "ensure accessible options for children to opt-out of religious classes and access appropriate alternatives to such classes, in accordance with the needs of children of minority faith or non-faith backgrounds". A step toward correcting this state of affairs was taken in January 2016 when the then minister for education abolished the 50-year-old official rule stating that religious instruction was the most important part of the school curriculum.[100] However, it remains the case that in practice the State has not to date funded the supervision of any children excused from participating in religious instruction. Arrangements for those who are opted out has been designated a parental responsibility; this is particularly difficult for parents of non-Catholic children in the 2nd and 6th forms of primary school when their classes are preparing for 'first communion' and 'confirmation'.

Faith schools

In Ireland, State education is faith-based: some 97 percent of primary schools and perhaps 50 percent of secondary schools are State-funded but managed by religious organisations: 90 percent of all primary schools are controlled by the Catholic Church.[101] In the above-mentioned *Greally v. Minister for Education (No 2)*,[102] Geoghegan J justified his decision to uphold a religiously biased staff recruitment system on the grounds that the parents had a constitutional right to have their children educated in denominational schools. The assertion of Barrington J, in *Campaign to Separate Church and State v. Minister for Education*,[103] that "the Constitution contemplated that if a school was in receipt of public funds any child, no matter what his religion, would be entitled to attend it"[104] has not always reflected reality and indeed was turned on its head by the unequivocal provision under the above-mentioned Equal Status Acts 2000–2012, s.7(3)(c) and s.7(2), which enable a school to refuse admittance to a pupil who is not of its denomination where it can prove that "the refusal is essential to maintain the ethos of the school". The much-delayed Equal Status (Admission to School) Act 2018, intended to address this situation, has now been introduced.

Right to non-discrimination in service provision

In Ireland, where so much public sector provision is delivered by religious organisations and where porous sector boundaries facilitate the permeation of Catholicism throughout the social infrastructure, discriminatory practices could in theory occur anywhere. In practice, there is little evidence of this in the cases processed by courts and regulatory tribunals.

Provision by religious organisations

The contribution of Irish religious organisations to building and maintaining basic social infrastructure – schools, hospitals, orphanages, homes for the elderly and so on – has been and continues to be probably greater than elsewhere in the common-law jurisdictions. This record has, however, been compromised by evidence of religious filtering of service access[105] and blighted by revelations of systemic abuse. In the latter case, for example, the care and training services provided in reformatories and industrial schools by religious organisations in residential institutions such as Letterfrack (where an estimated 147 boys died) were often subject to abusive management regimes.[106]

Provision of public services

Contemporary religious organisations engaged in public service provision are entitled to rely on their exemption to the statutory prohibition on discriminatory practice to lawfully discriminate in certain circumstances on the basis of religion, belief or sexual orientation. This can be evident in the resistance of staff in some hospitals, operating under the control of religious bodies but funded by the State, to perform abortions or be involved in IVF or other family planning procedures. Adoption, for example, is a national public service delivered by the Health Service Executive (HSE) and regulated by the Adoption Board, but has traditionally been dominated by religious organisations, several of which continue to provide services through their registered, religion-specific, adoption agencies. Following the publication of the Adoption (Amendment) Act 2016, same-sex couples in Ireland have been enabled for the first time to jointly adopt children and stepchildren. This is likely to trigger the same problems for Irish Catholic adoption agencies as it has for their counterparts in the UK, the US and elsewhere.

Private goods and service provision

The Equal Status Acts 2000–2015 prohibit discrimination in the provision of private goods and services, as well as in other areas, and the Workplace Relations Commission rules on complaints arising in that context with a right of appeal to the Circuit Court.

Service denial on grounds of conscientious objection

The Employment Equality Acts 1998–2011, s.16(1)(a) states that an employee's refusal to undertake the duties of their post, on the grounds of conscientious objection, will justify their dismissal; which provides an interesting contrast to the US "liberty laws".

Broadcasting services

The religious censorship of published material that dominated Irish media for most of the 20th century has now gone, but overt manifestations of religious belief are still in evidence. Perhaps the most obvious and enduring example of this, as mentioned earlier, is the daily two-minute mandatory broadcast of 'the angelus' by RTE, the national radio and television company: this State-sponsored, nationwide, 'calling to prayer' of the country's Catholic citizens, is open to interpretation as institutionalised religious discrimination and as violating the human rights of all those who find it oppressive.

In *Murphy v. Ireland*,[107] a pastor attached to the Irish Faith Centre, a Bible-based Christian ministry, wished to transmit an advertisement for his ministry on an independent commercial radio station. This was stopped by the national regulator on the grounds that the planned transmission would be in breach of the public interest requirement protected by s.10(3) of the Radio and Television Act 1988, a ruling confirmed first by the High Court where Geoghegan J took the view that "it is the fact that the advertisement is directed toward a religious end and not some particular aspect of a religious end which might be potentially offensive to the public". This was rejected by the Supreme Court, which did not accept that religious advertisements were *per se* offensive. Subsequently, the ECtHR, ruling in favour of the government, reiterated its established view "that even expressions which could be considered offensive, shocking or disturbing to the religious sensitivities of others fall within the scope of the protection of Article 10, the question for the court being whether any restriction imposed on that expression complies with the provisions of that Article".[108] The relevant Irish legislation was duly amended: s.41(4) of the Broadcasting Act 2009 now provides that a broadcaster shall not broadcast an advertisement addressing the merits or otherwise of adhering to any religious faith or belief or of becoming a member of any religion or religious organisation.

Conclusion

The national referendums in May 2015 and 2018 signalled a sea change in Ireland's willingness to comply with international human rights law on gay marriage and on access to abortion, respectively. The protracted tardiness in Irish human rights compliance has been the subject of repeated reports by international bodies. A legacy of historical abuse cases still require official investigation. Matters such as religious control over access to education, hospitals and other health and social care facilities and religious tuition in schools remain to be addressed. There is still some way to go before Ireland can be said to have fully acceded to the standards required by international human rights law.

The Constitution – framed to give clear precedence to theism, to Christianity and to Catholicism, in that order – has proved to be a considerable obstacle to modernising Irish law. While society has become noticeably pluralistic, multifaith and multicultural, domestic family law and modes of governance continue to be hampered by constitutional constraints. Government commitment to supporting the work of religious organisations in Ireland, for example, by means that include direct funding, has never been in question. As those organisations are predominantly Catholic, the constitutional ties between Catholicism and the State essentially remain in effect. Arguably, the pace of Ireland's continuing cultural transition owes much to the impact of human rights.

Notes

1 In particular: the International Covenant on Civil and Political Rights (ICCPR); the UN Convention on the Elimination of All Forms of Discrimination against Women (CEDAW) with its Optional Protocol; and the International Convention on the Elimination of Race Discrimination (ICERD).

2 See, in particular, the Equal Pay Directive (75/117/EEC), the Equal Treatment Directive (76/207/EEC), and the General Framework Directive (2000/78/EC).

3 See, for example, *Tsirlis and Kouloumpas v. Greece* (1997) 25 EHRR 1988 and the *Belgian Linguistic Case* (1968) (No. 2) 1 EHRR 252.

4 [1984] I.R. 36.

5 [1984] I.R. 36.

6 [1980] ILRM 167.

7 Op. cit., at p. 64.

8 (Commencement) Order 2003 (S.I. No. 483 of 2003).

9 See *Foy v. An t-Ard Chlaraitheoir & Others* [2007] IEHC 470, when a declaration of incompatibility was made concerning the lack of legal recognition for transgender people under Irish law.

10 See, for example, *Lithgow v. United Kingdom* (1986) 8 EHRR 329, *Fredin v. Sweden* (1991) 13 EHRR 784, *Abdulaziz, Cabales and Balkandali v. United Kingdom* (1985) 7 EHRR 471.

See further Legg, A., *The Margin of Appreciation in International Human Rights Law*, Oxford University Press, Oxford, 2012.

11 See *Refah Partisi v. Turkey* (2003) 37 EHRR 1 [2003] ECHR 87, when the ECtHR ruled that Shari'a law is not consistent with democracy and therefore the Turkish government was justified in banning a political party seeking to introduce such law.

12 UN Committee on the Rights of the Child, *Concluding Observations on the Combined Third and Fourth Periodic Reports of Ireland*, 2016, at paras. 35, 36, at: www.childrensrights.ie/resources/un-committee-rights-child-concluding.

13 *McGrath and Ó Ruairc v. Trustees of Maynooth College* [1979] ILRM 166, at p. 187.

14 In *Norris v. Attorney General* [1984] IR 36.

15 The Irish Church Act 1869 disestablished the Church of Ireland.

16 Op. cit., per Henchy, J., at p. 187.

17 As Gerard Whyte points out: "[T]his reasoning was subsequently relied on by MacMenamin, J., in the High Court in *McNally v. Ireland* [2009] IEHC 573". (Note to author, 17 February 2017).
18 *Corway v. Independent Newspapers (Ireland) Ltd* [1999] 4 IR 484.
19 *Campaign to Separate Church and State v. Minister for Education* [1998] 3 IR 321.
20 [1999] 2 IR 321 [1999] 2 ILRM 241.
21 See *Temple Street v. D. & Anor* [2011] IEHC 1, per Hogan, J., at para. 27.
22 Op. cit., at p. 502. Also see *Quinn's Supermarket Ltd v. Attorney General* [1972] IR 1 per Walsh, J., at p. 24.
23 Note, s.37 was amended in 2015; author acknowledges advice of Eoin Daly on this matter (note to author, 26 March 2017).
24 Note the Equality (Miscellaneous Provisions) Act 2015, s.11.
25 [1972] IR 1.
26 [1997] 2 IR 321, at p. 358.
27 See Casey J., *Constitutional Law in Ireland* (3rd ed.), Thomson & Maxwell, Dublin, 2000, at p. 698.
28 The 1996 Bill was declared unconstitutional on other grounds, but s.37(1) of the 1998 Act, its replacement, virtually replicates its predecessor. See also *Greally v. Minister for Education (No. 2)* [1999] 1 IR 1 [1999] 2 ILRM 296.
29 See further at: www.dcya.gov.ie/viewdoc.asp?fn=/documents/Child_Welfare_Protection/RyanImplementation.htm.
30 See further at: www.justice.ie/en/JELR/Pages/PB09000504.
31 (1847) 10 Ir. Eq. R. 295.
32 [1947] IR 277.
33 (1889) 23 L.R. Ir. 542 (Ch.).
34 *Burke v. Burke* [1951] IR 216 and *Re Blake, deceased* [1955] IR 89.
35 See further Casey, J., 'State and Church in Ireland', in *State and Church in the European Union*, Nomos Verlagsgesellschaft, Baden, 2005.
36 [1998] 3 IR 321.
37 Ibid., at pp. 241–242.
38 [1998] 2 ILRM 81, at p. 101.
39 [1999] 4 IR 484.
40 *Temple Street v. D. & Anor* [2011] IEHC 1.
41 [1943] IR 238.
42 [1940] IR 109 where Gavan Duffy J. stated:

> The assumption that the Irish public find no edification in cloistered lives, devoted purely to spiritual ends, postulates a close assimilation of the Irish outlook to the English, not obviously warranted by the traditions and mores of the Irish people.

43 See, for example, *Quinn's Supermarket v. Attorney General* [1972] IR 1 and *Campaign to Separate Church and State v. Min. for Education* [1998] 3 IR 321.
44 Ibid.
45 [1997] 2 IR 321, at p. 359.
46 See, for example, *Equality Authority v. Portmarnock Golf Club* [2009] IESC 73.
47 [1997] 2 IR 321.
48 Ibid., at p. 351.
49 *Tavoraite v. Dunnes Stores*, Unreported, Employment Appeals Tribunal, Dublin, 13 November 2012.
50 See *Heaney v. Ireland* [1994] 3 IR 531.
51 [2014] IEHC 388. Author thanks Gerry Whyte for bringing this case to his attention (note to author, 17 February 2017).

52 Citing: *McGee v. Attorney General* [1974] I.R. 284 *per* Fitzgerald, C.J., pp. 291–292 and Walsh, J., p. 303; also Henchy, J., at p. 326. It is difficult to contemplate "freedom of conscience" as excluding conscientious objection, which is in itself an obvious exercise of conscience rooted in religious or other moral or philosophical convictions.
53 See, for example, *Michael Lyons v. Longford Westmeath Education and Training Board* [2017] IEHC 272, when the court held that the refusal to allow legal representatives to appear on behalf of the applicant constituted a breach of Article 40(3) (1) and (2) of the Constitution.
54 See *O'Callaghan v. O'Sullivan* 1 IR 90 [1925].
55 The government announcement, in April 2017, of its intention to vest ownership of the new national maternity hospital in the Sisters of Charity provoked much controversy. See further at: www.thesun.ie/news/900916/new-national-maternity-hospital-must-obey-the-church-claims-bishop/.
56 See *Attorney General v. X* [1992] IESC 1; [1992] 1 IR 1, which established the right of Irish women to an abortion if their life was at risk because of pregnancy, including the risk of suicide; and *Re Article 26 and the Regulation of Information (Services Outside the State for the Termination of Pregnancies) Bill, 1995* [1995] 1 IR 1. The tragic death of Savita Halappanavar at the University Hospital in Galway in 2012 was attributed to a professional decision to deny her an abortion because Ireland was a Catholic country.
57 [2010] ECtHR (GC) (No. 25579/05) (16 December 2010).
58 Ibid.
59 See *IRM v. MJELR* (HC), 29 July 2016. See also *In re E* [2008] IEHC 68. Eoin Daly adds "[T]hese are isolated first-instance judgments, controversial and not yet confirmed by the Supreme Court" (note to author, 26 March 2017).
60 The government, in "A General Scheme of a Bill to Regulate Termination of a Pregnancy", has indicated that abortion may in future be legally available: on the recommendation of a doctor within the first 12 weeks of pregnancy; or outside that period, on the recommendation two doctors when there is "a risk to the life of, or of serious harm" to the physical or mental health of a pregnant woman, the unborn child is not viable and it is "appropriate" to terminate to avert that risk.
61 [1996] 2 IR 79.
62 In *Re a Ward of Court* (withholding medical treatment) (No. 2) [1995] 2 ILRM 401, per Hamilton, C.J., at p. 120.
63 [2013] IESC 19.
64 Ibid., at para. 108.
65 [2013] IESC 19, at para. 113.
66 *Haas v. Switzerland* Application No. 31322/07 (2011), at para. 51.
67 Although, as Gerard Whyte points out, some 56 sections have now been repealed (note to author, 16 February 2017).
68 See, for example, *The State (Nicolaou) v. An Bord Uchtála* [1966] I.R. 567, The then Mr Justice Walsh of the Supreme Court stated that "the family referred to in [Art.41 was] the family which is founded on the institution of marriage". See also *G v. An Bord Uchtála* [1980] I.R. 32; and *WO'R v. EH (Guardianship)* [1996] 2 I.R. 248.
69 In 1967 some 96.9 percent of non-marital births resulted in adoption.
70 See *The Irish Post*, and reports that the bodies of some 800 babies and infants were found in a burial pit at one mother and baby home in Tuam, at: www.irishpost.co.uk/news/philomena-journalist-lands-new-bbc-series-irelands-lost-babies.
71 See Milotte, M., *Banished Babies: The Secret History of Ireland's Baby Export Business*, New Island Press, Dublin, 2014.
72 Following an overwhelming majority favouring gay marriage in the May 2015 national referendum.

73 See the 2013 Oscar-nominated film *Philomena*, about an Irish mother forced into the care of Catholic nuns after she became pregnant and, like many thousands of other young Irish women, had her baby removed and adopted.
74 Following *Norris v. Ireland* (Application No. 10581/83) ECtHR 28th October 1988.
75 See the Criminal Justice (Sexual Offences) Act 2017.
76 [2007] IEHC 470.
77 See further at: www.nytimes.com/2018/05/30/world/europe/ireland-illegal-adoptions-apology.html.
78 [2014] IESC 60.
79 See further at: www.citizensinformation.ie/en/birth_family_relationships/adoption_and_fostering/surrogacy.html.
80 See the Report of the Commission on Assisted Human Reproduction, Dublin, 2005 which recommended that a child born through surrogacy should be presumed to be that of the commissioning couple. See also *M.R. & Anor v. An tArd Chlaraitheoir* [2013] IEHC 91.
81 See further at: www.aclsolicitors.ie/news-events/current-news/legal-status-of-surrogacy-in-ireland/.
82 *M.R. and D.R. (suing by their father and next friend O.R.) & ors v. An t-Ard-Chláraitheoir & ors* [2014] IESC 60, (7 November 2014), per Hardiman, J.
83 [2006] IEHC 359, (15 November 2006).
84 *M.R. v. T.R.* [2009] IESC 82.
85 Mainly, the General Framework (Council Directive 2000/78/EC) but also the Equal Pay Directive (75/117/EEC) and the Equal Treatment Directive (76/207/EEC).
86 [1997] 2 IR 32.
87 Ibid., at note 28.
88 [1999] 1 IR 1 [1999] 2 ILRM 296. See also *O'Shiel v. Minister for Education* [1999] 2 IR 321 [1999] 2 ILRM 241.
89 See, for example, UN HRC, "Concluding Observations on Ireland's Second Periodic Report under the International Covenant on Civil and Political Rights".
90 Unreported, Employment Appeals Tribunal, Dublin, November 13, 2012.
91 (Case No. DEC-E2016-063).
92 The Equal Status Acts 2000–2008, s.7(2).
93 [1980] IR 102. Author acknowledges advice of Gerard Whyte on this matter (note to author, 17 February 2017).
94 [1998] 3 IR 321 [1998] 2 ILRM 81.
95 Although, as Eoin Daly points out, primary school education is "*controlled* by Protestant as well as Catholic churches depending on demographics, and the State is constitutionally obliged to give equal funding to various faiths based on demand . . . the State set the curriculum" (note to author, 26 March 2017).
96 The IHREC recommended that the Bill should amend the Equal Status Acts in order to give effect to the principle that no child should be given preferential access to a publicly funded school on the basis of their religion and noted that the Bill could place children of non-Irish or new migrant communities at a disadvantage when compared with children of Irish parents, in "potential violation" of the EU Race Equality Directive.
97 Educate Together, a charity founded n 1984, promotes multi-denominational schools. As of 2016, it was the patron of 81 national schools.
98 [1985] ILRM 336.
99 Op. cit.
100 The rule delared: "Of all the parts of the school curriculum religious instruction is by far the most important, as its subject – matter, God's honour and service,

includes the proper use of all man's faculties, and affords the most powerful inducements to their proper use".

101 Ibid., which clearly established that the State could support denominationally controlled education in discharging its obligation to provide for free primary education.

102 [1999] 1 IR 1 [1999] 2 ILRM 296.

103 [1998] 3 IR 321.

104 Ibid., at p. 356.

105 See controversy surrounding the Sisters of Charity, and the proposed new national maternity hospital, at: www.independent.ie/irish-news/news/future-of-new-national-maternity-hospital-in-doubt-after-review-launched-over-controversy-35643178.html.

106 In the mid-20th century, the Catholic Church controlled 51 Industrial Schools cotaining some 6,000 children. See the Commission to Inquire into Child Abuse in Orphanages and Schools (the Ryan Report), 2009, at: www.dcya.gov.ie/documents/publications/Implementation_Plan_from_Ryan_Commission_Report.pdf.

107 Application No. 44179/98 [2004] 38 EHRR 212. See also *Colgan v. The Independent Radio and Television* [2000] 2 IR 490.

108 Op. cit., at para. 61.

5 United States of America

Introduction

The United States of America (US) has the distinction of producing the first Bill of Rights – The Virginia Declaration of Rights 1776 – Article 16 of which asserts that all men are equally entitled to the free exercise of religion. Subsequently, the separation of Church and State became an explicit constitutional requirement in the First Amendment, a requirement reinforced in due course by rulings of the United States Supreme Court (USSC) as it expanded its interpretation of the Fourteenth Amendment. These unique formative steps seemingly paved the way for the US judiciary to develop an acute awareness of laws governing the religion/human rights intersect and yet, as Ignatieff points out:[1]

> Since 1945 America has displayed exceptional leadership in promoting international human rights. At the same time, however, it has also resisted complying with human rights standards at home or aligning its foreign policy with those standards abroad.

This chapter explores the paradox of the contemporary relationship between the US and human rights, with particular reference to religion. It begins by outlining the contemporary legal framework, as governed by statutory and constitutional provisions, identifying the judicial and regulatory bodies and noting the extent to which the country is a signatory State to relevant international treaties, conventions and protocols. As in the other Part II chapters, it then examines in turn: the key issues in the relationship between the State and religion/human rights; the case law illuminating the nature and range of matters that typically cause conflict between religion and human rights; and the effect of equality and anti-discrimination legislation on key aspects of religion and human rights.

Current legal framework

The overarching provisions of the Constitution, particularly its Bill of Rights, provide a framework for the law relating to religion. However, there is no international or federal authority that can ensure a nationwide human rights regime; in that respect, as in others, each state enjoys considerable independence.

International legislation

The United States was a leading nation in ensuring the adoption of the Universal Declaration of Human Rights (UDHR) and in recent decades has become a signatory nation to most of the ten core international human rights instruments, some with optional protocols. It has also signed and ratified the International Convention on the Elimination of All Forms of Racial Discrimination (ICERD) and has signed but not ratified the Convention on the Elimination of All Forms of Discrimination against Women (CEDAW), the UN Convention on the Rights of the Child (UNCROC), the International Convention on Economic, Social, and Cultural Rights (ICESCR) and the American Convention on Human Rights. The failure to secure ratification is in part due to a technical issue: a two-thirds Senate majority is required, and in the current political climate this is almost impossible to achieve. Singularly among the common law nations, the US protects its sovereignty by denying international conventions any scope for superseding domestic legislation. Since the 1970s it has conducted an annual international human rights audit.

The International Covenant on Civil and Political Rights (ICCPR)

The US has signed and ratified the International Covenant on Civil and Political Rights (ICCPR), thereby undertaking to participate in an international review of its progress on human rights matters through the mandatory Universal Periodic Review process as outlined in Article 40 of the Covenant. However, it has not incorporated the Covenant into domestic law, nor has it adopted Optional Protocol 1.

Other

Having initially voted against adopting the UN Declaration on the Rights of Indigenous People 2007, the US ultimately removed its objections in 2010 (see further Chapter 2).

The Constitution and domestic legislation

The Virginia Declaration of Rights was proclaimed in 1776. The article on religion was initially crafted by George Mason and subsequently expanded by James Madison, who repudiated the institutionalised role of religion in England and set the US on its own singular path.

The U.S. Constitution

The constitutional basis for the Church/State relationship lies in the First Amendment of the Bill of Rights,[2] adopted in 1791, which declares: "Congress shall make no law respecting an establishment of religion, or prohibiting the free exercise thereof" – subsequently known as the Establishment Clause and the Free

Exercise Clause,[3] respectively. These, together with the Free Speech Clause of the First Amendment and the Fourteenth Amendment – which declares that the states may not "deprive any person of life, liberty, or property, without due process of law" – form the constitutional foundations supporting the contemporary federal and state laws governing the human rights/religion intersect.

The Religious Land Use and Institutionalised Persons Act 2000

This statute includes a section protecting individuals, houses of worship, and other religious institutions from discrimination in zoning and landmarking laws, and a section protecting the religious rights of persons confined to institutions, such as prisoners. It amended the 1993 Act by redefining an exercise of religion as any exercise "whether or not compelled by, or central to, a system of religious belief", which is to be "construed in favor of a broad protection of religious exercise, to the maximum extent permitted by the terms of this chapter and the Constitution". This was upheld by the United States Supreme Court (USSC) in *Gonzales v. O Centro Espirita*,[4] which emphasised that in establishing the existence of a "compelling interest" that would justify interfering with an exercise of religion, the burden of proof always rested on the government and if, as in that case, the evidence is in equipoise, the court must rule against the government.

The International Religious Freedom Act 1998

This requires the State Department to focus its international intervention on the humanitarian objectives of denouncing persecution and saving victims.

The Personal Responsibility and Work Opportunity Reconciliation Act 1996 (PRWORA)

Under s.104 of this Act, the "Charitable Choice" programme, which led to the creation of Faith-Based and Community Initiatives, was established.

The Religious Freedom Restoration Act 1993 (RFRA)

The RFRA, a legislative response to the USSC ruling in *Employment Division v. Smith*[5] (see further below), prohibits the federal government from applying its laws in a way that substantially burdens a person's religious conduct and requires all federal laws to satisfy a "compelling interest test" in circumstances where the protection of national security or of human life is at risk.[6] The prohibition applies "even if the burden results from a rule of general applicability" except when able to satisfy the compelling interest test: to "demonstrate that application of the burden to the person (1) is in furtherance of a compelling government interest; and (2) is the least restrictive means of furthering that compelling governmental interest".[7] Some states have introduced versions of the RFRA.

The Civil Rights Act 1964: Title VII

The Civil Rights Act, an iconic milestone for the US and for anti-discrimination laws everywhere, sought to prohibit discrimination in public life on a federal basis, including in commerce and education. Title VII prohibits employers with 15 or more employees from discriminating against employees or prospective employees on specified grounds, including religion, and also requires employers to "reasonably accommodate" the religious practices of employees provided that this does not cause the employer "undue hardship". All states have parallel laws.

Other legislation

The International Religious Freedom Act 1998 has been influential, as also have a number of federal statutes, particularly the Affordable Care Act 2010 (ACA).

Equality and non-discrimination

The proclamation in the Declaration of Independence that "all men are created equal" was the starting point for US equality laws, and this principle subsequently found endorsement in the "equal protection of the laws" provision in the Fourteenth Amendment. Currently, in practice, many of the associated issues are litigated under the provisions of the Civil Rights Act of 1964, particularly under Title VII of this federal statute, while each state has its own roughly similar framework of equality and non-discrimination laws. Litigation is also initiated directly under the Equal Protection Clause of the Fourteenth Amendment, under state law and under other federal statutes.

International courts and regulatory bodies

Issues involving religion are adjudicated on an exclusively domestic basis, to be heard and resolved in federal and state courts and administrative proceedings, though there is recourse to review on certiorari by the USSC, at its discretion. The US continues to refute the jurisdiction of the International Criminal Court in respect of its citizens.

The Human Rights Committee (HRC)

This body of international experts monitors the progress of States' parties, including in the US, in implementing the provisions of the ICCPR. The US submitted reports, pursuant to the Universal Periodic Review process, in 2010 and 2014 in both of which the State undertook to close the Guantánamo Bay detention facility (see further Chapter 2).

Domestic courts and regulatory bodies

The USSC is vested with a review jurisdiction, on certiorari, over all US courts. Throughout the course of its very many rulings on religious matters, this court has defined the key concepts and formulated and applied the principles that have become central to the law relating to religion and religious discrimination. Appointments to this court are made on the basis of nomination by the President and confirmation by the Senate, which leaves them open to political bias and has resulted in a very divided bench making some seemingly weak decisions.[8]

Each state has its own judicial and regulatory system, including a state Supreme Court.

The Equal Employment Opportunity Commission (EEOC)

This federal agency administers and enforces civil rights laws and as such is the regulatory body for matters arising under Title VII of the Civil Rights Act 1964. It mediates all complaints of discrimination, including those based on religion, and other statutorily prescribed indices of inequality. Many states have equivalent agencies with a right of appeal to the courts, which adjudicate on points of law and may grant leave of appeal to the state Supreme Court.

International reports on human rights in the US

In 2015, at the second Universal Periodic Review, concerns were expressed regarding the increasing restrictions on women's right to abortion in some states[9] and there were direct challenges regarding the abortion restrictions that the US periodically imposes on the disbursement of its foreign aid. It noted that previous undertakings to close the Guantánamo Bay detention facility had not been carried out. The HRC has expressed concern regarding the lack of free prior and informed consent of Indigenous people when decisions are taken in relation to issues such as sacred sites and mineral extraction on their lands.[10]

The State and the human rights/religion intersect

This relationship has come to be seen as represented in the starkest terms by US foreign policy. It is therefore associated with an overt transgression of human rights which has included drone strikes, 'extraordinary rendition', 'enhanced interrogation techniques' and detention in Guantánamo. In terms of domestic policy, the relationship has been largely concerned with much the same balancing of the interests of State, religion and secularism as in other modern developed nations, though this has been compounded by its home-grown, decades long and deeply divisive 'culture wars'.

Balancing the interests of Church and State

The First Amendment was intended to erect "a wall of separation between Church and State. That wall must be kept high and impregnable".[11] In practice, the USSC has evolved and applied a sequence of tests in an ongoing struggle to balance the interests of Church and State in keeping with First Amendment requirements.

The tests

The USSC, in *Sherbert*,[12] formulated and narrowly construed a "compelling interest test" requiring any law licencing State intervention in religious practice to be justified. Such a law, if it imposed an actual burden on the exercise of the religion in question, would only be valid if there was a "compelling interest" justifying the particular infringement and if there was no reasonable alternative that would achieve State objectives while causing a lesser degree of infringement. This test was severely constrained by the ruling in *Smith*,[13] when the court ruled that "the right of free exercise . . . does not relieve an individual of the obligation to comply with a 'valid and neutral law of general applicability on the ground that the law proscribes (or prescribes) conduct that his religion prescribes (or proscribes)' ".[14] This established the principle that the State could impose legal restrictions upon religious freedom provided the law was neutral and applied to all persons equally.

The legislature promptly responded with the RFRA, specifically in order to redress the onerous effects of that ruling by providing protection for religion and for those of religious belief when they were disproportionately affected by any such law of universal application. As Kennedy J explained in *Lukumi*,[15] "[R]eligious beliefs need not be acceptable, logical, consistent or comprehensible to others in order to merit First Amendment protection".[16] Indeed, as Kennedy J went on to say, "[A]lthough a law targeting religious beliefs is never permissible, if the object of the law is to infringe upon or restrict practices because of their religious motivation, the law is not neutral".[17] As was declared in *Grace United*, "[A] law is neutral so long as its object is something other than the infringement or restriction of religious practices" and a "law lacks facial neutrality if it refers to a religious practice without a secular meaning discernible from the language or context".[18]

As the USSC revealed in *Gonzalez*,[19] the RFRA requires "the government to demonstrate that the compelling interest test is satisfied through application of the challenged law to the person . . . the particular claimant whose sincere exercise of religion is being substantially burdened".[20] Proof must be adduced to show that the legislation does in fact unduly burden any such practice. This was demonstrated in *U.S. v. Winddancer*,[21] where the defendant, charged with six separate counts relating to having eagle feathers in violation of federal statutes, claimed he was a Native American and that the government was infringing his religious beliefs. As in *U.S. v. Tawahongva*,[22] on much the same issue, the court dismissed the claim of entitlement to RFRA protection because of a lack of standing. Interestingly, in the more recent case of *Salazar v. Buono*,[23] the USSC upheld a proposal that a cross and the land upon which it was erected should be transferred by statute from public to private ownership. Although this was an Establishment Clause case, where the issue was whether government was supporting Christianity and not whether the plaintiff's religion was being burdened, the resolution was viewed by many as compromised because all options considered seemed to discriminate in favour of a government-assisted solution to protect Christian interests (see further below).

In *McDaniel v. Paty*,[24] the USSC found that ministers could not be disqualified from becoming delegates to a state constitutional convention and held that special disabilities imposed due to religious status are subject to a test of strict scrutiny. This test was reinforced by the recent USSC ruling in *Trinity Lutheran Church of Columbia, Inc. v. Comer*,[25] which concerned the Trinity Lutheran Church Child Learning Center, a Missouri preschool and day-care centre which had been originally established as a nonprofit organisation but later merged with Trinity Lutheran Church. It sought to avail of a grant to replace its playground's gravel surface, but the state department had a strict, express policy of denying grants to any applicant owned or controlled by a church. The USSC determined that the policy violated Trinity's rights under the Free Exercise Clause by denying the Church an otherwise available public benefit on account of its religious status, emphasising that "it has remained a fundamental principle of this Court's free exercise jurisprudence that laws imposing 'special disabilities on the basis of . . . religious status' trigger the strictest scrutiny".[26] It declared that: the Department's discriminatory policy does not survive the "most rigorous" scrutiny that this Court applies to laws imposing special disabilities on account of religious status;[27] a standard which demands a State interest "of the highest order" to justify the policy at issue.[28]

State and religion related terrorism

Since the 9/11 twin towers atrocity in 2001, the US has been heavily committed to a global war against terrorism, involving the pursuit of Islamic fundamentalists in a number of Muslim countries. This has resulted in many Muslim citizens in those countries experiencing State directed warfare, which has destroyed much of their social infrastructure, and the human rights abuses of drone strikes and dehumanising treatment in detention facilities such as Abu Ghraib. All of this at least contributes to the migrant crisis, but it has also led to domestic Islamic terrorist attacks[29] and caused US Muslim citizens to feel socially exposed and vulnerable. The USA Patriot Act 2001, the Detainee Treatment Act 2005 and other generic antiterrorism measures have been supplemented by religiously discriminating policies and laws which, in early 2017, were joined by a ban preventing the citizens of seven specified Muslim countries from entering the US. Further, the 'America first' dictum of the present administration has been reinforced by the comment of the ambassador to the UN that US involvement in the European migrant crisis would be incompatible with US sovereignty.

State neutrality

"The Establishment Clause stands at least for the proposition that when government activities touch on the religious sphere, they must be secular in purpose, even-handed in operation, and neutral in primary impact".[30] It is deemed violated by government if an action by the latter has the purpose or effect of "endorsing" religion: that is, favouring religion per se, relative to secularism, or favouring one religion over another. As Souter J declared in *Kiryas Joel*,[31] "[G]overnment should not prefer one religion to another, or religion to irreligion". Increasingly, however, the evidence points to conservative judges eroding the State neutrality doctrine as they carve out more and more exceptions.

Christian symbols/prayers in State facilities

While the Christian heritage of the US is proclaimed on its coinage – 'In God we trust' – and in the Pledge of Allegiance – 'one nation under God', it has long been the case that the swearing of an oath or any other type of religious test is prohibited as a requirement for accepting a public post. The USSC affirmed this in *Torcaso v. Watkins*,[32] when it unanimously held that Maryland's requirement for a person holding public office to declare a belief in God violated the First and Fourteenth Amendments.[33] It had earlier ruled that the same principle applies to prayers or other religious ceremonies in State schools[34] (see further below) As the USSC explained some 30 years ago: "the prohibition against governmental endorsement of religion 'preclude[s] government from conveying or attempting to convey a message that religion or a particular religious belief is favoured or preferred' ".[35]

Protecting religion from the State

As declared in *Kedroff*,[36] religious organisations have the "power to decide for themselves, free from State interference, matters of church government as well as those of faith and doctrine". However, the Free Exercise Clause "does not prohibit governments from validly regulating religious conduct".[37]

The USSC in *Reynolds*[38] set an early benchmark for assessing the circumstances constituting a breach of the Free Exercise Clause. This case concerned George Reynolds, a Mormon residing in Utah, who challenged his 1878 polygamy conviction under federal law by arguing that this marital practice was sanctioned by his religion. In rejecting his argument, the USSC distinguished between religious belief and religious conduct: while the right to religious belief was absolute, the government had a responsibility to curb religious conduct that conflicted with the broader interests of the community.[39]

Intervention in church disputes

"The Establishment Clause prohibits government from abandoning secular purposes in order to put an imprimatur on one religion, or on religion as such, or to favour the adherents of any sect or religious organization . . ."[40]

A considerable body of case law attests to the fact that State intervention is, in theory, impermissible in relation to church property disputes.[41] Indeed the court noted in *Jones v. Wolf*[42] that "the First Amendment severely circumscribes the role that civil courts may play in resolving church property disputes . . . it prohibits civil courts from resolving (such) disputes on the basis of religious doctrine and practice". In fact, however, this ruling has subsequently been interpreted as giving the courts a wide remit to interfere with property disputes if they can do so without having to decide religious questions. The UK courts, in comparison, instead of regarding such matters as church business to be resolved by the church authorities, instead treat them as straightforward property disputes and adjudicate in favour of the faction found to represent the "true standard of faith".[43] The State is similarly constrained as regards its capacity to challenge a church's right to choose its minister: the Free Exercise Clause protects a religious group's right to shape its own faith and mission through its appointments.[44]

However, whether an issue presents as a church property dispute or as a religious organisation's employment dispute, a preliminary task is to determine if the parties can be defined as coming within the religious parameters required by the exemption privilege. This must necessitate some enquiry into the religious status of the organisation and of the parties involved. To that extent at least, a court or other body has to intervene in church matters – to establish the 'religiosity' of both organisation and parties while also analysing the functional roles of those concerned – notwithstanding First Amendment constraints.

State protection of the beliefs/culture of Indigenous people

The State record in relation to its treatment of the culture and beliefs of its Indigenous people is not dissimilar to that of its Canadian and Australian counterparts, involving: abuse and containment on reservations; a policy of enforced assimilation involving the use of boarding schools; and the outlawing of their language and culture. Far from offering protection, in the late 19th century, federal and state governments legislated to prohibit Indian culture and religious belief. Not until the Freedom of Religion Act 1978 was State-enforced religious discrimination – the threat of imprisonment for practicing their religious rituals – finally removed; though arguably it continues to be manifested in court cases regarding matters such as State constraints on the ceremonial use of eagle feathers and peyote and regarding issues where State intervention on land treated as a significant religious site is routinely sanctioned.[45]

State protection of its traditional religious/cultural identity

The Establishment Clause of the First Amendment would seem intended to operate as a roadblock to prevent any overt government initiative favouring its Christian cultural heritage, or any other. Arguably, however, the above evidence of preferencing Christianity in coinage, voluntary school prayers, and on State ceremonial occasions and so on indicates that this has not been wholly successful. Nevertheless, it remains the case that, unlike the corresponding European jurisprudence, there is a notable absence of superior court rulings on the existence or otherwise of any State right to protect its cultural/religious heritage.

State preferencing of religious organisations

Religious organisations, *per se*, are exempt from many regulatory mechanisms imposed upon other entities in the commercial and nonprofit sectors. Such exemptions and concessions apply not only to churches but also to the ever-extending religiously affiliated nonprofit facilities such as universities, hospitals, child care centres and homes for the aged.

It was the pivotal case of *Wisconsin v. Yoder*[46] that established the limits of State interventionism, under the First Amendment, in matters of religion. Although the effect of this decision has since been diluted by rulings in cases such as *Employment Division v. Smith*,[47] and by the overall ironing out of disparities achieved by equality and non-discrimination legislation, nevertheless the fact that religious communities can acquire such significant carveouts from the constraints imposed upon all other religious and secular entities constitutes an important characteristic of the Church/State relationship in the US.

The religious exemption

The 'exemption doctrine' emerged in the 1960s to provide special protection for religion under the Free Exercise Clause, as this seemed a permissible way of balancing the special disabilities imposed on religious activity under the Establishment Clause. It empowered courts to excuse individuals from complying with a neutral law of general application if they could show that the law unduly burdened their sincere religious practices, unless the government could show that mandating uniform obedience to the law was required by a compelling interest that could not be protected in any less intrusive manner.[48]

By the 1980s it had seemed that the exemption was being narrowly interpreted: religious entities were not as a matter of course able to claim immunity from state laws intended to have universal application,[49] as underlined by the USSC, in *Employment Division v. Smith*.[50] Following introduction of the RFRA in 1993, the USSC developed a more affirmative approach to the exemption in rulings which emphasised that the burden of proof continued to rest firmly upon the federal government to satisfy the "compelling interest" test established in *Sherbert v. Verner*[51] (see further below) if it was to justify any law that interfered with religious organisations. The *Smith* decision, however, has not been wholly legislatively overturned: it remains the case that at the state level, religion does not attract a blanket indemnity from the requirements of neutral laws of general applicability. The onus at the state level on an entity claiming exemption is to show both evidence of religious status and of the extent to which the entity functionally gives effect to it; the RFRA does not yet impose restrictions upon the states. The decision in *Gonzalez*[52] introduced further complications by ruling that in calculating whether a compelling interest justified exemption, the government should take into account the sincere belief of those likely to be affected: their subjective perception of what constituted a religious belief was to be the benchmark, which would vary from case to case.[53] The RFRA, it has been said, "forces courts into the awkward position of assessing the sincerity of a group's religious beliefs and then carving out exceptions to federal statutes in order to accommodate these beliefs".[54] The exemption is restricted to protect only those activities of a religious organisation which are religious in nature.[55]

However, in *Burwell v. Hobby Lobby*,[56] (see further below), the USSC greatly extended the potential scope of the religious exemption by ruling that commercial entities, if "closely held" (i.e. with few shareholders whose shares are not traded on public markets), were equally eligible. It then acknowledged "worries about forcing the federal courts to apply the RFRA to a host of claims made by litigants seeking a religious exemption from generally applicable laws. . . (citing the ruling in *Smith*)", but nevertheless asserted: "Congress, in enacting RFRA, took the position that 'the compelling interest test as set forth in prior Federal court rulings is a workable test for striking sensible balances between religious liberty and competing prior governmental interests'. . . . The wisdom of Congress's judgment on this matter is not our concern".[57] As noted by Ginsburg J in her dissenting opinion, the decision "gives commercial companies an opt-out from any law, except tax laws, considered to be incompatible with their sincerely held religious beliefs".[58] It is a decision that, by extending the religious exemption to include hybrid organisations – neither religious nor charitable, but mainstream commercial entities that happen to be owned by those with religious beliefs – sets the US on a different course to that followed in other common-law jurisdictions.

Implementation regulations exempted churches from the requirement in the Affordable Care Act 2010 that companies providing health insurance for their employees must include coverage for sterilisation procedures and birth control medication. Religious entities delivering public service such as Catholic hospitals, universities, schools, agencies and so on were required to allow their employees to freely choose whether or not to avail of such coverage.

The ministerial exception

The appointment of church ministers is governed by the so-called 'ministerial exception', which is grounded in the First Amendment and was first considered by the USSC in the landmark case of *Hosanna-Tabor*,[59] following some 40 years of unanimous decisions in the courts of appeal. Such matters are most likely to be raised in the context of alleged inequality or discrimination and tend to be adjudicated under the provisions of Title VII of the Civil Rights Act of 1964 and other employment discrimination laws.

In *Rayburn*,[60] the court found that "if the employee's primary duties consist of teaching, spreading the faith, church governance, supervision of a religious order, or supervision or participation in religious ritual and worship, he or she should be considered 'clergy' ".[61] Then *Elvig v. Calvin Presbyterian Church*[62] confirmed that the appointments of ministers and clergy are exclusively matters for determination by religious organisations – thus the Catholic Church may deny ordination to women – and are completely immune from a Title VII challenge. But it was in *Hosanna-Tabor*[63] that the USSC considered whether the Lutheran Church could avail of the exception in response to an unfair dismissal claim by an employee teacher at one of its religious elementary schools who had taught the full secular curriculum but also taught daily religion classes, was a commissioned minister, and regularly led students in prayer and worship. The court found that she had functioned as a minister – in part because her employers had held her out as such with a role distinct from that of its lay teachers, and in part because she held herself to be a minister by accepting the formal call to religious service required for her position – and concluded that her acquired status outweighed the secular aspects of her job. Roberts CJ explained that the exception privilege "ensures that the authority to select and control who will be minister to the faithful – a matter 'strictly ecclesiastical', – is the church's alone" and that its purpose is not limited to hiring and firing decisions made for religious reasons. He added that "we cannot accept the remarkable view that the Religion Clauses have nothing to say about a religious organization's freedom to select its own ministers . . .". The USSC reaffirmed that the Establishment and Free Exercise Clauses bar suits brought on behalf of ministers against their churches, claiming termination in violation of employment discrimination laws. It distinguished its *ratio decidendi* from that in *Smith* as follows:[64]

> *Smith* involved government regulation of only outward physical acts. The present case, in contrast, concerns government interference with an internal church decision that affects the faith and mission of the church itself.

As has been argued, "[T]he combination of *Smith* and *Hosanna-Tabor* means that religious individuals have absolutely no protection from neutral laws of general applicability, even if the laws bar them from participating in a sacrament (the *Smith* rule), while religious institutions may be protected absolutely, even if their acts have no religious basis (the ministerial exception approved by *Hosanna-Tabor*)".[65] However, this may be an exaggeration. As Gedicks points out, "*Hosanna-Tabor* applies only to ministers . . . while churches have been aggressive trying to classify employees as 'ministers', the courts have not given them carte blanche on this".[66]

Tax privileges

Based on an interpretation of freedom of religion in the First Amendment, churches generally are presumed to be charitable and tax-exempt.[67] Many religious congregations and thousands of churches are not required by law to register with the IRS and choose not to do so. Tax exemptions are available for all churches under IRS 501(c)(3), and any parishioner donations are tax-deductible. With the extension to encompass non-theistic religions and beliefs, this tax-exemption privilege has become even more significant. The reasoning in the *Schulman* case[68] clearly indicates that even anti-theistic organisations (with *locus standi*) are eligible to be grouped under 'religion and beliefs' and qualify for s.501(c)(3) exemption status.

Testamentary privileges

Testamentary dispositions subject to a religiously discriminatory condition have long been found to be valid. In *Shapira v. Union National Bank*,[69] for example, a father left his money to Israel, his wife and their three sons subject to the latter being married to a Jewish girl or marrying a Jewish girl within seven years of his father's demise. The court found that it was dutybound to honour his intentions. Similarly, in *re the Estate of Max Feinberg*,[70] the Illinois Supreme Court upheld a condition in the will of a deceased Chicago dentist which prohibited marriage outside the Jewish faith with the effect of disinheriting his four grandchildren.

State funding of faith-based facilities and services

Under the Establishment Clause of the First Amendment, the State is constitutionally prevented from providing direct funding or facilities for religious use, as this constitutes giving prohibited support to an institution of religion.[71] This has caused the courts to strike down many arrangements for government funding of schools.[72] Since 1986 and *Witters v. Washington Department of Services for the Blind*, the courts have moved toward interpreting the Establishment Clause as permitting government funding but only in a manner that maintains a position of 'neutrality'.[73] This was politically endorsed by the Charitable Choice initiative in 1996. As O'Scannlain J stated, in *Spencer v. World Vision, Inc.*,[74] the Establishment Clause commands "neutrality among religious groups". Following the initiative a decade ago by President Bush to establish federally *funded* partnerships between government and *faith-based* groups, the position now is that the:[75]

> federal government does not discriminate against non-governmental organizations on the basis that such organizations have a religious character. Faith-based organizations are eligible to compete for grant funds on the same basis as all other non-governmental organizations.

In *Young v. Shawnee Mission Med. Ctr.*,[76] the court determined that a religious hospital did not lose its Title VII exemption simply because it received thousands of dollars in federal Medicare payments, because such payments did not "transform [the hospital] into a federally funded institution". In assessing whether or not the State is acting properly when funding faith-based bodies, facilities or services, O'Connor J in *Mitchell v. Helms*[77] employed "the Lemon test" and concluded that religious organisations should monitor and "compartmentalize" government funding received in the form of aid for education programmes (see further below). Where the aid is used for secular educational functions, then there would be no problem. If, however, the aid flowed into the entirety of an educational activity and some "religious indoctrination [is] taking place therein," then that indoctrination "would be directly attributable to the government".[78] This issue may be viewed as less relevant in the light of the *Zelman v. Simmons-Harris* decision.[79]

Contention is noticeably acute in relation to programmes whose participants lack true freedom of choice (children and prisoners in particular)[80] and because they can in practice allow government funds to flow along channels that discriminate between recipients and non-recipients on religious grounds.[81]

Religion and the freedoms of association and expression

Rights awareness and religiosity are particularly strong phenomena in the US. This is where Christian fundamentalism and the threat of Islamic terrorism have grown to have a powerful influence on domestic social policy. Unlike in other countries, it is also where a significant volume of cases addressing issues on the human rights/religion intersect are determined by the nation's highest court.

Freedom of religion

This principle is enshrined in the Constitution but is also present in a number of supranational conventions to which the US is a signatory, including the UDHR (Article 18), ICCPR (Article 18), UNCROC (Article 14) and the American Convention on Human Rights (Article 12).

Definitions

A half-century has elapsed since the USSC determined in *Torcaso v. Watkins*[82] that an exclusively theistic definition of 'religion' was no longer sustainable and in *United States v. Seeger*[83] that any interpretation must exclude a "merely personal moral code" which is "in no way related to a Supreme Being". It subsequently added, in *Wisconsin v. Yoder*,[84] that for constitutional purposes a "religious" belief or practice is to be considered as "not merely a matter of personal preference, but one of deep religious conviction, shared by an organized group, and intimately related to daily living".[85] As elsewhere in the developed world, the definition of 'religion' has since extended well beyond the traditional institutional religions to include many different forms of 'belief'. It has, for example, been recently decided at federal level – in *Chenzira v. Cincinnati Children's Hospital Medical Center*[86] – that veganism could meet the definition because "religious practices . . . include moral or ethical beliefs as to what is right and wrong which are sincerely held with the strength of religious views".[87] It was enough that the plaintiff sincerely, and with conviction, believed as she did and did so with a commitment typical of a traditional religious adherent, a rationale that imported a subjective interpretation of belief as a crucial – if insufficient – determinant of what constitutes a 'religious belief'.

The USSC has retreated from the position it maintained in *United States v. Ballard*,[88] when it held that the question of whether the defendants' claims about their religious experiences were actually true should not have been submitted to a jury because the "freedom of religious belief . . . embraces the right to maintain theories of life and of death and of the hereafter which are rank heresy to followers of the orthodox faiths". As demonstrated in *Brown v. Pena*, it is now quite open to the courts to test the sincerity of a claimed belief, if not its veracity, and, as in that case, to rule that mere personal preferences do not constitute a religious belief. Even where they are found to be legitimate, this will be of little assistance to a defendant who seeks to shield his illegal actions by protests that he believed these to be a permissible means of giving effect to his religious beliefs, as in *S.D. v. M.J.R.*,[89] where a Muslim husband was held to have sexually assaulted his wife despite a plea that his beliefs negated the wilful intent necessary for him to have committed a crime (see further Chapter 1).

Indigenous beliefs

The traditional beliefs, customs and ritual ceremonies of the Indigenous people, or Native Americans, in the US varied from tribe to tribe, between bands and in the extent to which they succeeded in avoiding government prohibition and being undermined by Christianity. Their surviving belief systems centre on the worship of spirits associated with nature, the landscape and the seasons, and involve ceremonial dances, rituals and often animals. Customarily, religious beliefs are expressed and modes of group worship are led by a shaman or medicine man.

Manifestation of religion or belief

The religious clauses of the First Amendment confer both a freedom to believe and a freedom to manifest that belief, the former being absolute but not the latter.[90] The distinction has been the subject of many USSC rulings, including: *Reynolds*,[91] when it refused to grant an appeal against a conviction for polygamy; *Heffron*,[92] holding that state ordinances preventing Jehovah's Witnesses from door-to-door proselytising were "offensive, not only to the values protected by the First Amendment, but to the very notion of a free society"; *Gonzales*,[93] where a prohibition on the importation of a sacramental tea was judged to have failed the compelling burden test and was therefore invalid; and in *Salazar*,[94] when it refused to order the removal of a 7-foot-tall cross on government-owned property. The right to manifest, in conjunction with or in opposition to the right to freedom of expression, has also been explored in a litany of cases at the federal and state levels as referenced below in relation to matters such as the wearing of religion-specific clothing and more generally in equality disputes.

Religious discrimination

Religious discrimination occurs when someone is denied "the equal protection of the laws, equality of status under the law, equal treatment in the administration of justice, and equality of opportunity and access to employment, education, housing, public services and facilities, and public accommodation because of their exercise of their right to religious freedom".[95] It is prohibited on a federal basis under the First and Fourteenth Amendments and Title VII.

Freedom of association

As the USSC declared in *Roberts*:[96] "[I]mplicit in the right to engage in activities protected by the First Amendment" is "a corresponding right to associate with others in pursuit of a wide variety of political, social, economic, educational, religious, and cultural ends"; but this did not permit exclusion on the basis of criteria unrelated to an association's purpose, for example on the basis of gender. However, as subsequently clarified in *Hurley*,[97] this rule did permit the exclusion of those whose membership would seriously compromise an association's purpose (see further below).

The 'positive action' provisions

While there are no specific federal statutes targeting supplementary funding toward disadvantaged groups, many states have legislated for 'affirmative action' provision. In *Zelman v. Simmons-Harris*,[98] the USSC examined a school voucher scheme whereby public money was made available to pay for tuition at private schools, including religious schools. It found that the programme did not violate the Establishment Clause of the First Amendment because all schools were to be treated equally. The point of allowing parents to use public money to send their children to private schools was to enable parents in poor areas with failing public schools to get a better education for their children. The fact that in practice most used their vouchers to transfer to religious schools was incidental: they were entitled to make that choice. It did not mean that government was funnelling public dollars to religious institutions.

In 1990, Laycock[99] referred to what was then "the great national debate about affirmative action", citing the many academic contributors to that debate, but now, nearly 30 years later, equality case law has narrowed State affirmative initiatives to the point where they are so restricted in scope that they do little more than ease the admission of the socially disadvantaged into higher education. In *Fisher v. University of Texas*,[100] for example, the USSC upheld the university's admissions policy, which conferred a preferential weighting on the basis of race but warned that it must be subject to strict scrutiny.

Freedom of expression

Freedom of expression, constitutionally framed in the First Amendment[101] by clauses guaranteeing the free exercise of religion and of free speech, has long been viewed as the hallmark of democracy. In the US it is probably the single most staunchly defended of all human rights and enjoys much greater salience than anywhere else partly because it has acquired exemption from ICCP restrictions on free speech, including the prohibition on defamatory expressions directed at religious groups. However, not all views expressed qualify for First Amendment protection: they must touch upon a matter of public concern.[102]

Constraints upon the expression and dissemination of religious views[103] have been the subject of continuous judicial probing in the US,[104] particularly in respect of religious speech by Jehovah's Witnesses.[105] The USSC has ruled that laws which compel public disclosure of information that could attract threats or harassment, would breach the free speech clause of the First Amendment.[106] Some of the complexities involved in construing what amounts to 'expressing' in relation to religious belief, for the purposes of qualifying for First Amendment protection, became apparent in the recent *Masterpiece* case,[107] when a baker claimed that protection to justify his refusal, as a Christian and culinary 'artist', to bake a cake for a gay couple (see further below).

Religiously motivated conduct

Following the introduction of the RFRA, the USSC developed an affirmative approach toward defending religion-specific customs which manifest sincerely held beliefs.[108] In the above-mentioned 'eagle cases' where Native Americans have claimed an entitlement, on grounds of religious belief, to hunt, keep or take the feathers of eagles in contravention of neutral laws of general application – the test requires proof either that the legislation does not unduly burden any such practice or that, nonetheless, the government's interest is sufficiently compelling to justify the restriction imposed. So, in *U.S. v. Friday*,[109] where the defendant was charged with taking one bald eagle without asking permission from the Secretary of the Interior, he claimed that as a Native American he was exempt from the charges and even if the Bureau of Native Americans did not recognise him as such, the charges should still be dismissed, as his actions were protected by the RFRA. The court, having analysed the RFRA claim and citing *Gonzales*, ruled in favour of the defendant, specifically noting the following:[110]

> The Government may be able to meet [the compelling interest burden], as the Tenth Circuit considered the protection of bald eagles to be [a compelling interest]. Nonetheless, the RFRA test is not satisfied by generalized assertions.

The same principle grounded the ruling of Ambro J in the *Eruv Association* case,[111] where he found that as the borough had not enacted a genuinely general or neutral ordinance – it permitted a wide variety of attachments to utility poles for non-religious purposes, including posting signs and other items – it could not therefore selectively exclude attachments for religious purposes. In *Watchtower Bible and Tract Society of New York v. Village of Stratton*,[112] the court considered town ordinances which made it a misdemeanour to engage in door-to-door advocacy without first registering with town officials and receiving a permit. Jehovah's Witnesses argued that these ordinances violated their First Amendment right to canvass door-to-door as part of their religious belief that they should share the Gospel with others. The USSC agreed and stated that the ordinances were "offensive, not only to the values protected by the First Amendment, but to the very notion of a free society".[113] Again, in *Gonzales*,[114] the USSC ruled that the government – in prohibiting the importation of a sacramental tea, required for manifesting the beliefs of a Brazilian church – had failed to meet the burden imposed by the 1993 Act of demonstrating that its intervention served a compelling government interest; therefore the prohibition was invalid. In *Cutter v. Wilkinson*,[115] a case involving five Ohio prison inmates with quite different belief affiliations (2 Norse pagans, a Wiccan witch, a Satanist and an evangelical Christian), the plaintiffs collectively and successfully claimed that their access to ceremonial items and opportunities for group worship was not unconstitutional under the Religious Land Use and Institutionalised Persons Act 2000. More recently, the USSC refused to order the removal of a 7-foot-tall cross, which had stood as a war memorial for 70 years on a dominant rock on federal land in the Mojave desert,[116] as requested by a plaintiff who claimed to be "deeply offended by the display of a Latin Cross on government-owned property". Although the court ultimately ruled in favour of a government statute that ensured the retention of the commemorative cross by transferring ownership of it and the land on which it stood to a private party, the powerful dissenting judgment of Stevens J, joined by Ginsburg and Sotomayor JJ, indicates just how uncertain and divided the court was:

> it is undisputed that the "[L]atin cross is the preeminent symbol of Christianity. It is exclusively a Christian symbol, and not a symbol of any other religion." We have recognized the significance of the Latin cross as a sectarian symbol, and no participant in this litigation denies that the cross bears that social meaning. Making a plain, unadorned Latin cross a war memorial does not make the cross secular. It makes the war memorial sectarian.

Religious apparel

The weight of case law confirms that wearing religious apparel is not in itself sufficient to breach the Establishment Clause.[117]

Many cases concern pupils in state schools wearing religion-specific clothing while being taught, which in part is attributable to the bearing of established case law precedents upholding children's right to freedom of expression.[118] *Hearn and United States v. Muskogee Public School District*[119] concerned a Muslim girl who was suspended twice from school for wearing a hijab as required by her faith, but the court ruled that she was entitled to do so. The school authorities, by singling her out because of her Islamic faith, had intentionally discriminated against her, and the court quoted from the ruling in *Lukumi* that "at a minimum, the protections of the Free Exercise Clause pertain if the law at issue discriminates against some or all religious beliefs".[120]

The same principle is transferable to other settings,[121] as illustrated by the sequence of cases concerning the policy of clothing retailer Abercrombie & Fitch to ban the wearing of the hijab by its Muslim staff and job applicants. In the absence of any evidence that permitting Muslim employees to wear their hijabs placed an undue hardship on the employers, the latter were found to be guilty of religious discrimination.[122] The USSC made an important point: "Title VII gives favoured treatment to religious practices, rather than demanding that religious practices be treated no worse than other practices".[123]

Blasphemy and proselytism

Nationally, blasphemy laws in the US have been deemed unconstitutional, but they remain on the statute books in some states. In *Joseph Burstyn, Inc. v. Wilson*,[124] the USSC held that:

> the State has no legitimate interest in protecting any or all religions from views distasteful to them. . . . It is not the business of government in our nation to suppress real or imagined attacks upon a particular religious doctrine.

No one has been jailed in the US for blasphemy since 1838.

Proselytism finds stronger recognition in the US than elsewhere due to the protection offered by the First Amendment, although this will be breached if federal funds are used for that purpose.[125] Otherwise, any impairment of the right to distribute pamphlets, religious or otherwise, and even anonymously, is contrary to the First Amendment's Free Speech Clause, as was recognised in *McIntyre v. Ohio Elections Comm'n*.[126] Where, however, as in *Heffron v. International Society for Krishna Consciousness*,[127] such distribution would interfere with the State's legitimate interest in ensuring public health and safety, a state ordinance preventing this so as to allow for control of crowds at a fair will be upheld. When the proselytism becomes harassment, as in *Ng v. Jacobs Engineering Group*,[128] then the normal civil liberties of others will be upheld. In that case, an evangelical Christian, whose religious beliefs compelled her to share those beliefs with her co-workers in order to 'save' them, persisted in using company equipment and facilities for religious proselytising. When eventually fired, she filed a claim for religious discrimination based on her employer's failure to accommodate her religious beliefs and practices. The court found in favour of the employer: it considered that the company could potentially be liable for religious harassment claims by the plaintiff's co-workers if she were allowed to continue her proselytising and held that Ms Ng's proselytising violated the company's policies on anti-harassment and e-mail use (see further below at "Proselytism in the workplace").

Conscientious objection

The USSC, in *Seeger v. United States*[129] and *Welsh v. United States*,[130] established the right to refuse to join the armed forces on grounds that went beyond religious belief to include moral conviction. The judiciary then broadened the definition of 'conscientious objector' to include any person with "no particular sectarian affiliation or theological position . . . who has deeply held beliefs that cause them to oppose participation in war in any form". These rulings significantly extended the ambit of the right: in *Seeger* to a purely ethical creed "which occupies in the life of its possessor a place parallel to that filled by the God of those admittedly qualifying for the exemption"; and in *Welsh* to persons with deeply held moral or ethical beliefs who would have "no rest or peace if they allowed themselves to become a part of an instrument of war".

More recently, the USSC confirmation of the constitutionality of the Obama administration's Patient Protection and Affordable Care Act (ACA) brought with it considerable controversy as to public health measures which restrict personal choice: in particular, there were arguments that requirements of the Act violated the right to freedom of conscience by mandating access to contraception as a form of public service provision which breached the beliefs of many religious organisations and individuals. Some states responded by introducing so-called 'religious liberty' laws that provide opt-outs for service delivery staff, permitting them to decline involvement in services on the grounds of personal conscience.[131] This trend was consolidated by the Trump administration when it repealed crucial aspects of the ACA contraceptive provisions and established the Conscience and Religious Freedom Division, as part of the Office of Civil Rights, within the purview of the Department of Health and Human Services.

The remit of this new Division, tasked with enforcing federal laws protecting civil rights and conscience in health and human services, has been reinforced by the aforementioned "liberty laws". The most recent of these was the Religious Liberty Accommodations Act in Mississippi in respect of which the USSC declined to hear a challenge due to the plaintiffs lack of standing.[132] The Mississippi legislation is not untypical in that it permits state employees to refuse to participate in service provision to LGBT persons if doing so would contravene their religious beliefs (see further below). It specifies three beliefs that qualify the holder for exemption: that marriage happens only between a man and a woman; that sex should only take place in that kind of marriage; and that a person's gender is decided at birth and cannot be changed. The ramifications of this USSC decision not to grant a hearing are currently difficult to predict, but the law remains on the statute books, even if not yet implemented.

Human rights, equality and religion: the case law

The Equal Protection Clause of the Fourteenth Amendment places a legal obligation on the State, and therefore on all government entities, to ensure that similarly situated individuals are treated equally.[133] This constitutional liberty right has, arguably, been given such added weight by the *Smith* decision that many now view it as more of an equality right.

Right of access to justice

Equality of access to justice is fundamental to the rule of law. The provision of legal aid and representation, 'positive action' measures for facilitating access, are available throughout the US. A speedy and public trial and an impartial jury is a constitutional right protected by the Sixth Amendment. However, Guantánamo,[134] the Detainee Treatment Act 2005 and the 2017 immigration constraints – all impacting almost exclusively on Muslims – stand as reminders that access to justice is compromised in the US as far as religion is concerned. Given that foreign policy since 9/11 has been dominated by security concerns centred on Muslim countries, it is unsurprising that many Muslims within the US perceive domestic counterterrorist measures as being applied in a religiously discriminating fashion, largely directed toward them.

Religious law and courts

Religion-specific legal forums – tribunals and mediatory bodies – are well established in the US and have a long history of arbitrating family disputes. The Pew Research Center estimates that the Catholic Church has nearly 200 diocesan tribunals that handle a variety of cases, including an estimated 15,000–20,000 marriage annulments each year, while many Orthodox Jews use rabbinical courts to obtain religious divorce.

Shari'a law

Shari'a law and its associated courts have attracted State intervention. Between 2010 and Spring 2018 a total of 43 states introduced 201 anti-Shari'a legislative bills, and in 14 they have been enacted. Ostensibly, the legislative intent of such measures is to prohibit any foreign law which conflicts with rights guaranteed by the Constitution of the US or that of the state. In practice, it is Shari'a law which is being targeted, and this may leave states open to the challenge that they are engaging in religious discrimination which risks inflaming Islamophobia; interestingly, the Oklahoma statute has been struck down in federal court on constitutional grounds.

Right to life

In a country where State-sanctioned capital punishment has majority approval, a 'gun culture' is deeply embedded, and where the annual murder rate is greater than in any other developed nation,[135] a 'right to life' is arguably compromised. In relation to family related matters, however, the religion/human rights intersect as mediated through state equality legislation, has generated issues typical of those experienced elsewhere, though the 'culture wars' phenomenon driven by a strong evangelical Christian element has made them much more confrontational.

Abortion, contraception

Since at least the *Roe v. Wade*[136] decision in 1973, abortion has been the most long-running, socially divisive, family-related issue to test the Church/State relationship. It is an issue which may have been defused somewhat, or perhaps just further complicated, by improvements in contraception. The ACA brought into sharp focus the issue of access to contraception and triggered a flow of cases featuring religious employers protesting that to provide employees with a health plan that included contraceptives would be to impermissibly burden their religious beliefs.[137] Decades of pro-life/pro-choice confrontations, and the profound divisions in religious and secular principles represented by the strongly associated culture war issues, have resulted in voluminous case law[138] tracking a pattern of alternating victories and defeats notched up by pro-life and pro-choice protagonists. The introduction of the Religious Liberty Accommodations Act, followed most recently by contention over the *Bryant* case,[139] has done much to further the fracturing of US society.

Refusing medical treatment

The right of an adult to make an informed decision to refuse medical treatment is well established, was reaffirmed by the USSC ruling in *Mills v. Rodgers*[140] and has since been reiterated many times by that court. The exercise of this right, a fundamental aspect of personal liberty, is based upon respect for an autonomous adult to choose to live or die in accordance with their beliefs, subject only to a countervailing compelling interest of the State.[141]

Medically assisted death

In 2016, Colorado became only the sixth state to allow terminally ill patients to legally end their lives with medical assistance. The case law leading to this point had been protracted and cautious, with the USSC ruling: in 1990, in *Curzon*,[142] that while there is no constitutional right to suicide, there is a fundamental right to refuse medical treatment; in 1997, in *Glucksberg*,[143] that the Due Process Clause gives a terminally ill individual the right to commit suicide but not a right to medical assistance in doing so; and in 2006, in *Gonzales*,[144] that Oregon's

Death With Dignity Act, or "right to die" law, was constitutional and that physician-assisted suicide had a "legitimate medical purpose" – which paved the way for five other states to enact similar provisions. While these legislative steps are undoubtedly important – constituting significant milestones for both the neutrality doctrine and the culture wars – arguably they are outweighed by the fact that so far the vast majority of states have chosen not to follow suit.

Right to marriage and to found a family

Marriage, the social institution that traditionally brought sexuality and religious belief into legal alignment was, for religious adherents, naturally profoundly challenged by its extension to accommodate same-sex relationships. This challenge to social mores that had traditionally rested on a binary pattern of gender and sexuality naturally extended into changing parenting arrangements and transgender issues.

Marriage and family relationships

The basic definition of 'marriage' was first tested by the polygamous practices of the Mormons, and then by the prescribed roles and duties of the parties as laid down in religious law for Muslims (*shari'a*) and Jews (*ketubah*). The ongoing difficulties in aligning religiously defined divorce proceedings – particularly the Islamic *mahr* agreements[145] and the Jewish '*get*' – with statutory requirements can trigger allegations of religious discrimination from both those who believe their cultural traditions are being disrespected by being subordinated to statutory law and by those disadvantaged as a consequence of their enforced adherence to those traditions.

Same-sex marriage

The extension of the legally defined marital relationship to accommodate same-sex couples in *Obergefell v. Hodges*[146] presented the institutional religions with what has probably been their single most profound challenge in centuries, but while upholding the right to gay marriage, Kennedy J on behalf of the USSC then warned that the ruling should not be construed as undermining the First Amendment rights of those religions and their adherents:

> [I]t must be emphasized that religions, and those who adhere to religious doctrines, may continue to advocate with utmost, sincere conviction that, by divine precepts, same-sex marriage should not be condoned.

This was an equality ruling: both camps were entitled to equal judicial respect. The recent *Bryant*[147] decision is seen by some as a conservative pushback against the *Obergefell* ruling, but in reality it has simply left matters as they were. By standing aside, the USSC has left the partisan approach adopted by the Mississippi legislature unchallenged. *Obergefell* had set a national bar which this legislature chose to curb throughout its jurisdiction (though with effects which would be difficult to confine to religious/cultural groups) in order to affirm the equal rights of those with religious beliefs. However, if implemented, the consequences of this statute will be far-reaching: permitting an opt-out for all state employees whose beliefs align with one or more of the three specified in the statute will licence very many to withhold service provision, thereby discriminating against and disadvantaging some citizens relative to others. Inevitably, it will also set a precedent for the private and nonprofit sectors.

Sexuality and gender

In the US there are no federal laws that specifically afford protection to transgender people. Some limited federal initiatives have been taken: in 2009, the Hate Crimes Prevention Act added gender identity to the definition of a hate crime; in 2014, a Presidential executive order was issued prohibiting discrimination against transgender people employed by the federal government and its contractors; and in 2016, the Departments of Education and Justice issued informal guidance, since withdrawn by the Trump administration, that publicly funded schools should make the necessary arrangements for students to use bathrooms appropriate to their gender or transgender identities. Currently there is considerable variance in the extent to which states give legal recognition to gender identity where transgender people are concerned. This will often depend upon whether or not an individual has completed sex reassignment surgery.

Assisted reproduction, adoption, surrogacy and genetic engineering

Unlike the situation in other developed nations, IVF in the US is lightly regulated, very expensive and lacks a central agency with responsibility for providing a national overview and service coordination. Essentially, artificial reproduction technology has been treated as a matter best left to medicine and commerce rather than to the State.

Right to employment

Title VII[148] expressly forbids employers with 15 or more employees to discriminate on the grounds of race, colour, sex, religion, or national origin.[149] Employers may not make any employment decisions based on religious grounds, including hiring, firing, promoting, demoting and determining assignments and workloads. Title VII, as noted by Burger CJ in *Griggs v. Duke Power*,[150] "proscribes not only overt discrimination but also practices that are fair in form but discriminatory in operation".[151] Arguably, the veracity of this comment has been considerably undermined by the case law of recent years with the consequence that religion now has a much greater impact upon employment, and upon the interplay of human rights in the workplace, than previously and more so in this than in other common-law jurisdictions.

Hiring/firing staff and religious beliefs

The Free Exercise Clause of the First Amendment permits religious organisations to discriminate when hiring and firing, on the basis of religion, in addition to both the above 'ministerial exception' and the bona fide occupational requirement (BFOQ). This is also permitted by the Establishment Clause, as was confirmed in *Corp. of Presiding Bishop of Church of Jesus Christ of Latter-day Saints v. Amos*,[152] when the USSC upheld the constitutionality of a law permitting religious organisations to exercise a religious preference when making employment decisions. Schools established by religious organisations must comply with Title VII and the Equal Pay Act, though in practice disputes tend to revolve around their doctrines, and it is often issues that combine sex, gender and an organisation's ethos that lead to disputed firings. Where a teacher's duties are primarily secular, an employing religious organisation will be bound by Title VII and cannot rely on the 'ministerial exception' when firing staff for conduct inconsistent with its religious beliefs.[153] However, the effect of *Hosanna-Tabor*[154] has been to extend the protection of the 'ministerial exception' parameters available to religious organisations when they employ teachers to staff their schools. In short, the statutory exception is not confined to any particular kind of job but protects only religious discrimination, while the ministerial exception protects any kind of discrimination, but only for persons in positions of religious leadership.

In *Dodge v. Salvation Army*,[155] the court ruled that a Salvation Army Domestic Violence Shelter was wrong to terminate the employment of a counsellor because of her religious beliefs. As the employing religious corporation was in receipt of substantial government funding, it was not entitled to rely on the exemption normally available to such bodies from laws prohibiting religious discrimination. This ruling must now be viewed in the light of the "liberty laws" and bearing in mind the remit of the newly established Conscience and Religious Freedom Division of the Department of HHS.

Accommodating religious beliefs/practices in the workplace

Title VII, s.703(a)(1), in conjunction with the 1967 Equal Employment Opportunity Commission (EEOC) guidelines, requires an employer, short of "undue hardship," to make "reasonable accommodations" regarding the religious needs of employees. An employee's belief or practice can be "religious" even if the employee is affiliated with a religious group that does not espouse or recognise that belief or practice, or if few – or no – other people adhere to it. For example, in *Peterson v. Wilmur Communications, Inc.*,[156] the plaintiff's white supremacist belief system called "Creativity" was deemed to be a religion within the meaning of Title VII because it "functions as religion in [his] life". Again, in *Adeyeye v. Heartland Sweeteners, LLC*,[157] a federal court held that a Nigerian employee was wrongfully dismissed for having attended his father's funeral in Nigeria, which was conducted in accordance with tribal custom and practice – involving burial rituals and animal sacrifice – which he believed was an appropriate manifestation of his religion, a mixture of Christianity and tribal custom. The Court of Appeals attached great importance to the subjective nature of the plaintiff's beliefs: whether "the belief for which protection is sought [is] religious in [the] person's own scheme of things" and whether it is "sincerely held".

Title VII's protection also extends to those who are discriminated against or need accommodation because they profess no religious beliefs. An exception to this rule exists if an individual's religion is a BFOQ as when it is an essential part of their job description. The law applies to federal, state and local employers.

Right to education

Educational facilities are value-sensitive settings that cannot allow religion, a specific religion, or secularism to be preferenced – which can be particularly contentious in state schools where education is compulsory and information dissemination may be biased or used selectively for proselytising purposes.

Government funding and religious education: general overview

It is well established that government-funded public schools are required to have secular purposes and to avoid an excessive entanglement with religion.[158] They are prohibited from endorsing religion in general or any particular religion or belief.[159] No pupil should be compelled to participate in religious lessons or activities.[160]

Educational facilities: religion, staffing and pupil access

Title IV of the Civil Rights Act 1964 prohibits discrimination based on religion in public primary and secondary schools as well as in public colleges and universities. The Equal Access Act 1984 requires all schools receiving federal funds to ensure that any of its clubs – including religious clubs, associations or their members – have equal access to school facilities. The USSC has rejected allegations that this legislation violates the Establishment Clause.

In *Bob Jones University v. United States*,[161] the USSC found that a religious university with a racially discriminatory admissions policy, and other policies relating to religious beliefs against interracial dating and marriage, was not protected by the religion clauses of the First Amendment. Where a state university adopts a blanket policy that singles out, and thereby discriminates against, religious speech, then, as in *Widmar v. Vincent*,[162] it may find itself accused of religious discrimination. By way of contrast, in *Christian Legal Society v. Martinez*,[163] the USSC upheld the right of a College of Law to prohibit the

Christian Legal Society, a student organisation in the College, from restricting membership to those who agreed to comply with an explicit set of religious and lifestyle principles.

State schools, religion and educational content

The fundamental right of parents, based on freedom of religion, to direct the education of their children, was acknowledged in *Pierce v. Society of Sisters.*[164] It outweighs the public service duty of the State to ensure provision for the education of children and has been established since at least *Wisconsin v. Yoder*,[165] when the USSC ruled that Amish parents could not be compelled to send their children to high school.

Educational content may include a religious dimension on condition that it does not constitute persuasive views or amount to proselytism.[166] For example, the Bible may be taught for secular[167] but not for devotional purposes.[168]

The linking of religion to a state school, or to a teacher employed in such a school, is viewed as a governmental compromise to the neutral status of the State in education and its role in relation to religion. This was demonstrated in the decades of *School Prayer* cases which established that any memorial service, sponsored or organised by a school and involving mandatory participation in prayer, would compromise the neutrality of the public education system,[169] though group prayer is permitted in school if not school-sponsored.[170] It has also been evident in the judicial response to cases involving teachers wearing religious apparel in schools, though this has been less about apparel representing religion and more about employment discrimination decisions protecting teachers.[171] This is offset to a degree by the effect of the First Amendment right to free speech, which permits teachers and pupils some latitude to express their personal religious beliefs or opposition to such beliefs[172] and prevents any blanket rule prohibiting religious activity.

Faith schools

The USSC has often upheld the principle that parents have the fundamental right to direct the education and upbringing of their children,[173] most notably when it ruled that Amish parents were wrongly penalised for refusing to send their children to high school when they had "deep religious convictions" for not doing so.[174] Currently, tens of thousands of children attend Christian or Muslim private schools in the US, where knowledge is liable to be filtered through religious belief.

Right to non-discrimination in service provision

Private service provision is subject to the Equal Protection Clause of the Fourteenth Amendment and to state-based equality and non-discrimination legislation.

Both can generate allegations of religiously biased services affecting service users and causing human rights violations.

Provision by religious organisations

In all states where same-sex marriage has been legalised, the relevant legislation imposes no requirement upon religious organisations and their ministers to provide marriage services (i.e. a celebrant, use of church premises and so on) for such couples.[175] Most such states include exemption clauses for religious organisations and their ministers and exemptions from tax liability.

Spencer v. World Vision Inc[176] concerned a Christian humanitarian organisation that provided overseas aid to children, families and communities in need and was heavily funded by government. It terminated the employment of three staff because they had ceased attending daily devotions and weekly chapel services held during the workday and because they had denied the deity of Jesus Christ. The staff concerned sued World Vision for unfair dismissal, and the latter responded by claiming that it was a religious entity and therefore exempt from Title VII. Ultimately, the court ruled that even though World Vision was not a traditional house of worship, it was entitled to the institutional religious liberty accommodation. As a "religious corporation" it qualified for exemption from equality and non-discrimination constraints. This important decision was reinforced three years later by the USSC ruling in *Burwell v. Hobby Lobby*,[177] which extended the exemption to wholly commercial entities when it upheld the right of the evangelical Christian owners of Hobby Lobby not to provide health insurance coverage, which included contraception, to their female employees. It has now been further broadened and complicated by the legislative initiative in Mississippi and the associated *Bryant*[178] decision. These rulings greatly increase the potential protection available to companies engaged in religiously influenced service provision.

Provision of public services

Public services such as adoption and foster care traditionally provided by religious organisations have been negatively impacted by equality law. In 2006, Catholic Charities in Boston failed to gain exemption from the state's anti-discrimination statute and terminated its adoption work rather than continue to place children under the "guardianship of homosexuals". Similarly, in Washington, DC, in 2010, Catholic Charities took the same step when faced with a statutory requirement that government-funded religious entities providing public services do so by including same-sex couples. In 2012, the Illinois Department of Children and Family Services revoked its contract with Catholic Charities after its refusal to provide adoption and foster-care services to same-sex couples. This decision caused the transfer of more than 1,000 children to secular agencies. When religious organisations are contracted to provide services on behalf of government – acting as agents of the State – they have been wholly bound by State legislation but "liberty laws" are now challenging this proscriptive approach.

Private goods and service provision

As Justice Kennedy recently explained:[179]

> It is a general rule that [religious and philosophical] objections do not allow business owners . . . to deny protected persons equal access to goods and services under a neutral and generally applicable public accommodations law.

Private service providers (owners of hotels, boarding houses and so on), claiming exemption from equality and religious discrimination provisions on the protected grounds of personal religious belief, generate a great deal of controversy throughout the US. Cases include the refusal to bake a cake ordered to celebrate gay marriages[180] that led to the USSC decision in *Masterpiece*.[181] Unfortunately, the USSC was then unable to make any finding as to whether or not the baker's refusal to provide services was protected by the First Amendment, as it was deflected by process irregularities and had to confine itself to ruling that the Colorado Civil Rights Commission did not act "with the religious neutrality that the Constitution requires"[182] when it considered the bakery's arguments. The attempt to lever a service provider into First Amendment protection, on the grounds that he was a Christian and the service was an expression of his creativity as such and therefore he should be exempted from the obligation under civil liberty and equality laws to make his service available on a non-discriminatory basis, has failed, at least for now. Had this claim succeeded, the court would have thereby licenced similar discretionary religious/sexual discrimination from a limitless range of 'expressive' service providers including architects, hairdressers, tailors, designers and so on.[183] Arguably, the principle that a religious employer may restrict product availability on the grounds that to do so would violate sincerely held religious beliefs has already been conceded in *Burwell v. Hobby Lobby*.[184] So this matter is sure to return to the USSC.

It is difficult to gauge the overall significance of equality exemptions in a US retail context. Gedicks points out that "the definition of 'public accommodation' in Title II is quite narrow, restricted to hotels/motels, restaurants, and theatres and other 'places of public amusement' ".[185] While this is true, it must be added that state public accommodations laws are quite broad; most cover pretty much all forms of retail.

Service denial on grounds of conscientious objection

The number of doctors, nurses and other health care workers who decline to take part in health care service provision – because to do so would violate their religion, beliefs or morals – has increased in recent years. The newly established Division of Conscience and Religious Freedom, located within the Department of Health & Human Services and under the purview of the Office for Civil Rights, is intended to protect such professionals. Building upon recent USSC decisions[186] and state 'religious liberty law' initiatives, it marks an important point of departure from the law which generally does not permit public service providers to choose those aspects of legally mandated provision with which they will comply. There is an argument that such freedom of choice is prohibited under the Fourteenth Amendment.

While clearly aimed at offering protection to staff engaged in abortion and contraception services, the potential remit of this Division is uncertain. It seems likely that it extends to matters addressed in the Mississippi legislation – such as protection for those refusing to deal with LGBT and transgender issues – and may accommodate issues such as assisted suicide or capital punishment, and could possibly reach beyond direct service providers to those in ancillary positions such as radiographers or even receptionists. Differentiating between a justifiable right to protect beliefs and any unjustifiable resulting conduct that discriminates against others has become a dangerous fault line that runs throughout the 'culture wars'. This is rapidly becoming more complex. Establishing a rationale for limiting the potential scope of an opt-out for those who protest that service provision obligations compromise their consciences could prove difficult.

Broadcasting services

In multimedia broadcasting, the First Amendment is of central importance. However, the declaration that "Congress shall make no law . . . abridging the freedom of speech" is not absolute. *Thomas v. Chicago Park District*[187] although not concerned with religious matters, provides authority for the view that government can generally impose time, place and manner constraints on its exercise. The USSC then reasoned that the licencing scheme permitting use of a public park for events was not based on subject-matter censorship. Compliance with the First Amendment free speech guarantee only requires that any restrictions be content-neutral and reasonable rather than narrowly tailored to serve a significant government interest. Unless exercised in a manner that actually or potentially incites hatred or violence, is defamatory or is otherwise in breach of the law, the freedom to express religious views, or views about religion – however insulting – is constitutionally protected.

Conclusion

The paradox of the US relationship with human rights, alluded to by Ignatieff,[188] is perhaps particularly evident as regards the intersect between the State and human rights/religion. On the one hand there is no greater champion of the right to freedom of religion: the US conducts an annual international audit of how countries are managing religion-related responsibilities; it funds international religious NGOs; and on a domestic basis it has established government bodies, legislation and programmes to provide support for religion and religious entities in general. On the other hand, and for the past 15 years or more, the US focus on Islamic terrorism as a threat to national security has led it to flagrantly violate human rights through protracted warfare, including drone strikes, unlawful detention, torture and so on, directed almost exclusively at

Muslims, and by introducing border restrictions that deny entry to citizens of certain Muslim countries.

In addition, a very considerable volume of case law has been generated in relation to the protection of religious entities and the manifestation of their beliefs. More so than elsewhere, the case law engages equality issues and tends to confirm the Geddicks assertion that "freedom of religion in the United States is less a liberty right than an equality right".[189] The current mining of 'conscientious objection' jurisprudence by legislators, judiciary and regulators promises to broaden the range of equality disputes, further complicate the religion/human rights intersect and add fuel to the nation's culture wars. This is likely to be compounded yet further by political appointees to the USSC which will in all probability harden the tendency toward conservatism in relation to religion and toward proxy religious issues such as abortion.

Notes

1 Ignatieff, M., *American Exceptionalism and Human Rights*, Princeton University Press, Princeton, 2005, at p. 1.
2 The first 10 amendments to the Constitution make up the Bill of Rights.
3 *The Employment Division (Department of Human Resources of Oregon) v. Smith*, op. cit., per Scalia, J.
4 546 US 418 (2006).
5 494 US 872 (1990).
6 The non-applicability of the RFRA to state laws was confirmed in *City of Boerne v. Flores* 521 US 507 (1997).
7 Reference 42 US Code 2000bb, s.3(a) and (b).
8 For example, the USSC decision in *Burwell v. Hobby Lobby*, 573 US 134 S Ct 2751 (2014) was on the basis of a 5–4 majority.
9 See further at: www.wired.com/2014/03/united-nations-human-rights-committee-considers-report-united-states/.
10 Ibid.
11 *Everson v. Board of Education*, 330 US.
12 *Sherbert v. Verner*, 374 US 398 (1963).
13 *Employment Division v. Smith*, 48 US 872 (1990).
14 Ibid., at p. 879.
15 *The Church of the Lukumi Babalu Aye v. City of Hialeah*, 508 US 520 (1993).
16 Ibid., at p. 545.
17 *Lukumi Babalu*, op. cit., per Kennedy J at p. 533.
18 *Grace United Methodist Church v. City of Cheyenne*, op. cit., at pp. 649–650 (citing *Lukumi Babalu*, op. cit.). This summary of what *Smith* means is deeply contested, the subject of a circuit split, and probably inconsistent with *Masterpiece Cakeshop*, op. cit.
19 546 US 418 (2006).
20 Ibid., at p. 419–420.
21 435 F. Supp. 2d 687 (M.D. Tenn. 2006).
22 456 F. Supp. 2d 1120 (D. Ariz. 2006).
23 130 S Ct 1803 (2010).
24 435 US 618 (1978).
25 582 US (2017).
26 Ibid., at p. 533.

27 Citing *Lukumi*, 508 US, at p. 546.
28 Citing *McDaniel*, 435 US, at p. 628.
29 See, for example, 5 November 2009, when 13 people were killed and more than 30 injured in a mass shooting at Fort Hood in Texas by a US Army major claiming allegiance to Islamic militants.
30 *Gillette v. United States*, 401 US 437 (1971) per Marshall, J.
31 *Board of Education of Kiryas Joel Village School District v. Grumet*, 512 US 687 (1994).
32 367 US 488 (1961).
33 *Elk Grove Unified School District v. Newdow*, 542 US 1 (2004).
34 *McCollum v. Board of Education* 333 US 203.
35 *County of Allegheny v. American Civil Liberties Union (Greater Pittsburgh Chapter)*, 492 US 573 (1989), per Blackmun J citing *Wallace v. Jaffree*, 472 US at 70; but see also *Town of Greece v. Galloway*, 134 S. Ct. 1811 (2014).
36 *Kedroff v. St. Nicholas Cathedral*, 344 US 94, 116, 73 S.Ct. 143, 97 L.Ed. 120 (1952).
37 *Grace United Methodist Church v. City of Cheyenne*, 451 F.3d, 643, 649 (10th Cir. 2006).
38 *Reynolds v. United States*, 98 US 145 (1879).
39 See further Pepper, S., 'Reynolds, Yoder, and Beyond: Alternatives for the Free Exercise Clause', *Utah Law Review*, 309, 1981.
40 *Gillette v. United States*, 401 US 437 (1971) per Marshall, J.
41 See, for example: *Watson v. Jones*, 80 US (13 Wall.) 679 (1871); and *Presbyterian Church v. Mary Elizabeth Blue Hull Memorial Presbyterian Church*, 393 US 440, 441, 449–450 (1968).
42 443 US 595, 602 (1979).
43 See Corbin, C.M., 'The Irony of *Hosanna-Tabor Evangelical Lutheran Church and School v. EEOC*', *Northwestern University Law Review*, Vol. 106:2, at p. 956.
44 See, for example: *Watson v. Jones*, op. cit.; *Kedroff v. Saint Nicholas Cathedral of Russian Orthodox Church in North America*, 344 US 94; and *Serbian Eastern Orthodox Diocese for United States and Canada v. Milivojevich*, 426 US 696.
45 *Lyng v. Northwest Indian Cemetery Protective Association*, 485 US 439 (1988).
46 406 US 205 (1972).
47 48 US 872 (1990).
48 See Green, A., 'The Political Balance of the Religion Clauses', *Yale Law Journal*, 102, 1993, 1611.
49 For example, in *Alamo Foundation v. Secretary of Labor*, 471 US 290 (1985). See also *United States v. Lee*, 455 US 252 (1982).
50 48 US 872 (1990).
51 374 US 398 (1963).
52 546 US 418 (2006).
53 See *Multi Denominational Ministry of Cannabis and Rastafari, Inc. v. Gonzales*, 474 F. Supp. 2d 1133 (N.D. Cal. 2007).
54 Ibid., at p. 1145.
55 *Redhead v. Conference of Seventh-Day Adventists*, 440 F. Supp. 2d 211 (E.D.N.Y 2006).
56 573 US 134 S.Ct. 2751 (2014).
57 Ibid., at p. 54.
58 Ibid., at pp. 60–61.
59 *Hosanna-Tabor Evangelical Lutheran Church v. EEOC*, 565 US – (2012).
60 *Rayburn v. Gen. Conference of Seventh-Day Adventists*, 772 F.2d 1164,1166 (4th Cir.1985).
61 Ibid., at p. 1169.

62 397 F.3d 790, 790 (9th Cir. 2005).
63 *Hosanna-Tabor*, op. cit.
64 Ibid., at p. 697.
65 Corbin, C.M., op. cit., at p. 955.
66 Note to author, 19 April 2017.
67 See IRS Publication 1828, 'Tax Guide for Churches and Religious Organizations', at: www.irs.gov/pub/irs-pdf/p1828.pdf.
68 *American Atheists Inc. v. Schulman*, 2:2012cv00264 (United States District Court, Eastern District of Kentucky, Northern Division), 2014.
69 39 Ohio Misc. 28, 315 N.E.2d 825 (1974).
70 (2009) 235 Ill. 2d 256.
71 *Tilton v. Richardson*, 403 US 672 (1971). In fact State support for religious organisations has a long history in the US. See further Queen, E., 'History, Hysteria, and Hype: Government Contracting with Faith-Based Social Service Agencies', 2017, at: www.mdpi.com/2077-1444/8/2/22/pdf.
72 See, for example, *Meek v. Pittenger*, 421 US 349 (1975), government loans to religious schools; *Wolman v. Walter*, 433 US 229 (1977), government loans for services away from the religious school campus; *Illinois ex rel. McCollum v. Board of Education of School District*, 333 US 203 (1948), disallowed the use of public buildings for optional religious instruction; *Bowen v. Kendrick*, 487 US 589 (1989), disallowed the use of public buildings for optional religious instruction; and *Rosenberger v. Rector and Visitors of Univ. of Va.*, 515 US 819 (1995), required that equal funding be granted to evangelical Christian groups.
73 The IRS treatment of churches and religious organisations has been judicially scrutinised to ensure compatibility with the 'neutrality principle': see *Walz v. Tax Commissioner*, 397 US 664 (1970) and *Committee for Public Education v. Nyquist*, 413 US 756 (1973).
74 619 F.3d 1109 (9th Cir. 2010). See also *Epperson v. Arkansas*, 393 US 97, 103–104 (1968).
75 See Health Resources & Services Administration, at: www.hrsa.gov/grants/apply/eligibility/faith-and-community-organizations.html.
76 No. 88-2321-S, 1988 US Dist. LEXIS 12248 (D. Kan. 21 October 1988).
77 530 US 793, 120 S Ct 2530 (2000).
78 See also *Sch. Dist. v. Ball*, 473 US 373, 398–400 (1985).
79 536 US 639 (2002).
80 In recent years, several judges have concluded that children and teenagers, like prisoners, have too few options and too little power to make the voluntary choices the USSC requires when public money flows to programs involving religious instruction or indoctrination. See *Teen Ranch v. UDOW*, 389 F. Supp. 2d 827 (W.D. Mich. 2005), and *Freedom From Religion Foundation v. Towey*, No. 04-C-381-S, 2005 US Dist. LEXIS 39444 (W.D. Wis. 11 January 2005).
81 *Americans United for Separation of Church and State v. Prison Fellowship Ministries*, 432 F. Supp. 2d 862 (S.D. Iowa 2006). See also *Hein v. Freedom From Religion Foundation*, 551 US 587 (2007).
82 367 US 488 (1961).
83 380 US 163, 173, 186, 85 S. Ct. 850, 858, 864, 13 L. Ed. 2d 733 (1965).
84 406 US 205, 215–216, 92 S. Ct. 1526, 1533, 32 L. Ed. 2d 15 (1971).
85 See also *Thomas v. Review Board of the Indiana Employment Security Division*, 450 US 707 (1981) and *Frazee v. Ill. Dept. of Empl. Secur.*, 489 US 829 (1989).
86 No. 1:11-CV-00917 (S.D. Ohio 2012).
87 Federal regulation 29 C.F.R. § 1605.1.
88 322 US 78 (1944).
89 415 N.J. Super. 417, 427–429, 431 (N.J. Super. Ct. App. Div. 2010).

90 See further Pepper, S., 'Reynolds, Yoder, and Beyond: Alternatives for the Free Exercise Clause', *Utah Law Review*, 309, 1981.
91 *Reynolds v. United States*, 98 US (8 Otto.) 145 (1878).
92 *Heffron v. International Society for Krishna Consciousness*, 452 US 640 (1981).
93 *Gonzales v. O Centro Espirita Beneficente Uniao do Vegetal*, 546 US 418 (2006).
94 *Salazar v. Buono*, 130 S Ct 1803 (2010).
95 US Commission on Civil Rights, *1979: Religious Discrimination: A Neglected Issue; A Consultation Sponsored by the United States Commission on Civil Rights*, Washington, DC, 9–10 April 1979.
96 *Roberts v. United States Jaycees*, 468 US 609 (1984).
97 *Hurley v. Irish American Gay, Lesbian and Bisexual Group of Boston,* 515 US 557 (1995) and *Boy Scouts of America v. Dale*, 530 US 640 (2000).
98 536 US 639 (2002).
99 Laycock, D., 'Formal, Substantive, and Disaggregated Neutrality Toward Religion', *DePaul Law Review*, Vol. 39:4, 1990, at p. 993, 997. See further at: http://via.library.depaul.edu/law-review/vol39/iss4/3.
100 579 US (2016).
101 See the Virginia Statute of Religious Freedom 1777, drafted by Thomas Jefferson, guaranteeing freedom of religion to all, and endorsed by the USSC in *Reynolds v. United States*, op. cit.
102 *Pickering v. Board of Education*, 391 US 563 (1968).
103 See the 'clear and present danger' cases.
104 See, for example, *Good News Club v. Milford Cent. Sch.*, 533 US 98 (2001); *Rosenberger v. Rector*, 515 US 819 (1995); *Capital Square Review and Advisory Bd. v. Pinette*, 515 US 753 (1995); *Lamb's Chapel v. Center Moriches Union Free Sch. Dist.*, 508 US 384 (1993); *Bd. of Educ. v. Mergens*, 496 US 226 (1990); and *Widmar v. Vincent*, 454 US 263 (1981).
105 See, for example, *Marsh v. Alabama*, 326 US 501 (1946); *W. Va. State Bd. Educ. v. Barnette*, 319 US 624 (1943); *Martin v. City of Struthers*, 319 US 141 (1943); *Cox v. New Hampshire*, 312 US 569 (1941); and *Cantwell v. Connecticut*, 310 US 296, 309–310 (1940).
106 *Brown v. Socialist Workers Party* 459 US 87 (1982).
107 *Masterpiece Cakeshop v. Colorado Civil Rights Commission*, 584 US (2018).
108 See Currier, P., '*Freeman v. State of Florida*: Compelling State Interests and the Free Exercise of Religion in Post September 11th Courts', *Catholic University Law Review*, 53, Spring 2004.
109 2006 WL 3592952 (D. Wyo. 13 October 2006).
110 Ibid., at pp. 1–2.
111 *Tenafly Eruv Association v. Borough of Tenafly* (309 F.3d 144). An 'eruv' being an urban area enclosed by a wire boundary which symbolically extends the private domain of Jewish households into public areas, permitting activities within it that are normally forbidden in public on the Sabbath.
112 122 S. Ct. 2080 (2002).
113 Ibid., at p. 2087. See also Hare Krishna case.
114 *Gonzales v. O Centro Espirita Beneficente Uniao do Vegetal*, op. cit.
115 544 US 709 (2005).
116 *Salazar v. Buono* 130 S Ct 1803 (2010).
117 See further US Equal Employment Opportunity Commission (EEOC), 'Religious Garb and Grooming in the Workplace: Rights and Responsibilities', at: www.eeoc.gov/eeoc/publications/qa_religious_garb_grooming.cfm.
118 See, for example: *Tinker v. Des Moines Indep. Cmty. Sch. Dist.*, 393 US 503, 506 (1969), pupils wearing black armbands to signify dissapproval of Vietnam war; *Chalifoux*, 976 F. Supp. 659 (1997); high school students wearing white rosary

beads to signify their Catholicism; and *Alabama and Coushatta Tribes v. Big Sandy Schools District et al*, 817 F. Supp. 1319 (1993), Native American school children with long hair to signify tribal identity.

119 020, No. Civ. 03 598-S (E.D. Ok., 2003).

120 *Church of Lukumi Babalu Aye, Inc. v. City of Hialeah* 508 US (1993), at p. 532.

121 See, for example, *United States v. New York Metropolitan Transit Authority*, No. CV-04 4237 (2004) and *Axson-Flynn* 356 F.3d 1277 (10th Cir. 2004).

122 *Equal Employment Opportunity Commission (EEOC) v. Abercrombie & Fitch Stores Inc.*, 575 US (2015).

123 Ibid., at pp. 2–7.

124 343 US 495 (1952).

125 See *Hein v. Freedom From Religion Foundation*, 551 US 587 (2007).

126 514 US 334 (1995).

127 452 US 640 (1981). See also *Int'l Society for Krishna Consciousness Inc v. Lee* 505 US 672 (1992).

128 Super. Ct. No. BC320996, filed 10/16/06.

129 380 US 163 (1965).

130 398 US 333 (1970).

131 See further Laycock, D. (ed.), *Same-Sex Marriage and Religious Liberty*, Rowman & Littlefield, Maryland, USA, 2008.

132 Also known as the Patient Protection and Affordable Care Act 2016, or HB 1523. See *Barber v. Bryant* 17–547, and *Campaign for Southern Equality v. Bryant*, 17–642.

133 *Alford v. Consolidated Gov't of Columbus, Ga.*, 438 F. App'x 837, 839 (11th Cir. 2011); citing *Campbell v. Rainbow City, Ala.*, 434 F.3d 1306, 1313 (11th Cir. 2006).

134 Notwithstanding the USSC decision in *Boumediene v. Bush*, 553 US 723 (2008), that detainees at Guantánamo Bay have a constitutional right to habeas corpus.

135 Note the 'stand your ground' laws which legitimate the use of lethal force in self-defence.

136 410 US 113 (1973).

137 *Including Little Sisters of the Poor Home for the Aged, Denver, Colorado, a Colorado Non-Profit Corporation, et al., Applicants v. Kathleen Sebelius, Secretary of Health and Human Services, et al.*, 134 S. Ct. 1022 (2014), *Burwell v. Hobby Lobby Stores, Inc.*, 134 S. Ct. 2751, 2765 (2014) and *Zubik v. Burwell*, 135 S. Ct. 2924 (2015).

138 Including *Rust v. Sullivan*, 500 US 173 (1991) and *Planned Parenthood v. Casey*, 505 US 833 (1992).

139 *Barber v. Bryant*, 17–547, and *Campaign for Southern Equality v. Bryant*, 17–642.

140 457 US 291 (1982).

141 See, for example, *Georgetown College Inc.*, 377 US 978 (1964) and *Belchertown State Sch. v. Saikewicz*, 370 N.E.2d 417 (1977).

142 *Curzon v. Director, Missouri Dept of Health*, 497 US 261 (1990).

143 *Washington v. Glucksberg*, 521 US 702 (1997).

144 *Gonzales v. Oregon*, 546 US 243 (2006).

145 See Sizemore, C.A., 'Enforcing Islamic Mahr Agreements: The American Judge's Interpretational Dilemma', at: www.georgemasonlawreview.org/wp-content/uploads/2014/06/18-4-SIZEMORE.pdf.

146 576 US (2015). See also *United States* v. *Windsor*, 570 US 744 (2013), in which the USSC determined that an interpretation of "marriage" and "spouse" as applying only to heterosexual couples was unconstitutional under the Due Process Clause of the Fifth Amendment.

147 *Barber v. Bryant*, 17–547, and *Campaign for Southern Equality v. Bryant*, 17–642.
148 42 U.S.C. § 2000e-2(a)(1).
149 Congress in 1972 added an exemption, codified in s.702 of the Act, for "religious corporation[s], association[s], educational institution[s], or societ[ies]" to the prohibition against religion-based discrimination.
150 401 US 424, 91 S Ct 849 (1971).
151 Ibid., at p. 431.
152 483 US 327, 329, 339 (1987).
153 *Redhead* 440 F. Supp. 2d 211 (EDNY 2006).
154 *Hosanna-Tabor Evangelical Lutheran Church v. EEOC*, 565 US – (2012).
155 1989, WL 53857 (S.D. Miss).
156 205 F. Supp. 2d 1014 (E.D. Wis. 2002).
157 No.12–3820 (7th Cir. 2013).
158 *Lemon v. Kurtzman*, 403 US 602 (1971).
159 *Santa Fe Indep. Sch. Dist. v. Doe*, 530 US 290 (2000).
160 *Lee v. Weisman*, 505 US 577 (1992).
161 461 US 574 (1983).
162 454 US 263, 277 (1981).
163 130 S Ct (2010). See also *Ward v. Polite*, 667 F.3d 727 (6th Cir. 2012).
164 268 US 510, 45 S.Ct. 571, 69 L.Ed. 1070 (1925).
165 406 US 205 (1972).
166 *Altman v. Bedford Cent. Sch. Dist.*, 245 F.3d 49 (2nd Cir. 2001).
167 *Sch. Dist. of Abington Twp., Pa. v. Schempp*, 374 US 203 (1963).
168 *Hall v. Bd. Of Sch. Comm'rs of Conecuh County*, 656 F.2d 999 (5th Cir. 1981).
169 See *Santa Fe Indep. Sch. Dist. v. Doe*, 530 US 290 (2000); *Lee v. Weisman*, 505 US 577 (1992); *Wallace v. Jaffree*, 472 US 38 (1985); *Sch. Dist. v. Schempp*, op. cit.; and *Engel v. Vitale*, 370 US 421 (1962).
170 *Doe v. Duncanville Indep. Sch. Dist.*, 70 F.3d 402 (5th Cir. 1995).
171 *United States v. Board of Educ. Sch. Dist. Phila.*, 911, F.2d 882 (3rd Cir. 1990). See also *U.S. v. Bd. of Educ. of School D. of Philadelphia*, 911 F. 2d 882 (3rd Cir. 1990) and *Cooper v. Eugene School District No. 4J*, 301 Or. 358, 723 P. 2d 298 (1986).
172 *Tinker v. Des Moines Indep. Cmty. Sch. Dist.*, 393 US 503, 506 (1969).
173 See, for example: *Pierce v. Society of Sisters*, 268 US 510 (1925); *Farrington v. Tokushige*, 273 US 284 (1927); *Lehr v. Robertson*, 463 US 248, 257–258 (1983); *Hodgson v. Minnesota*, 497 US 417 (1990); and *Troxel v. Granville*, 530 US 57 (2000).
174 *Wisconsin v. Yoder* 406 US 205 (1972).
175 *Hosanna-Tabor Evangelical Lutheran Church v. EEOC* 565 US – (2012).
176 No. 08–35532, 2011 WL 208356 (9th Cir. 25 January 2011).
177 573 US 134 S Ct 2751 (2014).
178 *Barber v. Bryant*, No. 16–60477 (5th Cir. 2017).
179 *Masterpiece Cakeshop v. Colorado Civil Rights Commission*, 584 US (2018). Citing *Newman v. Piggy Park Enterprises, Inc.*, 390 US 400 (1968) and *Hurley v. Irish-American Gay, Lesbian and Bisexual Group of Boston, Inc.*, 515 US 557, 572 (1995).
180 See the decision of the Oregon Bureau of Labor and Industries to fine *Sweet Cakes by Melissa* for such a refusal at: Richardson, V., 'Oregon Panel Proposes $135k Hit against Bakers in Gay-Wedding Cake Dispute', *Washington Times*, 24 April 2015.
181 Op. cit.

182 *Church of Lukumi Babalu Aye, Inc. v. City of Hialeah*, 508 US (1993) and *Employment Division v. Smith*, 48 US 872 (1990).
183 See further Laycock, D. and Berg, T., *Symposium: Masterpiece Cakeshop – not as Narrow as May First Appear*, at: www.scotusblog.com/2018/06/symposium-masterpiece-cakeshop-not-as-narrow-as-may-first-appear/.
184 573 US 134 S Ct 2751 (2014).
185 Note to author, 19 April 2017.
186 *Burwell v. Hobby Lobby*, 573 US 134 S. Ct. 2751 (2014) and *Zubik v. Burwell*, 136 S. Ct. 1557–2016.
187 534 US 316 (2002).
188 Ignatieff, M., *American Exceptionalism and Human Rights*, Princeton University Press, Princeton, 2005, at p. 1.
189 See Gedicks, F.M., 'The Permissible Scope of Legal Limitations on the Freedom of Religion or Belief in the United States', *Emory International Law Review*, Vol. 19, 2005, at p. 1187. See also Kurland, P., *Religion and the Law: Of Church and State and the Supreme Court*, University of Chicago Press, Chicago, 1961.

6 Canada

Introduction

"Canada is founded upon principles that recognize the supremacy of God and the rule of law", proclaims the preamble to the Canadian Charter of Rights and Freedoms, thereby clearly asserting the primacy of Christianity and duly establishing a constitutional context that compromises the human rights of those of other faiths and none.

This chapter begins by outlining that constitutional and legal context,: specifying the current legal framework governing the relationship between religion and human rights on a domestic and international basis. It then examines the State and the human rights/religion intersect, giving particular attention to the established State support for Christian institutions as compared with its scant regard for the culture and beliefs of Indigenous people. This leads into a study of the case law that defines and illustrates the Canadian interpretation of the freedom of religion and identifies the issues arising as that freedom traverses those of association and expression. Finally, the chapter considers the religion-related case law generated by equality and non-discrimination legislation as this intersects with the human rights of access to justice, to life, to marriage and to found a family, to employment, education and to non-discrimination in accessing services.

Current legal framework

Canada has in place a modern domestic platform of law relating to human rights and to religion and belief. It is also a signatory State to most international treaties, conventions and protocols with a bearing on such matters.

International legislation

Canada signed and ratified the Universal Declaration of Human Rights in 1948 and has since played a leading role in endorsing other international treaties, conventions, protocols and so on.

The International Covenant on Civil and Political Rights (ICCPR)

Having ratified the ICCPR in 1976, Canada subsequently ratified Optional Protocol 1.[1]

Other

Ratification or accession has also been completed in relation to the International Convention on the Elimination of All Forms of Racial Discrimination (1970); the International Covenant on Economic, Social and Cultural Rights (1976); and the Convention on the Elimination of All Forms of Discrimination against Women (CEDAW) (1981).

The Constitution and domestic legislation

The Constitution Act 1982, containing the Canadian Charter of Rights and Freedom, is of central importance.

The Constitution

The Constitution of Canada consists of the Constitution Act 1982, together with its predecessor the Constitution Act 1867 (formerly the British North America Act 1867), and all other statutes and orders referred to in the schedule and any amendments. Unlike its US counterpart, the Canadian constitution does not have an anti-establishment clause.

The Canadian Charter of Rights and Freedoms

The Canadian Charter of Rights and Freedoms takes priority over all other federal and provincial legislation.

The Charter, s.2 declares that everyone has the following "fundamental freedoms: (a) freedom of conscience and religion; and (b) freedom of thought, belief, opinion and expression . . ." Under s.1, this is subject "only to such reasonable limits prescribed by law as can be demonstrably justified in a free and democratic society" and to a requirement that 'freedom' be interpreted in accordance with the "preservation and enhancement of the multicultural heritage of Canada" (s.27).[2] The specified freedoms are all subject to Clause 33, the "notwithstanding" caveat, which allows the federal or any provincial government to pass laws that breach Charter rights in relation to such matters. Section 15(1), provides a specific guarantee of protection from religious discrimination.

The 'Oakes test', established by the SCC in *R.* v. *Oakes*[3] for deciding when an infringement of a Charter right was reasonable and justifiable, has served that purpose for the past 30 years. Firstly, it requires the purpose of the infringing law to be of sufficient importance to warrant overriding a constitutionally protected right or freedom. Secondly, if that is the case, then there must be a "proportionality test" to establish that the means chosen are reasonable and demonstrably justified. The law must be rationally connected to the objective; the law must impair the right no more than is necessary to accomplish the objective, and the law must not have a disproportionately severe effect on the rights infringed. While the Oakes test remains the primary assessment tool, the *Doré* framework[4] is now also used when an administrative agency is involved (e.g. in *Loyola*).[5] As Guy puts it, in *Doré* the Supreme Court of Canada (SCC) held that administrative discretionary decisions implicating a Charter right "should be reviewed using a values-based, administrative law approach focused on proportionality, one that asks whether the decision-maker has properly balanced the relevant Charter values and statutory objectives at issue".[6] There is currently considerable uncertainty as to how the Oakes and *Doré* tests are to operate in conjunction.[7]

As has been noted, "no individuals or religious communities enjoy any less Charter protection than the major and recognizable religions".[8]

The Employment Equity Act 1996

The Employment Equity Act promotes equity in the workplace for the four designated groups: women, Aboriginal peoples, persons with disabilities, and members of visible minorities. In addition the Canadian government has passed into law a set of regulations, the Federal Contractors Program 1986 and the Employment Equity Act 1996, to address employment opportunities and benefits.

The Canadian Multiculturalism Act 1988

The Canadian Multiculturalism Act is a statute giving official recognition to multiculturalism as a fundamental characteristic of Canadian society and requiring federal institutions to take this into account when exercising their functions.

The Canadian Human Rights Act 1985

The Canadian Human Rights Act is a statute that improved and extended the largely ineffective Canadian Bill of Rights 1960. Section 3(1) broadened the law to ensure equal opportunity for individuals, to expressly prohibit discrimination on a federal basis (replicated at province and territory levels) and to prohibit discrimination on the grounds of national or ethnic origin, colour, race, religion, age, sex, sexual orientation, marital status, family status, disability and as regards any conviction for which a pardon has been granted or a record suspended.

The International Centre for Human Rights and Democratic Development Act 1985

As stated in the preliminaries, "[T]he purpose of this Act is to extend the laws in Canada that proscribe discrimination".

The Statutes of Canada 1841–1851

Statutes enacted prior to confederation in 1867 continue to have a resonance in some constitutional and contemporary statutory provisions. Included in that legacy is a guarantee given, under s.175 of the Statutes of Canada 1851, to ensure "the free exercise and enjoyment of Religious Profession and Worship, without discrimination or preference'.

Other legislation

The Criminal Code is a relevant federal statute, as it prohibits hate offences based on religion. Province level human rights legislation prohibits, among other things, discrimination on the grounds of race, religion or creed, colour, nationality, ancestry and place of origin.[9]

International courts and regulatory bodies

The Universal Periodic Review process provides an international peer monitoring forum for the ongoing review of Canadian progress in addressing human rights concerns, including those relating to religion and belief.

Domestic courts and regulatory bodies

The jurisdictional division between the federal and provincial government naturally affects the courts and regulatory machinery for law relating to religion: the system of Human Rights Tribunals with a right of appeal to a court is replicated in each province and territory.

The Supreme Court of Canada (SCC)

The Supreme Court of Canada is the final court of appeal and has a federal jurisdiction enabling it to adjudicate on, and to formulate governing principles in relation to, cases drawn from all areas of law, including those relating to religion and human rights. States and territories each have their own judicial and regulatory systems.

The Canadian Human Rights Commission (CHRC)

The Canadian Human Rights Commission, an independent body established at the federal level, was created to administer the Canadian Human Rights Act 1977, and subsequently undertook regulatory responsibility for the Employment Equity Act 1996.

The Canadian Human Rights Tribunal

Established under the Canadian Human Rights Act 1977, the jurisdiction of the Canadian Human Rights Tribunal is restricted to federally regulated activities, and thus most human rights claims come before the provincial tribunals. It is independent of the Canadian Human Rights Commission, which refers cases to it for adjudication under the Act.

International reports on human rights in Canada

In 1999, the UN Human Rights Committee condemned Canada, particularly Ontario, for exclusively funding Catholic schools in violation of Article 26 of the ICCPR. It did so again in 2005, when it published its Concluding Observations regarding Canada's fifth periodic report and observed that Canada had failed to "adopt steps in order to eliminate discrimination on the basis of religion in the funding of schools in Ontario". Canada's human rights record was not subject to further review until the 2015 sixth periodic report.[10] The Committee then expressed its concern regarding several issues, including the human rights of Indigenous people, and urged Canada to "renew its traditional commitment to the promotion and protection of the exercise of freedom of assembly, association and expression".[11]

The State and the human rights/religion intersect

Canadian society, in contrast to its US counterpart, is viewed by the State as comprised of a 'mosaic' rather than a 'melting pot' of cultures. The Standing Committee on Canadian Heritage, in Spring 2018, submitted a report to the national Parliament on its views as to some implications arising for the human rights/religion intersect.[12]

Balancing the interests of Church and State

Campbell J asserted in *Trinity Western*:[13]

> Canada is a "secular society". The State remains neutral on matters of religion. It does not favour one religion over another. And it does not favour either religion or the absence of it. While the society may be largely secular, in the sense that religion has lost its hold on social mores and individual conduct for many people, the State is not secular in the sense that it promotes the process of secularization. It remains neutral.

Evidence relating to this proposition, however, is at best mixed: cases such as *Big M*,[14] *Zylberberg*[15] and *Canadian Civil Liberties Association*[16] were all concerned with laws that gave preference to Christianity.

State and religion related terrorism

While adopting a policy of neutrality toward religion may place the State in a position to claim that it thereby offers equal recognition to all those who profess adherence to religion or belief, or to secularism, it can provide no protection to the State from domestic attacks by partisan religious zealots. Canada has suffered its share of religiously inspired violence: mostly 'lone wolf' Islamist attacks causing relatively few casualties, including one in 2014 on Canada's Parliament building. There was also the murder of six Muslim men praying at the *Centre culturel islamique de Québec* in Quebec City on 29 January 2017. It's not without irony to note that Canada has also been by far the leading common-law nation to offer refuge to Syrian migrants – necessarily almost exclusively Muslim – during the ongoing migrant crisis that began in 2015.

State neutrality

As Deschamps J noted in *SL v. Commission scolaire des Chênes*,[17] "[T]he gradual separation of Church and State in Canada has been part of a broad movement to secularise public institutions in the Western World . . . religious neutrality is now seen by many Western states as a legitimate means of creating a free space in which citizens of various beliefs can exercise their individual rights". The meaning of 'religious neutrality' was explained by *Mouvement laïque québécois* (a group in Quebec working to completely secularize the state and public institutions of the province) as follows:[18]

> The evolution of Canadian society has given rise to a concept of (this) neutrality according to which the State must not interfere in religion and beliefs. The State must instead remain neutral in this regard, which means that it must neither favour nor hinder any particular belief, and the same holds true for non-belief. . . . In a case in which a complaint of discrimination based on religion concerns a State practice, the alleged breach of the duty of neutrality must be established by proving that the State is professing, adopting or favouring one belief to the exclusion of all others and that the exclusion has resulted in interference with the complainant's freedom of conscience and religion.

This concept of State neutrality "allows churches and their members to play an important role in the public space where societal debates take place, while the State acts as an essentially neutral intermediary in relations between the various denominations and between those denominations and civil society".[19] It is an interpretation that permits State intervention to promote religion but only to the extent that it does so in an even-handed manner. This is held to be central to contemporary public policy, as it helps preserve and promote the multicultural nature of Canadian society.[20]

That State neutrality is subject to limits was made clear in *R. v. Jones*,[21] in which Wilson J stated that s.2(a) of the Canadian Charter "does not require the legislature to refrain from imposing any burdens on the practice of religion . . . the ultimate protection of any particular Charter right must be measured in relation to other rights and with a view to the underlying context in which the apparent conflict arises". No right is absolute. This was further illustrated by the *Hutterite* case,[22] which concerned the Alberta government's decision to withdraw an exemption previously available to Hutterites (whose religious beliefs prohibited them from willingly allowing their pictures to be taken) from the requirement that their driver's licences include photographs, an exemption clearly illustrative of State concern that a neutral law of universal application should not inadvertently burden a religious minority. In rejecting the applicants claim, McLachlin CJ acknowledged the perspective of religious claimants rights, but as she went on to explain, "[T]his perspective must be considered in the context of a multicultural, multireligious society where the duty of State authorities to legislate for the general good inevitably produces conflict with individual beliefs".

Christian symbols/prayers in State facilities

Religion has been constitutionally presumed to refer to Christianity and duly accorded special State recognition in various ways that include: reference to the 'supremacy of God' in the Charter preamble; the statutory recognition of Christian religious holidays; Christian inscriptions on coinage; and in the tax exemptions granted to what were initially Christian religious organisations. Nonetheless, the courts have assiduously sought to constrain what had become a customary inclusion of Christian prayers on ceremonial occasions in government facilities. For example, cases such as *Zylberberg v. Sudbury Board of Education (Director)*[23] and *Russow v. BC (AG)*[24] have established that the compulsory recitation of the Lord's Prayer in public schools – to the exclusion of prayers from any other religion – constitute an impermissible infringement of religious freedom. Such judicial stringency reached an apogee of sorts in *Mouvement laïque québécois v. Saguenay (City)*,[25] when the SCC, in allowing the appeal, prevented the Mayor of Saguenay from reciting a prayer in council meetings, warning that "the recitation of the prayer at the council's meetings was above all else a use by the council of public powers to manifest and profess one religion to the exclusion of all others".[26] By allowing the appeal, the SCC would seem to have come down in favour of equality and non-discrimination principles which are clearly antithetical to any public State endorsement of a particular religion or culture.

Protecting religion from the State

A right to "the free exercise and enjoyment of Religious Profession and Worship without discrimination or preference", as initially guaranteed under s.175 of the Statutes of Canada 1851, was continued by s.2(a) of the Charter of Rights and Freedoms; Article 1 of the Charter declares that religious freedom may be subject only to "such reasonable limits prescribed by law as can be demonstrably justified in a free and democratic society". As Côté and Brown JJ recently pointed out:[27]

> a s. 2 (a) Charter infringement is made out where a claimant establishes that impugned State conduct interferes, in a manner that is more than trivial or

insubstantial, with their ability to act in accordance with a sincere practice or belief that has a nexus with religion

When Dickson J, in *Big M*, pronounced on the freedom of religion, he did so in terms which emphasised the positive and protective role of the State:[28]

> Freedom in a broad sense embraces both the absence of coercion and constraint, and the right to manifest beliefs and practices. Freedom means that, subject to such limitations as are necessary to protect public safety, order, health, or morals or the fundamental rights and freedoms of others, no one is to be forced to act in a way contrary to his beliefs or his conscience.

Accordingly, in *Amselem*,[29] the SCC ruled that a condominium board had to allow a group of Orthodox Jewish unit owners to construct succahs on their balconies as part of the Jewish festival of Succot, despite the prohibition in their condominium contract prohibiting tenants from altering property. The property rights of secularists would have to give way to the rights of a minority to publicly celebrate their religion in a religious festival, in the same way that Christians would do at Christmas. This right has since been variously iterated in the human rights legislation of the provinces and it is there that much related case law has been generated.[30] Again, in *Loyola High School v. Quebec (Attorney General)*,[31] the SCC delivered a strong ruling affirming the State's duty to protect the identity and integrity of religious institutions and commented that secularism includes "respect for religious differences" and that "through this form of neutrality, the State affirms and recognises the religious freedom of individuals and their communities".[32]

More recently, in *Ktunaxa Nation*,[33] the SCC acknowledged that "where State conduct renders a person's sincerely held religious beliefs devoid of all religious significance, this infringes a person's right to religious freedom" and that because "in many Indigenous religions . . . land itself can be sacred . . . State action . . . (may then) interfere with the ability to act in accordance with religious beliefs and practices". In this case, the State decision to approve planning permission for a ski resort on a site considered by the plaintiffs to be sacred "interferes with the Ktunaxa's ability to act in accordance with their religious beliefs or practices". However, applying the proportionality principle, the court found that decision to interfere was reasonable. The SCC drew attention to some parameters on the State's protective duty when it noted the following:

> The State's duty under s.2(a) is not to protect the object of beliefs or the spiritual focal point of worship, such as Grizzly Bear Spirit. Rather, the State's duty is to protect everyone's freedom to hold such beliefs and to manifest them in worship and practice or by teaching and dissemination.

Again, in the most recent Trinity Western University (TWU) cases, the SCC emphasised that on the important issue of the threshold justifying State interference with religious freedom, the proportionality principle can play a critical role:[34] in a majority decision, the court found that the Law Society of British Columbia (LSBC), a State body, had interfered with the religious freedom of TWU but was justified in doing so because:[35]

> it was reasonable for the LSBC to conclude that promoting equality by ensuring equal access to the legal profession, supporting diversity within the bar, and preventing harm to LGBTQ law students were valid means by which the LSBC could pursue its overarching statutory duty.

However, the Chief Justice was in no doubt that this interference "cannot be characterized as minor . . . it precludes members of the TWU community from engaging in the practice of providing legal education in an environment that conforms to their religious beliefs, deprives them of the ability to express those beliefs in institutional form, and prevents them from associating in the manner they believe their faith requires".[36] This would seem to be a clear warning that the proportionality principle will not always justify State interference.

Intervention in Church disputes

In the words of Justice McLachlin:[37]

> As a general rule, the State refrains from acting in matters relating to religion. It is limited to setting up a social and legal framework in which beliefs are respected and members of the various denominations are able to associate freely in order to exercise their freedom of worship, which is a fundamental, collective aspect of freedom of religion, and to organize their churches or communities.

As was more forcefully expressed in *Amselem*, "[T]he State is in no position to be, nor should it become, the arbiter of religious dogma. . . . Secular judicial determinations of theological or religious disputes, or of contentious matters of religious doctrine, unjustifiably entangle the court in the affairs of religion".[38] Although reluctant to do so, the courts will adjudicate on church matters, including property disputes,[39] without preference for doctrine but with respect for trust law and for the right of Canadian religious organisations to manage their own affairs.[40] In *Diaferia v. Elliott*,[41] the court drew the line at reviewing decisions taken by members; it had "no intention of getting involved in how the ultimate meeting of the Church members proceeds . . . this court must circumscribe the extent to which it becomes involved in the internal affairs of a religious organisation".[42] In *Ktunaxa Nation*,[43] the SCC ruled that to determine how the plaintiffs' beliefs could be protected would require the State and its courts to assess the content and merits of religious beliefs, which was outside their remit. Most recently, in *Highwood Congregation v. Wall*,[44] the SCC held that the courts have no jurisdiction over disputes between members and their denominations.

State protection of beliefs/culture of Indigenous people

The failure of both the federal and provincial governments in *Tsilhqot'in Nation v. British Columbia*[45] to establish clear felling forestry rights in respect of land where a First Nations tribe had lived and worshipped for centuries was a significant SCC ruling. By finding that the tribe had acquired Aboriginal title by virtue of historical occupation, and that any intervention affecting it could only be with tribal consent or without such consent in restricted circumstances, the court by implication also seemed to extend the doctrine of State neutrality to accommodate aboriginal land disputes. This interpretation now needs to be reviewed in the light of the recent SCC decision in the above-mentioned *Ktunaxa Nation* case. This concerned a claim that a proposed ski resort development would drive the Grizzly Bear Spirit from a First Nation's traditional territory. While the SCC willingly conceded that s.2(a) of the Charter protected the appellants' freedom to hold and to manifest a religious belief in the Grizzly Bear Spirit, it was unable to share their view that s.2(a) extended to protect the presence of the Grizzly Bear Spirit in Qat'muk. The claim was not one seeking protection for the freedom to believe in the Grizzly Bear Spirit or to pursue practices related to it but one seeking to protect the Grizzly Bear Spirit itself, and the subjective spiritual meaning the claimants derived from it, which was beyond the scope of s.2(*a*). In a majority decision, the SCC found that the Ktunaxa's claim was not protected by s.2(a) of the Charter because neither the Ktunaxa's freedom to hold their beliefs nor their freedom to manifest those beliefs was infringed by the Minister's decision to approve the project.[46] A decision which, arguably, fails to give as much weight to the legitimacy of a subjective interpretation of 'belief' as is now required by human rights law.

State protection of its traditional religious/cultural identity

R v. Big M Drug Mart Ltd[47] was a landmark judgment in the politics surrounding Canadian religious identity. The case concerned a retail outlet that had been acquitted of violating the Lord's Day Act by opening for business on Sunday, but the issue was brought before the SCC to determine whether s.2 of the Charter of Rights and Freedom, had a bearing on the matter. The SCC ruled the Lord's Day Act unconstitutional because laws must have a secular purpose: a law based on religious reasons and favouring one denomination over others was deemed unconstitutional. As Dickson CJ then explained:[48]

> In proclaiming the standards of the Christian faith, the Act creates a climate hostile to, and gives the appearance of discrimination against, non-Christian Canadians. . . . The theological content of the legislation remains as a subtle and constant reminder to religious minorities within the country of their differences with, and alienation from, the dominant religious culture.

In *Mouvement laïque québécois*,[49] the SCC closely followed the sentiment expressed in *R v. Big M Drug Mart Ltd*,[50] that "[w]hat may appear good and true to the majoritarian religious group, or to the State acting at their behest, may not for religious reasons, be imposed upon citizens who take the contrary view". It took issue with Gagnon JA's reference in the Tribunal to "the State's duty to preserve its history, including its multireligious heritage" and to "the concept of 'benevolent neutrality' being more appropriate to define the State's duty of religious neutrality".[51] Instead, warning against a benign stance favouring Christianity (or any other religion/culture), the SCC advised the following:[52]

> If the State adheres to a form of religious expression under the guise of cultural or historical reality or heritage, it breaches its duty of neutrality . . . the State's duty to remain neutral on questions relating to religion cannot be reconciled with a benevolence that would allow it to adhere to a religious belief. . .

This valedictory dismissal of any recognition of a State duty of care for its cultural heritage is at variance with some ECtHR rulings and with the drift of current judicial rulings and legislative initiatives in the US.

State preferencing of religious organisations

In keeping with many other common-law countries, and despite the above evidence of State neutrality, Canadian religious organisations have long enjoyed special privileges: they may organise as they see fit, largely free from government regulatory requirements. This includes hiring staff on the basis of religious affiliation, and they enjoy other exemptions in relation to matters such as sexual orientation and gender parity. Indeed, religious communities such as the Hutterites have always been largely left to regulate their own affairs.

The religious exemption

In addition to the right to discriminate when employing staff in accordance with the "bona fide occupational requirements" (BFOR)[53] rule, the Constitution Act 1867, s.93(1) protects denominational school privileges from the anti-discrimination strictures of modern human rights law and the Canadian Charter of Rights and Freedoms.

When the Civil Marriage Act[54] was introduced, which extended the meaning of marriage to include same-sex relationships under Canadian federal law and inserted ss.149.1 into the Income Tax Act,[55] it provided that religious organisations would not have their charitable registration revoked solely because they or any of their members exercised freedom of conscience and religion in relation to the meaning of marriage. The SCC had also ruled to similar effect in *Reference Re Same-Sex Marriage*.[56] All of this was in keeping with an established acceptance, clearly evident in testamentary dispositions, that religious beliefs conferred a degree of immunity from the otherwise non-differentiating application of the law. As Campbell J pointed out in *Trinity Western University v. Nova Scotia Barristers' Society*,[57] the plaintiff university, "like churches and other private institutions, does not have to comply with the equality provisions of the Charter".

Regulatory privileges

In general, religious organisations are self-regulating. If they are incorporated and have charitable status, this renders them subject only to the compliance requirements of the Corporation Act and the Canadian Revenue Agency (CRA).

Tax privileges

The CRA grants charitable tax exemption to religious organisations in general and continues the traditional legal presumption that they are for the public benefit.[58]

Testamentary privileges

From at least *Laurence v. McQuarrie*,[59] with its forfeiture condition in the event of the beneficiary "embracing the doctrines of the church of Rome", until the introduction of the Charter of Rights and Freedoms, testamentary conditions in favour of religion had precedence over public policy considerations and went virtually unchallenged by the judiciary. It had seemed that the 1982 Act would inaugurate a new era, but this was not immediately forthcoming. *Canada Trust*,[60] the best known Canadian case on the issue of a religious trust being in breach of public policy, was determined by the Ontario Court of Appeal in 1990, which ruled that limiting scholarships to white, Protestant, British subjects, constituted racial discrimination and "is patently at variance with the democratic principles governing our pluralistic society in which equality rights are constitutionally guaranteed and in which the multicultural heritage of Canadians is to be preserved and enhanced".[61] However, shortly afterwards, in *Ramsden Estate*,[62] the court found that a testamentary gift to a university for scholarships for Protestant students presented "no ground of public policy which would serve as an impediment to the trust proceeding".[63] At much the same time, Galligan J, in *Fox v. Fox Estate*,[64] held that a trustee's use of a power of encroachment to punish the remainder beneficiary for marrying a person not of the Jewish faith was invalid. Most recently, in *Spence v. BMO Trust Company*,[65] the court firmly reiterated its support for testamentary freedom when it upheld the right of a testator to disinherit his adult child on grounds that were overtly discriminatory.

State funding of faith-based facilities and services

In recent years, the SCC has made it clear that "State sponsorship of one religious tradition" breaches the State's duty of neutrality, and is both discriminatory and destructive of religious freedom.[66] The State has a duty not to "create a preferential public space that favours certain religious groups".[67] A corollary is that the State must not deny to religious organisations the opportunities available to their secular counterparts to acquire public funding. However, it remains the case that the Constitution Act 1867, s.93 extends protection to denominational schools and permits partisan State funding (see further below). This anomaly was judicially acknowledged in *Adler v. Ontario*,[68] when Iacobucci J, on behalf of the court majority, ruled that government funding of both Roman Catholic and public schools, but not private religious schools, was entitled to special protection[69] under that constitutional provision.[70]

In *Mouvement laïque québécois*,[71] Gascon J acknowledged that "sponsorship of one religious tradition by the State in breach of its duty of neutrality amounts to discrimination against all other such traditions," and went on to explain that "the State (must) abstain from taking any position and thus avoid adhering to a particular belief . . . it may not use its powers in such a way as to promote the participation of certain believers or non-believers in public life to the detriment of others".[72] Nevertheless, the biased protections of the Constitution Act 1867, s.93 remain in effect.

Religion and the freedoms of association and expression

Freedom of conscience and religion, as guaranteed under s.2(a) of the Charter, includes "the right to entertain such religious beliefs as a person chooses, the right to declare religious beliefs openly and without fear of hindrance or reprisal, and the right to manifest religious belief by worship and practice or by teaching and dissemination".[73] These rights – to believe, to declare and particularly to manifest – expose the freedom of religion to possible violation along a wide front.

Freedom of religion

The right to freedom of religion is infringed, as the SCC stated in *Ktunaxa Nation*, when a claimant demonstrates:[74]

> (1) that he or she sincerely believes in a practice or belief that has a nexus with religion, and (2) that the impugned State conduct interferes, in a manner that is non-trivial or not insubstantial, with his or her ability to act in accordance with that practice or belief.

Adding that "where State conduct renders a person's sincerely held religious beliefs devoid of all religious significance, this infringes a person's right to religious freedom". This interpretation is in keeping with earlier decisions that have similarly emphasised a State duty not to breach the freedom of religion.[75] The corollary – whether there exists a State duty or discretion to provide support – has proven contentious in relation to the doctrine of State neutrality in a Canadian context.[76]

Definitions

Only in recent years, as McLachlin CJ noted, have the courts broadened their traditional interpretation of 'religion' to accommodate different belief systems: "[T]he reference to the supremacy of God in the preamble to the Canadian Charter cannot lead to an interpretation of freedom of conscience and religion that authorises the State to consciously profess a theistic faith".[77] Freedom of conscience and religion "must be given a generous and expansive interpretation".

'Religion'

Following the Dickson CJ ruling in *R. v. Big M. Drug Mart*,[78] the courts moved away from the orthodox institutional interpretation of 'religion' to embrace a wider view based on an individual's human right to choose their beliefs and how to express them:[79]

> The essence of the concept of freedom of religion is the right to entertain such religious beliefs as a person chooses, the rights to declare religious beliefs openly and without fear of hindrance or reprisal, and the right to manifest religious belief by worship and practice or by teaching and dissemination.

This view was further developed by Iacobucci J in *Syndicat Northcrest v. Amselem*:[80]

> Defined broadly, religion typically involves a particular and comprehensive system of faith and worship. Religion also tends to involve the belief in a divine, superhuman or controlling power. In essence, religion is about freely and deeply held personal convictions or beliefs connected to an individual's spiritual faith and integrally linked to one's self-definition and spiritual fulfillment, the practices of which allow individuals to foster a connection with the divine or with the subject or object of that spiritual faith.

In that case, the SCC stated that in determining the existence or otherwise of religious belief, a two-pronged test must be satisfied: it must be demonstrated that a person is engaged in a practice or a belief that has a nexus with religion, and the person has to be sincere in their belief.

'Beliefs'

A broad interpretation of what might constitute the freedom of religion was evident in *Morgentaler*,[81] when Wilson J advised that the freedom to hold and exercise beliefs was not restricted to beliefs of a religious nature: "[I]n a free and democratic society 'freedom of conscience and religion' should be broadly construed to extend to conscientiously held beliefs, whether grounded in religion or in a secular morality".[82] Again, in *Maurice v. Canada (Attorney General)*,[83] Campbell J was satisfied that vegetarianism, based on a belief that the consumption of animals is morally wrong, qualified for protection under s.2(a) of the Charter as a conscientious belief. As acknowledged by Iacobucci J in *Amselem*, this interpretation has permitted recognition of groups such as Falun Gong[84] and Wiccas,[85] (also, more recently, atheists),[86] and has now become a settled characteristic of the Canadian judicial approach to religion and belief.[87] He was of the opinion that it was unnecessary for the holder of that belief to show that it was "objectively recognized as valid by other members of the religion".[88] Essentially, if an individual's asserted religious belief "is in good faith, neither fictitious nor capricious, and that it is not an artifice"[89] and he or she sincerely believes that manifesting that belief by way of a certain practice has spiritual significance or connects them with the divine or spiritual realm, then this will be protected under s.2(a) of the Charter. It is "the religious or spiritual essence of an action" that attracts protection.[90] Moreover, all individuals and religious/belief organisations enjoy equal Charter protection. Further, in *Mouvement laique quebecois v. Saguenay (City)*,[91] the SCC held that for the purposes of Charter protection, the concepts of "belief" and "religion" encompass non-belief, atheism and agnosticism.[92]

Indigenous beliefs

The Indigenous people – the First Nations, Inuit and Métis – originally spread across all of Canada, each tribe with its own distinctive culture and set of beliefs, customs, ceremonies and rituals, usually with strong spiritual references to specific animals and to nature in general. "Religion is a matter of faith intermingled with culture", as McLachlin J noted in the *Hutterite* case,[93] and for the Indigenous people this largely became a matter of their traditional beliefs succumbing to, or fusing with, those of Christianity.

The Canadian Human Rights Act, s.35 of the Constitution Act, s.25 of the Charter of Rights and Freedoms and the United Nations Declaration of the Rights of Indigenous Peoples all include legal protections for the fundamental right of Indigenous peoples to freely practice their religious and spiritual traditions and to be treated equally and with dignity.[94] The SCC has a well-established track record of according *locus standi* to the beliefs of Indigenous people.[95]

Manifestation of religion or belief

As Iacobucci J has explained:[96]

> First, there is the freedom to believe and to profess one's beliefs; second, there is the right to manifest one's beliefs, primarily by observing rites, and by sharing one's faith by establishing places of worship and frequenting them. Thus, although private beliefs have a purely personal aspect, the other dimension of the right has genuine social significance and involves a relationship with others.

Adherence to a particular religion or belief does not imply that an adherent is restricted to manifesting their commitment in a preordained manner. It must, however, be more than a nominal gesture (e.g. the formal reciprocal bow of participants in a judo contest is not a manifestation of the Shinto religion/belief).[97] Otherwise the constraints on choice in the manner of manifesting adherence are only those generally pertaining to nuisance, health/safety and the rights of others in public places.[98]

Religious discrimination

As one of the 11 grounds listed in the Canadian Human Rights Act, religious discrimination attracts considerable judicial attention and asperity in this most multicultural common-law jurisdiction. This was clearly evident in the above-mentioned *Canada Trust* case,[99] when the court found it was "to expatiate the obvious" that a trust premised on notions of racism and religious superiority was obviously discriminatory and therefore void. As with other allegations[100] of a breach of rights, claims of religious discrimination must be evidenced, be objectively verifiable and be proven in accordance with the balance of probabilities test.[101] The comments of Gascon J must also be borne in mind: "I concede that the State's duty of neutrality does not require it to abstain from celebrating and preserving its religious heritage. But that cannot justify the State engaging in a discriminatory practice for religious purposes".[102]

Freedom of association

Freedom of association is guaranteed under s.2(d) of the Charter; this right entitles individuals to establish, belong to, maintain or leave any legal organisation. In *Mounted Police Association of Ontario v. Canada (AG)*,[103] the SCC agreed that:

> freedom of religion is not merely a right to hold religious opinions but also an individual right to establish communities of faith . . . and there is support for the view that the autonomous existence of religious communities is indispensable for pluralism in a democratic society and is thus an issue at the very heart of the protection of freedom of religion.

The SCC had earlier decided, in *Lakeside Colony of Hutterian Brethren v. Hofer*,[104] that the courts had jurisdiction to determine disputes over membership in religious associations. More recently, in *Wall v. Highwood Congregation et al.*,[105] the court concluded that members of a voluntary religious association should be able to ask a court to review decisions taken by that association so long as the decision in question is determined to be final. However, this Alberta Court of Appeal decision was subsequently reversed by the SCC and, as Harrington comments, "[T]here is now some uncertainty as to how the decisions in *Lakeside* and *Wall* are to be reconciled".[106]

The 'positive action' provisions

The equality provision in the Canadian Charter of Rights and Freedoms, s.15(1), is subject to the s.15(2) exception that it "does not preclude any law, program or activity that has as its object the amelioration of conditions of disadvantaged individuals or groups including those that are disadvantaged because of race, national or ethnic origin, colour, religion, sex, age or mental or physical disability". In keeping with the Canadian interpretation of State neutrality, government has a duty to both monitor policy and legislation and make such adjustments as may be necessary to ensure religious freedom is not unduly burdened and also to intervene with supportive assistance for disadvantaged religious entities. Far from having a 'hands off' approach, the State is encouraged to promote religion, provided it does so in an even-handed manner. As Dickson CJ put it in *Big M*:[107]

> The equality necessary to support religious freedom does not require identical treatment of all religions. In fact the interests of true equality may well require differentiation in treatment.

In the above-mentioned *University of Victoria v. British Columbia (A.G.)* case,[108] scholarships were used to positively discriminate in favour of Roman Catholics. This approach acknowledges that groups, including those defined by their religion or beliefs, may have distinct needs that are most effectively and efficiently addressed by that form of affirmative action.

Freedom of expression

The Canadian Charter of Rights and Freedoms proclaims the fundamental freedoms of thought, belief, opinion and expression, including freedom of the press and other media of communication. Conflict between the freedoms of expression and religion – as in 'Holocaust denial'[109] – is as prevalent in Canada as elsewhere.

Religiously motivated conduct

In *Ross v. Canada*,[110] the subject was a former teacher who in his spare time published books and pamphlets and made public statements reflecting his discriminatory views in relation to Jews.[111] The Human Rights Board of Inquiry concluded that he had contributed to a "poisoned environment" within the school district and recommended that he be transferred to a non-teaching position, which was endorsed by the SCC and also by the UN Human Rights Committee, which agreed that the disciplinary action did not constitute a violation of the freedom of expression as guaranteed by Article 19 (ICCPR).

In the *Hutterite* case,[112] but perhaps more so in *Amselem*,[113] the judiciary have wrestled with the weighting to be given to religious/cultural customs relative to neutral public benefit laws of uniform application. In *Hutterite* and *Amselem*, it would seem, the SCC resolved the issues by using the proportionality principle to gauge the significance of the custom for the religion/culture concerned against the overall importance of a neutral public benefit law in order to determine whether the latter had such a disproportionate adverse effect on the former as to be in breach of their freedom of religion. In such cases, including *Multani*,[114] (see further below) an adherent's subjective interpretation of the importance of a custom will need to be supported by hard evidence linking it to the religion/belief.[115]

In Canada as elsewhere, a conflation of religious belief and sexual orientation has generated considerable litigation. So, for example, *Boisson*[116] concerned a letter written by the appellant to a newspaper expressing disparaging comments about homosexuals. In overturning the HRC finding of incitement to hatred and upholding the relative importance of freedom of speech, Wilson J ruled that the language used must disclose a real intention to discriminate or incite others to discriminate. The same approach was taken in *Saskatchewan (Human Rights Commission) v. Whatcott*[117] regarding flyers that denounced gays and lesbians, when the SCC emphasized the need to pursue true hate speech, not just offensive language. It was a similar situation in *Trinity Western*,[118] when the court found no concrete evidence that holding beliefs about homosexuality would result in actions by its graduates that would be discriminatory.

Religious apparel

In *Saadi*,[119] the court considered the social issue, which presents in many jurisdictions and is viewed by some as a sensitive matter, of a Muslim female employee wearing her hijab at work. It pointedly overruled the following Tribunal finding: "The Code guarantees not only a woman's right to wear a religious headdress in the workplace, but also her right to choose the form of religious headdress, subject to any bona fide occupational requirements". Instead, it stated that the issue was whether the employee could have complied with the dress code without compromising her religious beliefs and what she was actually required to wear as part of her religion. Then consideration should be given to whether the employer's dress code, or the employer's enforcement or interpretation of it, conflicted with what the employee chose to wear. At variance with this approach is Quebec's recent adoption of Bill 62, the Religious Neutrality Law, which prohibits public workers, as well as those receiving public services, from covering their faces. This initiative attracted comment from the Canadian Human Rights Commission that "laws should be adopted to end discrimination – not promote it".[120]

The issue as to wearing the niqab when testifying in court was resolved in *NS*[121] by applying the following guidance: "If the judge concludes that the wearing of the niqab in all of the circumstances would infringe the accused's right to make full answer and defence, the right must prevail over the witness's religious freedoms and the witness must be ordered to remove the niqab". A very similar approach was recently taken in Australia in relation to the same issue.[122]

In the above-mentioned *Multani* case,[123] the SCC ruled that "a total prohibition against wearing a kirpan (a ceremonial dagger) to school undermines the value of the religious symbol and sends students the message that some religious practices do not merit the same protection as others".[124] The SCC considered that the freedom of a Sikh boy to carry his kirpan outweighed reasons (e.g. alleged safety concerns) to prohibit him from doing so, unlike an earlier tribunal ruling which held that safety reasons justified a prohibition against wearing it on an aircraft.[125] This exercise in balancing the unintentional adverse effects of a neutral rule on a religious/cultural minority against a general concern to promote the public benefit can be seen in a considerable number and variety of cases.[126] It should not, of course, distract attention from the blunt fact that an item of apparel – such as a turban – which identifies the religion/ethnicity of the wearer, is often sufficient to attract discrimination;[127] the policy decision permitting Sikh officers of the RCMP to wear turbans was, therefore, a potent political gesture neatly conflating religion and culture with nationalism.

Blasphemy and proselytism

The Criminal Code, s.296(1) declares that anyone who publishes a blasphemous libel is guilty of an indictable offence; Bill C-51 proposes the removal of s. 296.

In *Zundel v. Canada*,[128] which concerned Holocaust-denial publications, the SCC considered the limitations imposed on proselytism by s.181 of the Criminal Code. This stated that "[e]very one who wilfully publishes a statement, tale or news that he knows is false and causes or is likely to cause injury or mischief to a public interest is guilty of an indictable offence and liable to imprisonment". The court found that s.181 violated s.2(b) of the Canadian Charter of Rights and Freedoms because the restriction on all expressions "likely to cause injury or mischief to a public interest" was too broad, and imprisonment for expression was unreasonable. The parameters for proselytism were subsequently amended and are now set by s.319.(2) of the Code. In *Friesen*,[129] the Tribunal found that an employee had suffered religious discrimination when sacked because he refused to stop preaching in the workplace. But his sacking was justified, as other employees had a right to work in an environment where they were not subject to religious preaching, and the employer did not have a duty to accommodate an employee's beliefs. The observations of Iacobucci and Major JJ in *B. (R.) v. Children's Aid Society of Metropolitan Toronto*, seem apt:[130]

> Just as there are limits to the ambit of freedom of expression (e.g. s.2(*b*) does not protect violent acts),[131] so are there limits to the scope of s.2(*a*), especially so when this provision is called upon to protect activity that threatens the physical or psychological well-being of others.

Conscientious objection

The right to refuse to "bear arms" or otherwise serve in the armed forces, on grounds of religious or moral objection, is protected under s.2(a) of the

Charter – which extends protection to "freedom of *conscience and* religion" – and although not specifically mentioned in the National Defence Act is probably well established in Canadian law.

Conscientious objection to engagement in service provision is another matter. In Canada, as elsewhere, this is a rapidly growing area of jurisprudence, as national legislation prescribes a new set of social mores. *Moore*,[132] for example, concerned a Catholic public service employee who, having objected to abortion and on refusing to work with a client who sought a termination, was disciplined and eventually fired. The HR Tribunal found that because the employer knew of her religiously based objection, an onus rested on the employer to accommodate the employee by transferring the client to other employees. More recently, in *C. v. A.*[133] the HR Tribunal acknowledged that a family medical clinic had accommodated a Christian employee's pro-life beliefs by not requiring her to refer patients for abortions. Abortion referrals were processed by other individuals without compromising patient care. It is highly probable that the same difficulties will arise in relation to the legal right to a medically assisted death. Such matters have a singular weighting in Canadian law given the pointed constitutional reference to freedom "of conscience" in s.2(a) of the Charter (see further below).

Human rights, equality and religion: the case law

Provisions governing non-discrimination and equality are to be found in s.15(1) of the Charter which, as the SCC pointed out in *Andrews v. Law Society of British Columbia*,[134] requires a plaintiff to show differential treatment, an enumerated ground and discrimination in a substantive sense involving factors such as prejudice, stereotyping and disadvantage.[77]

Right of access to justice

Karakatsanis J, in *Hryniak v. Mauldin*,[135] warned that "ensuring access to justice is the greatest challenge to the rule of law in Canada today . . . that a culture shift is required"[136] and called for a realisation that access to the civil justice system must be proportionate, timely and affordable. Among the challenges facing the Canadian rule of law is that of bridging the disparity between national statutory family law and the parallel system administered by religious bodies.

Religious law and courts

Faith-based tribunals, established by Catholic, Jewish and Islamic communities, have been operational across Canada for many decades. Their rulings are sometimes brought before the national courts. For example, in *Bruker v. Marcovitz*,[137] the SCC found that a Jewish husband's 15-year-long refusal to grant his wife a *get*, thereby preventing her from divorcing him, was contrary to public policy, as "under Canadian law, marriage and divorce are available equally to men and women".[138] The court rejected the husband's defence that he was protected by the right to freedom of religion. Abella J warned that this well-established Jewish principle, confining the granting of a *get* exclusively to the discretion of a husband, was incompatible with Canadian law and that public policy supported the removal of barriers to religious divorce and remarriage. Moreover, in early 2018 the SCC agreed to hear the case of a Jehovah's Witness who was expelled from that religious organisation for alleged verbal abuse of his wife.

Shari'a law

In Spring 2018 a private members' motion – M-103[139] – was brought before the House calling for an amendment to the Constitution stating that "Shari'a Law or separate Shari'a family courts will never have a place in the Canadian Justice System".

Right to life

The Canadian Charter of Rights and Freedoms, s.7 states that "everyone has the right to life, liberty and security of the person and the right not to be deprived thereof except in accordance with the principles of fundamental justice".[140] The Canadian experience of the human rights/religion intersect, as it relates to such matters, has engaged courts at all levels across the country.

Abortion, contraception

Canadian ratification of CEDAW in 1981, followed a year later by adoption of the Charter, transformed the legal context of abortion which until then had been restricted by s.251 of the Criminal Code to life-threatening circumstances. Those twin events launched a period of many lengthy court battles involving anti-abortion groups,[141] an anti-pornography group,[142] campaigning pro-life groups,[143] abortion clinics[144] and addressing the uncertain status of the foetus in Canadian law.[145] The long history of *Morgentaler* prosecutions[146] records the changing legal status of abortion clinics in Canada. This is now a wholly legal procedure, and government-funded 'Well Woman' clinics, with 'safe zones' restricting protester harassment, are widely available throughout most of Canada. Nonetheless, in 2016 the CEDAW Committee expressed concern regarding the uneven access to abortion services across the country and recommended that Canada: "a) ensure access to legal abortion services in all provinces and territories; b) ensure that the invocation of conscientious objection by physicians does not impede women's access to legal abortion services".[147]

Refusing medical treatment

The SCC has found that a person over the age of majority and able to give or withhold informed consent "has the right to refuse treatment, even if that treatment is, from a medical perspective, in his or her best interest . . . the right to refuse unwanted medical treatment is fundamental to a person's dignity and autonomy".[148] It is a finding that consolidates the earlier decision of the court in *Ciarlariello v. Schacter*[149] that patients have a "clear legal right" to autonomy and self-determination in health care. This right is also available to a mature minor, meaning a child with the capacity to understand and reflect on their illness and the associated options. It is not, however, a right exercisable for religious reasons by a parent on behalf of their child, as illustrated by *B. (R.) v. Children's Aid Society of Metropolitan Toronto*,[150] when Jehovah's Witness parents refusal of a blood transfusion for their child was overruled by the court.

Medically assisted death

The SCC, in the 2015 landmark case of *Carter v. Canada*,[151] found that ss. 241 and 14 of the Criminal Code – prohibiting physician-assisted suicide, or euthanasia – violated s.7 of the Charter, and ruled that mentally competent adults, suffering intolerably and enduringly, had a right to a medically assisted death. In mid-June 2016, Parliament passed Bill C-14, which narrows the scope of the *Carter* decision by declaring that to qualify for a medically assisted death a person must be in an advanced state of irreversible decline and their natural death must be "reasonably foreseeable".

Right to marriage and to found a family

Freedom of religion and belief has been locked into the Constitution via the Charter: s.2(a) specifically prevents the legislature from discriminating against religious minorities, while s.1 qualifies this with the proviso that it be exercised subject to such "reasonable limits prescribed by law as can be demonstrably justified in a free and democratic society". This has provided a legal context for extending the legal definition of marriage, for addressing family related matters and in particular for clashes between human rights and religion on an array of gender, sexuality and reproductive issues.

Marriage and family relationships

The family model as traditionally known to Canadian law, and as long supported by the well-established religious institutions, has been Christian. Consequently, the issues arising in recent years have tended to be in relation to: homosexuality; same-sex marriages; abortion services; and as regards a range of gay,[152] lesbian and transgender[153] matters or the consequences thereof.[154]

One aspect of modern parenting increasingly contributing to the volume of family law litigation, in keeping with the corresponding rate of marital breakdown, is the right of a non-custodial parent to define the religious upbringing of their child, contrary to the wishes of the other parent. The courts have explored the respective rights of the parties in a number of cases,[155] including *Young v. Young*,[156] when the non-custodial parent – a Jehovah's Witness – protested that his freedom of religion, including his right to develop the children's religious beliefs, was being obstructed by the mother. The SCC took the view that the welfare of the child was the overriding principle and therefore the authority of the custodial parent to make decisions over religious activities must be secured in order to protect the children from any harmful stress.

Same-sex marriage

Enacting the Civil Marriage Act 2005 allowed Canada to become the first country outside Europe and the fourth country in the world to legalise same-sex marriage.

The SCC decision in *M. v. H.*[157] paved the way for recognition of the rights of same-sex couples to equal treatment under the Constitution, but not until *Halpern*[158] did the judiciary conclude that the common-law definition of marriage as "the voluntary union for life of one man and one woman to the exclusion of all others" infringed the equality rights of same-sex couples under s.15 of the Charter. It then rejected the claims of a Christian church that to redefine marriage would infringe its freedom of religion, contrary to s.2(a), and its equality rights as a religious institution. This was followed immediately by *Reference Re Same-Sex Marriage*,[159] where the SCC found that the meaning of marriage is not frozen in time, in accordance with its definition under s.91(26) of the Constitution Act 1867, but must be allowed to evolve with Canadian society, which currently represents a plurality of groups, a SCC principle with a capacity for limitless transferred application.

Sexuality and gender

"Being required by someone else's religious beliefs to behave contrary to one's sexual identity is degrading and disrespectful" as the SCC recently and rightly asserted.[160]

Bill C-16, prohibiting discrimination based on gender identity and gender expression throughout Canada, became law in June 2017 and makes it illegal to deny services, employment, accommodation and similar benefits to individuals based on their gender identity or gender expression within a federal-regulated industry. This initiative followed on from cases such as *C.F. v. Alberta*,[161] in which transgendered persons were prevented by state law from having their new gender officially recognised because they had not undergone sex-change surgery. The legislation is significant, as it gives gender identity the status of a separate and distinct human right. It also marks a clear line of departure from the US "liberty laws".

Assisted reproduction, adoption, surrogacy and genetic engineering

Altruistic surrogacy, without payment to the surrogate mother (other than for "expenses"), the creation of embryos for assisted reproduction procedures and the donation of embryos for stem cell research have all been legally possible since the Assisted Human Reproduction Act came into effect in 2004. Same-sex adoption has also become legal in all provinces and territories under varying rules, though in some there remain human rights issues around birth registration and the legal anomalies that necessitate birth parents adopting their own children.

In *Harvard College*,[162] the SCC found that higher life forms are not patentable: patents are applicable to inventions, including for "manufacture", which in turn denotes "a non-living mechanistic product or process".[163] A patent does not apply to "a conscious, sentient living creature"[164] because higher life forms have unique qualities and characteristics that transcend the particular genetic matter of which they are composed. This interesting ruling puts Canadian law at variance with other common-law countries and, it has been argued, the rationale being based upon a differentiation between higher and lower life forms, is "more properly a matter of religion than a matter of law".[165] The SCC adopted much the same rationale in its subsequent *Monsanto*[166] decision, when it confined itself to affirming that Monsanto had patent rights to products and processes if not to the plant itself. The court was plainly aware of the analogous implications for human reproductive research (use of stem cells, cultivation of embryos and so on), as it noted that "inventions in the field of agriculture may give rise to concerns not raised in other fields – moral concerns about whether it is right to manipulate genes".[167]

Right to employment

The Canadian Human Rights Act 1985 lists seven types of discriminatory practice that are prohibited in relation to religion, including: refusing to employ or continue to employ someone, or treating them unfairly in the workplace; following policies or practices that deprive people of employment opportunities; paying men and women differently when they are doing work of the same value; retaliating against a person who has filed a complaint with the Commission or against someone who has filed a complaint for them; and harassment. The legislative intent underpinning the Employment Equity Act 1995 was to achieve equality in the workplace by measures that would, where necessary, effect remedial intervention and accommodate differences.

Hiring/firing staff and religious beliefs

Human rights and religion can clash in the recruitment process. In *Qureshi v. G4S Security Services*,[168] for example, an employer was found to have religiously discriminated against an applicant when the recruitment process was terminated on learning of his need for time off for Friday prayers. Again, in *Widdis v. Desjardins Group*,[169] the Tribunal determined that a Seventh-Day Adventist applicant had suffered religious discrimination during an interview process when, after revealing her unavailability for work on Saturdays, as that day was her Sabbath, she was not called for an additional interview.

Many provincial cases have concerned religious schools and the hiring and firing of teachers and other staff in accordance with religious rules that were found to be bona fide occupational requirements. This was the case in *Caldwell v. St. Thomas Aquinas High School*,[170] for example, where the dismissal of a teacher from a Catholic school was upheld, as she had knowingly disobeyed fundamental Catholic rules, including marrying a divorcee. A rationale subsequently echoed in *Schroen v. Steinbach Bible College*,[171] when the right of a Mennonite College to dismiss a secretary who had converted to become a Mormon, was upheld. In *Daly v. Ontario (Attorney General)*,[172] the court acknowledged that restricting the recruitment of teachers to those of the Catholic faith was a valid consideration. However, the exemption privilege must be exercised reasonably and will not be available in circumstances of peripheral religious significance.[173]

Heintz v. Christian Horizons,[174] a landmark case, concerned a complaint of discrimination by a support worker employed by Christian Horizons who resigned after commencing a same-sex relationship, as she felt she could no longer honour her employer's beliefs but subsequently commenced proceedings alleging discrimination. Ultimately, the court found for the employers and, in an important ruling for all religious organisations in Canada, declared that there is an entitlement to exemption, from the law barring discriminatory hiring, "if they are primarily engaged in serving the interests of their religious community, where the restriction is reasonable and bona fide because of the nature of the employment".

Accommodating religious beliefs/practices in the workplace

In *O'Malley v. Simpson Sears*,[175] an early SCC human rights case, it was determined that a neutral rule requiring employees to work on Saturdays inadvertently discriminated against an employee because of her religious beliefs. This employee was negatively affected by the rule, as she could not, based on her religious beliefs as a Seventh-Day Adventist, work on a Saturday. In finding that her employers could readily have made adjustments to the work rota that would have allowed her to avoid working on a Saturday, the SCC thereby introduced a two-step test to determine whether adverse discrimination is really a *bona fide* occupational requirement and therefore permitted: is the rule/standard rationally connected to the necessities of the job, and have employers accommodated the individual to the point of undue hardship? There have been a number of such cases which have similarly decided that not to accommodate the religious holiday requirements of workers constitutes a form of religious discrimination.[176] In *Dairy Pool*,[177] the SCC found that undue hardship to an employer could take the form of anticipated poor staff morale that would result from having to make the workplace adjustments necessary to accommodate an employee's religious beliefs, while in *McGill University Health Centre*,[178] the court stressed the employer's obligation to customise the accommodation to fit the needs of the employee and the particular circumstances.

Right to education

Education, particularly public education, provides a value-laden context in which religion and human rights frequently intersect. However, as the SCC noted in *Loyola*:[179] "[I]n a multicultural society, it is not a breach of anyone's freedom of religion to be required to learn (or teach) about the doctrines and ethics of other world religions in a neutral and respectful way".[180]

Government funding and religious education: general overview

The Constitution Act 1867, s.93 – as preserved by s.29 of the Charter – explicitly guarantees the rights of denominational schools and thereby preferences Catholic and Protestant schools. These 'denominational privileges' continue in the constitutional obligation to fund Catholic schools in the provinces of Ontario, Alberta and Saskatchewan.[181] To that extent, the Constitution embeds a degree of religious discrimination which violates the human rights of all – including but not restricted to Sikhs, Muslims and atheists – who are thereby disadvantaged.

This archaic anomaly has often given rise to cases alleging religiously biased preferential treatment.[182] Consequently, in 1999 the UNHRC declared that Ontario's policy of fully funding Roman Catholic schools, while denying full funding to other religious schools, was discriminatory. It was of the view that if the State "chooses to provide public funding to religious schools, it should make this funding available without discrimination". Prompted more by cost-effective considerations than anything else, Newfoundland, New Brunswick, Nova Scotia and Prince Edward Island have in recent years moved toward unified secular school systems and no longer fund faith schools, but these continue to be partially publicly funded (typically 40–60 percent) in British Columbia, Alberta, Saskatchewan, Manitoba and Quebec, subject to rudimentary regulatory controls.

Educational facilities: religion, staffing and pupil access

The religious exemption from the constraints of equality and non-discrimination legislation applies to religious organisations that provide, staff and determine pupil access throughout Canada. That blatant religious discrimination will nevertheless not be tolerated was very evident in *Ross*,[183] when the SCC ruled that the removal of a teacher from the classroom was justifiable on the grounds that his distribution of antisemitic material created a poisoned environment for Jewish students and that schoolteachers must be held to a higher standard of behaviour. The court stressed that the freedom of religion is "subject to such limitations as are necessary to protect public safety, order, health or morals, or the fundamental rights and freedoms of others".

The slew of *Trinity Western*[184] cases are illustrative of the commonly accepted truth, as expressed by Iacobucci and Bastarache JJ on behalf of the majority during the SCC stage of those proceedings, that "the freedom to hold beliefs is broader than the freedom to act on them".[185] That case concerned a teacher training college – the Trinity Western University (TWU) – an emanation of the Evangelical Free Church of Canada, which chose to manifest its beliefs in a Community Standards Contract, stating its evangelical Christian values, including abstinence from sex outside marriage and rejection of homosexual relationships, that all students were required to sign. The British Columbia College of Teachers (BCCT) refused TWU accreditation on the basis that that graduates of this private institution would be inadequately prepared to provide educational services without discrimination in B.C.'s diverse public school classrooms. Ultimately, the SCC in a majority ruling held in favour of TWU. It found that the existence of the Community Standards contract, signed by the students, was insufficient to support the BCCT conclusion that TWU graduates would behave in a discriminatory manner toward future homosexual students and that there was no evidence that this in fact had ever occurred. In short, the court upheld the right of TWU to manifest its religious beliefs through its mandatory contract, even though this constituted an act of religious discrimination against those wishing to access its services but were unwilling to subscribe to the contract principles. Subsequently, TWU failed to gain accreditation from the Law Society of Upper Canada for its planned new law school, entry to which would again be via the contract gateway,[186] a decision upheld by the appeal court.[187] This was followed by the BC Court of Appeal ruling that the decision of the Law Society of British Columbia to refuse accreditation to graduates of a proposed TWU law school was unlawful.[188] The court found that the TWU community had a right to hold and act on its beliefs and that in the absence of any evidence of actual harm, this was a legitimate expression of the right to freedom of religion. Most recently, and perhaps finally, the SCC ruled in 2018 that the Law Societies were justified in their accreditation refusal because that decision represented a proportionate balance between the limitation on freedom of religion guaranteed by s.2(a) of the Charter and the statutory objectives pursued by the Law Societies as a regulating authority and was therefore reasonable; any interference with religious freedom was minor and the Law societies were entitled to take the view that the contract imposed "harm" on LGBTQ law students.[189] The majority view was that "it is inimical to the integrity of the legal profession to limit access on the basis of personal characteristics".[190] The dissenting view of the minority included the following:[191]

> In a liberal and pluralist society, the public interest is served, and not undermined, by the accommodation of difference. The unequal access resulting from the Covenant is a function not of condonation of discrimination, but of accommodating religious freedom.

In this instance, that view did not prevail. The debate did, however, highlight the relevance of the *Doré* framework as an assessment tool to aid adjudication where administrative agencies are involved.

State schools, religion and educational content

In *Chamberlain*,[192] the SCC considered the refusal of the Surrey School Board to approve three controversial books depicting same-sex parented families, which had been promoted as supplementary learning resources (as teaching aids in the family life education curriculum). The court found that "children cannot learn unless they are exposed to views that differ from those they are taught at home" and held that Board members, by refusing to permit the use of such books, were imposing their own religious values and seeking to deny children an important learning opportunity. However, it is the *Loyola* case[193] that now stands as a reference point for the competing tensions operating on the religion/human rights interface in Canada. It concerned the Québec government's mandatory core curriculum for high schools, the Program on Ethics and Religious Freedom (ERC), in respect of which Loyola, a Catholic high school, sought permission to teach from a Catholic rather than a neutral perspective. Ultimately, the SCC unanimously found that the refusal to release Loyola in any way from the requirement of strict neutrality in the teaching of the ERC disproportionately interfered with the religious freedom of the Loyola community. It reasoned that "requiring Loyola's teachers to take a neutral posture even about Catholicism means that State is telling them how to teach the very religion that animates Loyola's identity", which amounts to "requiring a Catholic institution to speak about Catholicism in terms defined by the State rather than by its own understanding of Catholicism".[194] In determining that the requirement to teach the ERC violated Loyola's religious freedom, the SCC in effect reprised its earlier ruling in *SL v. Commission scolaire des Chênes*,[195] when it had dismissed the appeal of Catholic parents who requested exemption for their children from the ERC course because its content was considered incompatible with their family beliefs and when it had added that "the early exposure of children to realities that differ from those in their immediate family environment is a fact of life in society".

Faith schools

The reputation of Canadian faith schools has suffered severely from their historical association with Indian residential schools, which were mainly emanations of the Catholic and Anglican churches, funded by the federal government and responsible for grave violations of human rights in the name of religion. In a policy of 'cultural genocide' consolidated by the Indian Act 1876, some 150,000 Aboriginal children were removed from their homes, communities and culture to residential educational institutions. The first such residential school was established in 1620, and the last one was closed in 1986, triggering what is now recognised as "the beginning of an intergenerational cycle of neglect and abuse".[196]

Under s.2(a) of the Charter, parents are said to have the right to oversee the spiritual welfare of their children, and many now do so by enrolling them in faith schools. In *Loyola*,[197] the SCC was clear that such a school – in this case a

Catholic private school – needed to be assured of State protection in order to safeguard "the liberty of the members of its community who have chosen to give effect to the collective dimension of their religious beliefs by participating in a denominational school".[198] This decision has clear implications for other religion-specific schools.

The *Adler* case[199] provides authority for the view that while the Charter creates no constitutional obligation to fund religious schools, neither does it impede State discretion to do so. Iacobucci J stated that the provinces are free to provide funding, and the dissenting L'Heureux-Dubé J added that public funding would "promote the value of religious tolerance in this context where some religious communities cannot be accommodated in the secular system".[200] Roman Catholic schools are by definition faith schools, but rather than forming part of the private sector, they are a wholly incorporated and fully funded component of the public school system.[201]

Right to non-discrimination in service provision

The Canadian Human Rights Act lists seven types of discriminatory service provision that are prohibited in relation to religion, including: denying goods, services, facilities or accommodation; providing goods, services, facilities or accommodation in a way that treats someone adversely and differently; retaliating against a person who has filed a complaint with the Commission or against someone who has filed a complaint for them; and harassment.

Provision by religious organisations

Canadian history reveals a shameful record of service provision by some religious organisations. It shows that the religious residential schools were implementing an enforced assimilation policy from at least the Indian Act 1876[202] and continued to do so for the next century, while records of child sexual abuse by Catholic Church clergy date back to Newfoundland in the 1980s and earlier.

More recently, the *Hall*[203] case concerned a Roman Catholic school board which had refused permission for a same-sex couple to attend a school graduation dance on the grounds that homosexuality is incompatible with Roman Catholic teaching and that any State interference with that decision would amount to denying the school its religious freedom. MacKinnon J, noting that "there is an obvious tension between the individual's free expression and equality rights when contrasted against the equality rights and the religious freedom of Catholic schools", and taking into account that "the Board is, in law, a religiously oriented State actor"[204] but side-stepping constitutional issues, ruled in favour of the plaintiff and ordered the school to admit the couple.

In *Knights of Columbus*,[205] a same-sex couple alleged religious discrimination when their rental application for a facility they wished to use to celebrate their marriage was rejected by the Catholic organisation that owned it. The tribunal concluded that renting out the hall for the purpose for which it was required would have forced the organisation to act against its religious beliefs and would breach its rights under s.2(a) of the Charter. Nevertheless, the organisation was fined, as it had failed in its duty of reasonable accommodation, as no consideration had been given to the consequences for the couple, and no attempt had been made to meet with them and explain the reasons for rejection.

Provision of public services

Religion is often a cause of public service disruption. Most recently, Bill 62, which was passed by the Liberal Quebec government in October 2017, arguably challenges Charter principles: s.10 requires Muslim women to remove face coverings in order to give and receive public services, such as accessing city transport; and s. 20 disqualifies child care providers, who engage in religious prayer or practices, from eligibility for public subsidies. Although the legislative intent is, purportedly, to foster adherence to State religious neutrality, as some provisions negatively impact upon particular religious groups, it may well be open to challenge on grounds of religious discrimination. On a nationwide basis, the Canada Summer Jobs program, which provides funding to help small businesses and charities create summer jobs for students, is also causing dissension. Changes recently introduced now require Canadian employers to "attest" that both their jobs and their "core mandate" "respect" certain "values" identified by the federal government, including access to abortion. Arguably, both Bill 62 and the Summer Jobs program penalise certain groups because of their religious beliefs, and by denying them the rights and benefits enjoyed by others, they may be guilty of religious discrimination. Disruption may also be caused by those whose religious beliefs, or lack thereof, motivate them to withhold or withdraw from particular services. As mentioned above, this has been very evident in abortion services, in family planning and in officiating at gay marriages.[206]

Teaching has also proven to be a sensitive area. In the above-mentioned *Ross* case,[207] the SCC ultimately upheld the decision of a Board of Inquiry that the Board of School Trustees had discriminated with respect to a public service because it failed to take appropriate action against the teacher. Most prominent, however, has been the above-mentioned case of *Trinity Western University v. British Columbia College of Teachers*,[208] which graphically illustrates the difficulties that can arise when the provision of an education service conflicts with religious principle.

Private goods and service provision

In Canada, as elsewhere, the provision of commercial services can provide a context for discrimination which is often rooted in a conflation of religious belief and sexual orientation. In *Brillinger v. Brockie*,[209] this involved the competing claims of sexual orientation discrimination and violation of freedom of religion. The Ontario Board of Inquiry found that Brockie, a born-again Christian, had discriminated against Brillinger (and the Canadian Lesbian and Gay Archives) on the prohibited ground of sexual orientation by refusing to provide printing services to homosexuals and homosexual organisations and ordered Brockie and his company to provide the same printing services to them as they provided to others. However, on appeal, the Ontario Superior Court of Justice held that the Board's order went further than was necessary and added a condition to the effect that the order should not require Brockie to print material of a nature that could reasonably be considered to be in direct conflict with the core elements of his religious beliefs. A judicial comment on this added caveat has noted that "on the above approach the believer is not required to undertake action that promotes that which the essence of the belief teaches to be wrong".[210]

In *Smith and Chymyshyn v. Knights of Columbus and others*,[211] the Tribunal found that the respondent's hall did meet the definition of a "service" or "facility" and dismissed the respondent's argument that in the light of their belief system and their own right to freedom of religion they could refuse to rent that hall for the celebration of a gay marriage. Again, in *Eadie and Thomas v. Riverbend Bed and Breakfast and others*,[212] a gay couple had reserved a room in a bed-and-breakfast accommodation offered by a Christian couple in their own home, but when the husband learned that the couple were gay, the booking was cancelled. The Tribunal ruled in favour of the gay couple who had been denied a service because the provider had unlawfully discriminated against them.

Service denial on grounds of conscientious objection

The above cases of *Brockie*, *Eadie* and *Moore*[213] are among the many instances where service refusal by individual providers, on the grounds of their conscientious objection to the values represented by prospective service users, have resulted in the former being found to have violated the human rights of the latter. The rationale being that generic laws of universal application cannot allow exceptions if their effect is to wholly negate legislative intent. However, the SCC in *Loyola* and the *TWU* cases can be seen wrestling with the issue of whether accommodation can be made for pockets of institutional beliefs that run counter to legislative intent. Building on the *C. v. A.*[214] decision, it may prove to be a short step to the "liberty laws" that now make allowances for individuals in the US to claim exemption from universal laws on grounds of conscientious objection.

Broadcasting services

Religious broadcasting has been a controversial issue for Canadian public law since the early days of radio in the 1920s and 1930s.[215] More recently, there have been a number of provincial cases involving individuals placing advertisements in newspapers protesting about LGBT issues. One such advertisement was *Owens*,[216] where the court ruled that although an advertisement connecting Bible verses related to homosexuality with gay marriage was "offensive and jarring to many", it did not constitute an offence. The court did, however, warn that statements designed to provoke "extreme emotions and strong feelings of detestation, calumny and vilification" may be deemed hate speech.[217] In *Dagenais*,[218] the leading Canadian case on the conflict between freedom of expression[219] and publication bans on trial information, the SCC stated:[220]

> Publication bans, however, should not always be seen as a clash between freedom of expression for the media and the right to a fair trial for the accused. The clash model is more suited to the American constitutional context and should be rejected in Canada.

Conclusion

Bill 62 and the Summer Jobs program, when considered alongside the SSC ruling in the latest of the Trinity Western cases,[221] would seem to indicate that Canada is distancing itself from the "liberty laws" approach currently being developed in the US and beginning to take shape in the UK. Although this is in line with other judicial reminders of the differences between Canadian and US society – resting largely on Canadian rejection of the US "melting pot" social policy – it may not prevail in the face of what appear to be strong social forces pushing back on the moral imperatives that have become aligned with equality legislation. As the "conscientious objection" jurisprudence builds up in other countries, it is becoming increasingly credible as a rationale for challenging what some see as the prescriptive dictates of equality provisions and is gaining traction as an argument for facilitating diversity in a democratic society.

Certainly, for so long as the 'denominational privileges' continue in the form of a constitutional obligation to fund schools in Ontario on an exclusively religious basis, the role of the Canadian State in relation to the religion/human rights intersect will differ from that of its neighbour.

Notes

1 See *Waldman v. Canada*, Communication No. 694/1996.
2 See, for example, *R. v. S. (R.D.)* (1997), 118 CCC (3d) 353 (SCC), per Cory, J., at p. 385.
3 [1986] 1 SCR 103.
4 *Doré v. Barreau du Québec*, 2012 SCC 12.
5 *Loyola High School v. Québec (Attorney General)*, 2015 SCC 12.
6 See Guy, T.R., 'Opening the Doré to Proportionality: Discretionary Administrative Decisions and the Charter', LLM thesis, University of Toronto, 2015, p. 1, at: https://tspace.library.utoronto.ca/bitstream/1807/69099/3/Guy_Trevor_R_201503_LLM_thesis.pdf.
7 Author acknowledges advice from Matt Harrington on this matter (note to author, 6 August 2018).
8 *R v. Laws* (1998) 41 OR (3d) 499 Ont. CA, per McMurtry, C.J.O., at para. 24.
9 The Canadian Multiculturalism Act 1985 and the Canadian Race Relations Foundation Act 1991 have also set benchmarks for legislation at provincial and territorial level.

10 See UN International Covenant on Civil and Political Rights, *Concluding Observations on the Sixth Periodic Report of Canada*, at: http://tbinternet.ohchr.org/_layouts/treatybodyexternal/SessionDetails1.aspx?SessionID=899&Lang=en#sthash.XzzyC1Bz.dpuf.
11 Ibid., at para. 15.
12 See 'Taking Action against Systemic Racism and Religious Discrimination Including Islamophobia', presented to Parliament 1 February 2018, at: www.ourcommons.ca/DocumentViewer/en/42-1/CHPC/report-10/.
13 *Trinity Western University v. Nova Scotia Barristers' Society* [2015] NSSC 25, at para. 19. See also Moon, R., *Law and Religious Pluralism in Canada*, UBC Press, Canada, 2008, at p. 231.
14 *R. v. Big M. Drug Mart* [1985] 1 SCR 295.
15 *Zylberberg v. Sudbury Board of Education* (1988) 65 OR.
16 *Canadian Civil Liberties Association v. Ontario (Minister of Education)* (1990), 71 O.R. (2d) 341.
17 [2012] 1 SCR 235, at para.10.
18 *Mouvement laïque québécois v. Saguenay (City)* [2015] 2 SCR 3. See also *Congrégation des témoins de Jéhovah de St-Jérôme- Lafontaine v. Lafontaine (Village)* [2004] S.C.J. No. 45 [2004] 2 S.C.R. 650, per LeBel, J., at paras. 67–68, 76.
19 *Congrégation des témoins de Jéhovah de St-Jérôme-Lafontaine v. Lafontaine (Village)*, 2004 SCC 48 [2004] 2 S.C.R. 650, per LeBel, J., at para. 67.
20 See further Ryder, B., 'State Neutrality and Freedom of Conscience and Religion', *Supreme Court Law Review*, 2005, pp. 178–194.
21 [1986] 2 S.C.R. 284, at pp. 313–314.
22 *Alberta v. Hutterian Brethren of Wilson Colony* 2009 SCC 37 [2009] 2 SCR 567.
23 (1988), 65 O.R. (2d) 641, 29 O.A.C. 23 (CA).
24 (1989), 35 B.C.L.R. (2d) 29. See also *Freitag v. Penetanguishene (Town)* (1999), 47 O.R. (3d) 301.
25 Mouvement laïque québécois, op. cit.
26 Ibid., at para. 118.
27 *Law Society of BC v. Trinity Western University,* 2018 SCC 32, at para. 318, citing in support: *Amselem*, at paras. 56, 65; *Multani*, at para. 34; *Loyola*, at para. 134 and *Ktunaxa*, at para. 68.
28 *R. v. Big M. Drug Mart* [1985] 1 SCR 295, at para. 95.
29 *Syndicat Northcrest v. Amselem* [2004] 2 SCR 551.
30 See, for example, *Rosenberg v. Outremont (City)* (2001), File No. 500-05-060659-008. See also *Chamberlain v. Surrey School District No. 36*, 2002 SCC 86.
31 2015 SCC 12.
32 Ibid., at paras. 43–44. See further at: www.carters.ca/pub/seminar/charity/2015/Renderings2015.pdf.
33 *Ktunaxa Nation v. British Columbia* [2017] SCC 54, at para. 71.
34 *Law Society of BC v. Trinity Western University*, 2018 SCC 32 and *Trinity Western University (TWU) v. Law Society of Upper Canada*, 2018 SCC 33.
35 *Law Society of BC v. Trinity Western University*, op. cit., at para. 40.
36 Ibid., at para. 134.
37 *Congrégation des témoins de Jéhovah de St-Jérôme-Lafontaine v. Lafontaine (Village)* [2004] 2 SCR 650, 2004 SCC 48.
38 *Syndicat Northcrest v. Amselem*, op. cit., per Iacobucci, J., at para. 50.
39 *Bentley v. Anglican Synod of the Diocese of New Westminster* 2009 BCSC 1608 (CanLII).
40 See. *Syndicat Northcrest v. Amselem* [2004] 2 SCR 551, per Iacobucci, J., at para. 67.

41 2013 ONSC 1363.
42 Ibid., per Edwards, J., at p. 22J.
43 *Ktunaxa Nation v. British Columbia*, op. cit.
44 2018 SCC 26. Author thanks Matt Harrington for advice on this case (note to author, 6 August 2018).
45 2014 SCC 44. See also *Delgamuukw v. British Columbia.* [1997] 3 SCR 1010.
46 *Ktunaxa Nation*, at para. 8.
47 *R. v. Big M. Drug Mart* [1985] 1 SCR 295.
48 Ibid., at para. 354.
49 *Mouvement laïque québécois v. Saguenay (City)* [2015] 2 SCR 3.
50 *Big M.*, op. cit., at para. 337.
51 *Mouvement laïque québécois*, op. cit., at paras. 69, 76.
52 Ibid., at para. 78.
53 See, for example, *Canada Trust Co. v. Ontario Human Rights Commission* (1990) 69 DLR (4th) 321, per Tarnopolsky, J., at para. 98.
54 SC 2005, c. 33.
55 RSC 1985, (5th Supp.), c. 1, as amended.
56 [2004] 3 SCR 698.
57 2015 NSSC 25, at para. 10 and endorsed in *Law Society of British Columbia v. Trinity Western University* 2018 SCC 32, at para. 335.
58 See CRA, 'Religious Charities – Exemption', *Policy Commentary*, CPC – O16, (17 October 2003).
59 (1894), 26 N.S.R. 164 at 166.
60 *Canada Trust Co. v. Ontario Human Rights Commission* (1990) 69 DLR (4th) 321.
61 Ibid., Harrington comments: "[T]the majority did not go as far as Tranopolsky. He argued that discrimination is illegal. That is not what the majority said. On the contrary, it said that *this trust* was illegal. It limited the decision to the facts of the case and refused to draw any larger conclusion." (note to author, 6 August 2018).
62 (1996) 139 DLR (4th) 746.
63 Ibid., at para. 13, per MacDonald, C.J.T.D.
64 [1996] O.J. No. 375 (Ont. C.A.).
65 2016 ONCA 196. Author acknowledges advice from Matt Harrington on this matter (note to author, 6 April 2017).
66 See, for example: *R. v. Big M. Drug Mart Ltd.* [1985] 1 SCR 295, at p. 337; *SL v. Commission scolaire des Chênes* [2012] 1 SCR 235, at para. 17, and *Mouvement laïque québécois*, op. cit., at paras. 64, 80.
67 *Mouvement laïque*, op. cit., at para. 64.
68 [1996] SCR 609.
69 Section 93 of the Constitution Act 1867 was deemed by Iacobucci J to be "immune from Charter scrutiny".
70 30 & 31 Victoria, c. 3.
71 *Mouvement laïque québécois v. Saguenay (City)* [2015] 2 SCR 3, at para. 64.
72 Ibid., at para. 88.
73 *R. v. Big M. Drug Mart* [1985] 1 SCR 295, per Dickson, C.J.
74 *Ktunaxa Nation v. British Columbia* [2017] SCC 54, at para. 68.
75 See *R. v. Big M*, op. cit. and *R v. Edwards Books and Art Ltd* [1986] 2 SCR 713.
76 See *Congrégation des témoins de Jéhovah de St-Jérôme- Lafontaine v. Lafontaine (Village)* [2004] 2 S.C.R. 650, 2004 SCC 48, per LeBel, J., who described freedom of religion as imposing "a duty of state neutrality."
77 Op. cit., per McLachlin, C.J.
78 [1985] 1 SCR 295. Citing Tarnopolski, J., in *R. v. Videoflicks Ltd.* (1984), 48 O.R. (2d) 395 (C.A.).

79 *R. v. Big M. Drug Mart*, op. cit., per Dickson, J., at p. 336. See also *R v. Edwards Books and Art Ltd* [1986] 2 SCR 713.
80 (2004) 2 SCR 576, at para. 39.
81 See *Morgentaler v. R* [1988] 1 SCR 30.
82 Ibid., at para. 251.
83 [2002] F.C.J. No. 72, 210 D.L.R. (4th) 186 (T.D.).
84 *Huang v. 1233065 Ontario*, 2011 HRTO 825 (CanLII).
85 *Re O.P.S.E.U. and Forer* (1985), 52 O.R. (2d) 705 (CA).
86 In *R.C. (Next friend of) v. District School Board of Niagara*, 013 HRTO 1382.
87 Ibid.
88 Ibid., at para. 43. See also *S.L. v. Commission scolaire des Chênes*, 2012 SCC 7 [2012] 1 S.C.R. 235.
89 *Syndicat Northcrest v. Amselem* [2004] 2 SCR 551, at para. 52.
90 *Law Society of BC v. Trinity Western University*, 2018 SCC 32, per Côté, J.J. and Brown, J.J., at para. 317, citing *Syndicat Northcrest v. Amselem*, 2004 SCC 47 [2004] 2 S.C.R. 551, at para. 47.
91 2015 SCC 16.
92 At para. 70. But there are limits, see *Blackmore v. The Queen* 2013 TCC 264 (CanLII).
93 *Alberta v. Hutterian Brethren of Wilson Colony*, op. cit., at para. 89.
94 *Kelly v. British Columbia (Public Safety and Solicitor General)* (No.3), 2011 BCHRT 183 (CanLII).
95 *Kruger and Manuel v. The Queen* (1977) [1978] 1 SCR 104, 75 DLR (3d) 434; *Simon v. The Queen (*1985) [1985] 2 SCR 387, 62 N.R.366; *Arthur Dick v. The Queen (*1985) [1985] 2 SCR 309, 62 N.R. 1 [1986] 1 W.W.R.1; and *Jack and Charlie v. The Queen (*1985) [1985] 2 SCR 332, 62 N.R. 14 [1986] 1 W.W.R.21.
96 *Syndicat Northcrest v. Amselem*, op. cit., at para. 137.
97 *Akiyama v. Judo B.C. (No. 2)* (2002), 43 C.H.R.R. D/425, 2002 BCHRT 27.
98 *Laws*, op. cit., at para. 23.
99 See *Re Canada Trust Co v. Ontario (Human Rights Commission)*; *Re Leonard Foundation; Canada Trust Co v. Ontario Human Rights Commission* (1990) 69 DLR (4th) 321.
100 See above-mentioned *Spence v. BMO Trust Company* 2016 ONCA 196. See also *Royal Trust Corporation of Canada v. The University of Western Ontario et al.*, 2016 ONSC 1143. Author acknowledges advice from Matt Harrington on this matter (note to author, 6 April 2017).
101 *S.L. v. Commission scolaire des Chênes*, 2012 SCC 7, at paras. 22–24.
102 *Mouvement laïque québécois v. Saguenay (City)* [2015] 2 SCR 3, at para. 116.
103 2015 SCC 1, at para. 64.
104 [1992] 3 SCR 165.
105 2016 ABCA 255 (CanLII).
106 Note to author, 68 August 2018.
107 *R. v. Big M. Drug Mart*, op. cit., per Dickson, J., at para. 124.
108 [2000] B.C.J. No. 520.
109 *R. v. Keegstra* [1990] 3 SCR 697.
110 (1996), 25 C.H.R.R. D/175 (SCC).
111 18 October 2000, Communication No. 736/1997 (UN Human Rights Committee).
112 *Alberta v. Hutterian Brethren of Wilson Colony*, op. cit., at para. 89.
113 *Syndicat Northcrest v. Amselem*, op. cit.
114 *Multani v. Commission Scolaire Marguerite-Bourgeoys* [2006] 1 S.C.R. 256, 2006 SCC 6.

115 See *Whitehouse v. Yukon* (2001), 48 C.H.R.R. D/497 (Y.T.Bd.Adj.).
116 *Boisson v. Lund* 2009 ABQB 592.
117 [2013] 1 SCR 467.
118 *Trinity Western University v. British Columbia College of Teachers* (2001), 39 C.H.R.R. D/357. 2001 SCC 31.
119 *Saadi v. Audmax* 2009 HRTO 1627.
120 Marie-Claude Landry, *Chief Commissioner, Canadian Human Rights Commission*, (20 October 2017), at: www.newswire.ca/news-releases/quebecs-face-covering-law-could-stray-into-federal-human-rights-jurisdiction-651935633.html.
121 *R. v. N.S.* 2010 ONCA 670 (CanLII).
122 *Elzahed v. State of New South Wales* [2018] NSWCA 103.
123 *Multani v. Commission scolaire Marguerite-Bourgeoys*, op. cit. See also *Singh v. Attorney General of Quebec*, 2018 QCCA 257.
124 Ibid., at p. 297.
125 *Nijjar v. Canada 3000 Airlines Ltd* 1999 CANLII (CHRT).
126 See, for example: *Grant v. Canada* [1996] 1 SCR vii, 130 DLR (4th) vii and *Peel Board of Education v. Pandori* (1991) 3 OR (3D) 531 (Div Ct).
127 *Randhawa v. Tequila Bar & Grill Ltd* 2008 AHRC 3 (CanLII).
128 [1992] 2 SCR 731.
129 *Friesen v. Fisher Bay Seafood* (2008), 65 C.H.R.R. D/400, 2009 BCHRT 1.
130 [1995] 1 SCR 315, at para. 226.
131 Ibid., citing *R. v. Zundel*, 1992 CanLII 75 (SCC) [1992] 2 SCR 731, at pp. 753, 801; *R. v. Keegstra*, 1990 CanLII 24 (SCC) [1990] 3 SCR 697, at pp. 732, 830.
132 *Moore v. British Columbia (Ministry of Social Services)* (1992), 17 C.H.R.R. D/426 (B.C.C.H.R).
133 (2002), 43 C.H.R.R. D/395, 2992 BCHRT 23.
134 (1989) 1 SCR 143.
135 2014 SCC 7.
136 Ibid., at paras. 1–2.
137 (2007) 3 SCR.
138 Ibid., at p. 3.
139 See further at: www.ourcommons.ca/Parliamentarians/en/members/Iqra-Khalid(88849)/Motions?documentId=8661986&sessionId=152.
140 See *Roger Judge v. Canada,* Communication No. 829/1998CCPR/C/78/D/829/1998.
141 E.g., *Human Life International in Canada Inc. v. Canada (Minister of National Revenue)* FCJ No. 365, 18 March 1998 *and Alliance for Life v. Canada (MNR)* 1999 FCJ No. 658, 5 May 1999.
142 See *Positive Action against Pornography v. MNR* [1988] 1 CTC 232.
143 See *Interfaith Development Education Association, Burlington v. MNR*, 97 DTC 5424.
144 *Everywoman's Health Centre Society (1988) v. Canada (MNR)* [1991] 136 NR 380.
145 *Tremblay v. Daigle* [1989] 2 SCR 530, at p. 533.
146 Including *R v. Morgentaler* [1988] 1 SCR 30 and *R. v. Morgentaler* 1993 CanLII 74 [1993] 3 SCR 463. Also see *Borowski v. Canada (Attorney General)* [1989] 1 SCR 342 and *Tremblay v. Daigle*, op. cit.
147 As cited in Dávila, I., 'Access to Abortion: An International Human Rights Perspective on Canadian Law', at: http://claihr.ca/2018/01/10/access-to-abortionan-international-human-rights-perspective-on-canadian-law/.
148 *Starson v. Swayze* [2003] SCC 32.
149 [1993] 2 SCR 119.

150 (1992), 10 O.R. (3d) 321 Ontario Court of Appeal.
151 2015 SCC 5.
152 See *Egan v. Canada* (1995) 2 SCR 513 where a statutory definition of "spouse" which excluded homosexual partners was deemed to discriminate against a homosexual couple.
153 See, for example, *Vancouver Rape Relief Society v. Nixon*, 2005 BCCA 601.
154 See *P. (S.E.) v. P. (D.D.)*, 2005 BCSC 1290 where the British Columbia Supreme Court ruled that the definition of adultery should include affairs between two people of the same gender.
155 *Hockey v. Hockey* (1989) 60 D.L.R. (4th) 765 (Ont. Div. Ct.). P.*(D.) v. S.(C.)* [1993] 4 S.C.R. 141 and *Young v. Young* [1993] 4 SCR 3.
156 [1993] 4 SCR 3.
157 [1999] 2 SCR 3.
158 *Halpern v. Canada (Attorney General)* [2003] O.J. No. 2268.
159 [2004] 3 SCR 698.
160 *Law Society of BC v. Trinity Western University*, 2018 SCC 32, at para. 101.
161 [2014] ABQB 237.
162 *Harvard College v. Canada (Commissioner of Patents)* [2002] 4 SCR 45, 2002 SCC 76.
163 Ibid., at para. 159.
164 Ibid., at para. 160.
165 See Burk, D.L., 'Reflections in a Darkling Glass: A Comparative Contemplation of the Harvard College Decision Symposium on the Harvard Mouse Decision of the Supreme Court of Canada', *Canadian Business Law Journal*, Vol. 39, 2004, at p. 221
166 *Monsanto v. Schmeiser* [2004] 1 SCR 902, 2004 SCC 34.
167 Ibid., at para. 93.
168 2009 HRTO 409 (CanLII).
169 2013 HRTO 1367.
170 (1984), 6 C.H.R.R. D/2643. See also *Sahota and Shergill v. Shri Gur Ravidass Sabha Temple*, 2008 BCHRT 269 which concerned the exclusion of members of a caste from a religious organisation representing a different caste.
171 (1999), 35 C.H.R.R. D/1 (Man. Bd. Adj.).
172 44 O.R. (3d) 349 [1999] O.J. No. 1383.
173 *Hall (Litigation guardian of) v. Powers* (2002) 59 O.R. (3d) 423.
174 2008 HRTO 22, 2010 ONSC 2105 (Div. Ct.).
175 [1985] 2 SCR 536.
176 For example, *Chambly (Commission scholaire régionale) v. Bergevin* [1994] 2 R.C.S. 525 and *HT v. ES Holdings Inc. o/a Country Herbs*, 2015 HRTO 1067.
177 *Central Alberta Dairy Pool v. Alberta (Human Rights Comm.)* (1990), 12 CHRR D/417 (SCC).
178 *McGill University Health Centre (Montreal General Hospital) v. Syndicat des employés de l'Hôpital général de Montréal* 2007 SCC 4 [2007] 1 SCR 161.
179 *Loyola High School v. Québec (Attorney General)* (2015) SCC 12.
180 Ibid., per Deschamps, J., citing *SL v. Commission scolaire des Chênes* [2012] 1 SCR 235, at para. 40.
181 Note also that many Canadian universities, including St. Francis Xavier University, Queen's University, McGill University and Concordia University College of Alberta, have long been religiously affiliated.
182 See, for example: *Tiny Township Catholic Separate Schools Trustees v. The Queen* (1928) A. C. 363; *Attorney General of Quebec v. Greater Hull School Board* [1984] 2 SCR 575; *Reference Re Bill 30* [1987] 1 SCR 1148; *Adler v. Ontario* [1996] SCR 609; and *Waldman v. Canada*, Comm No. 694/1996.

183 *Ross v. New Brunswick School Dist. No. 15* [1996] 1 S.C.R. 825.
184 *Trinity Western University v. British Columbia College of Teachers* (2001), 39 C.H.R.R. D/357. 2001 SCC 31.
185 *Trinity Western University v. British Columbia College of Teachers*, op. cit., at paras. 36–37.
186 *Trinity Western University (TWU) v. Law Society of BC* 2015 BCSC 2326.
187 *Trinity Western University (TWU) v. Law Society of Upper Canada* 2016 ONCA 518.
188 *Trinity Western University v. Law Society of British Columbia* 2016 BCCA 423.
189 *Law Society of BC v. Trinity Western University* (2018) SCC 32 and *Trinity Western University (TWU) v. Law Society of Upper Canada* (2018) SCC 33.
190 Ibid., per Abella, Moldaver, Karakatsanis, Wagner and Gascon, J.J., at para. 21.
191 Ibid., Côté, J.J. and Brown, J.J., at para. 81.
192 *Chamberlain v. Surrey School Board District 36* (2002), 221 D.L.R. (4th) 156 (SCC), at para. 19. Also, see *Hall v. Powers* (2002).
193 *Loyola High School v. Québec (Attorney General)* (2015) SCC 12.
194 Ibid., at para. 63.
195 [2012] 1 SCR 235.
196 See Saskatchewan Child Welfare Review Panel Report, 'For the Good of Our Children and Youth: A New Vision, a New Direction', at p. 18. See further at: http://saskchildwelfarereview.ca/CWR-panel-report.pdf.
197 *Loyola*, op. cit.
198 Ibid., at para. 62.
199 *Adler v. Ontario* [1996] 3 RCS 609.
200 Ibid., at para.10.
201 Matt Harrington adds: "Québec is a bit of an exception. Most of the province's Catholic schools were assimilated into the public system and function as public schools with religious names. However, the identifiable Catholic schools remain (Loyola, Marymount, Villa Maria, etc). These remain separate, private Catholic schools, but they still receive a large public subsidy" (note to author, 6 August 2018).
202 Not until 2008 did Parliament amend the Canadian Human Rights Act to give full human rights protection to those subject to the Indian Act.
203 *Hall v. Durham Catholic School Board* [2002] OJ No. 1803.
204 Ibid., at para. 57.
205 *Smith and Chymyshyn v. Knights of Columbus and others* 2005 BCHRT 544 (CanLII). See also *Whiteley v. Osprey Media Publishing*, 2010 HRTO 2152 (CanLII).
206 *Nichols v. M.J.* (2009) SKQB 299. Also, see *Marriage Commissioners Appointed Under The Marriage Act (Re)* (2011) SKCA 3 (CanLII).
207 *Ross v. New Brunswick School Dist. No. 15* (1996), 25 CHRR D/175 (SCC).
208 (2001), 39 C.H.R.R. D/357. 2001 SCC 31.
209 (No. 3) (2000), 37 C.H.R.R. D/15).
210 See *Christian Institute and Others v. Office of First Minister and Deputy First Minister*, Neutral Citation no. [2007] NIQB 66, per Weatherup, J., at para. 88.
211 2005 BCHRT 544 (CanLII). See also *Whiteley v. Osprey Media Publishing*, 2010 HRTO 2152 (CanLII).
212 *(No. 2)* 2012 BCHRT 247.
213 *Moore v. British Columbia (Ministry of Social Services)* (1992), 17 C.H.R.R. D/426 (B.C.C.H.R).
214 (2002), 43 C.H.R.R. D/395, 2992 BCHRT 23.
215 See Cook, P.G., 'Balance and Freedom of Speech: Challenge for Canadian Broadcasting', *Canadian Journal of Communication*, Vol. 17:1, 1992, at: www.cjc-online.ca/index.php/journal/article/view/647/553.

216 *Owens v. Saskatchewan (Human Rights Commission)* (2006).
217 See also *Ross v. New Brunswick School District No. 15* [1996] 1 SCR 825.
218 *Dagenais v. Canadian Broadcasting Corp* [2004] 3 S.C.R. 698, 2004 SCC 79.
219 See *Edmonton Journal v. Alberta (Attorney-General)* (1989), 64 D.L.R. (4th) 577 (SCC).
220 Ibid., at p. 839.
221 *Law Society of BC v. Trinity Western University* (2018) SCC 32 and *Trinity Western University (TWU) v. Law Society of Upper Canada* (2018), SCC 33.

7 Australia

Introduction

Following the format adopted in the preceding jurisdiction-specific chapters, this chapter begins by outlining the current domestic and international legal framework governing the relationship between religion and human rights. It then examines the State and human rights/religion intersect, giving particular attention to the established State support for Christian institutions as compared with its scant regard for the culture and beliefs of Indigenous People. This leads into a study of the case law that defines and illustrates the Australian interpretation of the freedom of religion and identifies the issues arising as that freedom traverses those of association and expression. Finally, the chapter considers the religion-related case law generated by equality and non-discrimination legislation as this intersects with the human rights of access to justice, to life, to marriage and to found a family, to employment, to obtain an education and to non-discrimination in accessing services.

Current legal framework

As has been noted, "Australia is largely alone among liberal democracies in taking a piecemeal, rather than a comprehensive, approach in the incorporation of its international human rights obligations into domestic law".[1]

International legislation

Human rights are statutorily defined at the federal level[2] to mean the rights and freedoms recognised or declared by: the International Convention on the Elimination of All Forms of Racial Discrimination 1965; the International Covenant on Economic, Social and Cultural Rights 1966; the International Covenant on Civil and Political Rights 1966; the Convention on the Elimination of All Forms of Discrimination against Women 1979; the Convention against Torture and Other Cruel, Inhuman or Degrading Treatment or Punishment 1984; the Convention on the Rights of the Child 1989; and the Convention on the Rights of Persons with Disabilities 2006. Australia is a party to all the above.

The International Covenant on Civil and Political Rights (ICCPR)

Ratified in 1980, although not assimilated into its domestic law, ICCPR provisions and the UPR process are fully binding upon Australia, and the country has acceded to Optional Protocol 1.[3] Article 18(1) protects the right to manifest religion or belief, which is further endorsed by the Declaration on the Elimination of All Forms of Intolerance and of Discrimination Based on Religion or Belief.[4] The ICCPR is supplemented by General Comment 22 (see also Chapter 2).

Other

Australia initially voted against adopting the UN Declaration on the Rights of Indigenous People 2007 but ultimately removed its objections in 2009 (see further Chapter 2). Also, because of the tendency for Australian litigation to conflate matters of racial and religious discrimination, ICERD has considerable relevance (see further Chapter 2).

The Constitution and domestic legislation

Australia has the distinction of having neither a national human rights statute nor a constitutional bill of rights. This singularity regularly attracts protests, most recently from the Australian Human Rights Commission (AHRC).[5]

The Constitution

Neither religion nor human rights are among the "heads of power" available to Parliament for legislative purposes. While this does not prevent Parliament legislating on some aspects of such matters, it can only do so incidentally. Although the Constitution does not contain a "bill of rights" it does provide, directly or implicitly, for certain rights and freedoms. For present purposes, the most relevant of these is s.116 which states:

> The Commonwealth shall not make any law for establishing any religion, or for imposing any religious observance, or for prohibiting the free exercise of any religion, and no religious test shall be required as a qualification for any office or public trust under the Commonwealth.

The limitations of this provision have often been noted, as has the fact that it applies only to the Commonwealth. Moreover, as Barwick CJ once explained, s.116 is "directed to the making of law . . . not . . . the administration of a law".[6]

The Marriage Amendment (Definition and Religious Freedoms) Act 2017 (Cth)

This statute amended the Marriage Act 1961, changing the definition of marriage and the protection of religious freedom to allow marriage between two persons of marriageable age regardless of their gender.

Sex Discrimination Amendment (Sexual Orientation, Gender Identity and Intersex Status) Act 2013 (Cth)

Amending the Sex Discrimination Act 1984, this statute makes it unlawful under federal law to discriminate against a person on the basis of sexual orientation, gender identity and intersex status.

The Human Rights (Parliamentary Scrutiny) Act 2011

This took effect on 4 January 2012 and requires all new legislation introduced to the Federal Parliament to be assessed for compatibility with human rights. It also established a new parliamentary joint committee on human rights, and a National Action Plan for implementing related commitments was launched in 2012. The Act implemented "Australia's Human Rights Framework" but did not create a Charter of Rights.

The Fair Work Act 2009 (Cth)

This protects freedom of association and extends the specific legal protection previously given to religious non-discrimination in the workplace.[7]

The Human Rights and Equal Opportunity Commission Act 1986 (Cth)

This statute established the Human Rights and Equal Opportunity Commission which, in 2008, was renamed the Australian Human Rights Commission (AHRC). It implements Australia's human rights obligations under the International Labour Organization Convention (No. 111) concerning Discrimination in Respect of Employment and Occupation. The Commission has the function of inquiring into and attempting to reach a settlement of complaints through conciliation.

The Sex Discrimination Act 1984 (Cth)

As amended, this legislation prohibits discrimination on the basis of sex, marital or relationship status, actual or potential pregnancy, sexual orientation, gender identity, intersex status or breastfeeding in a range of areas of public life.

The Racial Discrimination Act 1975 (Cth)

For clarification as to what constitutes "discrimination", s.9 refers to the rights established in Article 5 of ICERD, while s.10 establishes a general right to equality before the law. Section 18(c) prohibits speech that insults, offends or humiliates people based on their race. If a religious group can also be classified as an "ethnic" group, the racial hatred provisions may then cover direct and indirect discrimination and vilification against it or its members. Even if a religious group cannot be classified in that way, the Act may cover discrimination on the basis of religion in certain circumstances such as indirect race discrimination. In *Jones v. Scully*,[8] the court found that Jews constitute an ethnic group for the purposes of this statute and their vilification constitutes racial discrimination.[9]

Other legislation

At the federal level, equality and anti-discrimination provisions are to be found in a range of legislation of which some, such as the Fair Work Act 2009 (Cth), offer limited protection against discrimination on the basis of religious belief. In November 2012, the government released a draft of its Human Rights and Anti-Discrimination Bill 2012, but the Bill was suspended and the government settled for amending the more deficient features of the Sex Discrimination Act.

At the state and territory level: there are various laws that prohibit the vilification of persons, singularly or as a group, on the basis of their religion (Queensland, Tasmania and Victoria), while all except New South Wales and South Australia have legislation that makes "religious belief" a prohibited ground.

International courts and regulatory bodies

Australian judicial decisions are not amenable to any international judicial oversight. Australia is, however, subject to the HRC monitoring role conducted through the Universal Periodic Review process.

Domestic courts and regulatory bodies

The states and territories of Australia each have their own hierarchy of courts and tribunals with a right of appeal to a supreme court and thereafter to a federal court.

The High Court of Australia (HCA)

This is the supreme court and final court of appeal. Its federal jurisdiction is derived from authority vested in it by the Constitution, s.75 and s.76, and its appellate jurisdiction is defined by s.73. Appeals lie to it from the Federal Court of Australia (FCA).

The Federal Court of Australia (FCA)

This superior court has jurisdiction to deal with most civil disputes governed by federal law. It includes an appeal division, the Full Court, comprised of three judges.

The Australian Human Rights Commission

A national independent statutory body with responsibility for investigating matters protected by Australia's anti-discrimination legislation, including discrimination on the grounds of religion, the AHRC has also issued important reports on religious belief.[10]

The Human Rights and Equal Opportunity Commission

The Commission is the regulating body for such law and practice as is governed by: the Racial Discrimination Act 1975; the Sex Discrimination Act 1984; the Disability Discrimination Act 1992; and the Human Rights and Equal Opportunity Commission Act 1986. The latter gives rise to its responsibilities in respect of religious discrimination, which are informed by Articles 18, 20 and 26 of the International Covenant on Civil and Political Rights 1966 (ICCPR) and the Declaration on the Elimination of All Forms of Intolerance and of Discrimination Based on Religion or Belief 1981.

The Human Rights Law Centre

This is an independent, not-for-profit organisation which advocates for the protection and promotion of human rights in Australia. It works across a range of areas, including advocating for reform to anti-discrimination laws and stronger protection for human rights – including freedom of religion. It has called for "the introduction of a federal Human Rights Act that protects freedom of religion and belief, among other rights, and the addition of religious belief (including non-religious belief such as a humanist, atheist or other belief that is not religious in nature) to those attributes already protected under federal discrimination law".[11]

International reports on human rights in Australia

In 2009, the UNHRC reported its concern that "the rights to equality and non-discrimination are not comprehensively protected in Australia in federal law".[12] Concern was also expressed about specific matters – such as the high level of violence against women, the need for greater promotion and protection of the rights of people who are lesbian, gay, bisexual, trans, gender diverse and intersex (LGBTI) and the use of enforced sterilisation procedures. Most recently, in the 2015 URP second cycle, the UNHRC recommended that Australia "adopt comprehensive federal legislation giving full legal effect to all [ICCPR] provisions across all state and territory jurisdictions".[13]

The State and the human rights/religion intersect

The Australian constitution, unlike its US counterpart, fails to provide for the firm separation of Church and State, but the prohibition on the establishment of a church or religion, together with other s.116 clauses, has provided parameters to aid judicial navigation of the interests of both parties.

Balancing the interests of Church and State

Given the relatively strong and lasting public benefit service partnership between Church and State, it is unsurprising that in practice the government's avowed secularist public policy is quite constrained. This is evident in its continued funding of religious schools, hospitals, community service providers and so on, and in the unrepealed laws prohibiting blasphemy.

The alleged use of a 'religious test'[14] arose in *Church of Scientology Inc v. Woodward*,[15] which concerned advice supposedly given to government ministers by the Australian Security Intelligence Organisation (ASIO) claiming that certain persons employed or seeking employment in the Commonwealth posed a security risk due to their membership of the Church of Scientology. The plaintiff argued that, in effect, this amounted to the application of a 'religious test' by the ASIO. The court dismissed the application on a technicality of defective wording.

State and religion related terrorism

Australia is no stranger to religion related 'lone wolf' terrorist attacks,[16] but it was the 2002 Bali bombing by Islamic militants, which killed and maimed so many Australians, that prompted a decisive change in State domestic policy. The consequent introduction of the Australian Anti-Terrorism Act 2005 (revised) was followed in 2014 by the National Security Amendment Act and the Crimes (Foreign Incursions and Recruitment) Act, all intended to hamper the activities of any potential domestic terrorists and obstruct ISIS recruitment for Middle East jihadist warfare by measures such as banning organisations and the criminalisation of membership in certain associations. Inevitably, the freedoms of association and expression were thereby constrained.

State neutrality

The Australian constitution requires the State to treat all religions equally. This was acknowledged in *Canterbury Municipal Council v. Moslem Alawy Society Ltd*[17] by McHugh JA, who claimed that "the preservation of religious equality has always been a matter of fundamental concern to the people of Australia and finds its place in the Constitution, s.116." However, there is a school of thought which argues that the preferential treatment of one religion over another is permissible providing it falls short of seeking the establishment of that religion. It must also be recognised that the boundaries between Church and State proved sufficiently porous to permit the appointment of the Anglican Archbishop as Governor-General of Australia in 2001 and, as has been noted:[18]

> There are political parties in Australia that are specifically and openly religious in orientation. There are politicians who more or less openly profess religious faith and acknowledge its impact on their own political perspectives, deliberations and decision-making. And there are different views about

the proper content of religious belief, specifically in terms of its implications for political decision-making.

Christian symbols/prayers in State facilities

The Preamble to the Australian Constitution acknowledges the latter's Christian roots and the presumed Christianity of Australians in the proclamation that the Australian people, are "humbly relying on the blessings of Almighty God".

The fact that the establishment clause in s.116 states that "no religious test shall be required as a qualification for any office or public trust under the Commonwealth" has not prevented the parliamentary standing orders from requiring a full recitation of the Lord's Prayer by the Speaker of the House of Representatives and the President of the Senate at the commencement of each day's business. This is a practice that has been continued since 1901 – a practice that is plainly Christian and overtly Protestant and is most probably perceived by those of other faiths and none as discriminatory.[19] In the one recorded case concerning the taking of an oath as a requirement for public office, this requirement was found to constitute an interference with the free exercise of religion.[20] In *Attorney-General (Vic) ex rel Black v. Commonwealth*,[21] Stephen J seemed satisfied that the s.116 clause "prohibits the imposition, whether by law or otherwise, of religious tests for the holding of Commonwealth office".

Protecting religion from the State

Section 116 offers religion little protection from the State: its prohibition is restricted to an "undue infringement of religious freedom".[22] However, as Jackson J once declared, "[T]he true situation is that if an enactment permitted executive action under it which amounted to a prohibition upon the free exercise of any religion, the enactment to the extent that it permitted such action . . . would be invalid".[23] Another issue concerns the bodies entitled to protection. The St Vincent de Paul Society, for example, has been found not to meet the definition of 'religious body' and is therefore outside s.116 protection.[24]

The HCA has held that the only laws invalidated under the Establishment Clause are those which: entrench "a religion as a feature of and identified with the body politic"; "constitute a particular religion or religious body as a State religion or State church"; or require "statutory recognition of a religion as a national institution". Moreover, its constitutional protection applies only to the Commonwealth, not to the states:[25] in theory, the latter are free to establish their own religions, though none has ever done so. The limitations of s.116 are such that, as Justice Sir Ninian Stephen once said, it "cannot readily be viewed as a repository of some broad statement of principle concerning the separation of Church and State, from which may be distilled the detailed consequences of such separation".[26] Indeed its limitations were evident in *Krygger v. Williams*,[27] when the HCA held that compulsory military training for teenage boys did not prohibit the free exercise of religion, and again in *Adelaide Company of Jehovah's Witnesses Inc v. Commonwealth*[28] when, at the height of World War II, the court struck down wartime regulations and found that the freedom of religion had to give way to national security considerations. This in turn caused the Adelaide branch of the Jehovah's Witnesses to be dissolved and its property acquired by the government – notwithstanding the irony of Latham CJ's observation at the time that "s.116 is required to protect the religion (or absence of religion) of minorities and, in particular, of unpopular minorities".[29]

Intervention in Church disputes

It is well established that Australian courts are not competent to adjudicate on theological matters. Their inability to assess the validity or invalidity of the doctrines or tenets of any religion, or to differentiate between them, was acknowledged by Murphy J in *Church of the New Faith v. Commissioner of Payroll Tax*:[30]

> The truth or falsity of religions is not the business of officials or the courts. If each purported religion had to show that its doctrines were true, then all might fail. . . . It is not within the judicial sphere to determine matters of religious doctrine and practice.

This approach was confirmed in the Federal Court, in *Iliafi v. The Church of Jesus Christ of Latter-Day Saints Australia*,[31] when it found that if the respondent's argument concerned the correctness or disputes about the content – of ritual, doctrine or ecclesiastical issues – then the court would not have jurisdiction.

State protection of the beliefs/culture of Indigenous people

There is no domestic federal legislation which specifically protects the beliefs of Indigenous people.[32] While the Racial Discrimination Act 1975 (Cth) (RDA) does not prohibit discrimination on the ground of religious identity or belief, religious groups may be regarded as being covered by the RDA where they can establish a common 'ethnic origin'. In *Macabenta v. Minister for Immigration & Multicultural Affairs*,[33] the court stated that the following questions are relevant when considering 'ethnic origin' for the purposes of the 1975 Act:

> For example, is there a long shared history?, is there either a common geographical origin or descent?, is there a common language?, is there a common literature?, is there a common religion or a depressed minority?

The policies of conversion and assimilation, which continued up until the mid-20th century and included the tragically misguided "Stolen Generation" episode, were wholly prejudicial toward traditional religious and cultural practices. This scandal marked a significant milestone in the tangled relationship between State, Christianity and the Indigenous people.[34]

The importance of their sacred sites to Indigenous people has been judicially recognised, as has the justification for affording protection to lands of religious relevance from acquisition under the s.116 "free exercise clause".[35] In practice, as evident in the *Cheedy* case,[36] the protection has not always been effective. This case concerned provisions in the Native Title Act 1992 (Cth) allowing mineral extraction on the land of Indigenous people, if necessary without their consent, even if that land was regarded by them as an important site for spiritual beliefs. The provisions were found not to breach s.116, as they did not have the object of prohibiting the free exercise of religion.

State protection of its traditional religious/cultural identity

With the last remnants of the "White Australia" policy petering out in the 1970s, offset by a more positive pivot toward non-Christian Pacific Rim nations and a growing political awareness of the rights of Indigenous people, the present pluralism had become a feature of Australian society by the closing decades of the 20th century. However, a defensiveness in relation to its Anglo-Saxon Christian culture is still evident in the above-mentioned retained vestiges of allegiances to Crown and Christianity, in the institutional presence of the Church and in the policy of incarcerating would-be migrants from neighbouring non-Christian countries.

State preferencing of religious organisations

The institutions of Church and State have had, and continue to have, a particularly close relationship with State support for Christian religious organisations being a well-established policy.

The religious exemption

Federal exemptions are addressed primarily in the Sex Discrimination Act 1984 (Cth) and the Fair Work Act 2009 (Cth) but also in all state and territory anti-discrimination statutes.[37] These provide that religious organisations and religious educational institutions are granted an exemption where a discriminatory act or conduct has been required to ensure conformity with doctrines, tenets or beliefs of a religion, or is necessary to avoid injury to the religious sensitivities of adherents of that religion. It allows such bodies to discriminate: in the provision of accommodation; in the ordination or appointment of priests, ministers of religion or in the training or education of such persons or in the appointment of persons to perform religious duties or functions, and any other act or practice of a body established for religious purposes; and by educational institutions established for religious purposes in relation to the employment of staff and the provision of education and training, provided that the discrimination is in "good faith". In *Walsh v. St Vincent de Paul Society Queensland (No. 2)*,[38] the respondent was found to be a society of lay faithful closely associated with the Catholic Church, rather than a "religious body", and therefore not entitled to avail of the religious exemption. The 1984 Act has been amended by the Sex Discrimination Amendment (Sexual Orientation, Gender Identity and Intersex Status) Act 2013, which revises certain exemption privileges traditionally enjoyed by religious organisations but specifically exempts private schools and hospitals owned by such organisations from its gender identity and sexual orientation provisions, which, given the number of such facilities, has a significant human rights impact.

The religious exemption was clearly central to the lengthy proceedings that constituted the above *OV and OW* case and *Cobaw Community Health Services Limited v. Christian Youth Camps Limited & Anor.*[39] The exemption was also central to *Mornington Baptist Church Community Caring Inc*,[40] when a Baptist Church unsuccessfully sought to avail of the exemption privilege to restrict staff selection to those who had "publicly confessed Jesus Christ" and were "walking in daily fellowship with Jesus". Their claim failed because the organisation was unable to show why its religious beliefs required it to so restrict employment in order to fulfil the functional tasks of its community care projects.

In the light of the many international experiences of child abuse by clergy, the exemption privileges accorded to religious bodies have been called into question in Australia as elsewhere.[41] Indeed, in July 2015 the Royal Commission into Institutional Responses to Child Sexual Abuse noted that Jehovah's Witnesses (with approximately 70,000 Australian members) had failed to report any of its 1,006 alleged offenders over six decades of recorded child abuse.[42] This was followed in 2018 by committal proceedings against Cardinal Pell for alleged sexual abuse. As noted by the Human Rights Law Centre:[43]

> In Australian discrimination law as it currently stands, the permanent exemptions available to religious organisations do not strike the right balance. The mere existence of these exemptions operate as a barrier to vulnerable people – such as single mothers and transgender people – to access vital services provided by faith based organisations, organisations that often receive government funds to deliver these services.

This message was recently reinforced by the Australian Human Rights Commission, which recommended that "the Government examine alternatives to the current system of religious exemptions to anti-discrimination laws, including a general limitations clause, and that proposed changes should adhere to Australia's obligations under international law".[44]

Regulatory privileges

Privileges traditionally accorded to religion and religious organisations in Australia have been continued by the Charities Act 2013; they are subject only to standard incorporation requirements or to ATO processes if they seek tax-exempt status.

Tax privileges

Religious organisations invariably have charitable status, but this is more broadly interpreted than in the UK, as Australian charity law does not interpose a public benefit test as a determinant of entitlement to registration and to accompanying tax privileges. The extension of that status to "closed" religious orders, again unlike the UK, was established in *Assoc. of Franciscan Order of Friars Minor v. City of Kew*,[45] thereafter confirmed in relation to other religious entities[46] and is now endorsed by the Charities Act 2013.

Testamentary privileges

The principle that a testator has a right to make a bequest subject to an overtly discriminatory religious condition is well established in Australia as elsewhere in the common-law world.[47] So the bequest to sons, conditional upon their wives converting to Protestantism, in *Trustees of Church Property of the Diocese of Newcastle v. Ebbeck*,[48] was valid in itself. Indeed, Windeyer J, in making his determination, declared the general validity of testator-imposed religious restraints on marriage.[49] Under the Charities Act 2013, testators may continue to add religiously discriminating conditions to their bequests.

State funding of faith-based facilities and services

Section 116 of the Constitution does not prohibit the State from encouraging or giving aid to religion, and there is no constitutional obstacle to laws that indirectly assist the religious to further their religious goals. As mentioned above, this has permitted the channelling of government funds through church organisations, enabling them to run schools, hospitals, social care facilities and so on. It necessarily gives the Christian churches, relative to all others, an institutional presence and influence – on government and local communities – that may be perceived as overbearing by those of other faiths and none.

The appointment of chaplains to the armed forces requires the prospective appointee to be "a member of a church or faith group approved by the Religious Advisory Committee to the services". This, clearly being a 'religious test', has triggered some debate as to whether it could be s.116-compliant and whether non-Christians or atheists are thus unfairly treated. However, considerably more controversy was generated by the National School Chaplaincy Programme which was introduced in 2007 and by 2016 was using some $60M of federal public funds per annum to provide a school chaplaincy service to nearly 3,000 schools across Australia. Debate has focused on the provision of a service that is: religious (no equivalent secular service is available); almost exclusively Christian; delivered mostly by evangelical organisations in the main to State schools; and which is paid for by taxpayers, some of whom are atheists, agnostics or belong to non-Christian religions, and many of whom argue that schools should be strictly secular. In *Williams (1)*,[50] the plaintiff challenged the constitutionality of the programme, claiming that he had a right to secure a secular education for his children. The High Court held that while the chaplaincy programme was not in breach of the s.116 religious test, the Commonwealth's funding arrangements were unauthorised by statute and therefore unconstitutional. Within days of the decision, the Commonwealth Parliament passed the Financial Framework Legislation Amendment Act (No. 3) 2012 (Cth), which sought to regularise the funding arrangements and secure the national network of chaplaincy posts, but this was challenged by the plaintiff in *Williams (II)*[51]. Again the court found the funding arrangements to be unconstitutional, though this time on the more fundamental grounds that the statutory provisions purporting to authorise the programme were invalid because they did not fall within any of the Commonwealth's legislative powers. Since then, the programme has been centrally funded by the federal government to enable all states and territories to place and administer chaplains in public and private schools: the "placing" being contracted to evangelical Christian organisations such as Scripture Union; the service is to counsel troubled children. Understandably, the overall impact may well be perceived as discriminatory by non-Christian parents.

Religion and the freedoms of association and expression

While the freedom of religion intersects no less regularly with the freedoms of association and expression than happens in other Part II jurisdictions, in Australia the related issues are settled with greater reliance upon the provisions of international conventions, protocols and so on.

Freedom of religion

There are long-standing HCA rulings to the effect that s.116 does not function as a free-standing individual right to freedom of religion.[52]

In *Grace Bible Church v. Reedman*,[53] the court gave short shrift to the appellant's claim that "there was an inalienable right to religious freedom". Parliament, as White J commented, had "an absolute right to interfere with religious worship and the expression of religious beliefs at any time that it liked"[54] and indeed had done so when the nation was at war, as illustrated in the Jehovah's Witnesses cases. Nonetheless, the "freedom of religious belief and expression" has been judicially declared to be an "important freedom generally accepted in Australian society,"[55] although an academic has claimed that "Australia has only relatively weak constitutional and legal protection of freedom of religion or belief and prohibition of discrimination on the basis of religion or belief".[56]

This claim seemed to be endorsed by the above-mentioned *Iliafi* case, which concerned an internal dispute regarding language, when the full Federal Court confirmed that in such circumstances an individual's freedom of religion was protected only by the right to leave the Church.[57]

Definitions

There are no domestic legislative provisions that provide a basis for defining and differentiating forms of religion, beliefs and their associated organisations.

'Religion'

In *New South Wales Stewards' Co Ltd v. Strathfield Municipal Council*,[58] the court relied on orthodox principles to determine whether a company, which had among its objects the promotion of the true welfare of humankind in Christian or benevolent principles and the teaching of the word of God, was a 'religious body' and on that basis entitled to a rating exemption. Noting that 'religious body' and 'religion' were not defined in the rating statute, the court found that these terms were to be given their popular meaning – which imputed a belief in a supreme being. Forty years later, in *The Church of the New Faith v. Commissioner of Pay-roll Tax*,[59] when considering whether a particular set of beliefs and practices would constitute a religion, Mason ACJ and Brennan J suggested that:[60]

> for the purposes of law, the criteria of religion are twofold: first, belief in a supernatural Being, Thing or Principle; and second, the acceptance of canons of conduct in order to give effect to that belief. . . .

More recently, *OV and OW*[61] was significant from many perspectives, including for its exploration of what constitutes a 'religion'. The Wesley Mission had sought to rely upon the "fundamental Biblical teaching that 'monogamous heterosexual partnership within marriage' is both the 'norm and ideal' ",[62] but the Tribunal (NSWADT) initially found, given the diversity of views across Christendom on this issue, that "it does not follow, and nor is it asserted, that that belief can properly be described as a doctrine of the Christian religion". Ultimately, the Court of Appeal held that the search for such a doctrine, and the need to establish its conformity or otherwise with the act or practice of the Mission, was "misguided"[63] and referred the issue back to the Tribunal. In reconsidering the matter, the NSWADT took the view that "doctrine" ' was broad enough to encompass, not just formal doctrinal pronouncements such as the Nicene Creed, but effectively whatever was commonly taught or advocated by a body, including moral as well as religious principles, in a contemporary time frame rather than as traditionally prescribed.

Subsequently, Hampel J, in *Cobaw Community Health Services Limited v. Christian Youth Camps Limited & Anor*,[64] heard expert evidence from theologians on the meaning of "doctrines of religion". She found that the beliefs of the Christian Brethren about marriage, sexual relationships and homosexuality could not be construed as "doctrines of the religion". Not everything in the Scriptures amounts to "doctrine"; the prevailing cultural beliefs at the time must also be taken into account.[65] The Court of Appeal, endorsing Hampel J's ruling, held that CYC was not "a body established for religious purposes" and therefore could not rely on the religious exemption.

Among the implications of these decisions is an awareness that the Australian courts and regulators will focus on any declared doctrines of an organisation claiming to be a religious body. This focus would seem more pronounced than in other jurisdictions, and this may be attributed to the fact some Australian legislation makes explicit reference to "doctrines". When a legal issue arises which makes it necessary to ascertain the doctrines of a religion, it will be the formulation of those doctrines at the time the issue arose which is crucial. This is an approach that concurs with HRCommittee advice and which, by requiring the doctrine to be contextualised within contemporary cultural values and norms, may allow traditional religious dogma to be side-stepped.

'Beliefs'

In *Church of the New Faith*, the court considered whether the doctrines and beliefs of Scientology could be construed as meeting the definition of religion. Although unable to agree on what might constitute such a definition, there was consensus that it should extend to philosophies which "seek to explain, in terms of a broader reality, the existence of the universe, the meaning of human life and human destiny".[66] The indicia of religion as discussed by Wilson and Deane JJ were: that the particular collection of ideas and/or practices involved belief in the supernatural, that is, a belief that reality extended beyond that which was capable of perception by the senses; that the ideas related to man's nature and place in the universe and his relations to things supernatural; that the ideas were accepted by adherents as requiring or encouraging them to observe particular practices having supernatural significance; and that, however loosely knit and varying in beliefs and practices adherents might be, they constituted an identifiable group or identifiable groups.[67] In unanimously concluding that Scientology is a religion, the HCA reached the opposite decision to that made in England & Wales on the same set of facts (as also occurred in relation to closed religious orders).[68]

Where, however, the purposes of an organisation are clearly antithetical to religion, the Australian judiciary has adopted the same approach as their British counterparts. The *Freethinkers* case,[69] for example, concerned a society the beliefs of which included that "science provides for life and that materialism can be relied upon in all phases of society". The court considered that as the purpose of the organisation was to work against already established religions or against the idea of religion, the organisation could not be construed as 'religious'.

Latham CJ's assertion, in *Adelaide Co of Jehovah's Witnesses Inc v. Commonwealth*,[70] that "it is not an exaggeration to say that each person chooses the content of his own religion" in determining what constitutes a religion or belief, was treated with some caution by Mason Acting CJ and Brennan J in the *Scientology* case.[71] Australian law has not strayed far from its roots in the *Scientology* case.[72] Being alert to the dangers of overstretching the interpretation of religion, both warned that "the mantle of immunity would soon be in tatters if it were wrapped around beliefs, practices and observances of every kind whenever a group of adherents chose to call them a religion".[73]

Indigenous beliefs

For Indigenous people, recognition of their distinctive ethnicity and culture is particularly important and has occasionally been acknowledged: "the Nyungah elders are an ethnic group in that they have a shared history, separate cultural tradition, common geographical origin, descent from common ancestors, a common language and a religion different to the general community surrounding them",[74] as was "the freedom of certain Ngarrindjeri people to hold and practise their religion".[75]

There are no statutory provisions designed to recognise and accommodate the Dreamtime rites – which vary from tribe to tribe in accordance with tribal boundaries, topography and ancestor narratives – that constitute the religious beliefs of Indigenous people. The case for extending such recognition has been well made.[76] Enquiries undertaken to establish whether such beliefs could be construed as religious were the subject of judicial scrutiny in *ALRM v. State of South Australia*.[77] The Supreme Court of South Australia then held that an inquiry into the genuineness of the belief of Ngarrindjiri women was lawful, notwithstanding that those beliefs were, under Aboriginal rule, confidential to women.

In *Kruger v. Commonwealth*,[78] Gaudron J alluded to the parallels between the beliefs of Indigenous people and those of more orthodox religious adherents when, in considering whether the removal of Aboriginal children breached s.116, she stated that "the Aboriginal people of the Northern Territory, or at least some of them, had beliefs or practices which are properly classified as a religion". This was endorsed by Toohey J, her colleague on the bench, who in relation to the State-sanctioned removal of children commented that "it may well be that an effect of the Ordinance was to impair, even prohibit the spiritual beliefs and practices of the Aboriginal people in the Northern Territory".[79]

Manifestation of religion or belief

Latham CJ, in *Adelaide Company of Jehovah's Witnesses Inc v. Commonwealth*,[80] was certain that s.116 protection extended beyond holding beliefs to include their manifestation, as were Mason ACJ and Brennan J in *Church of the New Faith v. Commissioner of Pay-roll Tax (Vict)*.[81] However, the right to manifest is constrained in at least two respects. Firstly, the action must be appropriately linked to the belief: clearly not all action taken by a religious person or organisation is necessarily related to, let alone a manifestation of, their religious beliefs. Secondly, any such action must be proportionate, comply with freedom of speech standards and be respectful of the rights of others. As Hampel J noted in *Cobaw*,[82] the right to hold a belief is broader than the right to act upon it. In particular, she emphasised that the right to freedom of religious belief does not confer a right on members of a religion to impose their beliefs on a secular society.[83] The protracted 2004 controversy over the building of a mosque in Bendigo county, Victoria, provides a good illustration of the general give-and-take approach to overt expressions of religious differences in this very pluralist society; it was resolved without any need for judicial involvement.

Religious discrimination

Neither the Constitution nor any federal legislation specifically prohibits discrimination on the ground of religion and neither does statute law in NSW. In practice, the relevant domestic federal legislative framework consists of s.351 of the Fair Work Act 2009 (Cth), the Human Rights and Equal Opportunity Act 1986 (Cth) and the Racial Discrimination Act 1975 (Cth). The latter omits any explicit prohibition of discrimination on the ground of religious belief, although certain religious groups – Jews and Sikhs – are recognised as having a common "ethnic origin" and as such have some protection under these laws. Given the evidence of increased Islamophobia,[84] there is concern that protection is not extended to Muslims and increasing demands that s.18(c) of that Act be amended to include a specific reference to religious discrimination and to prohibit religious vilification.[85]

The absence of federal legislation prohibiting discrimination on the basis of religion in areas such as employment, accommodation or education, forces reliance upon international conventions – particularly the ICCPR.[86] Article 3 of the Declaration on the Elimination of All Forms of Intolerance and of Discrimination Based on Religion or Belief is potentially relevant, but in practice, as Gaze comments, "this has no significance at all in Australian law".[87] As noted above, the relevant case law is equivocal as to the extent to which religious and racial discrimination can be conflated.

Freedom of association

There is no express constitutional right to freedom of association, but nonetheless its importance has been confirmed by the HCA,[88] and protection is ensured by recourse to international law (the ICCPR and the ICESR). As in other countries, this right is subject to statutes governing public order and safety. Parkinson is of the view that there is an undue tension between the freedoms of association and religion. He argues that faith-based organisations should have a right to select staff that fit with the values and mission of the organisation, just as political parties, environmental groups and LGBTI organisations do.[89]

The 'positive action' provisions

This term refers to action taken that aims to foster equality by providing targeted support to offset the particular disadvantages suffered by certain specific groups. An anomalous instance of what might be construed as 'positive action' was the subject of judicial scrutiny in *Kay v. South Eastern Sydney Area Health Service*,[90] which concerned a fund for the treatment of white babies. The court ultimately upheld the fund as charitable on grounds that included the banal rationale that "the receipt of a fund to benefit white babies would just mean that more of the general funds of the hospital would be available to treat non-white babies so that, in due course, despite the testatrix's intention things will even up".

Freedom of expression

This right is one to communicate and receive opinion, information and ideas without interference and it often conflicts with the right to religious freedom.[91] In *Francis v. YWCA Australia*,[92] a complaint against the YWCA for selling and distributing T-shirts bearing the slogan 'Mr Abbott, get your rosaries off my ovaries' was dismissed. Manifesting the organisation's religious beliefs in that manner was construed as within the confines of free speech and insufficient to incite hatred of Catholics. Similarly, in *Evans v. NSW*,[93] the right to free speech was found to be obstructed by statutory provisions intended to prohibit the "annoying" of Roman Catholics participating in World Youth Day celebrations in 2008. Again, in *Deen v. Lamb*,[94] a pamphlet inferring that all Muslims were obliged to disobey the law of Australia was held to be permissible as it was published "in good faith". However, in *Menzies & Ors v. Owen*,[95] the court upheld a charge of publicly vilifying homosexuals and incitement to hatred despite an assertion that this was sourced in "ancient religious text such as the Bible, the Torah or the Koran".[96]

Where the statements stray beyond being offensive to become "errors of fact, distortions of the truth and inflammatory and provocative language", as when a blogger named persons whom he claimed were "fair-skinned Aborigines" trading on their self-identified status for personal gain, then this is impermissible.[97] In *Sisalem*,[98] a Muslim who claimed that a newspaper article constituted religious intolerance and vilification when it suggested, after the Paris attacks, that Islam needed to undergo fundamental change, had his claims dismissed on the grounds that the article could not be shown to have generated the degree of hatred and contempt of Muslims necessary to negate the paper's exercise of its right to free speech.

Religiously motivated conduct

In *Catch the Fire Ministries Inc v. Islamic Council of Victoria Inc*,[99] the Victorian Court of Appeal considered whether the conduct of Catch the Fire Ministries, an evangelical religious organisation, contravened s.8 of the Racial and Religious Tolerance Act 2001 (Vic). The conduct concerned statements made at a seminar in 2002, in a newsletter in 2001 and in an article on their website in 2001 that included: the Koran promotes violence and killing; the Koran teaches that women are of little value; Allah is not merciful; that Muslims practising Jihad are following the Koran and a number of other similar statements. The ruling that there had been no incitement to hatred of Muslims because of their faith – as opposed to possible hatred of the religious beliefs of Muslims – (a distinction the significance of which may not be readily apparent to Muslims) places a high value on the relative importance of freedom of speech.[100] Not dissimilarly, in *Adelaide Preachers*,[101] the HCA upheld the validity of a local by-law that prohibited "preaching, canvassing and haranguing" in a public place without a licence from the city, adding that it did not breach any right to free speech under s.116. Recently, *Gaynor*[102] concerned an officer in the armed forces who had his commission terminated when he refused to stop publicly expressing offensive views, which he claimed were related to his Catholic religion, on matters such as LGBTI rights and Muslim extremists. While the court found that the plaintiff was entitled to exercise his right to freedom of speech in the way he did, and duly set aside the decision terminating his commission, Buchanan J made the point that he was "satisfied that the applicant acted by choice to make the statements which he did" and did not accept "that even as a matter of conscience, he felt he had no choice but to defy the instructions and orders given to him".[103]

Religious apparel

There is no Australian federal legislation, and virtually none among the states and territories, that deals with matters of religious dress and symbols. As a general rule, there is no restriction on wearing religious apparel in the workplace, school or college unless doing so constitutes a safety hazard or confirmation of personal identity is required. Unusually, there would seem to be a dearth of case law relating to such matters, an exception being *Elzahed v. State of New South Wales*,[104] when the Court of Appeal upheld the earlier ruling of Balla J that the Muslim plaintiff was not entitled to keep her face covered while testifying, as the judge could not be "completely deprived of having the assistance of seeing her face to assess her credibility". This balancing of respect for religious freedom with the needs of justice would seem a proportionate means of achieving human rights compliance.

Blasphemy and proselytism

Blasphemy continues to be a criminal offence in some states and territories. In 2016 the Australian Capital Territory amended the Discrimination Act 1991 to introduce the offence of inciting hatred toward, revulsion of, serious contempt for, or severe ridicule of a person or group of people on grounds which include religious conviction. This amendment was ostensibly introduced for the protection of Muslims but has a potential application in respect of all religions.

Proselytism is as permissible under Australian law as it is in other common-law countries and has been defended in the HCA by Kirby J.[105] Possibly, however, the Commonwealth-funded school chaplains programme, mandating government-funded exclusively Christian counselling (which in practice facilitates proselytising) on a nationwide basis, could be considered discriminatory.

Conscientious objection

The Defence Act 1903 granted total exemption from military service to "those who could demonstrate a conscientious objection to bearing arms", but this did not prevent the court, in *Krygger v. Williams*,[106] from finding that a conscientious objector could not object to compulsory military service on the ground of religious belief. The then Chief Justice, Sir Samuel Griffith, described such a proposition as "absurd" and added that s.116 only protected "the doing of acts which are done in the practice of religion. To require a man to do a thing which has nothing to do with religion is not prohibiting him from a free exercise of religion".

In *Judd v. McKeown*,[107] the appellant, a committed socialist who as a matter of conscience had refused to vote, was convicted of failing to do so "without a valid and sufficient reason" contrary to the compulsory voting provisions of the Commonwealth Electoral Act 1918 (Cth). Although Higgins J expressed the view, at variance with the *Krygger* decision, that if the appellant had had a religious objection to voting, then this would have been protected under s.116.[108] More recently, conscientious objection on religious grounds to paying taxes that could be used to provide for abortions[109] and to revealing the contents of a religious confession were summarily dismissed.[110]

Human rights, equality and religion: the case law

In Australia, as in all Part II jurisdictions, it would seem to be equality issues that are most frequently testing the tension between religion and human rights and generating the bulk of religion-related case law.

Right of access to justice

The failure to ensure that Indigenous people and detained asylum seekers have adequate access to justice has been repeatedly criticised by the HRC.[111]

Religious law and courts

Religious courts can operate in parallel to national courts in Australia. There is, for example, no obstacle preventing an Orthodox Jewish or Muslim couple from divorcing in accordance with their religious rules. Many such couples marry or divorce under both sets of laws.

Shari'a law

The above liberal Australian approach, which accommodates religion-specific laws and courts, is subject to the caveat that their operation does not inflict undue disadvantage on any party compared to equivalent litigation in the national legal system. Family proceedings in Shari'a courts may well result in adverse outcomes for those parties who happen to be female and/or gay.

Right to life

This most basic of human rights, proclaimed in Article 6 of the ICCPR, remains unacknowledged in Australian federal law. It has long been the focus of much attention from anti-abortion protestors, a focus that has more recently also turned toward matters such as medically assisted death and the use of embryos for research.

Abortion, contraception

The law relating to abortion varies across the states and territories and remains criminal in some. In *Fraser v. Walker*,[112] a person displaying a poster featuring pictures of aborted foetuses outside an abortion clinic in Melbourne was convicted of "displaying an obscene figure in a public place". The judicial comment that "assuming the appellant's stance on abortion comes from her religious belief, the display of obscene figures is not part of religion nor can it be said the display is done in furtherance of religion"[113] is interesting, as it treads the uncertain line that separates the right to manifest personal religious belief from the duty to do so in a manner compliant with the freedom of expression. That line has been complicated by political involvement in determining the legal availability of RU-486 (an abortifacient) and significantly adjusted by the recent introduction of "protest free zones" in a number of states and territories, to exclude anti-abortion activity within 50 metres of a clinic.

Refusing medical treatment

Australia, in keeping with many other countries, respects an 'advance directive' given by an adult refusing medical intervention[114] but allows health authorities to apply for a court order to overrule a parental veto on the provision of treatment for their child. The Supreme Court (WA) recently ruled that staff at the Princess Margaret Hospital for Children could give a teenage cancer patient blood transfusions despite parental objection on religious grounds. Again, in *X v. the Sydney Children's Hospital Network*,[115] when dismissing an appeal in respect of a parental refusal to permit intense chemotherapy for a child suffering from Hodgkin's disease, because it would probably lead to a blood transfusion contrary to their religious beliefs, Basten J said: "[T]he interest of the State in preserving life is at its highest with respect to children and young persons who are inherently vulnerable, in varying degrees". This principle was also in play in 2015, when the federal government terminated the long-standing exemption enjoyed by some religious groups – most notably the Christian Scientists – from national child vaccination programmes.

Medically assisted death

The Northern Territories became, if briefly, the world's first jurisdiction to legalise euthanasia[116] with the Rights of the Terminally Ill Act 1996, but nevertheless there has never been any enabling federal legislative provision, and since the Euthanasia Laws Act 1997, it has been illegal[117] in all states and territories. In November 2017, legislation to allow assisted death was passed in the Parliament of Victoria to take effect in 2019.[118]

Right to marriage and to found a family

Australia has a well-documented history of non-traditional family units, including polygamy (unlawful in that a bigamous/polygamous marriage cannot be entered into in Australia). It is also a country in which there tends to be a significant time lag between established practice – such as single-parent families or same-sex parenting – and the introduction of legislation, particularly federal legislation, to recognise that practice and protect the parties involved.[119]

Marriage and family relationships

In *Simpson v. Brockmann*,[120] the Family Court ruled that persons other than biological parents were parents for the purposes of the Family Law Act and held that a lesbian couple, living together as partners with their children for more than nine years, met the definition of 'parents'. Since then, the legal definition of what constitutes a family unit has been broadened by legislation such as the Sex Discrimination Amendment (Sexual Orientation, Gender Identity and Intersex Status) Act 2013, which amended the 1984 Act to provide new protections from discrimination on the basis of sexual orientation, gender identity and intersex status.[121]

Same-sex marriage

Not until the introduction of legislation enacted after *Toonen v. Australia*[122] were same-sex relationships finally decriminalised nationwide, and not until the Marriage Amendment (Definition and Religious Freedoms) Act 2017 amended the Marriage Act 1961 did marriage between two persons of marriageable age, regardless of their gender, become possible. The 2017 Act not only exempts ministers of religion from any obligation to officiate in marriage ceremonies, as in other Part II jurisdictions, but extends the exemption to: civil registrars, where to do so would compromise their beliefs (e.g. same-sex marriages, or involving previously divorced or interfaith couples) and to religious organisations, enabling them to refuse to provide facilities, goods or services if to do so would compromise either their beliefs or those of their religious communities.

Sexuality and gender

The *Sex Discrimination Act 1984* (Cth), as amended, makes it unlawful to discriminate against a person on the basis of their sex, sexual orientation, gender identity, intersex status, marital or relationship status, pregnancy, breastfeeding and family responsibilities in areas of public life, including employment, education and the provision of goods, services and facilities.

The long-established Australian practice of surgical intervention to "correct" physiological anomalies in small children, often involving their sterilisation, has been much criticised. Such intervention achieves physical gender alignment but only by reducing a complex psychosocial matter of sexual identity to a simple one of surgically induced gender conformity: with all the eugenic connotations of enforced engineering, on the authorisation of parents but without the consent of the child. In 2013, the Australian Senate published a report which condemned the practice of "normalising" surgeries and made 15 recommendations, including ending cosmetic genital surgeries on infants and children and providing for legal oversight of individual cases.[123] Australia's reputation of being the only nation in the world that required transgender teenagers to get court authorisation before they could start taking transitioning drugs, usually around the age of 15, came to an end in November 2017 with the decision of the court in *Re Kelvin*.[124]

Giving legal recognition to the status of transgender and intersex Australians has also been problematic. In *Attorney-General for the Commonwealth & "Kevin and Jennifer" & Human Rights and Equality Commission*,[125] the Family Court recognised the reassigned gender status of a transsexual person and their consequent right to marry someone of the now opposite sex but did so only after taking into account evidence of hormonal therapy and irreversible surgery. *Hanover Welfare Services Ltd (Anti-Discrimination Exemption)*[126] concerned the ruling of a regulatory authority that a women's shelter was exempted from the relevant anti-discrimination legislation, thereby allowing it to reject male-to-female transgender persons as "women" for the purposes of providing shelter. In the more recent *G v. Australia*,[127] the UN HRCommittee ruled that the State breached its human rights obligations under Article 26 of the ICCPR by not providing a means for a transgender person to have their birth certificate amended in accordance with their new gender identity.

Assisted reproduction, adoption, surrogacy and genetic engineering

Commercial surrogacy is banned nationwide, although surrogacy is legal on an altruistic basis within all Australian jurisdictions – except Western Australia (where it is illegal for singles and same-sex couples). Surrogacy arrangements very often involve adoption proceedings, and with the passing of the Adoption of Children Legislation Amendment (Equality) Bill 2017 in the Northern Territories, same-sex and unmarried couples are now able to adopt children anywhere in Australia.

Whether the law should permit research or patenting of inventions that involves hES cells (human embryonic stem cells) has been disputed on religious grounds in Australia as in many other jurisdictions. In 2007, remarks made by an Australian Catholic Cardinal opposing such research were referred to the New South Wales parliamentary privileges committee for allegedly being in "contempt of parliament". The Cardinal was cleared of the charge and described the move as a "clumsy attempt to curb religious freedom and freedom of speech".[128]

Cancer Voices[129] was the first Australian decision on the issue of whether a valid patent may be granted for naturally occurring DNA and RNA that had been isolated and separated from human cells; the isolated gene was BRCA1. The HCA[130] found that isolating a gene did not in itself constitute a manufacturing process and, in overturning the earlier decisions, brought Australian law on this matter into conformity with that in the US[131] but away from the European approach. While this decision turned squarely on legal technicalities, the underlying issue in Australia, as in other countries, has been and will continue to be the extent to which the law of patents may permit companies to carve out commercial monopolies in the use of genetic material.

Right to employment

The International Labour Organisation's Discrimination (Employment and Occupation) Convention, ratified by Australia in 1973, requires the removal of employment-related discrimination on grounds which include religion. The Workplace Relations Act 1996 (Cth) prohibited the termination of employment on the basis of religion, while its replacement – the Fair Work Act 2009 (Cth) – in s.351(1) prohibits any adverse action based on religion, but in s.351(2)(c) exempts employers from prosecution in respect of action taken against staff in good faith and on the basis of religious doctrine or to avoid injury to the religious susceptibilities of adherents. "Discrimination," in the context of employment or occupation, is as defined in the Human Rights and Equal Opportunity Commission Act 1986.

Hiring/firing staff and religious beliefs

Staff selection on the basis of criteria that include an applicant's religious belief does not constitute religious discrimination for the purposes of the 1986 Act if: this is necessitated under Part (d) of the definition of 'discrimination' in s.3 to ensure compliance with the doctrines, tenets, beliefs or teachings of a particular religion, and is made in good faith, and in order to avoid injury to the religious susceptibilities of adherents of that religion, or is necessary to fulfil the inherent requirements of the post.[132]

In *Thompson v. Catholic College Wodonga*,[133] the plaintiff teacher who had been summarily dismissed on return from maternity leave due to her unmarried status being at variance with the beliefs of her employing organisation, had her unfair dismissal complaint upheld by the EOC. So, also, in *Griffin v. Catholic Education Office*,[134] when the complaint of a LGBTI activist teacher who had been refused employment in Catholic schools for the same reason was similarly upheld.

However, when an irreligious employee is placed in an invidious position in the form of a new contract requiring them to become an active church member of their employing religious organisation (Baptist Community Church) then – with legal recognition now extending to those with no religious belief – such an employee will be entitled to protection against discrimination.[135] Also, state laws (e.g. in Victoria) provide protection not only against discrimination based on religious belief or activity but also on the absence of such belief or activity.[136]

Australian case law, as in other jurisdictions, reveals the legal significance attached to the closeness of the relationship between the functional duties of a post and the religious beliefs of an employing religious organisation. So in *Ciciulla v. Curwen-Walker*,[137] the complaint of discrimination by an employee who had resigned in response to pressure from her employer to attend services at their Pentecostal church was upheld because of the lack of any such relationship. This rationale was also evident in *Walsh v. St Vincent de Paul Society Queensland (No. 2)*,[138] when the tribunal rejected the respondent's claim that being a Catholic was a "genuine occupational requirement" for the post of president of that society; particularly given that the respondent knew that the claimant was not a Catholic, welcomed her as a member and saw her elected as president of three of its conferences, saw her inducted as a president of a conference by a priest of the church and allowed her to work without challenge for years as a conference president.

While grounds of religious belief can also play its usual role in the firing of staff, this may be complicated in Australia by a racial/ethnic component. For example, in *T v. Dept of Education (Vic)*[139] and in *Kapoor v. Monash University*,[140] the plaintiff teachers, a Sikh and a Hindu, respectively, were both the subject of ridicule and harassment by their pupils, and ultimately their employment contracts were terminated or not renewed because their employers took the view that their appearance and communication skills undermined their teaching capacity, despite the plaintiffs' protests that their roles in the classroom were conditioned by their religious beliefs. In *Marett v. Petroleum Refineries (Australia) Pty Ltd*,[141] the claim of religious discrimination by an employee who refused to pay union dues on the grounds of his religious beliefs, resulting in his being ostracised by his co-workers and eventually sacked, was upheld.

Accommodating religious beliefs/practices in the workplace

Employers are generally required to make reasonable accommodation for the religious practices of employees in the workplace. In *Ahmad McIntosh v. TAFE Tasmania*,[142] an allegation of religious discrimination, made by a Muslim teacher who had not been provided with a dedicated prayer room nor was released from duties on Fridays and on Islamic holy days, was dismissed, as was the claim in *D'Urso v. Peninsula Support Service Inc*[143] by an employee who was asked to remove a notice to hold a prayer service during work hours in a secular workplace. That "reasonableness" is a two-way street was illustrated in *Fox v. Canberra Television Pty Ltd*,[144] when the Tribunal declined to issue an order preventing the dismissal of a manager who refused to work on Saturdays for sincerely held religious reasons. The Tribunal found that given the financial circumstances of the company, it was impracticable for it to provide staff to relieve the manager every Saturday and that it would not be financially feasible for it to close the store on that day.

In *Abdulrahman v. Toll Pty Ltd T/As Toll Express* (2006) EOC 93–445, an Australian Muslim from Lebanon, subject to taunting from his work colleagues on the basis of spurious 'terrorist' sympathies, was found to have been unlawfully discriminated against – though on ethno-religious grounds because the relevant legislation did not provide for religious discrimination, as also was the case in *Trad v. Jones and Anor (No 3)*.[145] Again, in *Swamy v. Percival*,[146] a Hindu employee in a smelting plant was successful in his claim that he had been unfairly dismissed following his complaints of the bullying and harassment endured from his foreman, who had ridiculed his religious beliefs.[147]

Right to education

A primary area of concern in the Australian education system relates to the freedom of government-funded religious schools, in an increasingly religiously diverse and secular society, to claim exemption from religious discrimination laws, a privilege that inevitably brings greater benefits to the established Christian religious organisations relative to all others.

Government funding and religious education: general overview

In the landmark case of *Attorney-General (vic) (Ex rel Black) v. Commonwealth*,[148] the plaintiffs sought a court order declaring that State funding of Church schools amounted to establishing a religion, contrary to s.116. This was rejected on the grounds that s.116 does not prevent the "giving of aid to or encouragement of religion" and therefore could not prevent the government from providing financial assistance to schools operated by religious organisations on the same basis as that assistance was provided to other private schools. Such funding was deemed constitutionally compliant because it was intended for educational rather than religious purposes. There was consensus among six of the seven judges that s.116 differed from the corresponding US First Amendment clause in that it did not presume to represent a liberty right but was limited to suppressing any initiative by the Commonwealth government to impose a law giving preference to any one religion or church.

That a failure to satisfy the definition of 'religious school' could entail forfeiting an entitlement to government funding was demonstrated in the interesting *Best Practice* case.[149] This concerned a non-denominational school which espoused religious beliefs in general but none in particular and for that reason found itself disadvantaged as regards funding arrangements. In justifying the ruling that this did not constitute religious discrimination, Peedom DP cited the Mason CJ and Brennan J dictum in the *Scientology* case to explain that the school approach to religion lacked the crucial component that it be "based upon a supernatural being, thing or principle". This rationale is questionable because: it relies upon a theistic definition of what constitutes a 'religion' or 'belief'; ignores an equality interpretation which would give equal status to secularism; and raises the issue of the presence or absence of a legislative reference to religious belief, which varies across the states and territories. It also, of course, seemingly rests on a 'religion test' which, although confined by the fourth clause of s.116 to the Commonwealth, is contrary to that principle. The scope of s.116 was recently examined in *Hoxton Park Residents Action Group Inc v. Liverpool City Council.*[150] This concerned the channelling of Commonwealth funding to the state of NSW (in accordance with s.96 of the Constitution) for the running of the Malek Fahd Islamic School, a school run on Islamic principles. The court held that the federal government did not thereby breach the Constitution by "establishing" a religion: providing funds to a religious school (where such funds are conditioned on objective, secular, educational criteria and also provided on a needs-based and in an even-handed manner to other religious schools from different traditions) did not amount to the establishment of a State religion. Section 116 will only be breached by a law which has as its clear purpose an outcome prohibited by that provision.

Educational facilities: religion, staffing and pupil access

It could, perhaps, be argued that the National School Chaplaincy Programme constitutes a State-funded form of religious discrimination within the public school system because the service is restricted to provision by qualified religious personnel: who are Christian and are employed by Christian organisations such as Scripture Union, and who provide evangelical programs and activities such as Bible Clubs. Some secularists, adherents of non-Christian religions and others may perceive it at best as anomalous and at worst as intimidating to have such a programme defined as an in-built constituent part of their children's education. That the option to withdraw a child from scripture classes may not resolve this issue was demonstrated in *The State of Victoria, Department of Education & Early Childhood Development (Anti-Discrimination)*,[151] when parents claimed that such a 'singling out' would also give rise to religious discrimination, a claim rejected on the grounds that there was no evidence of adverse impact upon the children. A reverse instance of 'singling out' arose in the *Patka* case,[152] which concerned a five-year-old Sikh boy who was not allowed to enrol in a Christian primary school unless he conformed to the school dress code by cutting his hair and removing the small turban worn, as religiously required for Sikh children. The Tribunal concluded that it was "not reasonable to accept enrolment applications from students from non-Christian faiths only on condition that they do not look like they practise a non-Christian religion".

State schools, religion and educational content

Classroom-based religious instruction, usually one hour per week, is provided in most states and territories, often by volunteers, and has been for many years. The content consists of materials approved by the relevant religious organisation, none of which is subject to approval by the Department of Education and Training.[153] The efforts of Safe Schools Coalition Australia to introduce a nationwide programme offering guidance on how to combat anti-LGBTI abuse or bullying has generated much controversy. Christian organisations have lobbied, sometimes successfully, for the use of conceptual material relating to gender and sexuality to be prohibited in primary schools.

Faith schools

Faith schools in Australia, as noted above, are not a distinct category outside the public education system. Nonetheless, they are: free to require religious affiliation when employing staff and enrolling students; have a discretionary capacity to require adherence to the tenets and ethos of their respective religious organisations; and can integrate theories such as 'creationism' into the school curriculum. All of these characteristics may be perceived as having a detrimental effect on those pupils or their families with different values for example in relation to sexual orientation. Such overt government endorsement for faith schools was reinforced by the rejection of the plaintiff's claim in *Williams v. the Commonwealth of Australia*[154] that he had a right to secure a secular education for his children.

Right to non-discrimination in service provision

In Australia, whether as a cause or effect of the lack of any federal legislation specifically prohibiting religious discrimination, Christian organisations continue to dominate public benefit service provision as they do in Ireland. Some, by virtue of their size and longevity, have managed to remain true to their roots as local providers while also acquiring a nationwide brief; almost all are engaged in the delivery of social services.

Provision by religious organisations

Australian religious organisations act as government-funded service providers across many sectors in all Australian jurisdictions; they are responsible for the largest non-government grouping of hospitals, facilities for the aged and community care services. They have more than 760,000 students in their schools. The Marriage Amendment (Definition and Religious Freedoms) Act 2017, in keeping with the Sex Discrimination Act 1984, exempts religious organisations from providing facilities, goods or services if to do so would compromise either their beliefs or those of their religious communities. However, s.38 of the 1984 Act ties that exemption to the "doctrines, tenets, beliefs or teachings of a particular religion or creed'; thereby narrowing the ambit of application.

The above mentioned *OV and OW*[155] and *Cobaw Community Health Services Limited v. Christian Youth Camps Limited & Anor*[156] cases both centred on alleged discrimination by religious organisations. The first concerned the right of Wesley Mission to withhold services, by not accepting an application to place a child in the foster care of a same-sex couple, on the grounds that its religious beliefs would be breached if it treated them the same as it did those whose status complied with the core Wesleyan doctrine of "monogamous heterosexual partnership within marriage". Ultimately, the court rejected the allegation of discrimination on finding that the Wesley Mission was able to avail of the statutory exemption as, at the relevant time, its doctrines were binding upon the Mission and could be construed as religious (see further above). In the second, the issue was whether Christian Youth Camps, a religious charity, could withhold services to people because of their sexual orientation but claim statutory exemption from what would otherwise be discriminatory practice. Justice Hampel's conclusion, endorsed by the Court of Appeal,[157] that it was not necessary for the respondents to refuse the booking in order to comply with their genuine religious beliefs, and in taking that step they had discriminated in breach of the Act.

Recently, the Sex Discrimination Amendment (Sexual Orientation, Gender Identity and Intersex Status) Act 2013 has imposed constraints on the discretion of religious organisations to deny service provision on grounds of a conflict with religious beliefs. Care homes owned by such organisations are no longer able to exclude people from aged care services based on their LGBTI or same-sex relationship status. However, in most other respects their discretionary discriminatory practices remain in place: Catholic hospitals, for example, are free to continue their embargo on conducting vasectomies, tubal ligation and abortions; faith schools maintain their religious access filters and are exempt from gender identity and sexual orientation provisions; and family planning services provided by religious organisations, even if receiving government funding, provide advice and information that excludes access to contraception or abortion.

Provision of public services

The piecemeal effects of disparate state and territory legislation on matters of equality and non-discrimination are particularly apparent in relation to public service provision and associated anomalous case law. For example, while an Orthodox Jew was unsuccessful in alleging that it was discriminatory for the relevant authority to fail to provide him with a house within walking distance of a synagogue, he succeeded in his claim that his refusal of other accommodation should not be deemed to be 'unreasonable' by the authority.[158] Again, while it was accepted that the public school system did not accommodate the religious beliefs of many parents, forcing them into having their children schooled outside that system, the parents were successful in their appeal against the refusal of public transport concession cards to fund the additional travel costs.[159]

Private goods and service provision

The above-mentioned 2013 Act prohibits discrimination on the basis of sexual orientation, or gender identity or expression, throughout Australia. Aside from the above-mentioned *Cobaw* case, there do not appear to be reported judgments, at any rate none known to this writer, on issues that elsewhere typically relate to the refusal of commercial services – such as accommodation – on religious grounds.[160]

Service denial on grounds of conscientious objection

In some states and territories, such as Victoria, medical practitioners can refuse to undertake or participate in an abortion procedure if to do so would be against their religious belief. However, little credence was given to a challenge to the introduction of the GST (goods and services tax) that to comply would breach the obligation of Muslims not to collect taxes on behalf of government. The court held that "the importance of maintaining a sound tax system is of such a high order that the religious belief in withholding GST tax is not protected by s.116".[161]

Broadcasting services

In the absence of any cases specifically dealing with public broadcasting and religion, the *Threewisemonkeys*[162] decision is of relevance as it illustrates a legal conflation of sexual orientation with religious belief and the weak constitutional protection afforded to religion. It also indicates the related legal constraints on broadcasting. The case concerned a pamphlet, published by a representative of an organisation known as the 'Threewisemonkeys', and distributed in the Sandy Bay area of Hobart in 2013. It stated that "homosexuality should not be tolerated" and that "Scripture rejects homosexuality as utterly abominable", and set out alleged statistics on lifespan expectations and causes of death for gay men and lesbians compared to heterosexual men and women. The complainant claimed that publishing and distributing this pamphlet constituted incitement to hatred on the grounds of sexual orientation under the Tasmanian Anti-Discrimination Act 1998, s.19, while the respondent claimed that such conduct was protected by the right to freedom of religion under s.116 of the Constitution. The court found that the latter:[163]

> does not amount to a complete guarantee of protection. In particular, it does not provide individuals with any avenue of legal redress if their perceived right to freedom of religion has been violated. In any event, any "freedom" must be balanced against the rights of others, as is the case with the rights to freedom of speech and freedom of association. Accordingly, the Tribunal finds no basis for the respondent's reliance on a right to freedom of religion by way of response or defence to this complaint.

Somewhat ironically, the respondent's defeat was due to his reliance upon the weak protection afforded by s.116.

Conclusion

There is a lack of coherence in the Australian approach to both national legislation relating to religious discrimination and to incorporating international human rights law into national legislation. For almost two decades, the Australian Human Rights Commission has been making submissions to government on the desirability of a federal Religious Freedom Act, and in its 2018 report it again "urges the Australian Government to consider expanding the circumstances in which federal anti-discrimination law protects against discrimination and vilification on the basis of religion".[164] It is also interesting that there would seem to be little indication that there is the same wrestling with a need to consider "liberty laws" in Australia as there is in the US and, if more tentatively, in the UK.

Notes

1 Australian Human Rights Commission, *Religious Freedom Review*, 2018, at para 131. See further, at: https://www.humanrights.gov.au/submissions/religious-freedom-review-2018.
2 See the Human Rights (Parliamentary Scrutiny) Act 2011, s.3(1).
3 See *Toonen v. Australia,* Communication No. 488/1992, U.N. Doc CCPR/C/ 50/D/488/ 1992 (1994).
4 GA Res 36/55, UN GAOR, 36th sess, UN Doc A/36/684 (25 November 1981).
5 Australian Human Rights Commission, *Religious Freedom Review*, 2018, at para. 90. See further, at: https://www.humanrights.gov.au/submissions/religious-freedom-review-2018
6 *Attorney-General (vic) (Ex rel Black) v. Commonwealth* (1981) 146 CLR 559, per Barwick, C.J., at pp. 580–581.
7 Neil Foster points out that the protections in the employment area in relation to discrimination on the grounds of religion only apply where the relevant State provides such protection, citing s.351(2)(a) (note to author, 20 February 2017).
8 [2002] 120 FCR 243.
9 *Jones v. Tonen* [2002] FCA 1150.
10 See the Australian Human Rights Commission, *Freedom of Religion and Belief*, (1998); *Freedom of Religion and Belief in the 21st Century*, (March 2011); and *Religious Freedom Review*, (February 2018). See further, at: https://www.humanrights.gov.au/our-work/race-discrimination/projects/freedom-religion-and-belief-21st-century
11 See Human Rights Law Centre, at: www.hrlc.org.au/news/2017/6/7/freedom-of-religion-or-belief-should-have-federal-protection-with-appropriate-mechanism-for-balancing-competing-rights.
12 See UNHR Committee, *Concluding Observations: Australia* (2009), at para. 12.5.
13 See further at: www.ag.gov.au/RightsAndProtections/HumanRights/United-Nations-Human-Rights-Reporting/Pages/Australias-Universal-Periodic-Review.aspx.
14 See further Beck, L., 'The Constitutional Prohibition on Religious Tests', *Melbourne University Law Review*, Vol. 35, 2011, at pp. 323–353.
15 (1979) 154 CLR 79. See also *Sykes v. Cleary* (1992) 176 CLR 77.

16 Dating back to the 1915 'battle of Broken Hill', involving Islamic militants.
17 (1985) 1 NSWLR 525.
18 Aroney, N., 'The Constitutional (In)validity of Religious Vilification Laws: Implications for their Interpretation', *Federal Law Review*, Vol. 34:2, 2006.
19 See further Puig, G.V. and Tudor, S., 'To the Advancement of Thy Glory? A Constitutional and Policy Critique of Parliamentary Prayers', *Public Law Review*, Vol. 20:56, 2009 at pp. 8–9.
20 *R v. Winneke; Ex parte Gallagher* (1982) 152 CLR 211.
21 (1981) 146 CLR 559, at p. 605.
22 *Jehovah's Witnesses Case* (1943) 67 CLR 116, per Latham, C.J., at p. 131.
23 *Minister for Immigration and Ethnic Affairs v. Lebanese Moslem Ass'n* (1987) 71 A.L.R. 578, at p. 584.
24 *Walsh v. St Vincent de Paul Society Queensland (No. 2)* [2008] QUADT 32.
25 *Grace Bible Church Inc v. Reedman* (1984) 54 ALR 571 when the Supreme Court of South Australia decided that the s116 right did not apply to state laws.
26 *Attorney-General (Vic) (Ex rel Black) v. Commonwealth* (1981) 146 CLR 559.
27 (1912) 15 CLR 366.
28 (1943) 67 CLR 116.
29 Neil Foster points out that the regulations were struck down as invalid, but not on s.116 grounds (note to author, 20 February 2017).
30 (1983) 154 CLR 120, per Murphy, J., at pp. 150–151.
31 [2014] FCAFC 26.
32 The Territory Acts do provide some protection: Discrimination Act 1991 (ACT) s. 11; Anti-Discrimination Act 1992 (NT) s.4(4), which expressly includes Aboriginal spiritual belief.
33 (1998) 90 FCR 202.
34 See the Human Rights and Equal Opportunity Commission, *Bringing Them Home: A Guide to the Findings and Recommendations of the National Inquiry into the Separation of Aboriginal and Torres Strait Islander Children from Their Families*, Australian Government Publishing Service, Sydney, NSW, 1997. On 13 February 2008, Prime Minister Kevin Rudd delivered an official apology on behalf of the Parliament of Australia to those affected by the Stolen Generations policy. See further, at: https://www.humanrights.gov.au/sites/default/files/content/pdf/social_justice/bringing_them_home_report.pdf
35 See *Milirrpum v. Nabalco Pty Ltd* (1971) 17 FLR 141 (the Gove Land Rights case) and *Coe v. Commonwealth* [1979] HCA 68.
36 *Cheedy on behalf of the Yindjibarndi People v. State of Western Australia* [2010] FCA 690; [2011] FCAFC 100.
37 Tasmania being the only exception. The absence of a religious exemption in its anti-discrimination legislation means that it is illegal to discriminate there on the grounds of sexuality or gender identity.
38 [2008] QADT 32.
39 [2010] VCAT 1613 (8 October 2010).
40 (2006) EOC 93–422 (VCAT).
41 See Royal Commission, *Institutional Responses to Child Sexual Abuse*, 2017, at: www.abc.net.au/news/2017-02-06/child-sex-abuse-royal-commission:-data-reveals-catholic-abuse/8243890.
42 See further at: www.childabuseroyalcommission.gov.au/media-centre/media-releases/2015-07/public-hearing-into-the-jehovah's-witnesses.
43 See Human Rights Law Centre, at: www.hrlc.org.au/news/2017/6/7/freedom-of-religion-or-belief-should-have-federal-protection-with-appropriate-mechanism-for-balancing-competing-rights.

44 Australian Human Rights Commission, *Religious Freedom Review*, 2018, at para. 152. See further, at: https://www.humanrights.gov.au/submissions/religious-freedom-review-2018
45 (1967) VR 732.
46 *Council of the Municipality of Canterbury v. Moslem Alawy Society Limited* (1987) 162 CLR 145 and *Crowther v. Brophy* [1992] 2 VR 97, 100.
47 See, for example, *Omari v. Omari* [2012] ACTSC 33. See further Butt, 'Testamentary Conditions in Restraint of Religion', *Sydney Law Review*, Vol. 8, 1977, p. 400.
48 (1960) 104 CLR 394; [1961] ALR 339.
49 (1960) 104 CLR 394, at para. 5. Neil Foster questions whether s.116 would apply to State Supreme Court decisions on matters of succession (note to author, 20 February 2017).
50 *Williams v. the Commonwealth of Australia* [2012] HCA 23.
51 *Williams v. Commonwealth of Australia* [2014] HCA 23.
52 See *Adelaide Company of Jehovah's Witnesses Inc v. Commonwealth* (1943) 67 CLR 116; *Krygger v. Williams* (1915) 15 CLR 366.
53 (1984) 54 ALR 571.
54 Ibid., at p. 385.
55 *Evans v. New South Wales* (2008) 168 FCR 576, per French, Branson and Stone, J.J., at p. 596.
56 Evans, C., 'Legal Aspects of the Protection of Religious Freedom in Australia' (paper prepared for the project 'Freedom of Religion and Belief in the 21st Century') 2009, at p. 8. See further, at: https://www.humanrights.gov.au/sites/default/files/content/frb/papers/Legal_%20Aspects.pdf
57 Op. cit., at pp. 85–86.
58 (1944) 15 LGR 139.
59 [1983] HCA 40; (1983) 154 CLR 120 (27 October 1983), at p. 137.
60 *OV and OW*, op. cit., at para. 40.
61 *OV v. QZ (No. 2)* [2008] NSWADT 115; *Member of the Board of the Wesley Mission Council v. OV and OW* (No. 2) [2009] NSWADTAP 57; *OV & OW v. Members of the Board of the Wesley Mission Council* [2010] NSWCA 155.
62 *OW & OV v Members of the Board of the Wesley Mission Council* [2010] NSWADT 293 (10 December 2010) at para 54.
63 Ibid., at para. 40.
64 [2010] VCAT 1613 (8 October 2010).
65 See also *Ananda Marga Pracaraka Samgha Ltd v. Tomar* (No. 6) [2013] FCA 284.
66 *Church of New Faith v. Commissioner of Pay-Roll Tax* (1983) 1 VR 97, at para. 13.
67 (1983) 154 CLR 120, at para. 18.
68 For a critique of the decision, see Sadurski, W., 'On Legal Definitions of Religion', *Australian Law Journal* 63 (December 1989) pp. 834–843. See also *Nelson v. Fish* (1990) 21 FCR 430. Note that in *R (on the application of Hodkin and another) v. Registrar General of Births, Deaths and Marriages* [2013] UKSC 77 the Supreme Court adopted much the same approach.
69 *Re Jones* [1907] SALR 1990 (Incorporated Body of Freethinkers of Australia).
70 (1943) 67 CLR 116, at p. 124.
71 *Church of New Faith v. Commissioner of Pay-Roll Tax* (1983) 1 VR 97.
72 Ibid.
73 Ibid., at p. 132.
74 *Wanjurri v. Southern Cross Broadcasting (Aus) Ltd* (2001) EOC 93–147, per Commissioner Innes.
75 *Aboriginal Legal Rights Movement Inc v. State of South Australia and Iris Eliza Stevens* (1995) 64 SASR 551, per Doyle, C.J., at pp. 552–553.

76 See, for example, Gallois, W., 'On Dreaming Time', in *Time, Religion and History*, Pearson Education, London, 2007.
77 (1995) 64 SASR 551.
78 See (1997) 190 CLR 1.
79 Ibid., at p. 86.
80 (1943) 67 CLR 116, 124.
81 (1983) 154 CLR 120, 135.
82 Ibid., citing both s.14 of the Charter and Art 18 of the ICCPR. Endorsed by the Victorian Court of Appeal in *Christian Youth Camps Limited & Ors v. Cobaw Community Health Services Limited & Ors* [2014] VSCA 75.
83 Citing Laws, L.J., in *McFarlane v. Relate Avon Limited* [2010] EWCA Civ B1.
84 In September 2014, an Islamophobia Register was launched, in which 243 verified incidents of abuse and discrimination of Muslims were logged in the first 14 months.
85 See, for example, Amnesty International, *Submission to the Religious Freedom Review*, (13February 2018), at: www.amnesty.org.au/wp-content/uploads/2018/02/Religious-Freedom-Review-Submission.pdf.
86 As, for example, in *Evans v. NSW* [2008] FCAFC 130 and *Iliafi v. The Church of Jesus Christ of Latter-Day Saints Australia* [2014] FCAFC 26.
87 Note to author, 22 February 2017.
88 *Unions NSW v. New South Wales* [2013] HCA 58.
89 Parkinson, P., *Traditional Rights and Freedoms – Encroachments by Commonwealth Laws* (ALRC Interim Report 127), *Submission 9*, 2015.
90 [2003] NSWSC 292.
91 See, for example: *Fletcher v. Salvation Army Australia (Anti Discrimination)* [2005] VCAT 1523 (1 August 2005); *Bropho v. Human Rights and Equal Opportunity Commission* [2004] FCAFC 16; *Judeh v. Jewish National Fund of Australia Inc* [2003] VCAT 1254; and *John Fairfax Publications Pty Ltd v. Kazak* [2002] NSWADTAP 35.
92 [2006] VCAT 2456.
93 [2008] FCAFC 130.
94 [2001] QADT 20.
95 [2008] QADT 20, at para. 129.
96 *Youssef v. Khani* [2006] TASADT 8.
97 *Eatock v. Bolt* [2011] FCA 1103.
98 *Sisalem v. The Herald & Weekly Times Ltd* [2016] VCAT 1197.
99 [2006] VSCA 284.
100 See further Parkinson, P., 'Enforcing Tolerance: Vilification Laws and Religious Freedom in Australia', 2005, at: http://sydneyanglicans.net/blogs/indepth/enforcing_tolerance_patrick_parkinson.
101 *Attorney-General (SA) v. Corporation of the City of Adelaide* [2013] HCA 3.
102 *Gaynor v. Chief of Defence Force (No. 3)* [2015] FCA 1370.
103 Ibid., at p. 215.
104 [2018] NSWCA 103.
105 See *NABD of 2002 v. Minister for Immigration and Multicultural and Indigenous Affairs* [2005] HCA 29; (2005) 216 ALR 1; (2005) 79 ALJR 1142, at p. 121.
106 (1912) 15 CLR 366.
107 (1926) 38 CLR 380.
108 See further Foster, N.J., 'Religious Freedom in Australia', keynote address at 2015 Asia Pacific JRCLS conference, Sydney, at: https://works.bepress.com/neil_foster/94/.
109 *Daniels v. Deputy Commissioner of Taxation* [2007] SASC 431 (Unreported, Debelle, Sulan and Vanstone, J.J., 7 December 2007).

110 *SDW v. Church of Jesus Christ of Latter-Day Saints* (2008) 222 FLR 84.
111 See, for example, the 2015 UPR, at: https://documents-dds-ny.un.org/doc/UNDOC/GEN/G16/004/89/PDF/G1600489.pdf?OpenElement.
112 [2015] VCC 1911.
113 Ibid., at para. 49.
114 See *Qumsieh v. GAB* (1998) 14 VAR 46.
115 [2013] NSWCA 320.
116 See *Toonen v. Australia* CCPR/C/D/488/1992 (4 April 1992) and *Christopher John Wake and Djiniyinni Gondarra v. Northern Territory of Australia and the Honourable Keith John Austin Asche AC, The Administrator of the Northern Territory of Australia* (Unreported judgment of the Supreme Court) No. 112 of 1996 (24 July 1996).
117 See, for example, *R v. Shirley Justins* [2011] NSWSC 568.
118 For an overview of Australian law on this subject see Foster, N., 'Euthanasia and Assisted Dying: The Law and Why It Should Not Change', at: https://lawandreligionaustralia.files.wordpress.com/2018/05/euthanasia-paper-hunter-bible-church.pdf.
119 See further Evans, C. and Gaze, B., 'Between Religious Freedom and Equality: Complexity and Context', *Harvard International Law Journal*, Vol. 49, 2008.
120 [2012] FamCAFC 37.
121 See further the Australian Human Rights Commission, *Same-Sex: Same Entitlements*, 2007, at: www.humanrights.gov.au/our-work/sexual-orientation-sex-gender-identity/publications/same-sex-same-entitlements.
122 Communication No. 488/1992, UN Doc CCPR/C/50/D/488/ 1992.
123 See The Senate: Community Affairs Reference Committee, 'Involuntary or Coerced Sterilisation of Intersex People in Australia', October 2013, at: http://www.aph.gov.au/~/media/Committees/Senate/committee/clac_ctte/involuntary_sterilisation/second_report/report.ashx.
124 [2017] FamCAFC 258.
125 [2003] FamCA 94. See also *Re: Wakim ex parte McNally* (1999) 198 CLR 511.
126 [2007] VCAT 640.
127 CCPR/C/119/D/2172/2012 (2017).
128 See further at: www.catholicculture.org/culture/library/view.cfm?id=7801.
129 *Cancer Voices Australia v. Myriad Genetics Inc* [2013] FCA 65.
130 *D'Arcy v. Myriad Genetics Inc & Anor* [2015] HCA 35.
131 See *Association for Medical Pathology v. Myriad Genetics Inc* 596 – (2013).
132 See *X v. The Commonwealth* (1999) 167 ALR 529, per Justices Gummow and Hayne; where the discrimination concerned disability rather than religion.
133 (1988) EOC 92–217 (Vic ESCAB).
134 (1998) EOC 92–928 (HREOC).
135 See *Dixon v. Anti-Discrimination Commissioner of Queensland* (2004) EOC 93–327 (SCQ).
136 Author acknowledges advice of Beth Gaze on this matter (note to author, 22 February 2017).
137 (1998) EOC 92–934 (Vic ADT).
138 [2008] QADT 32.
139 [1997] HREOC 38.
140 (1999) EOC 92–971 (VCAT).
141 (1987) EOC 92–206 (VCAT); *Petroleum Refineries (Australia) v. Marett* (1988) EOC 92–237 (SCV).
142 [2003] TASADT 14.
143 [2005] VCAT 871 (Unreported, Member Davis V-P, 11 May 2005).
144 (1999) VCAT, Tribunal No. A328 of 1999.
145 [2009] NSWADT 318.

146 [2013] AusHRC 66.
147 Contrary to Australia's international obligations under ILO Convention (No. 111) concerning Discrimination in respect of Employment and Occupation and to the Australian Human Rights Commission Act, s.3(1).
148 (1981) 146 CLR 559. Also known as the State Aid or Defence of Government Schools (DOGS) case.
149 *Best Practice Education Group Ltd T/as Blue Gum School v. Dept of Education & Community Services* [2002] ACTDT 1.
150 [2016] NSWCA 157.
151 [2012] VCAT 1547.
152 *Arora v. Melton Christian College (Human. Rights)* (2017) VCAT 1507.
153 Beth Gaze adds that "this has now been abolished in Victoria and challenged in NSW" (note to author, 22 February 2017).
154 [2012] HCA 23. See further at: www.hcourt.gov.au/cases/case-s307/2010.
155 *OV v. QZ* (No. 2) [2008] NSWADT 115; *Member of the Board of the Wesley Mission Council v. OV and OW* (No. 2) [2009] NSWADTAP 57; *OV & OW v. Members of the Board of the Wesley Mission Council* [2010] NSWCA 155.
156 [2010] VCAT 1613. See further at: www.austlii.edu.au/au/cases/vic/VCAT/2010/1613.html.
157 *Christian Youth Camps Limited & Ors v. Cobaw Community Health Services Limited & Ors* [2014] VSCA 75.
158 *Azriel v. NSW Land & Housing Corporation* [2006] NSWCA 372. Mr Azriel was an Orthodox Jew who could not drive or travel by public transport on the Sabbath.
159 *Christian Family Schools Association of Australia v. Public Transport Corporation* (1990) EOC 92–300.
160 Though see *Burke v. Tralaggan* [1986] EOC 92–161 when a Christian couple were held to have unlawfully refused to rent a flat to an unmarried couple.
161 See *Halliday v. Commonwealth of Australia* [2000] FCA 950, per Sundberg, J., at p. 20. See also *Daniels v. Deputy Commissioner of Taxation* [2007] SASC 431 where the challenge, on religious grounds, to paying tax was in relation to government funding of abortion services.
162 *Williams v. 'Threewisemonkeys' and Durston* [2015] TASADT.
163 Ibid., at para. 50.
164 Australian Human Rights Commission, *Religious Freedom Review*, 2018, at para. 126. See further, at: https://www.humanrights.gov.au/submissions/religious-freedom-review-2018.

Part III

Evaluation

8 Themes of commonality and difference

Introduction

"Substantive equality and equal impact are not wholly equivalent" as Laycock has pointed out,[1] quoting "the law, in its majestic equality, forbids the rich as well as the poor to sleep under bridges, to beg in the streets, and to steal bread".[2] Against a contemporary background of radically changing social norms and cultural contexts that differ across the Part II jurisdictions, the truth of that observation as it relates to the impact of law on religion and belief has seldom been more starkly apparent.

This chapter considers the significance of such areas of jurisdictional commonality and difference, in relation to the intersection of religion and human rights, as were found to characterise the Part II jurisdictions. Rather than painstakingly follow the structure used in the format for those chapters, with the repetition this would entail, the chapter extracts and discusses the main themes emerging from the four sections: the legal framework; the State and the religion/human rights intersect; religion and the freedoms of association and expression; and the case law relating to human rights, equality and religion.

The legal framework for religion/human rights

Human rights law focuses on the individual. It confers upon each person a set of uniform entitlements in respect of which they are authorised to seek recognition and protection from their national courts and, if necessary, enforcement from international bodies.

While the national and international legal frameworks of the Part II jurisdictions provide fully for recognising and giving effect to such entitlements, including those that fall on the religion/human rights intersect, this by no means ensures their uniform operational effectiveness. The existence of a globally recognised legal framework may reflect a global consensus on what should constitute inalienable human rights, but the daily news provides a constant reminder of the extent to which this fails to translate into uniform international compliance with agreed normative rules.

Legislation

Contemporary international human rights law derives from the governing principles outlined in the United Nations Declaration of Human Rights as enlarged by the ICCPR. That inner core has been extended to ten international treaties and by innumerable additional international, regional and local legal instruments, though these are not uniformly acceded to by all jurisdictions: there are various abstentions, reservations and failures to ratify. This is most apparent in relation to the ECHR,[3] which is confined (for present purposes) to the UK and Ireland, where it has had a profound and lasting effect on the development of national legislation. As the court noted in *Tyrer v. the United Kingdom*,[4] the ECHR "is a living instrument which . . . must be interpreted in the light of present-day conditions", and it has often proven to be an effective resource for challenging outdated laws at the religion/human rights intersect in those jurisdictions.[5] The ICCPR, which is viewed in similar terms by the UN HRCommittee,[6] provides a common platform for all contracting States, most of which have fully incorporated its provisions into national law. It is firmly focused on the individual as a rights holder, rights which the State has a legal obligation to protect, but the ability of the UN HRCommittee to hold State parties to account for human rights violations is constrained by the fact that neither the UK nor the US have adopted Optional Protocol 1. The growth of this body of law has been organic: there is no classification of free-standing rights which are added to from time to time. Instead, there is a corpus of complex interdependent laws that evolve in response to changes in social context and whose application is often subject to political exigencies.

National law governing the religion/human rights intersect is generally to be found in much the same raft of legislation comprising statutes on human rights, equality and non-discrimination, employment equality and racial hatred. Some countries have chosen to constitutionally embed core human rights principles or to assimilate convention provisions into statute law. In recent years, this has been added to by not dissimilar national provisions for gay marriage and transgender matters, with some jurisdictions also legislating for the right to a medically assisted death. The US is singular in that the principle of equality is firmly established as a primary foundation stone of its constitution. Arguably, this gives it an overriding legal weighting when it comes into conflict with other human rights, and the consequences may be seen in the forensic judicial sifting of related interests when adjudicating on allegations of religious or sexual discrimination. It is, of course, singular also in the firm constitutional stand against any State 'establishment' of religion, in sharp contrast to the position taken, and being maintained, by the progenitor common-law jurisdiction. Given the latter singularity, it seems somewhat paradoxical that it is the US which has initiated policies (e.g. Charitable Choice and the Conscience and Religious Freedom Division) and legislation (e.g. the Religious Freedom Restoration Act 1993 and the International Religious Freedom Act 1998) permitting State protective measures toward religion and the religious, measures which leave the State in a weak position to claim that it respects the neutrality principle.

The areas of jurisdictional difference are interesting: Ireland, most noticeably, has only very recently initiated steps to legislatively address the human rights shortcomings repeatedly noted by the UNHRC, while Australia conspicuously lacks a human rights statute and, with no federal legislation specifically prohibiting religious discrimination, is often forced to rely upon race hatred statutes and/or the provisions of international treaties, conventions and protocols. The US and the UK can to some extent be differentiated from other jurisdictions by the attention now being given by the judiciary and legislature to developing the conscientious objection jurisprudence as a means of recalibrating the balance hitherto struck between equality rights and freedom of religion.

The majority of the Part II jurisdictions (the CANZUS nations) have a socially disadvantaged Indigenous population for whom the United Nations Declaration on the Rights of Indigenous Peoples (UNDRIP) 2006 is particularly important. However, despite the bearing of that dedicated set of provisions on their circumstances, in addition to the protection available under all other human rights instruments, the Indigenous people in all relevant jurisdictions continue to suffer from a higher incidence of human rights violation and a lower regard for their belief systems, relative to their fellow citizens.

Supranational bodies

The varied adherence to international instruments is matched by a similar jurisdictional disparity in acceptance of international courts. Most obviously, the US rejects the possibility of any international court having jurisdiction over its citizens, while assiduously pursuing extrajudicial processes against the citizens of many, mostly Muslim, countries. Both the UK and Ireland accept the jurisdiction of the ECtHR and respect its rulings on issues arising from the domestic litigation of 47 member States, even if the decisions have no binding effect on their domestic law. The resulting considerable body of jurisprudence has included formative principles – such as 'proportionality' and 'necessary in a democratic society' – which have proven influential in all Part II jurisdictions.

The UN is the world's largest and most powerful human rights organisation. It works on behalf of its almost 200 member States and it has been responsible for formulating many foundational human rights instruments. The work of the UN HRCouncil in managing the Universal Periodic Review process has significantly raised awareness as regards deficits in international human rights law and its avoidance or abuse by certain nations, though such a 'name and shame' practice has had little impact, for example, on the domestic policy of the US (e.g. closure of the Guantánamo Bay facility) and the UK (e.g. respect for ethnic minorities) or that of Ireland and Canada (e.g. State funding of Catholic schools in the public sector). The Council has developed a practice of adding 'Concluding Observations' as an addendum to national UPR reports, under the aegis of the Article 40 reporting requirements, which has evolved to become an important means for encouraging consistency and guiding the normative application of international human rights law. The withdrawal of the US in 2018, citing dissatisfaction with the number of member States with a poor human rights record, such as Algeria and Saudi Arabia, and also for reasons to do with the constant passing of resolutions criticising Israel, can only weaken the Council.

The quasi-judicial function exercised by the UN HRCommittee has resulted in many influential adjudications that have added weight and some controversy to the jurisprudence on the religion/human rights intersect.[7] In at least two areas, that controversy is likely to prove significant for the future: as regards the "margin of appreciation" rule, and in relation to the advice that "the Covenant should be interpreted as a living instrument and the rights protected under it should be applied in context and in the light of present-day conditions" (see further below). The "General Comments" issued from time to time by the Committee in respect of ICCPR implementation have also proven to be influential in guiding national practice.[8]

National courts and regulatory bodies

In all Part II jurisdictions, the flow of issues on the religion/human rights intersect very largely runs through regulatory bodies, with a relatively small proportion passing to the courts. Of the latter, their volume and the rate at which they end up in the national Supreme Court would seem to be greater in the US than elsewhere. In recent years, the force of that flow has been generally driven by equality legislation, and within that, by an increase in ethnic/religious- and LGBT-related issues.

The State and the human rights/religion intersect

The presumptive dominance of Christianity – its institutions, cultural attributes and moral imperatives – relative to the standing of all other religions and despite the increased prominence of secularism and government or judicial assurances of State neutrality, is unquestionably the strongest area of jurisdictional commonality in the relationship between human rights and religion, but there are others.

State neutrality

The importance of maintaining "the State's duty of impartiality and neutrality toward various religions, faiths and beliefs"[9] is well established by the ECtHR[10] (see further Chapter 2). It has also been judicially proclaimed in each of the Part II jurisdictions,[11] perhaps excepting Ireland, and with some vigour in Canada,[12] where paradoxically it is constitutionally compromised.[13] Further, the HRCommittee has recognised that proactive State intervention may be required in order to redress an imbalance and promote greater equality in the social presence of different religions:[14]

> The principle of equality sometimes requires States to take affirmative action in order to diminish or eliminate conditions which cause or help to perpetuate discrimination prohibited by the Covenant. For example, in a State where

> the general conditions of a certain part of the population prevent or impair their enjoyment of human rights, the State should take specific action to correct those conditions.

In practice, however, affirmative action – or positive discrimination – is not just more contentious in the field of religion and belief than in other areas; its purpose is also much more difficult to achieve. This is largely due to the intergenerational number and networks of adherents, the weight of associated outreach facilities and artefacts, and the duration of the social roles established by the main institutionalised religions relative to all others. The newly emerging religious groups suffer not only from the disadvantages of scale and of being unfamiliar to the general public but from the fact that there is such a wide range of them, many of which mutate and re-form, with overlapping memberships. Their variety, fluidity, reliance on websites and cross-border membership would frustrate any State strategic intervention designed to orchestrate a more equitable balance between religions.

Any prospect of State neutrality in the Part II jurisdictions is mostly compromised by an institutionalised deference to Christianity, despite the HRCommittee admonition that "limitations on the freedom to manifest a religion or belief for the purpose of protecting morals must be based on principles not deriving from a single tradition".[15] This deference is particularly evident in England and Wales where the Church of England is formally bound to the State, but in all Part II jurisdictions there is evidence, in terms of symbols and practices – constitutional references, national anthems, prayers on government occasions/premises, coinage and so on – of continuing State homage to its traditional Christian culture. It is embedded in their shared common-law roots, language, legislation and architecture. It is demonstrated in the same pattern of State privileges – regulatory, testamentary, taxation and statutory religious exemptions – present in all jurisdictions, which together with State funding, overwhelmingly benefit Christian religious organisations and have done so for a very long time. Indeed, the channelling of taxpayer revenue – from contributions made by adherents of many different religions and by atheists – to churches and religious organisations, the majority of which will have hiring or service policies favouring a specific religion and its adherents that significant numbers of taxpayers would not necessarily be in sympathy with, inevitably casts doubt on any State assertion of neutrality. Such doubt would be intensified by evidence of structural State support and funding for religious entities, for example, for school chaplains in Ireland and Australia. While State preferencing of Christianity and religion in general is most evident in England and in Ireland, it is least so in the US, where the Establishment and Free Exercise Clauses of the First Amendment in theory foreclose the prospect of such selective treatment,[16] although in practice do not prevent government from initiating policies and programmes that provide general support for religion.

Any inclination to follow HRCommittee advice toward achieving State neutrality is being undermined by an emerging development in the Church/State relationship: the judicial affirmation now being given to the right of the State to protect its established cultural identity. While this has been accepted for some time by the Irish judiciary,[17] it has since been endorsed by the ECtHR[18] which, together with recent US decisions upholding the opt-out rights of those with traditional religious beliefs,[19] may well indicate a resurgent legitimacy for protectionist State measures favouring a Christian cultural identity, though it has to be said that the Canadian judiciary strongly refute any such trend.[20] For the Special Rapporteur, there is a link between the trend and government policy in countries such as Slovakia, Poland and Romania toward the migrant crisis. In the closing sentence of his report he warns as follows:[21]

> The pretext that hosting certain refugees would erode the traditional religious make-up of a country amounts to a "territorialization" of religion or belief, which violates the spirit and the letter of the universal right to freedom of religion or belief.

As things stand, State neutrality in the short term would seem to be an unrealisable aspiration: no institution of the State is completely insulated from religion, all States fail to treat religions equally and none have clear rules for balancing the interests of secularism and religion. Secularism may well be growing and consolidating in the Part II jurisdictions, but in all likelihood the millennia of Christianity, strengthened by the recent populist revival of traditional national cultural norms, will slow any further steps toward a social consensus in favour of State neutrality.

Protecting religion from the State

In England, the constitutional recognition of an 'established' Church provides that religion with the strongest possible State guarantee of protection and, equally, thereby acknowledges that others will be regarded as of less importance. In the remaining Part II jurisdictions, there are constitutional prohibitions on 'establishment' which give all religions the protective assurance that none will be awarded preferential State status.

State intervention in religious matters, including in relation to the manifestation of religion or belief, is subject to constraints imposed by international conventions and national constitutional or statutory provisions. Such intervention, as the ECtHR stressed in *Chapman v. the United Kingdom*,[22] "will be considered 'necessary in a democratic society' for a legitimate aim if it answers a 'pressing social need' and, in particular, if it is proportionate to the legitimate aim pursued". It is not sufficient that an interference is deemed necessary in a "democratic society"; any restriction "must be directly related and proportionate to the specific need on which it is predicated". When directed toward matters held to be quintessentially religious – doctrines, tenets and so on – then State interference has traditionally been held to be unwarranted. However, while the courts in all Part II jurisdictions continue to uphold the principle of non-interference in Church disputes, the judiciary in England and Wales have recently indicated a willingness to intervene even as regards matters of doctrine.[23]

One aspect of the 'necessary in a democratic society' principle is 'the living instrument' caveat which has emerged from ECtHR and from HRCommittee case law to suggest that the provisions of the ECHR and the ICCPR should be interpreted and applied with regard to the current social context. The authority for this guidance is cited as sourced in the wording of Article 31 of the Vienna Convention, which broadly advises that the meaning of a treaty's terms should be determined in the light of the treaty's purpose, while taking into account the context and any relevant rules of international law.[24] Unfortunately, for the purposes of consistency in applying the law, social context varies considerably and is prone to rapid change in the Part II jurisdictions: the 'living instrument' approach is likely to require a different legal response to the same issue across different societies and in the same society from time to time. Moreover, for adherents of the traditional institutional religions – the doctrines and tenets of which are essentially predicated on being immutable and relatively impervious to changing social context – this advice is problematic and challenging for any State wishing to offer protection to those religions, their adherents and associated organisations. It must also be borne in mind that Indigenous people are citizens of the same democratic society, and there is little evidence of State willingness to offer parity of recognition and protection to their particular beliefs. How to reconcile the verities of religion with those of human rights, in a society where the mores are in flux, is a characteristic problem for all Part II jurisdictions but one most clearly evident in the US culture wars and in the contrasting circumstances of Indigenous people.

Allied to that principle, and again of fundamental significance for an appreciation of jurisdictional variations in judicial treatment of the religion/human rights intersect, is the "margin of appreciation" doctrine. The proposition includes the following:[25]

> States Parties enjoy a margin of appreciation in how they apply and implement the Convention, depending on the circumstances of the case and the rights and freedoms engaged. This reflects that the Convention system is subsidiary to the safeguarding of human rights at national level and that national authorities are in principle better placed than an international court to evaluate local needs and conditions.

This, it has to be said, does not sit easily alongside the much-vaunted doctrine of State neutrality, but decades of ECtHR decisions and the Protocol 15 amendment have firmly embedded this approach in the Convention jurisprudence of the 47 member States. The UN HRCommittee, however, has pointedly rejected the margin of appreciation.[26] Instead, the Committee argues that equality of treatment before the law is a basic precept and one of overriding importance. In the light of the burgeoning "conscientious objection" jurisprudence (see further below) this difference of opinion is one of real importance in relation to the scope legally available to the judiciary to protect religious adherents and organisations from the prescriptive State equality measures that are increasingly impacting on the religion/human rights intersect.

Judicial readiness to offer protection from State interference has been clearly demonstrated in relation to laws of universal application which are judged to disproportionately burden those of particular religious beliefs. Arguably, this is little more than a further permutation of the rationale underpinning the above principle and doctrine, but it does more fully engage with the proportionality principle. So in *Karnel Singh Bhinder v. Canada*,[27] the HRCommittee ruled that public safety concerns, under Article 18 of the ICCPR, did not warrant an employer's insistence that a Sikh workman wear a hard hat instead of his turban on a construction site, because any risk would not extend to the public. Again, in *Prince v. South Africa*,[28] it considered the prohibition on the use of cannabis to be a disproportionate burden on the freedom of religion for a Rastafarian who used it in compliance with his religious beliefs and whose criminal conviction for possession compromised his career. This approach has received little judicial attention in Australia but a great deal in the US. Rulings of the USSC from *Sherbert*,[29] as qualified by *Smith*[30] and further developed in the post-RFRA era,[31] have brought US law[32] to similarly establish the principle that laws of universal application which disproportionately affect those of religious beliefs place a heavy onus on the State to justify any such interference in the right to freedom of religion. So, also, in Canada, where the SCC in *Amselem*[33] ruled that laws prohibiting tenants from altering property imposed an undue burden on Jews whose beliefs required succahs to be constructed on their balconies.

While the extent and duration of State privileges – regulatory, testamentary and taxation – all of which focus on religious entities, is enough to demolish any pretence of State neutrality in all Part II jurisdictions, it is the religious exemption that has become particularly contentious. This may be due in part to a generalised adverse public reaction to the evidence of systemic sexual abuse perpetrated by the same religious organisations claiming an entitlement to be excused from the constraints of equality and non-discrimination legislation on the grounds that their transcendent beliefs are thereby unduly burdened. The range of entities entitled to rely on the religious exemption has become so much wider in the US than elsewhere that this is now a distinct area of jurisdictional difference. The *Hobby Lobby*[34] ruling, coupled with the "liberty laws" now introduced in eight states (as of June 2018), and reinforced most recently by the decision in *Masterpiece*,[35] has sharply differentiated US law governing the privileges available from the law prevailing in all other Part II jurisdictions. A "closely held" commercial company with a religious owner in the US is now free to discriminate on grounds of religion or belief or sexual orientation in the way they operate. In the UK, an employer with a 'religious ethos' but without a commercial sole or main purpose may only discriminate on the grounds of religion or belief or sexual orientation when appointing staff if such religion or belief is a 'determining' requirement of the post. In Canada, religious exemption is constitutionally extended to grant denominational school privileges, while in Ireland and to some extent in Australia the number of service providers benefitting from the exemption is particularly high, but this may simply reflect the higher proportion of religious providers.

Another aspect of the principle that religion should be protected from State interference is interesting if only because of the general lack of contention it generates in the US, Canada, Australia and elsewhere. Theoretically, the right to freedom of religion and to human rights protection applies as much to the beliefs/culture of Indigenous people as to adherents of institutional religions and to those of all other faiths and none, a principle given international recognition.[36] In practice, their beliefs have at worst been subject to sustained systematic State persecution and at best have attracted fairly rudimentary State recognition and protection. The resulting case law reveals considerable jurisdictional commonality in the cursory weighting given to their beliefs and in the judicial failure to protect these from State interference.[37]

A final area of jurisdictional commonality lies in the failure to protect religion from State interference that is given effect through national and international antiterrorism measures. Since 9/11, all modern developed nations, especially the Part II jurisdictions, have initiated policies and laws to address terrorism, much of which is generated by Islamic fundamentalism. The consequent failure to ensure adequate protection for religion is evident in certain antiterrorism measures – 'stop and search', deportation, use of extraordinary rendition and Guantánamo and so on – deployed mainly against adherents of a particular religion. In relation to the Part II jurisdictions, two extremes are apparent: Ireland, which did not join the counter-insurgency alliance of Western powers against Islamic militants, and the US, which led that alliance and perpetrated human rights abuses such as drone strike executions, torture and dehumanising treatment in Abu Ghraib and detention without trial in Guantánamo.

Religion and the freedoms of association and expression

Within the past two decades or so, our understanding of what in law constitutes a religion has undergone a radical change: beliefs that had seemed immutable for millennia are no longer necessarily so regarded; some current interpretations would be incomprehensible to all previous generations. Such changes to the freedom of religion have impacted upon the freedoms of association and expression.

Freedom of religion

In all Part II jurisdictions, the institutional religions have traditionally been legally recognised through supportive evidence supplied by doctrines, tenets and practice of worship, rituals and so on. In Ireland and Canada, this has largely continued to be the case. In Australia, however, as in the UK and the US, the judiciary would seem convinced that there is no longer a necessity for an entity to have, or hold to, such a body of liturgical and ecclesiastical teachings in order to substantiate its status as a 'religion'.[38] Moreover, there is judicial consensus that doctrines, tenets and so on are to be interpreted in accordance with a contemporary social context, not as when first formulated. This legal rationale, if not necessarily theologically accepted, has obvious implications for religions such as

Islam. A person, therefore, need not necessarily subscribe to any particular set of doctrines in order to be considered in law an adherent of the related religion; a subjective interpretation, sincerely held but contemporaneously contextualised, may suffice. Indeed, that subjective interpretation may well be legally valid even if it is not recognised as legitimate by relevant religious authorities.

The opinions of judiciary and regulators have converged to suggest that certain elements are crucial if a 'belief' is to acquire a status commensurate with 'religion'. Beliefs must amount to more than mere opinions, views or deeply held feelings; they must involve holding a spiritual or philosophical conviction which has an identifiable formal content, and the subject matter has to be sufficiently weighty. They also require supporting evidence that the holder had invested a personal and strong commitment to upholding the beliefs; a demonstrable degree of sincerity is required. Attention has shifted from religion as an institution to the authenticity of an individual's subjective interpretation and experience of it.[39] So cogency, seriousness, cohesion, importance and commitment have come to be viewed as essential. This approach has made it possible to extend regulatory recognition to organisations (such as Druids and Pagans with a spiritualist or faith healing focus) and to persons (such as believers in climate change). One indicator of creeping jurisdictional commonality in the legal definition of 'religion' and 'belief' is the credence now given to Scientology: currently legally recognised in all Part II jurisdictions except Ireland. Another is the delayed and grudging acceptance of UNDRIP by the CANZUS nations, which has at least assured that they are now formally committed to recognising the rights of Indigenous people to have and to practice their beliefs on the basis of legal parity with other religions.

Clearly, as the legal definition of 'religion' and 'belief' has broadened so, too, have the ways and means by which they may be legitimately manifested. The right to do so is subject to much the same constraints, regarding the rights of others and public health or safety considerations, in all Part II jurisdictions. Increasingly, this right is being exercised and challenged from the perspective of its conflation with rights of equality or sexual orientation. A significant area of jurisdictional difference in relation to the law governing the manifestation of religion and belief is the growth in carve-outs provided in the US from equality provisions which then feed into that country's culture wars. Allied to this is the jurisdictional difference in the scope for conscientious objection, as exercised by health care professionals in relation to matters such as abortion, IVF or transgender service provision: a greater span of discretionary exemption is now statutorily available in the US and UK than in other jurisdictions.

Freedom of religion includes the right not to be discriminated against on religious grounds and is a right which is prone to becoming entangled with other fundamental rights. Where a universal policy or law, though couched in neutral terms, has a disproportionately prejudicial effect on the interests of a minority ethnic or religious group and there are no public health and safety concerns, then there is jurisdictional consensus that this will constitute unlawful discrimination.[40] Where, however, religiously motivated conduct is not human rights-compliant – such as in *talaq* divorce, *nikah* marriage or FGM – then the strictures of domestic anti-discrimination law should prevail, which has not to date been the case in the UK in relation to FGM. Indeed, an area of jurisdictional commonality lies in the degree of latitude extended to ethnic/religious practices: this includes a shared inability to ensure that a coherent relationship prevails between national and Shari'a laws; and, equally, a shared lack of policies to address the jurisdictional 'creep' of Islamophobia. Australia is singular among the Part II jurisdictions in not having any national statutes specifically prohibiting religious discrimination which results in litigation that relies unduly upon domestic racial discrimination laws and on international conventions, particularly the ICCPR.

Freedom of association

The freedom to associate is now increasingly in conflict with the freedom of religion. As the law extends recognition to the right of religious entities – persons, churches, religious organisations – to be excused from involvement in an ever-broadening sweep of activities – public health care duties, commercial service provision, officiating at gay marriages and so on – so it simultaneously licences breaches in the freedom to freely associate. This would seem set to become a shared feature of contemporary life in the Part II jurisdictions.

Respect for the freedom to associate, for the accompanying obligation to exercise positive action to offset a disadvantage suffered by a particular group and for both to be deployed in relation to religious entities is held to be important in all the jurisdictions studied, perhaps particularly so in the US, where this First Amendment right has always been staunchly defended. Where matters become less clear is when it comes to the right of any group to exclude others on the grounds of differences in religious belief or as regards LGBT issues. Contemporary examples include the right of Christian service providers (bakers, florists, bed-and-breakfast proprietors and so on) to refuse their services, on religious grounds, to members of the LGBT community. The succession of *Trinity Western* cases,[41] for example, illustrates the difficulties involved when a professional association founded on religious principles with exclusionary conditions seeks regulatory recognition on a par with other professional associations. Again, the right of an association formed for secular reasons (e.g. a St. Patrick's Day parade, to celebrate feminism or the suffragette movement, or to protest against racism) to exclude a group to join them under an evangelical Christian banner or an LGBT banner is becoming contentious in all Part II jurisdictions. Arguably such actions constitute discrimination and at times come close to segregation. The innate tension between the rights to associate and to freedom of religion would seem prone to breakdown when equality rights come into play.

Affirmative action, or positive discrimination, is also not without its problems. The use of quotas to increase the proportion of a minority group – such as Muslims – in employment or higher education and so on can have negative effects both on those who resent having to forgo an opportunity and on those who feel stigmatised at being at being offered it.

Freedom of expression

Not restricted to speech, but accommodating all forms of expression through all types of media in what is becoming an increasingly digital, multimedia context,[42] this right applies wherever a communication is being transmitted or received. As one of the most important indicators of a healthy democratic society, its exercise has been granted a generous latitude in the laws of all Part II jurisdictions, which are now generally free of religious censorship and where the law is guided by the principle that no one has a right not to be offended. Permissiveness is tolerated up to the point where an offensive expression becomes one of hate, which then leaves it subject to criminal sanctions under race or hate speech legislation. Blasphemy, once the archetypal criminal law threshold for freedom of speech in relation to religious matters, is now a national statutory offence only in Canada[43] as it has now been replaced in Ireland.[44] Proselytism, on the other hand, continues to be legally upheld in all jurisdictions as constituting an important aspect of the freedoms of both religion and expression. Arguably, however, Islamic proselytism – or *dawa* – is not ICCPR-compliant, as it goes far beyond information dissemination and persuasion to licence indoctrination.[45]

For most adherents, giving effect to religious beliefs and values through their behaviour in everyday life is mandatory. When this is manifested in public or private by wearing religion-specific clothing or ornaments, prayer, adherence to religious ceremonies and customary practices, then, provided it does not unduly impact upon the rights of others, this is commonly acceptable in all Part II jurisdictions. In particular, the right to express religious belief through the wearing of religion-specific clothing – if not in breach of health and safety requirements or the requirements of justice – is not usually problematic, at least in the common-law countries.[46] Issues commonly arise where such a demonstration of private religious adherence is made by a State employee such as a teacher in a State school when it could be open to interpretation as improper proselytism or a breach of the State duty of neutrality toward religion.[47] The case law reveals a common jurisdictional tendency toward conflating religious belief and sexual orientation and a growing awareness that the law needs to accommodate – under freedom of speech and freedom of religion – conduct that reflects genuine opposition, based on religious belief, to newly legislated social mores.

The traditional protection afforded by the principle of conscientious objection to those who choose to do or not to do something, in keeping with the dictates of their conscience, has become increasingly contentious in the current climate of change in relation to LGBT and other issues. Arguably, the introduction of "liberty laws" which extend exemption from equality and non-discrimination requirements to public service providers whose beliefs conflict with the nature of the service by formally legitimising a dual morality code, may well cause long-term incoherence to the relationship between the State and the religion/human rights intersect (see further below).

Human rights, equality and religion: the case law

Both Parkinson in Australia and Geddicks in the US have expressed concern regarding a "new fundamentalism about 'equality' ".[48] Insofar as this alludes to a general tendency for the levelling effect of equality law to undercut other legal rights, it's probably fair comment. However, in reality it seems impossible to reconcile equality dictates with religion. The latter, after all, has always been self-referential, hierarchical and given to operating within and by its own set of values: accommodating the stratifying and reductionist effects of equality law was guaranteed to present difficulties. Consequently, there is now a serious structural incoherence in the interrelationship between human rights, religion and international law. This is readily apparent in the pattern of issues arising where equality legislation intersects with religion and human rights.

Right of access to justice

This is often conditioned by the terms set by statutory law for legal aid and representation to be available in regulatory and judicial proceedings, which in practice is restrictive in ways that are prejudicial to the exercise of that right by those who are poor or who belong to marginalised communities such as the Indigenous people. It is also compromised, mostly in the US, by security issues.

In all Part II jurisdictions, there are religion-specific tribunals the rulings of which may be at variance with the principles applied in the official court system. The Shari'a and Beth Din courts, and to some extent those of the Protestant and Roman Catholic religions, provide forums and processes for mediating disputes – mainly marital and other family problems – and are intended to provide an alternative to national legislative remedies but may do so to the detriment of the human rights of women and such others as members of the LGBT community.[49] Specifically, in all jurisdictions, the disparity between the national legal system and Shari'a in relation to family law matters is such as to suggest that this anomalous situation needs to be specifically addressed by the legislature.

Right to life

Matters of life and death have always been of central importance to religion. This has led to abortion and euthanasia being for many years the focus of heated contention in all Part II jurisdictions.

In Ireland, the laws governing the availability of contraceptives and abortion have been and continue to be more restrictive than in any other nation currently being considered, resulting in well-founded allegations that Irish law on such matters violates women's basic reproductive rights. In the other jurisdictions, the comparable laws are much more permissive, if socially divisive, but only in the US have they generated decades of culture wars, violent protests and several deaths.

In all Part II jurisdictions, it has long been the case that a competent adult can refuse a blood transfusion, can choose to stop chemotherapy and can make informed choices about their medical treatment; such a decision must be respected by medical practitioners. Most case law has been in relation to the right of a parent to take such a decision on behalf of their child, and the courts have been uniformly of the view that the child's right to life-saving medical treatment outweighs all other considerations.

In relation to the issue of the availability of medical assistance to further death, Irish law is possibly the most regressive in the developed common-law nations, as assisted suicide continues to be a criminal offence punishable by up to 14 years imprisonment. Despite a recent ECtHR ruling[50] upholding its legality, a medically assisted death remains illegal in the UK, as it also does in Australia and in all but eight states in the US (as of summer 2018). Only in Canada is it legally available nationwide, and even there it is subject to tight statutory constraints.

Right to marriage and to found a family

Neither the right to marry and to found a family, nor the right to private and family life, nor any other right guaranteed by international human rights law, implies a right to procreation. Curiously, neither does such law recognise any right to divorce.

Legislation permitting same-sex marriage is now the new norm in most developed nations, but it presents fundamental challenges for many of those with religious beliefs. While it conflicts with the traditional values of Protestants, Catholics and Jews, it poses particularly serious problems for Muslims, as Islam is centred upon a model heterosexual marital family unit which ascribes gender roles and sexual orientation, and directs severe punishments for any breach of the related rules. The common jurisdictional exemption permitting ministers not to officiate at gay marriages – on the grounds that participation would be contrary to their religious beliefs – has become something of a weathervane for statutorily extending the conscientious objection of professionals across a range of religion-related service provision. The "liberty laws" as reinforced by the *Bryant* ruling[51] in the US, a development which the UK legislature would seem ready to follow, has legitimised the broadening ambit of conscientious objection on religious grounds. It must also, inevitably, raise the question as to whether the State is slipping into licencing a form of religious discrimination.

The tension between the right to freedom of religion or belief and the right not to be discriminated against on the basis of sex, sexual orientation, gender identity or intersex status gives rise to many issues which the "Yogyakarta principles",[52] compiled in 2007 and updated in 2017 by the International Commission of Jurists together with the International Service for Human Rights, seek to address. All Part II jurisdictions have in common the fact that they have recently introduced legislation that provides legal recognition for the acquired gender of transgender persons, though this varies according to whether or not surgery is involved, and have duly extended the ambit of legal prohibition from discrimination to provide protection for such persons. Currently, in the US, some revision of equality rights for transgender people is under way with, for example, a Presidential initiative to remove their eligibility to join the armed forces.

Reproductive rights continue to generate religious contention in all jurisdictions studied. While developments in artificial reproduction have been a matter of serious concern to many Christians, they are wholly reprehensible to those Muslims who respect the Qur'an injunction that "their mothers are only those who conceived them and gave birth to them (*waladna hum*)".[53] To some extent, there is a fundamental conflict between the human right to create a family and Islamic beliefs, as the latter would seem to present an insurmountable obstacle to doing so by relying on artificial means – such as IVF, statutory adoption and surrogacy – even if sanctioned by domestic law.

Again, while developments in medical intervention present difficulties for many Christians, they can be anathema to Muslims, as the Qur'an requires the genetic integrity of family lineage to remain inviolate.

Right to employment

Equality legislation intersects with the human rights to employment and to religious freedom largely with the effect of exempting religious organisations and persons of religious belief from certain constraints.

Religious organisations in all Part II jurisdictions are legislatively permitted to discriminate by restricting staff recruitment to those who share the organisation's religious belief where this is a genuine occupational requirement for a particular post or is necessary in order to be in accord with the organisation's religious ethos. This is qualified by the significant caveat that the post must be one that gives fairly direct effect to the organisation's religious standing – for example, teachers in a school or doctors in a hospital, but not secretarial or janitor staff – where such facilities are owned by a religious organisation. The firing of staff on discriminatory grounds for violating an organisation's religious beliefs is similarly subject to that caveat: the post must be one in which the employee's conduct would directly impact upon the employing organisation's religious purpose, and an employee bears some responsibility for having placed themselves in such a position. Problems in this employment context can often arise where religion is conflated with sexual behaviour or orientation. The hiring and firing practices of religious organisations, protected by statutory exemption privileges, can then have a disproportionately adverse effect on the human rights of staff belonging to the LGBT community, or divorcees, single parents or persons of another religion or none. In the US, the consequences of the decisions in *Hobby Lobby* and *Bryant*, the state "liberty laws" and the remit of the newly established Conscience and Religious Freedom Division of the HHS have yet to fully materialise. The parameters of the protection provided by the 'ministerial exception' have been extended[54] and the right to discriminate now includes those organisations that are only "connected" with the activities of a religion and those that are secular but "closely held" by religious owners.[55] Inevitably, religion will have a greater role in US employment practices, and upon the interplay of human rights in the workplace, than previously, and more so in this than in any other Part II jurisdiction.

In weighing the balance between the right of an employee to manifest religious beliefs – or lack of same – in the workplace as against the rights of colleagues to be spared unwanted exposure to such beliefs and an employer's right not to have interference in either work processes or marketing, the courts have developed a sympathetic understanding of the detrimental effects caused by those who foist their views on religion, belief or secularism on others. In doing so, the judiciary in all jurisdictions have applied the proportionality principle to assist in that determination, and in the US[56] and the UK[57] they have demonstrated a willingness to accept a subjective interpretation of what constitutes a 'religious belief' and its associated required rituals. In the latter, the case law[58] indicates that religious beliefs – or conscientious objection – will not justify a refusal to perform contractual duties if they disproportionately affect the rights of others.

Right to education

Government franchising out of public benefit services – such as education – to commercial and charitable providers, including religious organisations, has become a well-established practice in all developed nations in recent decades. The latter's delivery capacity, and obvious market advantage, is enhanced by tax exemption privileges and by equality legislation which permits a range of exceptions to discriminatory practice on the grounds of religion.

The doctrine of State neutrality requires a State to either refrain from supporting religious teaching in public schools or to provide it on an even-handed basis so that pupils of all religious denominations receive parity of support.[59] The fact that practice fails to reflect theory is a strong area of jurisdictional commonality. In the UK, where the Church of England has long had a dominant contribution to religious tuition in the public school system, the judiciary have advised that "the State may legitimately give priority to imparting knowledge of one religion above others, where that religion is practised or adhered to by a majority in society".[60] Most obviously, this is also the approach in Ireland,[61] Canada[62] – and, if less overtly, in Australia[63] – where it has been found to be justifiable on the ground that a State has the right to give primacy to its traditional cultural heritage.[64] It is an approach which ripples through the public provision of education, surfacing particularly in the religious preferencing given to staff selection, pupil access and in curriculum content. It is present in the customary requirement that all children be provided with some religious education, if not instruction, and in the usual daily classroom prayers and other collective religious practices. It can be seen in the policy of State funding for school chaplains, who are almost always representatives of Christian organisations. Again, there are often problems when children choose to wear non-Christian items of religious clothing in the classroom, or whose parents want to have creationism treated as scientific or object to educational material depicting

LGBT relationships. In all jurisdictions, there would seem to be a problem in arranging non-stigmatising opt-outs for pupils not wishing to participate in religious activities. The general jurisdictional priority that the State demonstrates in its support of Christianity throughout the public educational system is most clearly evident in relation to Catholicism in Ireland and Protestantism in England and Wales, and most obviously absent in the lack of equivalent State institutional support for the beliefs of Indigenous people.

From the perspective of all citizens adhering to religions other than the national dominant one, or to none, this approach may well seem discriminatory. The right of the State to confer such primacy is arguably open to challenge not just on the grounds that it can become a platform for State proselytism but also: because it subverts the 'positive action' principle; because it infringes the freedom of religion rights of all others; and because, in a democracy, it might seem inequitable to some that all citizens should be mandatorily required to fund, through taxation, a continuing caste system of religious education not for public benefit but for that of a particular social group. However, unquestionably there is a difficulty in squaring the internationally recognised parental human right to determine the religious upbringing of their child with the non-discrimination provisions of equality legislation and with recognition for the rights of a child.

The proliferating spread of faith schools in all jurisdictions may well be viewed as the answer to that difficulty, but in fact could be compounding an already significant problem of religious discrimination in the education of children. In some Part II jurisdictions – most noticeably in England, Canada and Ireland – faith schools are incorporated into the public school system but continue to function very largely on a religion-specific basis. Their exclusiveness can be exacerbated when there is no cap, or a very high one, on the percentage of religion-specific pupil admissions, where teaching staff are hired and fired in accordance with a religious ethos and where the school actively promotes an indoctrination of beliefs and values which are alien to its social context. Whether or not they are in receipt of government funding, and most receive at least some, then in order to ensure parity of standards and to avoid allegations of discriminatory treatment on religious grounds, all faith schools should be set up solely in accordance with statutorily established definitional criteria and thereafter be fully subject to national registration and regulatory processes. This has not been the case with, for example, all Islamic madrassas in England and Wales. Indeed, Islamic schools in general present problems in terms of compliance with some of the more basic human rights – including equality and freedoms of speech and association – which are not furthered by practices such as gender segregation in the classroom and the rejection of pupils and curriculum content that represent non-Islamic values. Such problems are not, of course, solely associated with the Islamic religion; schools established to further evangelical Christian values can also be non-compliant with contemporary human rights. Religious fundamentalism in any form is going to conflict with human rights and with the pluralism necessary to sustain a democratic civil society.

Right to non-discrimination in service provision

Because so much public benefit service provision – such as social housing, hospitals, general health care and community care facilities – is now franchised out to religious organisations, this has become a particularly sensitive interface between Church and State. Private service provision, complicated to a varying extent by a legitimising of conscientious objection as grounds for service refusal, is also rapidly becoming a legal minefield.

Public service provision by religious organisations has, historically, a well-established dark side. Each of the Part II jurisdictions has its own record of systemic human rights abuse perpetrated by clergy in residential schools and other facilities established and run by religious organisations to provide child care and family support but also to reinforce their religious ethos to service users. Service provision was then on a religiously discriminating basis. Contemporary service provision by religious organisations, if funded by government, is now required to comply with statutory equality and non-discrimination legislation; if not so funded, then they are entitled to rely upon the religious exemption. Having lost their traditional right to condition public service provision in accordance with their religious beliefs, and being confronted with the constraints of changing social mores, many organisations are left with the choice of either withdrawing from that role or be embroiled in successive court cases as they claim protection from equality dictates on the grounds of religious exemption or within such wriggle room as may be permitted by an evolving conscientious objection jurisprudence. Catholic adoption agencies, for example, in various countries have opted to shut down their adoption services rather than make them available to gay couples;[65] others such as the Scouts have successfully availed of statutory exemption privileges,[66] while some private religious colleges are continuing to plead their case that they have an equality entitlement to provide education conditioned by religious beliefs and that the resulting degrees should be acceptable to the relevant regulatory bodies.[67] It is worth noting, perhaps, that the current Canadian approach to public service provision would seem to be a tightening of equality constraints at the expense of religious freedom,[68] a development which is the reverse of that evolving in the US.

Private service provision by religious persons, or by organisations owned by those with religious beliefs, are frequently the subject of alleged discrimination in all jurisdictions. Much the same range of services seem to provide settings for much the same conflict of personal beliefs and public equality rights: the beliefs are most often rooted in a blend of religion and sexual orientation with a focus on LGBT issues, and the services tend to involve bed-and-breakfast accommodation, hotels and social function venues, bakers, florists and outdoor pursuit centres and so on. The law in this area, where equality rights are entangled with the rights to freedom of religion, freedom of expression and freedom of association, has by no means settled down yet, and predictions as to the shape it might ultimately take are difficult to make. In the US, the judicial decisions to extend the religious exemption[69] leave unchallenged the introduction of the Religious Liberty

Accommodations Act in Mississippi[70] and the not dissimilar liberty laws in eight other states. while developing the grounds of conscientious objection, is beginning to mark out entitlement to equality legislation exemption – on grounds of religion, belief or conscience – as an area of significant jurisdictional difference.

The law relating to service denial on grounds of conscientious objection in the Part II jurisdictions is currently in a state of flux. As regards public services, the jurisprudence of the ECtHR[71] and the European Committee of Social Rights[72] is now at variance with that emerging in the US[73] and the UK,[74] where courts and legislators are beginning to grant some latitude to health care professionals who decline to provide services on grounds of conscientious objection. As regards private or commercial service provision, the US[75] and UK[76] 'gay cakes' rulings have raised a serious challenge to the constraints of equality legislation. This turmoil seems very reminiscent of the divided ECtHR ruling in *A, B and C v. Ireland*,[77] when six dissenting judges challenged the decision of the majority that because the issue (access to abortion) was one of "acute sensitivity" and because of "the importance of the public interest at stake" in relation to "profound moral views", the court should therefore avoid directing a particular course of action but should instead leave the issue to be resolved at the discretion of the parties. The argument of the 6 dissenters asserted that the rationale articulated by the majority justified precisely the opposite outcome. Because the moral views were complex, the law had been formulated around a consensus; that consensus should therefore prevail as legislatively intended. Unquestionably, for all jurisdictions, there are real difficulties in framing law to address what at any point in time appear to be moral imperatives and which, as such, are inevitably also inextricably entangled in religious beliefs. Equality legislation necessarily confronts a barrage of such imperatives – either in the form of explicit religious beliefs or in their proxy substitutes – and, as is becoming ever clearer, choices need to be made by the legislature as to whether the majority consensus given effect by existing legislation should prevail or whether conscientious objection carve-outs are to be allowed space to evolve. The US culture wars have some way to run and show every sign of spreading.

Broadcasting is another area where service provision can be contentious. In a contemporary social-media context where so much communication occurs globally, in real time and via an assortment of media, including by radio, television, cinema, internet, twitter and blogger transmissions, there are now very many opportunities for misunderstandings and for wilful abuse. This is an area in which the rights to freedom of speech and to the freedom of the press are crucially important to manifesting religious belief and to the life of democratic society more generally. However, as the ECtHR has ruled, the exercise of these rights is conditional upon a duty to avoid gratuitous offensiveness or profanity to those of religious belief.[78] In the light of the Charlie Hebdo massacre and other lethal responses to perceived offensiveness to religious beliefs, there may well be good reason to reflect on the 2018 Irish initiative to repeal the criminal offence of blasphemy.

The right to broadcast, being an aspect of the right to freedom of expression, has acquired topical prominence in the light of the recent 'gay cakes' cases which engaged the claim that an artist should be free to express their creativity through whatever medium they think appropriate. Dissemination is clearly essential for the appreciation and affirmation of any artistic work as well as to the livelihood of the artist. Whether communicating their artistry by means of baking a cake or by other means, the mode of expression should be unconstrained by law unless exercised in a manner that actually or potentially incites hatred or violence, is defamatory or is otherwise in breach of the law. The 'gay cake' cases would seem, perhaps, to have established two things. Firstly, that an artist is entitled to express and to broadcast their artistry – provided this avoids conveying actual hatred – without fear of violating the provisions of equality and non-discrimination legislation. Secondly, that while holding him or herself out as open for business to the general public, an artist may refuse business without thereby violating such provisions, where the buyer is requiring that the product be loaded with an additional component that compromises the artist's freedom of expression which – in turn – may include their religious beliefs. In such circumstances, as Lady Hale pointed out, where the "less favourable treatment was afforded to the message not to the man", the seller will not have discriminated against the buyer.[79]

Conclusion

As Van Burren rightly points out, "[I]t is the universality of human rights, as fundamental to our sense of being human, which distinguishes human rights law from other areas of law".[80] This is matched by the parallel universality of religion as a belief in the transcendent that distinguishes religion from other areas of philosophy and personal commitment. Both, being fundamentally about shaping and maintaining the moral integrity of citizens, are experiencing difficulty in holding traction in an increasingly fluid and diverse society. They are each currently undergoing great changes, and the common ground for their mutual engagement is becoming decidedly slippery. The effects of this can be seen in the above discussion of areas of jurisdictional commonality and difference.

Arguably, two factors are primarily responsible for the current disjunction in the relationship between human rights and religion. Firstly, equality legislation is producing difficulties for law and religion as a consequence of its unremitting levelling and reductionist effect. Secondly, religion has become so attenuated in terms of legal definition that it is increasingly difficult to distinguish it from other subjectively held beliefs. The two co-exist in liberal Western democracies by expanding to accommodate diversity. When they collide, as they can do when there is a blunt confrontation between Islamic misogyny and domestic family law or when both traverse morality-laden and loosely defined areas where there is a range of moral choices – such as in relation to matters of gender, sexuality and the ever-growing nexus of LGBT-related issues – this may have consequences that are unforeseen, inconsistent and sometimes unfair.

Notes

1 Laycock, D., 'Formal, Substantive, and Disaggregated Neutrality Toward Religion', *DePaul Law Review*, Vol. 39:4, 1990, at p. 993, 1016. See further at: http://via.library.depaul.edu/law-review/vol39/iss4/3.
2 Citing Bartlett's familiar quotations 802a (14th ed. 1968) (quoting A. France, *Le lys rouge* [1894]).
3 The diverse constituency of the ECHR's 47 member States includes Russia, Turkey, Iceland and Azerbaijan.
4 Application No. 5856/72, (1978). Wording derived from Article 31 of the Vienna Convention on the Law of Treaties, 23 May 1969, United Nations Treaty Series, Vol. 1155, p. 331.
5 See, for example: *Dudgeon v. United Kingdom*, Application No. 7525/76 [1981] 4 EHRR 149 [1981] ECHR 5; *A, B and C v. Ireland,* Application No. 25579/05 [2010] ECtHR (GC); and *Eweida and Others v. the United Kingdom,* Application Nos. 48420/10, 59842/10, 51671/10 and 36516/10 [2013] ECHR 37.
6 The terminology in both instances being loosely derived from the rules of interpretation in Article 31 of the Vienna Convention on the Law of Treaties, 1969.
7 For example, in *X v. Colombia*, Communication No. 1361/2005, UN Doc CCPR/C/89/D/1361/2005 (2007) the Committee found that the State had unfairly discriminated against same-sex partners, by denying them pension rights which were available to unmarried heterosexual partners.
8 See, for example: CCPR General Comment No. 34, Freedoms of Opinion and Expression (2011); No. 22, Freedom of Thought, Conscience or Religion (1993); and No. 18, Non-discrimination (1989). See further at: http://ccprcentre.org/ccpr-general-comments.
9 *Hasan and Eylem Zengin v. Turkey* [2007] ECHR 787.
10 *Dahlab v. Switzerland*, Application No. 42393/98 (2001) and *Leyla Sahin v. Turkey*, Application No. 44774/98 (2005).
11 See *England and Wales, McFarlane v. Relate Avon Ltd* [2010] IRLR 872; US, *Board of Education of Kiryas Joel Village School District v. Grumet*, 512 US 687 (1994); Canada, *Mouvement laïque québécois v. Saguenay (City)* [2015] 2 SCR 3; and Australia, *Canterbury Municipal Council v. Moslem Alawy Society Ltd* (1985) 1 NSWLR 525.
12 *Trinity Western University v. Nova Scotia Barristers' Society* [2015] NSSC 25.
13 State funding for Catholic schools in Ontario may be constitutionally mandated under s.93(1) of the Constitution Act 1867 but cannot be compliant with any concept of State neutrality.
14 See United Nations Human Rights Committee, 'General Comment Relating to Discrimination under the ICCPR', 1989, (No.18, at para. 10).
15 See General Comment 22, at para. 8.
16 *Sherbert v. Verner*, 374 US 398 (1963), *The Church of the Lukumi Babalu Aye v. City of Hialeah*, 508 US 520 (1993), *Board of Education of Kiryas Joel Village School District v. Grumet*, 512 US 687 (1994) and *Trinity Lutheran Church of Columbia, Inc. v. Comer*, 582 U.S. (2017).
17 Campaign to Separate Church and State [1998] 3 IR 321.
18 *Folgerø & Others v. Norway*, Application No. 15472/02 (2007), *Members of the Gldani Congregation of the Jehovah's Witnesses and Others v. Georgia*, Application No. 71156/01 (2007) and *Lautsi v. Italy*, Application No. 30814/06 (2011).
19 *Barber v. Bryant*, No. 16–60477 (5th Cir. 2017) and *Masterpiece Cakeshop v. Colorado Civil Rights Commission*, 584 U.S. (2018).
20 *Mouvement laïque québécois v. Saguenay (City)*, op. cit.
21 See Report of the UN Special Rapporteur on Freedom of Religion or Belief, A/HRC/34/50, 2017, at para. 78.

22 Application No. 27238/95 (2001), at para. 90.
23 *Shergill v. Khaira* [2014] UKSC 33, per Neuberger, L.J., at paras. 45–59.
24 For Article 31, see, at: https://treaties.un.org/doc/publication/unts/volume%201155/volume-1155-i-18232-english.pdf.
25 See Explanatory Report to Protocol No.15 amending the Convention for the Protection of Human Rights and Fundamental Freedoms (CETS No.213, Protocol No. 15, 24 June 2013), para 9, at: https://rm.coe.int/CoERMPublicCommonSearchServices/DisplayDCTMContent?documentId=09000016800d383d.
26 For example, *Toonen v. Australia*, Communication No. 488/1992. See UN Commission on Human Rights, *The Siracusa Principles on the Limitation and Derogation Provisions in the International Covenant on Civil and Political Rights*, 1984, E/CN.4/1985/4. See also *Bikramjit Singh v. France*, Communication No. 1852/2008, CCPR/C/106/D/511/1992.
27 Communication No. 1876/2009, CCPR/C/102/D/1876/2009 (2011).
28 Communication No. 1474/2006, CCPR/C/91/D/1474/2006 (2007).
29 *Sherbert v. Verner*, 374 US 398 (1963).
30 *Employment Division v. Smith*, 48 US 872 (1990).
31 *The Church of the Lukumi Babalu Aye v. City of Hialeah*, 508 US 520 (1993), *Gonzales v. O Centro Espirita Beneficente Uniao do Vegetal*, 546 US 418 (2006).
32 *Trinity Lutheran Church of Columbia, Inc. v. Comer*, 582 US (2017).
33 *Syndicat Northcrest v. Amselem* [2004] 2 SCR 551.
34 *Burwell v. Hobby Lobby*, 573 US 134 S.Ct. 2751 (2014).
35 *Masterpiece Cakeshop v. Colorado Civil Rights Commission* 584 US (2018).
36 See Article 14 of the ECHR and Article 12 of the UN Declaration on the Rights of Indigenous Peoples.
37 See, *US, U.S. v. Winddancer*, 435 F. Supp. 2d 687 (M.D. Tenn. 2006); *Canada, Ktunaxa Nation v. British Columbia* [2017] SCC 54; and *Australia, Cheedy on behalf of the Yindjibarndi People v. State of Western Australia* [2010] FCA 690; [2011] FCAFC 100.
38 See *The Church of the New Faith v. Commissioner of Pay-roll Tax* [1983] HCA 40; (1983) 154 q CLR 120 (27 October 1983).
39 See Edge, P.W., 'Determining Religion in English Courts', *Oxford Journal of Law and Religion*, Oxford University Press, January 2012.
40 See in Europe, *Cha'are Shalom ve Tsedek v. France*, Application No. 27417/95 (2000); the US, *Gonzales v. O Centro Espirita Beneficente Uniao do Vegetal*, 546 US 418 (2006); Canada, *Syndicat Northcrest v. Amselem* (2004) 2 SCR 576; and in Australia, *Church of New Faith v. Commissioner of Pay-Roll Tax* (1983) 1 VR 97.
41 See *Trinity Western University v. British Columbia College of Teachers* (2001), 39 C.H.R.R. D/357. 2001 SCC 31; *Trinity Western University (TWU) v. Law Society of BC* 2015 BCSC 2326; *Trinity Western University (TWU) v. Law Society of Upper Canada* 2016 ONCA 518; and *Trinity Western University v. Law Society of British Columbia* 2016 BCCA 423.
42 *Delf AS v. Estonia*, Application No. 64569/09 (2015).
43 See s.296(1) of the Criminal Code.
44 See Article 40.6.1 of the Constitution and the Defamation Act 2009.
45 See further Ali, A.H., *The Challenge of Dawa*, at: www.hoover.org/sites/default/files/research/docs/ali_challengeofdawa_final_web.pdf.
46 Rulings of the ECtHR, HRC and ECJ are mixed on this issue, particularly in relation to the *laïcité*, cultural context of France.
47 Quebec's Bill 62, the Religious Neutrality Law, prohibits public workers, as well as those receiving public services, from covering their faces. This practice is already well established in the police and armed forces of the Part II jurisdictions where it is presumably open to challenge on the same principle.
48 See Parkinson, P., *Traditional Rights and Freedoms – Encroachments by Commonwealth Laws* (ALRC Interim Report 127), *Submission 9*, 2015; and Geddicks, F.M.,

'The Permissible Scope of Legal Limitations on the Freedom of Religion or Belief in the United States', *Emory International Law Review*, Vol. 19, 2005, at p. 1187.

49 See Bano, S., *Muslim Women and Shariah Councils: Transcending the Boundaries of Community and Law*, Palgrave MacMillan, UK, 2012.

50 *Haas v. Switzerland* (2014) 58 EHRR 7.

51 *Barber v. Bryant* 17–547, and *Campaign for Southern Equality v. Bryant*, 17–642.

52 See 'Principles on the Application of International Human Rights Law in Relation to Sexual Orientation and Gender Identity', as updated in 2017. See further at: www.refworld.org/pdfid/4a783aed2.pdf.

53 See the Qur'an, *ayah* in *Surah al-Mujadalah* (58: 2).

54 *Hosanna-Tabor Evangelical Lutheran Church v. EEOC* 565 US – (2012).

55 *Burwell v. Hobby Lobby,* 573 U.S. 134 S Ct 2751 (2014).

56 *Adeyeye v. Heartland Sweeteners, LLC,* No.12–3820 (7th Cir. 2013).

57 *Grainger v. Nicholson* [2010] IRLR 4 (EAT) and *Eweida v. British Airways plc* [*2010*] EWCA Civ 80 CA.

58 See, *Ladele v. London Borough of Islington* [2009] EWCA (Civ) 1357; *McFarlane v. Relate Avon Ltd* [2010] EWCA Civ B1; and *McClintock v. Department of Constitutional Affairs* [2008] IRLR 29.

59 As stated, for example, by the ECtHR in *Savez crkava « Riječ života » and Others v. Croatia,* Application No. 7798/08 (2010).

60 *R (Fox & Ors) v. Secretary of State for Education* [2015] EWHC 3404 (Admin), per Warby, J., at para. 39.

61 *Crowley v. Ireland* [1980] IR 102.

62 *Loyola High School v. Québec (Attorney General),* 2015 SCC 12.

63 *Hoxton Park Residents Action Group Inc v. Liverpool City Council* [2016] NSWCA 157.

64 *Folgerø v. Norway* [2007] ECHR 546 and *Osmanoglu and Kocabas v. Switzerland,* Application No. 29086/12 (2017).

65 *Catholic Care (Diocese of Leeds) v. The Charity Commission for England and Wales* [2011] EqLR 597.

66 *Boy Scouts of America v. Dale*, 530 US 640 (2000).

67 *Trinity Western University (TWU) v. Law Society of Upper Canada* 2016 ONCA 518.

68 See Bill 62 passed by the Quebec government in October 2017 and the Summer Jobs program.

69 *Burwell v. Hobby Lobby,* 573 US 134 S Ct 2751 (2014).

70 *Barber v. Bryant* 17–547, and *Campaign for Southern Equality v. Bryant*, 17–642.

71 *Pichon and Sajous v. France,* Application No. 49853/99 (2001) and *R.R. v. Poland,* Application No. 27617/04 (2011).

72 *IPPF v. Italy,* Complaint No. 87/2012 (2014) and *FAFCE v. Sweden,* Complaint No. 99/2013 (2015).

73 *Zubik v. Burwell,* 136 S. Ct. 1557–2016 and various and state 'religious liberty' laws.

74 See the Conscientious Objection (Medical Activities) Bill 2017.

75 *Masterpiece Cakeshop v. Colorado Civil Rights Commission*, op. cit.

76 *Gareth Lee v. Ashers Baking Company Ltd*, McArthur and McArthur, Neutral Citation: [2016] NICA 39.

77 [2010] ECtHR (GC), Application No. 25579/05 (2010).

78 *Otto-Preminger-Institut v. Austria,* Series A no. 295-A, (20 September 1994) and *Wingrove v. The United Kingdom,* (19/1995/525/611) 25 November 1996.

79 *Lee v. Ashers Baking Company Ltd and others* [2018] UKSC 49, at para. 47.

80 See Van Bueren, G., *The Human Dignity Trust v. Charity Commission for England and Wales* [2014] UKFTT, 2013/0013/B (GRC), at para. 94.

9 Conclusion

The ECtHR,[1] in common with many national courts,[2] has often advised that maintaining State neutrality in relation to religion, its adherents religious organisations, and indeed secularism, is essential for the preservation of pluralism and the proper functioning of democracy. It would seem that both are now buckling under the pressure of responding to the traumatising effects of Islamic terrorism, a migrant crisis and a climate of populism. This points up another strong area of jurisdictional commonality, albeit one with some important aspects of difference.

The foreign policy of the Part II jurisdictions – excepting Ireland – has been dominated, for at least the past 17 years, by a US-led counter-insurgency strategy in Iraq, Afghanistan and other Islamic countries. This ever-expanding theatre of a war[3] that shows no sign of ending represents the 'sharp-end' of a relationship between State and religion/human rights. There is no avoiding the fact that this conflict is drawing more countries into a gradually polarising cultural nexus in which the forces of the State in largely Christian countries are arraigned against Islamic fundamentalists in largely Muslim countries.[4] Advice as to the desirability of achieving State neutrality seems of doubtful relevance and concern for human rights somewhat misplaced in a context where the full might of the State is being specifically directed toward obliterating a particular 'religious' group: "removing ISIS from the face of the earth".[5] While the short-term domestic repercussions of this policy are very evident in the random acts of Islamic violence, intrusive security measures and constraints on human rights, the alienation of many Muslim citizens and in generalised social insecurity, it is the longer-term consequences for the State and the human rights/religion intersect that may prove most damaging for pluralism and the proper functioning of democratic society.

The migrant crisis, largely Muslim in character, as it emanated from and followed hard on the heels of Western bombing of eastern Muslim countries (though other factors were also in play), has been challenging for the Part II jurisdictions. Aside from Canada, which opened its doors to displaced refugees, most other jurisdictions have responded defensively by increasing border controls and the deportation of those defined as illegal immigrants. Some, specifically the US, have adopted much the same approach as Hungary, Slovakia and Poland and sought to deny migrant access. Whether welcoming or rejecting, the Western experience of responding to the largest population movement since WWII and to murderous violence perpetrated on the streets of their capital cities – both being Muslim phenomena – has had a divisive and destabilising effect. In particular, it has left Muslim citizens in the Part II jurisdictions feeling set apart, vulnerable and exposed to a growing Islamophobia.

This possible unravelling of the pluralism that had come to characterise Western democracies has been exacerbated by the trend toward populism. In the US and across Europe – Turkey, Poland, Austria, Spain and elsewhere – traditional, seemingly settled democratic political systems have been disrupted by the sudden emergence of more radical, authoritarian political leaders and parties. The rise of populism may well be linked to a perceived threat to the traditional national culture posed by Islamic fundamentalism and a surge in Muslim immigrants, but its roots lie in a more basic disenchantment with the liberal democratic political system. This is widely viewed as having failed to protect: ordinary citizens from terrorism; society from the financial crisis of 2008 and the consequent slump in living standards; and the environment from pollution and the public services from being debased. It is also seen as having been too forgiving as regards corruption in political, financial and religious institutions, and being permissive in relation to the growing gulf between rich and poor. The danger that populism presents can be seen in policies that include building frontier walls, denying members of certain religious/cultural groups entry to a country, banning religious apparel in public and in rewriting equality and non-discrimination laws. As populism reasserts the virtues of the nation State, sovereignty and cultural heritage, it also explicitly or by implication suggests that other cultures and religions are of lesser importance or can only be accommodated if fully assimilated. This would seem to be a fairly direct route toward the end of both pluralism and to the proper functioning of a democratic society.

The threat to civil society posed by the above combination of destabilising forces suggests that some form of binding morality and authority is needed to forestall any further slide into defensive conservative insularity. Judt, in his chastening book *Ill Fares the Land*, refers to the "magic of universalism" as the means whereby Western democracies became more confident and stable in the decades that followed the fear and destruction of two world wars.[6] This he saw as a consequence of the State assuming responsibility, through higher taxation, for ensuring a fairer and more bonded society in which most had access to a better standard of public services and opportunities for social advancement: Keynesian socio-economic planning had proven to be more efficient and socially uplifting than its fascist or communist counterparts, which bred the dissatisfaction that led to war. As a first step, however, citizens had to trust that the State, after imposing the universalism of a just tax system, would then deliver the public benefit goods that all could see made their society a safer and better place.

Any such "magic of universalism" is clearly no longer to be found in contemporary market-led economies with their sanctions, protectionism, tariffs, trade wars and with tax systems manipulated as deemed expedient by government. At a time when many feel that the world is becoming less safe, it might be expected that they would turn to religion. However, religion has become somewhat desiccated – fading in numbers of adherents and in the authority of its institutions, fragmented and mutating as new belief systems emerge, sublimated into culture wars, corrupted domestically and problematic internationally – so citizens are now perhaps less ready to place their trust in the Church. Instead, they may feel that State-sanctioned human rights, embedded in international law, could have more to offer. Those who are citizens of common-law nations are in the strongest position to put this to the test. Because of their deep and shared characteristics – including a Christian cultural heritage, parliamentary democratic governance and their investment in initiating and developing an international human rights regime – these are the States where it should become most apparent whether or not such a regime could bring the "magic of universalism" to stabilise Western society in the 21st century.

As this regime beds down and there is a growing acceptance of the universality, indivisibility and interdependence of human rights, so a heavy onus rests on the State to deliver related benefits: citizens are entitled to feel they are in a safer and more equitable society where everyone is mutually bound by respect for the same rules, domestically and internationally. The task for this book was to examine just how that is now working out for several leading common-law nations. It may be possible to draw some broad, if brief, conclusions. For example, while it is difficult to guess how much worse international tensions would be without human rights safeguards, the evidence is that despite the existence of this considerable body of law, the world is no safer. Many countries are now engaged in actual or proxy warfare, including the US, Russia, Turkey, Iraq, Iran, Afghanistan, Syria, Somalia and Libya; ethnic cleansing is under way in India, Hungary and Myanmar; and presidential powers are eroding civil rights and the rule of law in China, Rwanda, Venezuela, Thailand and the Philippines. Negative monitoring is, of course, unfair or insufficient: we will never know, for instance, what might have happened without UN HRCouncil negotiations, if peacekeeping forces mandated by human rights provisions were not in place and if the ICC did not stand as a deterrent to potential human rights transgression. The world may not yet be safer, but most of it has agreed to the normative standards and the forums to which transgressors can be held accountable and this in the long run may induce greater safety awareness. Domestically, the outlook is a good deal more positive. Social diversity within a Christian common-law culture requires the rights of all minority groups to be protected. If these democratic societies are to be sufficiently robust to accommodate difference and survive the above-mentioned destabilising forces, then they must ensure that their institutions are equipped to mediate between the many different sets of interests. The case law surveyed in Part II, complicated as it is by the interweaving of equality rights, shows the judiciary and regulators assiduously balancing competing rights with the help of principles such as 'proportionality'. Other principles – such as "the margin of appreciation", "the religious exemption" or "respect for traditional culture" – are more difficult, as they can be used to undermine equality and non-discrimination rights, particularly in relation to LGBT issues. This tends to point up the important role of the State and the "doctrine of State neutrality". It is difficult to see how the institutions of a democratic society can embrace and fully apply human rights unless mandated to do so by a rigorously impartial State. For human rights and international law to bring a much needed "magic of universalism", citizens will need to trust that the hands of the State are not tied by historical religious/ cultural commitments.

Notes

1 *Metropolitan Church of Bessarabia and Others v. Moldova*, Application No. 45701/ 99, §§ 115–16, ECHR 2001-XII and *Savez Crkava "Riječ života" and Others v. Croatia*, Application No. 7798/08 (2010).
2 England and Wales, *McFarlane v. Relate Avon Ltd* [2010] IRLR 872; US, *Board of Education of Kiryas Joel Village School District v. Grumet*, 512 US 687 (1994); Canada, *Mouvement laïque québécois v. Saguenay (City)* [2015] 2 SCR 3; and Australia, *Canterbury Municipal Council v. Moslem Alawy Society Ltd* (1985) 1 NSWLR 525.
3 The 'Costs of War' report estimates that as of 2017 the US was engaged in counterterrorism activities in 76 countries, see further at: http://watson.brown.edu/ costsofwar/.
4 See further Polk, W.R., *Crusade and Jihad*, Yale University Press, New Haven, CT, 2018.
5 See President Trump's 2018 'State of the Union' speech, at: www.vox.com/ world/2018/1/30/16945312/state-of-the-union-2018-isis.
6 Judt, T., *Ill Fares the Land: A Treatise on Our Present Discontents*, Allen Lane (now Penguin Random House), UK, 2010, at p. 52.

Index

For Product Safety Concerns and Information please contact our EU representative GPSR@taylorandfrancis.com Taylor & Francis Verlag GmbH, Kaufingerstraße 24, 80331 München, Germany

Batch number: 10725973

Printed by Printforce, the Netherlands

TRANSNATIONAL CORRUPTION AND CORPORATIONS